Praise for *Poetics for the More-than-Human World*:

This amazingly capacious and intelligent collection of poems and essays is the first extended work I know to take completely seriously where poetry comes from ... Eco-concerns make us hear multiple musics in endless varied assemblages that allow us to become attuned to the many kinds of intelligences that sponsor them.

—Charles Altieri, Stageberg Professor of English, UC Berkeley

This significant collection of the latest ecopoetic thinking and practice brings together a diverse representation of twenty-first-century poetry and commentary to speak truth to both the peril and hope of the present moment. The voices in this anthology—whether urgent cry or sibilant whisper—need to be heard ...

—Scott Edward Anderson, author of *Dwelling: an ecopoem*

This phenomenal gathering of writers makes a collective pledge that will serve a generation of readers. This anthology pauses the insufficient verbiage of environmental policy and regulation by borrowing language's ability to imaginatively represent and alter how we speak about and frame current ecological challenges. These poems and essays widen the berth by which we understand, absorb, and begin to face with courage and hope the consequences of several centuries of inattentive human behaviors that have proven harmful to the planet. By displaying a complex of approaches and styles, the anthology points us to a greater regard for life with as much diversity and as manymanifestations as what is found on land, in oceans, and in the air.

—Major Jackson, Richard A. Dennis Professor of English, University of Vermont

... a volume for everyone who loves our planet and reveres its extraordinary biodiversity and balance; it also informs us, as Tyrone Williams points out, of *the connection between capital and ecology* and of humans as *the abstract figure of the global consumer* accelerating climate change. These poems and commentaries encourage us to live more consciously and sustainably and, perhaps, propel us into necessary action to ensure it.

—Karen Neuberg, author of *the elephants are asking*

This astonishingly capacious gathering is proof that the shadow of the Anthropocene is the biggest, darkest game in town (read: planet). The luminous delicacies of the human imagination seem kindled to a keener wattage here, as if the proverbial hive mind had summoned all these poets for an uncannily mutual resonance, like the sound of frogs around a pond: these poets ... invite new ways of listening, new ways of hearing what hearing can mean.

—Jed Rasula, author of *This Compost: Ecological Imperatives in American Poetry*; Helen S. Lanier Distinguished Professor, Department of English, University of Georgia

I0380743

Poetics for the More-than-Human World

Mary Newell, Bernard Quetchenbach, Sarah Nolan
Editors

Dispatches Editions

ISBN 978-1-952419-56-0 pbk. | 978-1-952419-30-0 hdc.

Cover design: Allyson Pang

Photo collage on back cover: Rosalind Schneider's "River of Dreams" (http://rosalindschneiderart.com/)

Book design: Brie Barron

Library of Congress Control Number: 2020949987

Summary: An anthology of ecologically oriented poetry and commentary by 140 contemporary writers from a wide range of bioregions, nations, and life situations who include the more-than-human world in their vision of accountability.

May some of these words leave footprints
for those who come after

Table of Contents

Poetry

Essays and Critical Responses

Introduction

"Poetics for the More-than-Human World": a phrase that we hope reveals significant features of the writing selected here. For one thing, "More than human" implies a broad swath of human cultures and traditions. Though we can't claim to speak for all of humanity, this collection features a diverse slate of poets practicing a variety of twenty-first-century approaches; selections represent beat-inspired rebelliousness, deep image-inflected perceptual psychology, projectivist field composition, and l=a=n=g=u=a=g=e dynamics, culminating in Hinge and other genres of innovative avant-garde work, as poets respond to increasingly challenging and complex environmental circumstances. We feature work that spans the globe from North America to Amazonia to South Korea to a transcontinental collaboration linking Australia and the United Kingdom, including writing by members of several indigenous nations and communities. But "more than human" places the poetry in a far more sweeping context that includes birdsong, insect calls, even the patient shrugs and pulses of geology. And it does so from a place of humility, recognition, and kinship. These voices may represent "other nations," in Henry Beston's phrase, but they emerge from the same reality that we ourselves belong to, from neighbors and relatives sharing DNA, chemical composition, and mutual embeddedness in a cosmic history leading to the present moment. In some of these works, they share authorship as well.

That present moment has, needless to say, become dangerously unstable, in large part because we humans have understood the voices we hear around us as less than rather than more than human, or at least as hopelessly foreign. It is our hope that the voices gathered here will sound as natural as the Great Horned Owl calling from my backyard and as inevitable as the physical and chemical processes that govern the universe. Earth's chorus needs all of its constituent voices; even if the result is dissonance rather than a harmonious music of the spheres, the song of the creation is never irrelevant, trivial, or devoid of meaning. It is a music of imminent danger and immanent resilience, time-bound but transcendent, and always more than human.

Some Thoughts on Ecopoetics

The term "Ecopoetics" describes creative writing that engages in the complex interrelationships within the ever-shifting, endangered ecosphere. In their comprehensive *Ecopoetry Anthology*, Ann Fisher-Wirth and Laura-Gray Street divide ecopoetry into three categories: nature poetry, in which the natural world is the subject matter, but might function as a source of imagery for purely human interests; environmental poetry, concerned with "active and politicized environmentalism"; and ecological poetry, which emphasizes linguistic formulations and self-reflexivity and may challenge "a form historically taken for granted–that of the singular, coherent self" (xxix). In this anthology, our primary focus has been on the third category, writing that aspires to ecocentric inclusiveness. Of course, poems need not conform to categories. Since writers are constrained by human perceptual and cognitive faculties, along with interpretive habits, an ecocentric perspective may remain more of a pathway than a destination. Along with disputing the authoritative viewing position of a unified "I," ecopoetics challenges the classic mind/body split. Further, any belief in an interiority sequestered from the external world confronts the permeability of bodily boundaries to toxins and disease. Yet the sense of more flexible personal boundaries can support encounters of intersubjectivity or co-creation. In Harriet Tarlo's words, "the avoidance of the lyric 'I' also involves a shift towards a more communal rather than individual human perspective, one in which we see the human animal's own endangering of itself alongside the rest of the non-human residents of earth." When we find ourselves implicated and equally at risk, the response may resound with more profound emotional intensity or its irony prick more deeply.

If the preferred scenes of romantic nature writing were pristine views of nature as respite from the sociocultural realm or nature as emblem of human sentiment, those of ecopoetry are as diverse as ecosystems, encompassing scales from the microscopic to the planetary. The proposed Anthropocene epoch is by definition a time when the human touch has altered whatever natural systems pre-existed. The places of ecopoetry might include toxic dump sites, pipelines, and polluted waters as well as wildlife niches, urban nature sites, and neglected "third landscapes." Poets might wander through places with media assistance, imaginally, or physically, as participant observers. Relation to place may be evoked by means of momentary snapshots; a stream of ruminations while passing through; or, as Jonathan Skinner notes for fieldwork-based writing, with "serial composition extended over time, to convey the complex, intermeshing, and endlessly variable dimensions of a place." Research and documentation can extend such explorations into historical or deep time, perhaps captured in the poetry through a layered, "thick time" perspective, as discussed by David Farrier; both science and imagination inspire projections into possible futures.

Ecopoetics can give voice to inequalities and troubled histories among human populations, alongside the urgent needs of the more-than-human world. It may invoke the restorative power of language to reclaim disrupted connections or forge new ones. It becomes multi-vocal, perhaps multi-lingual, dialogic, or intersectional, providing a synchronous breadth.

Ecopoetics can foster connections across delimiting boundaries, partly through its grounding in dynamic views of biological and neuro-cognitive systems which, as Forrest Gander notes, "suggest ways of being in the world that might lead to less exploitative and destructive histories." He queries, "What if structures of perception are not 'subjective' (i.e., added by humans to raw data) or 'objective' (i.e., provided by things in themselves), but are articulated within media of relation and interaction such that to speak is to surge up into a medium that isn't projected, but is ongoing, like an environment. Might we see ourselves then as participants in a noninstrumental language?"

Beyond whatever paradigms we develop to elucidate ecopoetry, its inspiration flows from those moments or hours of attuning to the vital cadences and vortices that surround us. The poets' concerns may be specific to a single species, locale, or region, or can be more global; they can evoke transience or invite readers to share a present moment expanded through heightened attentiveness. The emotive tone traverses a wide range, from anger to zeal, no doubt influenced by one's relative vulnerability to physical or cultural danger, oppression, and bigotry as well as one's compassion, altruism, and focus. In any case, ecologically oriented writers enter a shared field of inquiry into what it means to be living in precarious times, in bodies with permeable boundaries, on a globe whose regions and populations are inter-implicated.

Bibliography

Farrier, David. *Anthropocene Poetics: Deep Time, Sacrifice Zones and Extinction*. Minneapolis: University of Minnesota Press, 2019.

Gander, Forrest. "The Future of the Past: The Carboniferous & Ecopoetics." *Chicago Review*, 56, no. 2/3 (Autumn 2011): 216–21.

Skinner, Jonathan. "In the Field with Ecopoetics: New Pastoral Procedures, Objectivist to Newlipo." In *Proceedings of the 2008 Poetic Ecologies Conference*, edited by Franca Bellarsi. Brussels: Peter Lang, forthcoming.

Tarlo, Harriet. "Women and Ecopoetics: Some Thoughts in Context." *How2* 3, no. 2 (2008). https://www.asu.edu/pipercwcenter/how2journal/vol_3_no_2/ecopoetics/index.html

Poetry

JUANA ADCOCK

Steller's Use of Verbs When Describing the Sea Cow, Hunted to Extinction within 27 Years of Its Discovery by Europeans. De bestiis marinis, 1751.

captured / resisting / put to uses / detached / masticates / lies prone / grows / increases / grows / grow / take the place / masticates / move as do the lips of cattle / tear off / cut / cut / softened by boiling / cut like a checkerboard / boiled / yield / may be moved / can be moved / to move / masticate

set in the palate / expressed by no known name / cannot call it / is inserted / are perforated / are inserted / excavated / fit into / will explain / stretch back / perforated / grows / take the place / takes the place / cut / grows / grows / excavated / extend downward like a bow / make a double hollow / grows / is frayed out / ends / is inserted / it agrees / with an up-and-down motion drives itself violently forward / struggles to escape / this happened by mere chance

walks as with feet / fights / resists / swimming prone / embraces / holds and permits herself in turn to be embraced / are exactly as man / have not yet given birth / is not swollen / to get the milk in large quantities from dead ones in the same way as from cows / cut / give out milk / collected by squeezing / boiled / reaches clear to / ends / enter / cut / cut / were not found / were found / given this round form / seen / is inserted / move / to happen / was done / was perforated / had penetrated / cut / took / thought / cut / saw / it happened /cut / had been hired / took the place of money / became tired / inspect / make tessellated like a checkerboard / present a pleasing spectacle / cut

did not make the boast to have found / found / argued from utterly false premises / lay opposite / are not kept / but are kept / was unquestionable proof / was thoroughly cleansed / are not everywhere equal / is hollowed out to receive / cut / cut / it occurred

am very sorry / did not think / was not possible without the help of many men to do so / thought / saw / cut / neither saw nor wish to conjecture / is detached / forms rather a species of cavity / feeding / rests / ended / cut / found / secreted in consequence of the slow and distressing death of the animal / detached / shine through like a tree / cut

trust / observed / saw only through a lattice / seen / stating / explaining / observed / captured / spoil with teeth / steal / studying / worried / writing / hire / tear to pieces / commended / to bring home with / saw / to bring at least the spoils / narrating / feed / never saw / never heard / saw / misinformed / describe / make like the Platonic man / bears resemblance / impresses as being like / feeds / say nothing / moving / it happened / was helpless and unable to get away / should be tamed / can be tamed
through stupidity and greediness / it happened

hook / secured / took / entered / held / stood / holding / struck / held inspite of frantic efforts at resistance / dragged / held / wore out by constant blows / rendered thoroughly passive by spears / finished by knives and other weapons / drawn to land / cut while still alive

did not find / think / it happens / breathe differently from fishes / can better swallow / more easily taken / move about / get free by tearing hook out of skin / saw / caught / endeavor to assist / try to upset boat / endeavour to extract the hook from the back of wounded companion with a blow from their tails / several times proved successful / cut / found still waiting / utters no sound / only breathes heavily and seems to sigh when wounded / will not venture to assert how much their eyes and ears are worth / see and hear little / seem to neglect and despise the use of these organs

have written / published in English in London / correspond / says / says / hunting / approach without noise and without speaking / caught in great numbers / eat / called by the inhabitants, in their language / must tell the uses / are put to use / stretch it / use in the same way as / use / becomes yellow like May butter / cannot be compared

can be kept / approximates / nearly can be used for / its use is not to be despised / it moves gently, producing / can be kept / lives / prevents / preserving / work even more powerfully / cooked / to distinguish / resembles / can hardly tell the difference / when boiled it soon becomes tender / boiling / swells up like young pork / takes up / does not really refuse / becomes quite like corned beef / did not try to do much / had a great abundance / it moves

Italian Tourism Bureau Draws Up Plans for the Regeneration of the Cinque Terre Landscape

I am land –
cut into terraces my earth
hugged together by roots my water
inking through gaps my stones
holding together neatly my walls
tidy in vineyards and olive groves.

Contadino, you made me beautiful.
From afar

I was paradise. From up close
I was back-breaking work.
From the golden mean I was indifferent
market stalls.
Imports and exports.

Contadino, my love, you left me
for the city.
My stonewalls crumbled
my wild boar stamping
my maritime pines invading
with their high tops and bare masts
swooping in the wind.

My legs were too prickly
for your taste, O Contadino.

You were ridiculed for your dialect of scrub.
You ironed it out like a shirt.
Your clean fingernails tapped at the keyboard
in air conditioned rooms
atop staircases made of marble carved out
from my sisters' mountains.

And me, abandoned, returning to my wild
state shaking off your cuttings and divisions
with a few landslides and storms
to wipe my slate clean.

And as the dinghies sink
and those fleeing from war drown
wordlessly in my picturesque sea
the functionaries hold long meetings
at the Tourism Bureau
puzzling over how to reignite
my Contadino's love for me –

they know I am worth more
as a terraced olive grove.

We don't have enough hands
for all the things we need
to hold onto

Omar Al-Nakib

Eavesdrop

on malaised roots
of its one-tenth of an acre
eavesdrops the crocus

:::

no longer mild the peril
of dollops
from
o, a tad

the hare now is moving
by the snore of
lettuce cutters

fodient
blackward

terra dragglesacked
to the aural collocation
of *clopfh, eclopfh*
&
lumpenprole
with
fahrhut,
a shovel

reddle dyestuff
sets to blend
the horror vacui

and above
the sun grandly apportions
and
albedo parts
then
anatomy on the floe

its eating by proxy the moribund panes
and

miscellaneous nips
will make it water

Pre-Existing Planes and Fragments

So as to accelerate quasi-neural lightning that ignites levels other than psychic astigmatism and its related detritus engages collective telepathy. Thus the human energy field is charged via intangible language that at first seems scrambled according to one's rational grasp where impalpable proto power squares itself via transfigured embranglement that at a prior state once seeded the cells. Within this realm an inner micro-diagnosis emerges via squared suns and ravines not in the sense of structural density or menace and certainly not as some protracted after-thought that rules by inoperable mechanics, but by rise of inner burning, prior to times of time, prior to known thought, prior to hyper-ventilated evolution with its dire eras, prior to an evolved nexus sans human visibility. I am thinking of the subtext our strange electrical animation. Because our subtext remains largely nonhuman we struggle with psychic interstice, with transhuman agglomeration, so that we more and more claim kinship with the unmarked biota of Qingjiang* strata via its ferocious dousing by mystery. Thus this plane authors invisible gales from an alphabet proto to suns.

The above is certainly not a wayward chronicle of rhetoric but impalpable extension into invisible density, into ceaseless extension that is the great collective density of humanity so that alchemical tautology spins and explodes the great residue of itself so that collective power breaks through partial vacuums of mystery as a variant of invisible density. Common thought can only go so far as gold and iron shapes the mind into hardened matter accruing power according to tangible waste with beings cunningly affected sending signals of prematurity thereby blunting complexity. Thus the mental range takes on the character of a dark and wandering orb. It remains empowered by polluted inner powers that issue through sluices capable of listening to themselves as an ensemble of Saturns. These powers never capable of listening via the anterior at the precipice of their appearance or are they capable of listening to Saturn's 82 lunar configurations that ignite as interior warrens.* The latter being charisma counter to fecund emptiness condensed according to the charisma of voltage with its parallels and reflections, condensed being anterior to palpable distance and any notion of measurement. One does not speak of measurable space, but of existence sired as abnegation of itself.

Perhaps I now evince myself as energy via carrier ray, perhaps one can now speak of oneself as a bold and enamored riddle, as burning intangible anomalous registration that senses pre-existence. Not as a curious ray of staged Jungian theatre slipping through partial dimensions enlisting a view barely beyond obstreperous personal kindling igniting psychic residue that continues to obstruct primal contact with the self that ignites never capable of exploring ancestors' riddles.

Via ancestor's riddles thought never devolves by allegation but simply exists as refraction when attempting to declare allegiance to all there is. Thus one evolves beyond sundered realms naturally enlightened by anomalous registration. Then one can say that one functions as a bold enamored riddle, via an intangible cast of thought scripted via parallel sub-causes that remain like and unlike inner observation all the while roving inner hamlets of seeming darkness.

Not private oxygen as such but its mirrored preamble far beyond earthly dusk and its various stages of dawn as the mind projects backwards into unbound blankness projecting and at the same time retrieving various destinations from seeming mists and scatterings. Not crass or optimum power but indiscriminate understanding. Say one places the genes of a she-dog side by side with one that enters a parallel realm replete with hallucination as if breathing fumes from auras collapsing around a main sewuene sun. These being auras that re-ignite themselves ad-infinitum until higher darkness is broached. Not statutes that issue from reprehensible parliaments but shadows kindled by pre-existing planes and fragments.

Perhaps one may see my view as trans-personal and remorseless integral with debility. I am attempting a higher forecast perhaps pre-emptive and non-clinical freed from stunning mirrors of itself. Never an acrobatics tuned by emblems of crass material nostalgia honed according to measured objects.This being vertiginous summons spontaneously coded by pre-existence. Not precautionary suffocation sired by errorless minimums but copies that rise above errorless minimums of themselves. This being carnivorous tautology pure and simple. Yet existence remains connected to itself as totalic resource never unconnected to the mysterious field that we experience as kinetic imbalance. Thus our living field is never promulgated as consequence from the anterior being a curious flare that erupts as refracted motion broaching consciousness via what is sensed as glints from pre-existence.

Never a psychic acrobatics delimited and tuned to itself as crass aromatics but as vertiginous summons. I am speaking of signals from that which has no possibility of linear definition. Thus I am not speaking in defense of pre-cautionary definition that attempts to define errorless minimums. Not blazing inevitable language come to form quanta, but eclipse via glints, via staggering implication sired by creation itself. This ignites a staggering ripple concussive as pre-classification sans boundary as we've come to know it through cognition.

Pre-classification ignites in the human field as unknowable colloquy with oxygen being none other than the riddle that eclipses all riddles. The latter remains the central fatigue of the modern human corpus always guided by its fear of inevitable blood drain. For the modern soul this is not unlike re-ignited infamy seeping through erratic cellular locales invaded by collective distance being barbaric and fundamental always exclusively sired by material consciousness. Yet for higher states of mind this kinetics fails as insight. This latter insight understood via interior psychic ballet, a ballet empowered by transmuted neural summons.

The anterior consisting of unknowable reality cannot be countenanced as cognitively created fragment seeded by appearance as unalterable functioning. Within this tenor measurement functions as inescapable circularity. I'm thinking of the mind as a torrent of fundamental sounding always at one with anomalous pre-engendering. And this pre-engendering being synonymous sans torrential Alpha particles that falsely pre-engender reality as we understand them to be cells, as restrictive energies that triangulate themselves via hard and fast data. This is certainly not pre-ignited or rational at the human level. Our anterior state remains a mysterious and capacious opening if you will. In terms of cognitive understanding its zone is consistently conjured as something barbaric and fundamental. According to material consciousness life is scripted as drafts in sudden regions of the mind being something fundamental and barbaric. This being none other than psychic obsidian that remains subsequent and territorial. Energy from the proto-realm being seemingly blind and distorted possibly based on the notion of an omni-directional vortex with its solar planes and attendant cometary debris. As for occulted warrens and their parallels via data the proto plane can be agitated by the senses so that gods are seen according to squid.

The anterior consisting of a plane no fragment can countenance. As superior christening one can never extend one's physical appendage into non-existence at the same time having the human neural field remain intact as it was before its appendage was extended.This scenario is never based on an isolate neural image trending as an isolate fragment attempting to combine itself as essence.

As I register my human subsequence through brackish neural glass I come to myself as an alchemical powder streaking through space. To this degree I can never speak of myself as a dazed green comet peering through an aperture of itself streaking as an aperture of negation. Within such casted tolerance I can cast no relevant neural display or action. Perhaps I am reflected squid-like to myself as an apparition streaking across the infernal waters beneath Phobos.* Or perhaps I can easily add to this list the Japanese Spider Crab,* or the blue dragon* as nudibranch, or Ctenophores* that seem to flare then drift as aurorae into human stratification that flare and spin as cellular rotation. Perhaps one can speculate that diamonds are blood spills alive with lands and unions of lands prior to Laurasia and Gondwanaland* Perhaps one can claim to recall an a-cellular canvas where the void resembles its own interval say, depicted by the difference between sea eagle and iguana where the interval teems with potencia. Perhaps we are speaking of a void that teems with equivocal larvae without pattern gleaned from unknown evidence exploded and prior to coagulation. This being the plane of what I consider to be human dis-evidence with its reflexive reciprocity.

What I say remains awkward incandescence to myself and the cells inside my cells therefore I am illumined by projections from emptiness, by glints from pre-atomic eternity that remain endemic with its own obliteration sustaining its own motion as evidence. Perhaps mantra exists as mediation not unlike a coral ignited by spiders that self-ignite themselves via higher mnemonics based on what I consider to be sub-causes and their synonymous parallel reflections that fail to monitor themselves according to classification or metrics. According to human rote as the proto plane wrought by compositional peril being dark geographic blending with itself. This being the plane active with trans-functional irrationality quoting itself via curious question or plague. Not every living episode transmutes according to alchemical pressure. I am simply enunciating pressure perhaps via bellicose and terrestrial scorpions gelatinous with toxicity and not unlike poisonous sea worms under the auspices of trans-galactic law. This being what the greater part of humanity considers as toxic and void enacting itself as transposed strength making equation with uneven marshes. Perhaps I remain nothing other than derelict energy emblazoned and riddled by traps and glowing deficits.

The unknown replete with horizonless suns, with antipodes buried in blankness that exists as unclaimed rivulets where blood begins to blaze and assassinate itself in differing dimensions. This being not unlike a teeming proto-sun that silently explodes symbolized by super novae exploding above the Earth remaining a conundrum of brilliance espied in its private solar pasture according to rogue or shifting account. The latter reality wedded to protracted neon deserts on Saturn coldly burning, symbolized as a trans-galactic particle that en-veins itself as trans-galactic neurology that float like the demographic maps of Ibn Khaldun.* Thus any map of the cosmos can only be lighted for a time. As for exo-planet and their wilderness it remains naive and immature galactic understanding. The commercial mind presently exists as flight within dulled lightning sheafs. I could speak of lighted oceans on exo-planet K2-18,* of feral rays pouring from unknown uranian infernos. This brings to view the darkness of uranian mystical fields with these mystical fields being akin to higher states where the sky disappears where we sense a mingling of rays non-existent as metaphors that seep beyond equation. It is my contention that existence exists not as tautology but as a kind of evidence blazing as motif by interior witness.

Not simply extinguished visual metrics but impalpable scent that circulates beyond the invisible, beyond the entry root of graves. This is not about the repetition of lives that have turned back on themselves floating as blinded loopings beyond themselves breaking beyond causality. Not broken grace but higher consciousness suffused by differing dawns. Let me state consciousness as a wilderness of infinitely fingering dawns. Let me evince a spate of local suns. Let us make note of main sequence stars, in short, common aerial suns that includes our personal Sun. I am thinking in this regard of the Hertzspruung-Russell diagrams* that include 90% of the stars in our known universe. I can speak of T Tauri, Rigel, our local Sun, Aldeberan, Antares, Lamda Bootis, Fomalhaut.* Not strangely shaped forms but conventional aerial balance based on anterior seepage that reveal all solar mass to be at one with erasure. This does not condone erasure sans the staggering realia that condenses cosmic complexity. Suns are not grainy industrial ciphers that release from themselves overwhelming animation and blight but gather into themselves as explosive founts of erasure. Even considering visible tactility suns are understood to be rife with staggering complexity always pointing the way to their own invisibility. The latter understood to be their furtive index, their disappearance unto themselves symbolized on a lesser scale by the Jupiterian Red Spot only alive via truncated time when considered within the light of human evidence. All the suns named symbolise powers far in advance of the particular evidence garnered by humans.

When the human mind extends to the understanding of giant molecular clouds it recognizes over a million solar masses. Typical cloud densities are 100 to 1000 molecules per cubic centimeter since suns have an overwhelming but truncated life span.* Here I am only considering their visible habitability because ultimately they are maps of condensed uncanny power, and because their winds and lesser winds continue to condense as imperious power I have never been released into the ultimate whirl of their alien seismicity. This is not some pseudo-medicinal construct on my behalf ushered along by uninhabitable ciphers and flares, but irrigated by the proto reflex that is emptiness. Not emptiness chronicled by localized belief but by a proto sun risen above suns whose energy magically releases itself into a blank and uncertain grace. Not simply physical iridescence poised as barbarous counterparts of metal, but of self-release according to problematical osmotics.

The latter not as the stenography of demise based on territorial cinder but of power that never registers itself according to our fragmented nexus charged as it is by calumny. This being far beyond the energy cast searching for derelict waters on Mars. The latter endeavour not unlike a truncated pattern that explores itself as cognitive progression. Instead I am speaking of climate as gregarious inner research being bells that ring and disentangle their own nightmares so as to enter scorching crystalline pastures of purity. An inner pathway not according to sainthood or psychic parity with demons but breakage into erasure where a compass of splendour hurls itself beyond the terror of reason, beyond all its beings, and waters, and volcanoes. This being mathematics with links to their natural perspicuity opening onto a state sans sound and colour resounding.

Glossary

Qingjiang biota– province in southern China where over 20,000 over fossilized remains from the Cambrian period (over 500 million years ago) were found palpably intact many of them unknown.

Saturn's lunar fields– now total 82 moons the highest number in our solar system.

Phobos– innermost moon of Mars "and is seven times as massive as the outer moon Deimos." It is irregularly shaped.

Japanese Spider Crab– largest known species of crab that can live up to 100 years. It reaches 18 feet from "claw to claw."

blue dragon– shelless blue sea slug that floats upside down using the surface tension of the water to stay afloat. It is a nudibranch.

Ctrnophores– resembling jellyfish "having biradial symmetry swimming by means of eight bands of transverse ciliated plates." They are also called comb jellies.

Laurasia/Gondwanaland– continents that broke off from the supercontinent Pangaea some 200 million years ago. Laurasia was the northern half and Gondwanaland was the southern.

Ibn Khaldun– Islamic historian and original demographer who provided essential characterics of collective populations that remain in use.

K2-18b– exo-planet 110 light years from Earth. An uninhabitable water world having an atmosphere closer to that of Neptune than that of Earth.

Hertzspruung-Russell diagram– A "chart that revolutionized the study of stars." Devised by Enjar Hertzsprung and Henry Norris Russell "in which the absolute magnitudes of stars are plotted against their spectral types."

T Tauri, our Sun, Aldeberan, Antares, Lambda Boothis, Fomalhaut– mean sequence suns that represent 90% of suns in the heavens.

truncated star life– stars being not unlike human beings are born evolve and die. For instance our Sun at 5 billion years is in the midst of its lifetime.

Findings

A Gift from the Universe:
This message has no content.

*

In this animation someone
has personified the synapses.

*

A raindrop,
pendulous,
at the end
of a long twig,

I

have great respect
for the recalcitrance
of objects.

For

This tree's a paradise
of glass and plastic
icicles, raindrops

lit by winking (ticking)
stars.

Stay here.

Red is for ripe
and green for forest.

Now green is for go
and red is for stop.

Blue is for cold
and for heaven above.

"Live for," they say.

Who does?

Ghost World

Memories are ghosts
of people not yet dead.

Everyone believes in them
(believes them.)

When they disappear,
they let the cold in.

*

In the cold, things
come closer
without moving,

becoming more and more
distinct.

It's not possible to touch them.

*

The conjunctions are frozen;
the hinges:

"now."

*

Now tiny birds
are bouncing

through the corpse
of the wisteria.

Whistle

The Empire Builder rolls through,
its "whistle" a groan.

A scream is rounded out
in poems, given
a smooth finish.

"Respect the drink!"

In how many recent films
does the hero get his power
from venom,
radiation, or exposure
to chemicals?

How many have been made to host
a hostile symbiont
against their will?

These are moments
that can be flipped, dropped
into 4-Chan.

By naming its vape flavor
"Unicorn Poop," DripStar
parodies marketing,

thus appealing
to children.

III.

Tonight I'm going to show him how I got good
at petitioning for rain, how I came to handle
drowning, and how I came to turn away from candle
light because the flicker simply overwhelmed me. Could
I, in his absence, pass my hands over limbs of wood—
Tonight, though we're walking in years between us, a candle
brings us a cloud closer to a deeper hue, and we can handle
any breeze that turns us inside out. I leave on my hood,
afraid I'll forget I even changed. Forget his whorl.
If he were rain, I'd quit him before he even fell.
I was taught not run when it finally came, but to take
it all in; I couldn't. It's the way my hands and face whirl
off like utterance in the wind, and my drowning quells
like rain off the leaf of a boy's flower, or muscle ache.

XII.

The lace hem of my skirt has become worn.
Or maybe it's always been this way: like wind,
we never felt the cracks of morn

that summer. I told him I'd turn them, wind
them even, if he wanted me to, until he'd think
I was making music—sometimes when I bind

them, they can be tuned beautiful still. Just a wink,
and I'll come wearing mountains over my shoulders,
come bearing lakes about my legs. Then in a blink

we'll tune ourselves to a field of lace, our shoulder
blades thrusting into the white, and our wrists—
they'll finish going round, ready to shoulder

the day we yellow together into old lace, old wrists.
Our lives rounded out like arcs of our wrists.

Stacey Balkun

Dead Pregnant Whale Found with 48 Pounds of Plastic in Stomach, April 2, 2019

How do I show you this phone screen
conjures more than mirror? It scries my face
over a whale, breached like I breached,
both of us turned around in the salt-murk
between birth and death, our lungs burning.
I was adopted, bottle-fed limp formula, the plastic
nipple tossed once I was grown, thrown
to the ocean and lodged in the belly
of this whale. Everything I've held
turned weapon against her, baby
bottle to ballpoint pen. How could it add up
to 48 pounds, as much as six well-fed infants,
of plastic? Yesterday's whale, pregnant,
would never give birth even if she had
lived. Her dead calf was rotting inside her,
the plastic not rotting inside her
as her mammal-flesh decays against
wind-brittle sand. The lump
and cut pushed against her womb,
the empty that maybe she felt, too,
sometimes, thinking about her own mother
or what home means, slipping wetly
from the hungry mouth of the Gulf
where absence should be left for krill and water
and salt. This story is a pattern, not a spell
and there is no tide. The ilium, a clamshell,
broken. The story breaking against the shore
and again against the front page
of my smartphone and yours. Look.
The sun still blares against the surface,
the silver-painted pen in my hand glinting
like a fillet knife—can it save
anything? It might be too late to dive in
with our soft hands, to turn it
around. I don't know what to call upon
and sometimes I want to give up.

The problem is I was born
to it, the water already warming
to a briny murk. Before I knew it,
my bones were white, my skin soft
and the small trash can in the nursery full.
The problem is I already have.

Joan Baranow

Drought

These hills are green again
with grasses fine and fleeting—
like lanugo, it won't last.

Each year the rain recedes
over the ocean,
the ocean churns its plastics.
Almond trees and cattle feed
drink the ground dry.

On this parched lip of land
we watch the signs,
pocket profits, project
the desiccations of earth.

When the water's gone,
when the hills are stripped
of deer and birdsong,
we will wander across
the cracked valley
on unbalanced accounts,

east from San Joaquin,
towards Reno.

Michael Basinski

Frog Medley

Frog Medley is a multi-voice sound poem in celebration of frog transformations from egg to maturity. There must be a quartet of frog voices and an auxilium of frog voices that could be the audience. The more participants there are, the more effective the poem is realized.

Notes:
The frog quartet performs the score with a primary performing frog voice that manifests the majority of the vocal labor, while the remaining frog voices recite various facets of the poem and improvise. The primary frog is part of the quartet.
The auxilium fully participates in the frog cacophony, and the auxilium is encouraged to randomly and variously deposit frog noises throughout the Frog Medley as the quartet of frog voices presents the medley.
The frog quartet and the frog auxilium could use frog clicker toys.
The frog quartet and the frog auxilium could use some of the following instructions in Frog Cacophony to improvise and realize frog noises throughout the poem.
Expressively repeat improvisations and manifestations as desired. Space each realization with some silent seconds. General realizations suggest raspatory airflow going from the lungs, passing through the larynx, and into the oral cavity as the vocal cords oscillate.

What the audience needs to know. The primary frog recites: *Hi, Frog Medley is a multi-voice sound poem celebrating the life cycle of a frog which begins with courtship and proceeds to the laying of eggs, then transmutes to full maturity and returns to courtship. You should know that in the original story, the princess or prince does not kiss the frog but tosses the frog at a wall: splat. Please join in this manifestation.*

Frog Cacophony

(Tone: Frogs advertise their location in the mating process. Pitch: intense. Frog quartet and frog auxilium present this facet. Improvise. Express. For variable duration.)

Frog instructions:
Sharp woody raps: cut-cut-cut-cut!
An explosive nasal utterance of rolling grrrrrruut-grrrrrrrrruut-grrrrrrrrrrrrrrruut!
Gagging this word errrrrrrrah!
A rapid series of metallic clicks that rise in pitch: crrrrrreeeeeeeeeeeeeek!
An aggressive stuttering trill rising in pitch at the end:
purrrrrrrrreeeeeeeeeeek! Squeaky peeps.
Soft duck-like rolling cackling: ca-ha-ha-ac, ca ha ha ac!

Nasal, buzzy trill of about 5 seconds: waaaaaaaaaaaaaaaaaaaa!
Loud, resonant bass sound: rummmm, rummm, rummm, which sounds like jug-a-rum.
Drawn-out rattling snore lasting three seconds starting soft and growling
louder followed by soft grunts or chuckling: brekekekex koax koax. Classic
frog sounds such as ribbit and croak.

(As the frog auxilium finds its zenith the frog quartet begins a recitation of the following lines. Each performer reads at a rapid pace until all the passage is complete. The cacophony semi-resides into the background as egg depositing begins.)

Ribbit rabbet ribber rubber rubbar ranparykus rabber robbur ribbiet croak Coke folk hokes hooks jamoke joke
Rutter rybat ribbot rabber rebut rabble rethar ramble rancor ribbon
croak Crock clack coat broke choke cloak croak
Random rubbar ratter rattler raddle rearing reating ripping ribbit croak
Stroke toke toke toke toque yogh yolk yoke
Rytling rutting rutter ribald ranger rabbler
rambler ramparyncus croak
Oak poke reque smoke toak stoke spoke soke soak
Ribbit rabbet ribber rubber rubbar ranparykus rabber robbur ribbiet croak
Coke folk hokes hooks jamoke joke
Rutter rybat ribbot rabber rebut rabble rethar ramble rancor ribbon
croak Crock croak coat broke choke cloak croak
Random rubbar ratter rattler raddle rearing reating ripping ribbit croak
Stroke toke toke toke toque yogh yolk yoke
Rytling rutting rutter ribald ranger rabbler
rambler ramparyncus croak
Oak poke reque smoke toak stoke spoke soke soak

(Seamlessly continue from Frog Cacophony to Frog Repo.)

Frog Repo

(Realized by frog quartet with frog auxilium accompanying. Tone: Some frogs lay egg clusters usually attached to emergent aquatic vegetation forming a jelly-like blob, and frogs do not have penises. Females discharge eggs into the water and the male sheds sperm on the eggs. An egg is the letter e. Improvise. Deposit eggs and sperm randomly for some duration. Pitch: sensual.)

E e e e E e e e e e e e e e e e e e e e e e e e e e e e
e e e

Or Eeeeeeeeeeeee eeeeeeeeee eeeeeeeEeeeeeeeeeeeeeeee
And then Eeeeeeeeeeeeeeeeeeeeeeeeeeeeeeeeeeeeeeeeeeeeee
Or Eeee e e e e e e e e e e e e e e e e e
And then Eeeeee Ee e e e e

(Seamlessly continue from Frog Repo to Frog Metamorphosis.)

Frog Metamorphosis

(Realized by frog quartet with primary frog voice realizing far left column. The other frog quartet voices recite cuing off the primary voice recitation. Listen. Tone: metamorphic machine. Pitch: fast. Frog auxilium accompanies.)

The embryo leaves			
His jelly shell			
The embryo leaves	jelly shell	the tiny black spots	21 days
Her jelly shell	jelly shell	the specks will hatch	20 days
The embryo leaves	jelly shell		
His jelly shell	jelly shell	the spawn will wiggle	19 days
The embryo leaves		the spawn will wiggle	
Her jelly shell		the spawn will wiggle	18 days
The embryo leaves	jelly shell		
Their jelly shell	jelly shell		17 days
The embryo leaves	jelly shell	the spawn will wiggle	
They jelly shall	jelly shall		16 days
The larvae that			
Emerges			15 days
The lava that	gills		
Emerge	gills	Hormone thyroxine	14 days
The Larva larvae	GILLS	Hormones hormones	
The larva that	gills	Hormone thyroxine	13 days
Emerges	gills	Hormones hormones	
The larvae that	gills		12 days
Emerges	GILLS		
The larva that			11 days
Emerge			
A torrent of tadpoles	they have	two arms four legs	10 days
A torrent of tadpoles	no lips	two arms four legs	
A torrent of tadpoles		two legs for arms	9 days
A torrent of tadpoles	they have	two legs four arms	8
With tiny black legs	no lungs	fingers like webbed	7
A torrent of tadpoles		webbed webbed	6
A torrent of tadpoles	toothless	fingers	5

With tiny black legs		1,2,3,4,5,6		4
A torrent of tadpoles		1,2,3,4,5,6,7,8		3
Glands are formed		9,10		2
Hope away		9,10		2,1
Eat flies and reproduce	absorb your tail			2,1
Hope away	absorb your tail	hop away		1
Eat flies and reproduce	absorb your tail	hop away		1
Hope away	absorb you tail	hop away		
Eat flies and reproduce	hop away	hop away		1
Hope away	hop away			hop away
Eat flies and reproduce	hop away			
Hop away				
Hop Away			you nasty frog	you silly frog
Alas, Alas	if I could get my ball		you nasty frog	you silly frog
again			you nasty frog	you silly
again			you nasty frog	
If I could get my ball	again		you nasty frog	you silly frog
	again			

If you will love me and let me eat from your golden plate and sleep upon your silken bed

Tap	tap	plash	plash
Tap	tap	plash	plash
Tap	tap	plash	plash
Tap	tap	plash	plash
Tap	tap	plash	plash

(Seamlessly continue from Frog Metamorphosis to Froggie Went a Courtin.)

Froggie Went a Courtin

(Realized by frog quartet with primary frog voice realizing far left column first singing and then keeping rhythm until gadzooks. The other frog quartet voices recite cuing off the primary voice recitation. Other frog voices need not recite each phrase or recite each phrase exactly. However, all end in repo as primary voice enters gadzooks. Listen. Tone: methodical and chanty. Pitch: semi-fast. Frog auxilium accompanies.)

♫ Froggie went a courtin and he did ride. Mhmm
♫Froggie went a courtin and he did ride. A sword and a pistol by his side. Mhmm. Mhmm. Mhmm.
♫Froggie went a courtin and she did ride. Uh-huh
♫Froggie went a courtin and she did ride. A sword and a pistol by her side. Uh-huh. Uh-huh Uh-huh

♫Froggie went a courtin and we did ride. Hey-hey
♫Froggie went a courtin and we did ride. A sword and a pistol by our side. hey-hey

hey-hey			
uh-huh			
uh-huh			
mhmm-mhmm			
ergh-ergh		frog clog hog flog analog	
orrck-orrck		frog fog drub haag jog blog dialog	
ecgee-ecgee			
eha-eha		frog bog glove hedgehog	
yupo-yupo		bog frog cog haag hog	
agog-agog			
egad-egad		hog cub hoog bub maag moog nog	
utoo-utoo		nog plog shog skog smog	
ika-ika			
chacha-chacha		togue tog wag zog metagog	
yeah-yeah		bog clog bubb flog dog frog analogue	
yeah-yeah			
okay-okay		loc blog logs jogs frog	
fooey-fooey		blog bog clague clog dague flog fog	
fiddle dee-fiddle dee			
right on-right on		dog's flog nog fog glove	
ouch-ouch		log hog chubb dialog	
ouch-ouch			
o dear-o dear		log smog lapdog	
o my-o my		bog clog cog dog fog hog jog	
o well-o well			
oopsey-oopsey		agog befog club incog prolog	
okey-dikey		unclog sled-dog grub	
okey dokey	repo	repo	repo
okey-dikey	re	po	rib
okey dokey	it	re	po
gee whiz-gee-whiz	rib	it	re
golly-golly	po	rib	it
goodbye-goodbye	re	po	rib
good grief-good grief	it	re	po
geepers-geepers	repo	repo	repo
gadzooks-gadzooks			

(Seamlessly continue from Froggie Went a Courtin to Frog Splat.)

Frog Splat

(All realize splat with the sound of splat multiple times and all then end in ribbit. Tone and pitch: expressionistic and loud.)

splat splat splat splat splat splat splat splat

rrribbit.... rrribbit....rrribbit....rrribbit

Lesley Battler

redundant

my hometown, north of here, withers along a lake but i'm used to leaving it, this time following the guard to a small hot room covered with time clocks. steam machines hiss, saws bark and choke, wire service tickets clatter, the day starts babbling. i usually work in a musical format but the office is full of arithmetic dressed in powdered wigs, rouged cheeks paling under the display model of a hydrocarbon. loud perfume of starch and bleaching fluid, redundant stories run by compressed air pumps. the idea is always make a tree into a log, a log into a plank

crypto

summer packs all its wallop in a bindle, hops
a train. snow waits for the day-labour trucks then drops
into a box, everywhere skies walking into windows

i polish the tarnished horizon clasping my ankles
and pass the fascists breeding in potholes. clash of side
streets. cops stroll on patrol in pilled sheets axe
handles swinging

dusk creeps along the banks of ancient
jests and tiltyard escapades. midnight flashes my family
of paving stones. moon, mean as a clipped coin
oversees the falling children

clouds sloop into mucilage pools. i claw out
the riptide of family photos, score a dime bag of air
miles, reap today's gibbering from the monocle
glued to my pineal gland

unmatched femurs jam laundry chutes, pallets
of tinned narratives are loaded on wagons, rolling
into sponsored float camps moored at the mouth of
disappearance

the who-cares arrive salting carelessness
down QAnon Sound. not one, but countless
serpents rustling under my feet. 8chan aliases peer
through blockchain visas

self-reproach drifting in from the river, every
no one lurking in verges. i have just enough crypto-
night to buy balaclavas for all the pixels hiding in
the barrows

an ampersand walks through a phrase, attacks
the A-frames. the driverless Model T picks up a
crate of sisyphean roll-your-owns. lawyers stand on
the shoulders of assault rifles

what tumbles out next, a rootball of untold
tales, implications camped along empirical shores
sent to you alone, Private and Confidential under
separate cover

i can hear the Late carrying their ropes, baskets
and spades. i am not myself, i never had a self in
that real where White Beard holds the sickle and
ghosts flee the ovens

Jeffery Beam

The Folk

nurses
          tending nymphs and larvae

honored ladies
                    waiting on the Queen
house bees
          airing refreshing heating the hive
                    fanning with wings

architects
                    masons wax-workers sculptors
                    constructing combs
foragers
                    sallying forth
chemists
                    preserving honey
                    formic acid dropped from sting-tips

capsuled males
                    sealing cells
sweepers
                    irreproachably cleaning
bearers
                    removing the dead

amazons

          watching thresholds day and night
          questioning comers and goers
          welcoming novices home from first flights
          scaring away vagabonds marauders loiterers
          expelling interlopers
          attacking foes

Hive's minions
                              of the One Mind

          individual indistinct

to the sweet mass you inhabit
invent
I bring you a human smoke to show you how
unconsciousness works

to show you

men and women claiming universal love
seeking the flowery field with compasses broken

around you and your spheres of endeavor
we lord over ruling nothing

your constellations remain
subtle abstracted

when the sun falls
star-bomb into our world
you like us will flare
into smoke
but unlike us
knowingly together

but then
what then of us

perhaps when the sun
falls terrible ball terromoto *onto us*
we will see as one
explode into whitefire whitedust

platinum honey

making the cosmos glow
into

eternal hexagonals of being

Parnassus, the Barren Cleft

For Jonathan Williams, after Andrew Young

We should
of course
be grateful
from such an elevation—
distracted
by some plant—
saxifrage
among the rocks
urging us on:
after the wind—
a still small
voice
The clouds—
tired—
hang low to the hills
In them
a tempting brightness
making us short-sighted
god-like
Mountains
smoking
on all sides
Pastures below—
a steaming cauldron
The earth on fire
The river
a serpent winding
from wet fire
Our eyes
trespassed
to dim distance

Above all
the mountain
huger than itself

The Flies

They visit a country where flesh is only a language. A country of wide vistas, brown prairies, where air currents are impassioned, young and unencumbered. They have prepared for this carefully, remembering their ancestors, some wingless, who became anonymous as milk. They prepare to never again be anonymous. Somewhere their hungry secrets accumulate, debtless, waiting for a signal from below.

Our destiny is to witness. The first place we are taken is familiar, the small pain from a needle. Lessening our will, they invade, pouring sulfur into the windows. This is the original country. The fluid nation. Beyond boundaries. The Flies pinch and sting. Their anger knows no solace. They dress in green and purple robes. Afterwards, the sun sets. The moon comes out, thread in the undergarments of the drowned.

In a fortnight, the Flies are gone. We discover their final instructions: a few detached wings, crushed antennas, a green puddle of inner antagonisms. We wonder at their brevity, whether their soul's wit is as delicate as ours, and whether we will follow. We visit a country where flesh is known only as language. A country of narrow stone streets, windless and stale. Some of us, wingless, accumulate hungry secrets. We wait for a signal from above.

Mei-Mei Berssenbrugge

Jump Circle

For Marthe Reed

1.

I fall like a meteorite through the dark.

A flute of light streams from the hole I make in the sky.

People looking up see a dot in this beam, arms and legs spiraling, and grow still and widen their sight like a halo around me.

When I land, I see crystals have fallen from my bag, and I look up at stars.

Seven crystals gather to the north; I draw the Pleiades for human memory.

My first task is to look across night in such a way that each crystal has a place.

The story's both myth and prophecy, just as starlight reaching us already happened; the void, space-time, comes before.

Then Milky Way with its four corners of dark, ascending and descending, gives time scansion.

Looking up, you engage with elemental transparence.

Pleiades, light in space-time, distance, suddenly takes the form of being.

This state-change is intrinsic to experience and reveals itself by circumstance, what happens.

I desired to see how what happens conforms to cycle, place, when our mesa was lit by a flash, wherein my wish, rain, fell.

2.

Think of stars as ecologies of beings, substantive as angels.

Up there, matter and consciousness exist as bounded levels of frequencies.

Aliveness is both shared and particular to our dimension, like the light of day.

There's no distinction between intent and space, because dimension is a frequency like light not a space, as when I was a husband in previous time or my poem was once recognized as a star.

A boy points out the route his grandmother will take to the Milky Way at death; to one backlit star he assigns her returning soul.

She falls through the quantum plenum ahead of us and behind us, teleporting from a "jump" circle on our land, maybe to Venus or a freestanding mesa in space.

Solstice, equinox demonstrate this coherence, frame for story to extend.

Its intelligibility is transparence in the mind of an angel, fragment of green consciousness that gives circumstance living form.

I ask to connect by matching frequencies with her.

She was already painting me with leaves, and everywhere she touched me, we grew.

Sally Bliumis-Dunn

Echolocation

The whales can't hear each other calling
in the noise-cluttered sea: they beach themselves.
I saw one once—heaved onto the sand with kelp
stuck to its blue-gray skin.
Heavy and immobile,

it lay like a great sadness.
And it was hard to breathe with all the stink.
Its elliptical black eyes had stilled, were mostly dry,
and barnacles clustered on its back
like tiny brown volcanoes.

Imagining the other whales, their roving weight,
their blue-black webbing of the deep,
I stopped knowing how to measure my own grief.
And this one, large and dead on the sand,
with its unimaginable five-hundred-pound heart.

Sean Borodale

Crickets and Noise of Grasses and Perseids

The coast of night hoops overhead.
I can hear
streaked light too fast to interrupt;

can feel the friction of a meteor;

crickets
setting out nodes, that will constellate later.

Under the helmet of dawn,
their milliseconds will strike.

There is nothing tentative.
The cold fever
cannot accomplish heat.

What am I lying in?
A body, breathing.
A sharpening that pins me to the boards of the table;
saw-chafed and frozen.

The cloth I wear
is made of listening to my skin.

I smell the damp dead-grass;
a saturated decay of dripping woods,
nearer than my blood.

I breathe to rescue ruined air.

Earth moves.
I am not afraid of being broken, or hit.

My dry bones will make a sound;
their snaps will configure

the spasm(s) of a future.

Devil's Coach Horse Beetle slowly through a moment of Witness

Even here, its artery is of black silence
juddering over painted concrete
of the kitchen floor.

A silent siren;
carrying a consequence of its entering.
The beetle articulates furiously, on.

Time, so still so thickened
I cannot cross it after it
  but hold it

opening across me,
closing across me.

Is it a kinship?
What will I do with an 'us' that absorbs me?

Have I mentioned the barbs,
  the fringed bristles along the legs,
the segments of antennae?
The prismatic sheen across blackness?
Each part immaculate;
un-bruised, un-chafed as something born.

No.
But in the slow whirlpool of the room:
to have passed a beetle on nearly equal terms.

May-Flies Unfinished

Bandages of flesh.
Bodies in tourniquet.
Engrossed cupid-white.
Growing towards wings.

Not yet colour; they do not know yet.

They know nothing of flight.
Their bodies know for them.

But I keep watch:
  scared;
  re-attuned.
Will they turn full-palette,
  like a watch
reaching an hour?

Noon is the bleached hour.
Dusk is the time to exist.
The faults cannot be seen at dusk.

I fizz in the woods when I walk.
I think, *this is the nymph;*
I think, *this is me;*
in wood under fungus, in mud under death.

The emergency of the urge to be born.

Nymph-blood beats in my feathered ears.
I will have to learn to create
a shadow from a feel for the air.

It is almost an apprenticeship
to grow under stones.

One thread of me manages.
My lungs stop and they start
like a monastery dinner bell.

It remains to be seen
if I will alarm the air and lift to the sun.

The blue foil of a future day
will arrange me like flowers around a coffin;
a one-day carnage to which plants are invited.

The body causes its own trivia;
its own unmentionables;
distracting an urgency towards sex:

the red fungus of the phallus;
the lips of the dewpond.

I think, *this is it.*

Our babies will be buried, too, in muds
under slow-moving streams;

live colourless, translucent
cot lives as cold as corpses.

With the defect of a future
that will sometimes be furious.

Cindy Botha

Ticking

Orang-utans are the new homeless. Stray and starved they wander the red-dust bulldozed wastelands. Their eyes are abyssal. Thundering timber trucks, hundreds a day, gobble the track as leftovers burn. Hectares of black heat, the fizz and spurt of ancient stumps. The ash is a suffocating ubiquity. 'There is no fire like greed' said the 14th guru. His cupped hand holds rice—but burger on the hoof makes a happy meal and 760 million tons of grain fodder exact a wide wide stretch, lakes of water running dry while the slaughterhouse floor runs with blood and terror. Despite his bodyguard of four, submachine guns hefted, the last male white rhino slumps – it's decades since he regarded his mirror-self. A horn's a sure curse in a world of quasi-cures. Unless you're a unicorn, non-biodegradable plastic, mass-produced, extinction impossible. But the tired factory workers don't know unicorn myth, and they've never heard of fair trade. Unconcerned, the mannequin celebrities are preened for approval. They Instagram their golden bath-tubs, gelled fingernails, velvety buttocks like strange giant peaches to a tsunami of likes. The worship and whinny of a billion restless fingers is powered by fuels too ancient to fathom: the last bottom-of-the-barrel scrapings of primordial plenty. A polar bear, second cousin to the orang-utan, vacates at last his crumbling biscuit of ice and launches into the ink-black water to swim and swim until exhaustion and hunger stall his limbs, as the ice shelf shrugs its massive shoulder, miles of frozen blue, and births a calf the size of Belgium. 420 houses on a Pacific island – golden, a dropcloth of Paradise – sense the water lap their doorsteps, children splash at the fickle tideline. Right on time the sun will rise, the clock's ticking.

Michael Boughn

Eglinton at 5

It's never through with you, never
done with the deaths original
to your own figurations
of happy trails or another

stroll through the garden
of shattered hearts, pieces
crunching under relentless
reflections on the nature

of metaphysics. Examined
traffic patterns yield
crusading misprisions in place
of flows when deflect

enters the picture. When the picture
enters deflect confusions
confound patterns claim
to assigned seat. The light

changes and no one moves
because distant incursions
of injected greed breeds
entropic fixations normal

stasis and no one really wants
to get there knowing pensioned
conclusions offer little hope
beyond brief visits to distant

unapproachable worlds
of bad teeth, crushed goats
writhing in dust, and another
beautiful day in the light

stolen from time at a cost
calculable only in utter

disregard for what passes
for decency, a concept ripped

from pages of unique
literary merit. Repeated adjectival
superlatives ring bells
in alien belfries rousing objections

anticipated well before approaches
to various ramps announce
impassable blockades of jammed
up steel and rubber founding economies

of pain and routine passages
through unthought habits against blank
skies of late February. Food
and roof wander into labyrinth's

multitude of reasons and become
stone. Not stoned, which would reopen
negotiations with traffic patterns
toward possible, what? entropic

fibrillations or analogical
eruptions into parking lots across
GTA, little gestures of love oozing
into front seats with hot pizza

after game's folderol? Sheer unlikeliness
of the sky caught up in rivers
of red lights, silent and still
over stabilized motion interruptions

stretching into fields of grief
for unrecognized iron fortune's
rendition of *almost there if it*
weren't for the damned traffic

announcements leave it likely, in fact
newsworthy for broadcasts
across temporal grid interstices
every night at six while economies

quiver thinking of arrangements
opening, beginning to move
into the night, shifting constellations
flowing toward another long day.

JOHN BRADLEY

Once and Always

A stray galaxy settled in
the voice box, bits of charred
star in everything we say.

And You Shall Know Us by Our Trash: An Ecopoetics for the Moon

Ninety-six plastic bags of human urine, feces, and vomit (*I sure feel bad,*
said Buzz Aldrin, *for whoever finds my bag*). More than seventy spacecraft,
including modules and crashed orbiters. Twelve pairs of space boots.

Six nylon American flags (complete with artificial wind ripples) now bleached
solar white. Six gnomons. Five electric generators, each containing eight
pounds of plutonium. Three lunar rovers, one with a small Bible

(James Irwin's) on the dashboard. Two golf balls (struck by Alan Shephard
with a six iron. *Miles and miles and miles*, said Shepherd on the flight
of the second ball), location unknown. One bar of soap.

A falcon's feather (from Baggin, the Air Force mascot falcon) and a hammer
(dropped simultaneously to demonstrate Galileo's theory of falling objects).
A color photo of James Irwin and another of Charles Duke,

his wife, and two kids—all bleached solar white. A polycarbonate urn containing
human ashes (geologist Eugene Shoemaker). Empty packages of space food.
Insulating blankets. Several (improvised) javelins.

TV cameras, film magazines, tripod, zoom lens. Shovel, trenching tools, rakes,
tongs, drills, brushes. Towels (red and blue), wet wipes, tissue dispenser,
anti-bacterial ointment, a pair of nail clippers. Earplugs, watchband,

tie tack. Several hammocks. One document proclaiming: *University of Michigan
Alumni of the Moon*. One hundred $2 bills (forgotten by James Irwin
and Dave Scott, who planned to auction them—*Lunar-Infused*

$2 Bills!—once back on Earth). *I sure feel bad,* said Buzz Aldrin, kicking from
the door of the lunar lander those *collection devices* full of human
feces, urine, and vomit onto the moon, *for whoever finds my bag.*

Marc Brightside

A Beetle

Disgusting, artless creature,
aesthetically and functionally useless,
the embodiment of entropy
and brutal in its biological desires,
now inverted, twitching and convulsing
on the edge of platform three.

I watched it strain, and lurch,
and twist against the pavement.
Tonight, its primitive design,
tested against bombs and poison,
would prove to be the nails
pinning it before the executioners,
those drunks and tired salesmen
departing from the midnight train.

My back towards the window,
discretely as I could, I tapped once,
twice, my toe against its shell,
until the creature fell onto its feet,
re-ordered its axes, and sped off,
away from our aloof machines.

It was just a bug, one of a billion,
but character is what you are
in the dark, and in the darkness,
they know light, an ancient sanctitude
that still eludes us, in our higher state
of uniform, methodical refrain.

Laynie Browne

Practice Has No Sequel

I searched for a sentence to repeat in peril. A sentence immune to flares of memory or invented daggers. This sought sentence transports me to a series of auricles, absolute volition, regardless of circumstance, unscathed by relentless uncertainty or misfortune.

So many sentences are not the sentence I can say to myself in an attempt to lean toward equanimity while not avoiding sorrow. Why remain loyal to loss? Is willful movement away dishonest? Is a walk through blighted fields an encounter with blindness? If I am not here regarding the actual (which has never yet occurred and is not repeatable) then aren't I missing a series of pressing moments—each precisely vast—if attended?

Now I've stumbled on ancient thresholds real not only in mind. How does this happen? Stillness translates concepts to essence. A butterfly circles the body. A red fox pauses and looks into your eyes. Yesterday I spoke with a bird, and several hemlock trees adorning a roadside whose pendulous depths nod blue shade.

Today I've found a sentence, pulled it over my head, listened to the rush of language. Falls in waves over face and torso. Syllables brush knees—graze floors, delicate tracery of sky. The sentence is weightless contour—follows closely—detaches easily. These words belong to any attempting return—to altar and solace—to residence of now.

Let another run away with false concepts. Carried untold distances. The essential 'I' never enters another's false story.

Psithurism is the sound of wind through trees.

The sentence is filigree, leaf become ground. Demulcent concepts fall silently in cobalt forests beyond form. I am not another's story. I am not even my own self-concept. Thousands of miniscule false portraits we clutch may depart—softly as rain returns to rivulets and capillaries—or discordantly—as spines clash.

Joseph Bruchac

Walking Over Ice to Valcour Island

Petonbagok, the waters between, is
  breathing underneath this skin of
  white, no thicker than the space
  from one frost to the next.

The rumble of an army bomber
  throbs overhead practicing war.
It passes as quickly as all human sounds
  while the lake's thrum continues.

I walk on bear paws,
splayed like the feathered feet of grouse,
  following the hieroglyphic prints
of deer and coyote in new snow.

I walk and as I walk I listen
to the drumbeat that began far away
  growing closer, closer,
the horizon underneath my feet
  widening into sky.

As a crack opens, moving toward me
like a strike of lightning caught in slow motion,
  spreading the ice between my feet
and, one last heartbeat before I fall in,
  closing the gap again.

The ice subsides as I stand still on
  the chest of this great being—
ignoring my passage, simply waiting for
  a stronger sun to open its lungs.

As I wait for strength to return to my limbs
  Petonbowk rumbles and hums beneath me, a
  song older than human certainty,
deeper than all our memories, stronger
than our quick presence on earth and water.

Mikwaldam

My palm is filled with dust
  like that same dust
sprinkled from Great Mystery's hands
  onto the moist glacial sand

where it shaped itself a body
  arms, hands, fingers,
a neck and head, blind and deaf
  but unable to speak
until the sacred lightning arrows
  pierced flesh and skull

making ears, eyes, nostrils
  and a single mouth.

As I pour this dust, I
  pray the lightning
  may once more
to us restore those
  seven sacred
  openings that we
  may see, hear,
  smell again

that we may chant for
  all that breathes for the
  stolen waters, the
  wounded land,

that we may rise together
  this time to walk singing
  mikwaldam, mikwaldam,
  mikwaldam, mikwaldam,
  mikwaldam, mikwaldam,
  we remember.

The Last Stand

Just one paved road back then led
from east to west
across the Adirondacks.

We took it in the Cornell bus.
It was 1960, so many things then just
begun, like the feathered seeds
of milkweed lifted in a scattering wind.

It had been clearcut, that forest
not only once but more than twice.
What trees there were,
beech, spruce and pine, all
were second growth save
in that one place the
loggers had missed, as if
their eyes
had been blinded by
some ancient spirit.

Professor Hamilton led us there,
to a hill not far from Saranac Lake. His
face looked different in the light that
sifted down from the canopy, dust
motes dancing like pollen around his
bowed head.

His voice was so quiet
that our own words
vanished like the sound
of steps muffled by needles
piled in centuries beneath our feet.

These pines were here
before the first white man
stepped anywhere upon this land.

I remember nothing of words after that
only the touch of rough bark to my cheek,
my arms around a grandfather tree,
praying that their roots might be strong enough to
continue to hold their ancient peace.

Oded Carmeli

Hating Animals

Translated from the Hebrew by Maayan Eitan & Oded Carmeli

*

A dove is a winged rat

a cat is furred cockroach

and it's killing me

how chickens taste like chicken

dinosaurs tasted like chicken

it sickens me

that carnivores are not vegan

and omnivores not picky

it's eating me up

the way grasshoppers rape and pillage

and ducks don't pay taxes

and never vote

and all the microorganisms combined

have not contributed a single verse

to modern Hebrew poetry

how can they live like that

how can I live

after something like that

*

Animals

what a bunch of primitives

the Archaea kingdom a monarchy

the Arthropod phylum a technocracy

the Maxillopoda class still waging

class warfare

the Lepidoptera order a cult

the Liliaceae family values

family values

the Ailuropoda genus all racists

and the species Homo Sapiens

a subspecies of subhumans

still discriminating against

women.

*

In the worst storm

in twenty years

and there's one

just about every year

you see people

standing their ground

you see people

running around

you hear the sirens

wailing

which means people

are at work

are at war

and a tree falls

but the people

raise it back up

you see people rise up

you see people

up and running

never even thinking

of ever leaving earth

in the worst storm

in twenty years

and there's one

every year

you see people

standing

you see people

withstanding

you see people

what you don't see

what you never see

are hedgehogs

no hedgehogs

where are all the hedgehogs

where's the dove

where's the crow

one fly to feed upon our dead

there's not a dog

in sight.

Catherine Carter, illustrated by Sara Method

Luna

LUNA

A mouse has gnawed this dead luna moth,
leaving only the celadon sails
raised to cross the black lakes
of these few nights—devoured sailor and ship,
and the pale shores of evening,
and even the crescent's spring-green
sickle, so that tonight, if you meet with that mouse,
you'll know which mouse it was:
the one whose silver ears trim and turn
to catch the May wind, the one who shines like the moon.

—Catherine Carter
CW Carter

From *Larvae of the Nearest Stars*, copyright 2019 by Catherine Carter. Letterpress printed using Kennerly & Century Schoolbook type on Stonehenge. Original illustrations & typesetting by Sara Method, School of Art & Design, Western Carolina University, Cullowhee, NC. Limited edition of 100, of which this is copy 1/100, signed & numbered by the poet.

Cara Chamberlain

35—Bromine

By 2100, ocean will drown the keys, killing all sea-fringing, margin-adapted
Red mangroves of South Florida. In memoriam, we'll have (if we have anything; if we "are")
Old photographs, "Red Mangroves" by Clyde Butcher, for instance, that
Materialized in a darkroom using, perhaps, photosensitive silver nitrate or bromide.
In his image, the trunk of a single tree lunges open-armed over its own filigreed
pNeumatophores, a witch's tracery of bleached and bone-worn phalanges,
Edging into the water, the main trunk a contortionist's tangle of spine and breast

Black and white, and more exquisite for that; in the background, a silver-toned batik confusion of
Rangeless foliage, extended bolts of pattern, and the water a white-topped wash, satin-smooth since the lens was open so long,
Only a hint of a splash against the photo's vortex, which is located on what you could call the genitalia or 7th chakra of the tree if you see it as somewhat human—or lizard,
Maybe, which it might be judging by the rough and warty appearance of the bark/skin mottled by accretions of moss or bromeliads, and encrustations of tiny shelled creatures basking in a humid languor above the ocean—
Its unrelenting battle against the land being waged, right here, on the battle-scarred old mangrove forging its own offensive against the gently rising, if sly, incoming tide, warm and welcoming to the bonnethead shark, grouper fry, trumpetfish, and other creatures of the wet, which, though well-adapted, may not survive the rising
Nitrogen levels of our catastrophe with which turquoise waters of the Gulf of Mexico darken even now, the red tides, a Biblical-scale plague of death and stench causing respiratory distress in tourists whose vacation plans, alas, will degenerate into a week indoors at amusement parks and restaurants, Hog Heaven, for example, where silver look-down fish used to circle the pier like ponies of a carousel, and, in all its rising horror, the coming-in-for-good of the tides seems
Enough to remind me of dangerous bromine, bloody brown, named for its stink, and quick to emit potentially fatal vapors, an element that, apparently, has no completely safe applications as the only thing that makes it less awful than chlorine seems to be its propensity to exist at room temperature as a liquid rather than an infiltrating gas, and, of course, I'm reminded when I think of these chemical dangers of the Mayan Lords of Xibalba (the afterdeath kingdom), who have names like Pus and Flying Scab, but who today could be called bromine, chlorine, uranium, and plutonium, and may only be defeated the way the twin heroes of the Popul Vuh won, which is by trickery and virtuoso dancing (as in Butcher's photo).

47—Silver

Sybarite, he of golden toilet fame, and his simpering daughter, and
Imago of a gimlet-eyed wife—emerging full rich with her arms in the wings of her coat
Like she hasn't done a lick of work since she met him, lucky girl—and those
Voodoo-looking sons who love to kill large mammals (it takes a big man…). In opposition,
    unknowing
Eremite, our true hero pushes his homeless body like a coracle into a sidewalk sea
Reavers plunder, and I, embarrassed, can't meet his eye because I failed him,

Saw him bleeding, long complex braids of bright blood down the channels of his face,
Implicating me and all like me—ah, but we're past that guilt (or not there yet).
Let's ignore him if he's that sketchy Native—was he?—the clerk said,
Very pretty young woman who wouldn't call an ambulance (I'd left my phone in the car),
Encamped as she was on his home and hearthstone, her feet in his guts ensconced forever
Raking in, or hoping to, since on $10 an hour she probably wasn't, what he'd been robbed
    of then and now.

Somewhere high up in those mountains to the west, the foundational tailings gleam
In mendicant sunlight, dabs of metal in the waste that will be gathered with the last seal,
Left for a while, too insignificant to transport and smelt to purity, sub-rich, maybe, less than
    gold, but still
Validating the Anglo-American project of might makes right and always has, kingdom
    come on a Liberty dollar,
Engelmann spruce curling round them like a dragon on treasure, poison tail tight, breath
    held
Really not for long. Economy, swaggering god, will come for those cast-offs, too.

112-118—The Superheavy Elements

Slovenly wilderness surrounded that hill,
Uprose when, like nothing else, they
Placed on it a jar of tennessine (like nothing
Else at Oak Ridge National Laboratory), and
Round it was (or maybe not—that
Hybrid of calcium and berkelium basically
Eluding space and time, and, I mean, how could it ever be "tall"?)
And of a port in air (and, as I said) sprawling all around was Southern
Verdure (that became, at that very moment) no longer wild. That jar
(Yes, that Mason jar of copernicium, flerovium, etc.) took dominion

Everywhere
Like nothing else in Tennessee (or Dubna, Russia, or the University of Nevada–Las Vegas, for that
matter).
(Even now in experimental groves of pink and starry-stamened almond flowers robotic bees in
Murmurous haunts are pollinating [because real bees are dying], clumsily and with little
Esthetic appeal, to be sure, and, in the face of biological collapse, this fiddling with monstrous
electro-chemical combinations seems
Nonsensical in its sheer extravagance. Such calcium-on-curium, calcium-on-plutonium recipes!)
The jar (as I said) being gray and bare and giving not of bird or bush (marking the boundary
Staked by slovenly human minds sprawling like happy gulls at a landfill) took dominion
everywhere.

Melting Glaciers

for
M any centuries of settled freeze,
E ven millennia, and more, these delicate flakes, sheets, chunks of
white and blue have been
L eft stacked up (though ebbing and flowing) in a very cool ecosystem on
T op of the world, home to polar bears and seals… but lately,
I n the wink of a geologic eye, this lovely
N ever-never-land is rapidly coming un-
G lued,
sailing
down
to
meet us
in beautiful
fragile
ships.

Non-Equation:

Volumetric Measure of
Human <u>Effects</u>

(doesn't equal)

Volumetric Measure
Human <u>Thought</u>

((Picture the near immor-
tality of plastic products
vis-à-vis the handful of
time any public ecological
action might last.))
(Picture a rainforest thr-
ough a chronological zzz-
oom lens.)
[Picture us as a bubble
in the Sea of Biodiversity.]

Sunnet

for Peter Warshall

So bioluminescence is rebellion;
I'll take some more of that, for danger's sake.
For danger CHANGES spots, a "leopard" hellion:
Local beauty's always on the make.

I mean, I mean, review iambic swing
From lip to line and back again—half dead
With poison from excessive light (the Sting);
But white reflects while black absorbs, and red

Is Long enough to govern half a life.
Enchanted by the sun, this bullseye range
Refines itself in terms of tonal strife,
Which livens up romance: home <u>in</u> the change.

Do shadows merely blot the multitask
Of shifting hues? (You thought I'd never ask.)

James Cook

The Positions

now that the polis / has dreamed its ruin
shadows mineral,
animal, vegetable,
live out their days
as overexposed photographs
posing complicated theorems
on the nature of 'nature' : Pliny

the Elder, from shrieking lobe
cut w/volcanic glass
circumscribes our summary gnosis
in wound & phylum leaked

from garish spaces where
a species learns to convert
spiral galaxies to strips
of pulpy skin flowing from
winter trees

cutting awareness with
rough translations
spliced into nativity's
ecliptic

near the belong of hammered deer

where blue trucks
carry across
lodestone red snow
in disintegrating saliva grails

fallopian discord shrieking
with the new weather enables
16th century smiths to reckon
a shattered grafting of topaz onto
Baudelaire's skull

because this bloody town is dull

my own magicks access
  the world of the blue trucks
reality insurance granting
black tendrils back to Scythia

(remember how they took off
Hypatia's skin in strips
  scraping bone
    with clamshell) my own

  diagrams excavate
narcotic tapestries
inscape tropic transit
enter the street provisionally
  embedded into texts passed
hand to hand
  titled 'Lilypad Trample'
    or 'Oxide Shoal'

& later // at the world poetry awards
in Reno
an oil tanker is slowly birthed
from the moist blue mouth
of an owl   (quoting Nero—

affectionately dubbed LORCA or ORACL)

(star date
unknown
subtle
perceptual

changes take
effect wet

pavement
brain fold

estuary
parallel

I parallax this episteme
strip mall syncope

if you don't weaken
sipping the medicine

fugitive stagger
Soledades of Gongora

when churchbells sine-wave this
                                        glassy
                              profane
                    mumble

microphones
mold
in 11/8
time

& poetry takes over everything !

issues to articulate
subterranean
voltage
from three
four
five
crows
eroding in *mindbeamwind* / **o** paul
        your knots rampart
        crystal figures razor-
            wise glandular inter-
                  planetary systems passed thru
            before finally returning to
        rooms, backroads,
                                                  dollar store
                                                  carwash
                                                  ATM
                                                  the varieties
                                                              and uses
                                                            of concrete

& then poetry
overtakes
everything :

the blue trucks
carry me across i
episteme this parallax

cross-bedding evident
w/ sedimentary origin

far drum of possibility columns
detached ear
off to murmur
                    watery street
          absorb my writings
          or let
          the strolls flee
                              con-
          fronted by concepts :

          empire demented
            winter rain

BRENDA COULTAS

from "The Writing of an Hour"

Heating soup in the kitchen, even though this is the hour of writing, glance at three french baguettes that need to be tossed into the woods for animals to eat: back on the bed, propped up and keyboarding, sniffles, and looking at blue socks on my feet, and this view of green grass despite the season, leaves of curled brown, like brown butcher's paper and the summer lawn chairs. Seed heads of overgrown border weeds, and what about that humpback whale videoed in Hudson River, a singular traveler, through heavy boat traffic and if the whale is lost or sick, how lonely or maybe not, is this mammal, who surfaces to breathe.

Late hours/another hour/early hours/happy hour/visiting hours

All the elements of the dying hour surround my laptop, in the dying blades of cut grass and in the dying battery. Finches continue their making of a nest of twigs and grasses, but I know the nest is early paper, the raw ingredients and pulp. I know the world is a page turner, a paper globe, and I know that the birds are the great writers of the sky.

Thomas Rain Crowe

Fall in Big Cataloochee Valley
An Ecology

for Wayne Caldwell

For a hundred and fifty years
only one road out of 'Big Catalooch,'
dug by hand. Built on buffalo trails
that crawl like a blacksnake on a rough-cut wall
up Half Acre Ridge to Cove Creek Gap.

In the valley the small elk herds graze
side by side with turkey and crows.
Sharing fields that Caldwells cleared
on the bottoms 'long Shanty Branch.
Along Cataloochee Creek, the old church
and schoolhouse stand alone like widowed ghosts
with open doors that answer the bugling
of the bison-sized males like Sunday's bells.

How many Caldwells, Messers and Woodys lived here
hidden between these two old hills?
And how many elk, deer, bear and beaver
once called this place home?
Now we drive by in large gas machines
looking for graves. Spoiling for a fight
and the crash of antlers from the rutting bulls.
Going where the history of humans
and the flora for ancient animals have forever been.
From what the hell these eyes have seen:
the subtle passing of the green.

Bradley David

Should I Go Back Out There?

There are cigarettes on the highway
There is not enough rain
There are cats hit by cars
There are nubs of burnt-out Independence Day
It smells like sulfur and rotting cats
This place is going up in smoke
I'm choking on souls
I'm ankle deep
I've come too far
I've hit the water
I'm out of apologies at the edge of the sea
There are killers on the loose
There is not enough rain
Cars are piling up
Cats are piling up
The shelves are buckling
I can't tell heartbeats from earthquakes
The birds stopped singing
Children are beating on pots and pans to fell sparrows
Birds are piling up
If I go back out there
I'll be knee deep in sparrow
This time tomorrow

In the Midst of a Flock

There was that day
when I took this same walk
and my cluttered mind hiccupped
as I became aware of the flurry of
back and forth.

It was late fall then
when animals are busy
and that day it was the Robins
darting from rock to rock
and tree to tree
criss crossing the path like a haywire cat's cradle.

That feeling
when you think that there is only one
or maybe even two
and slowly realize
that you are in the midst of a flock
and perhaps even part of it.

Owl Eye

All thinking stop
for a moment, at least,
so I might look this owl in his pitch black
eyeball of shine and sorrow and
ask him please,
to show me where he lives.

Tree hole lined
with tuft of squirrel
with mouse pelt
with feathers plucked from
softest bellies
of Chickadee and Nuthatch,
Robin and Wren,
perhaps even a pillow of
Hummingbird down.

My binoculars follow
your broad winged flight
of swoop and swift
and gratitude, gratitude,
lifts my heart, it aches
in this moment of distraction.

Silent Pink Moth

The honeybee has found me out.
Lean back slow
this is uncharted territory,
barely charted at all.

Wood thrush so sullen
so sudden, so full of
birdsong, hornet
and three feathered caterpillar,
little ant and bullfrog,
snorting deer and

silent pink moth
perched on the door frame
for a day and then gone.

I float on my back in the center of the pond
I am still, I am flotsam,
water swallowing all sound.
Even bird chatter cannot reach me,
I hear nothing but heartbeat.

Janine DeBaise

Inside my head

Every year after trucks
come through our neighborhood

spraying pesticides onto lawns,
I find dead songbirds

who escaped too late to my yard.
I never understood this need to kill weeds

and wildflowers. In childhood, I sat
on our lawn to pick dandelion greens

for my father—his favorite salad.
When the plant bloomed and the leaves

turned bitter, my sisters and I wove
the yellow flowers into necklaces

Now in early spring, a migraine slug creeps
into my brain, spinning grey matter until I vomit.

When I open my kitchen window
I smell penicillin from the smokestacks

of the pharmaceutical company next door.
I want to move but no one will buy my house.

Chemists say that toxins
creep through milk and cheese

stew inside cans and bottles
drift from smokestacks

to poison me slowly
exploding in my brain

until I can't stand the sound

of my children's voices.

Biologists say that mammals
pass toxins on to their children.

Firstborn dolphins die from the ingestion
of a lifetime of toxins from their mother's body.

This explains why I never got migraines
when I was breastfeeding.

I feed my kids organic vegetables and grains.
I try herbs: feverfew and ginger root and don quai.

But still, the headaches persist.
I can change what I eat, but not what I breathe.

Toxins touch all of us. My kids. My neighbors.
And the songbirds that nest in my lilacs.

Seventh Generation

Dangling a baby, they pose on
this broken curve of beach
that lies east of Gary. They have rich tans,
blond hair, teeth the color of foam.
The photographer pushes his tripod
hard into sand, his back
to the stacks that breathe thick dragon
smoke.

I turn to admire the holiday picture,
the cropped scene. But my children
run through, chasing waves that brush
evening sun onto sand. They stomp puddles
to scatter glisten. I can't stop them
or keep up with them. The wind erases
my voice as they run faster
and faster.
At the end of the beach loom
the smokestacks, a sunlit haze.

Seagulls swoop above the shore
edge of seaweed and litter. The young
woman squints at the silhouette of my children
running into the yellow industrial smudge.
Smile, the photographer says to her,
smile.

Vivian Demuth

Live Earth

The concert goers gather where the earth is slanted,
sheltered from city lights—
Where the land still grows verdant words,
not slick pavement and glowing machines
who fear and suffocate poems.
The wandering moon fills their refugee mouths.
The homeless wind sprinkles a rouge of cosmic
dust on their skins to magnetize their memories.
An orphaned grizzly cub taps his claw three times
on a fire-tower woman's arthritic shoulders.
Gray wolves lick Cree words hidden beneath buffalo horns.
There are no police with their song and dance—
that's for the birds who punctuate the budding
text from their nests and cover any half-naked chicks.
Pine beetles spit three times at the evergreens who cough
and remind all that the word "pristine"
died invisibly in the grey rain long ago.
Shadow dinosaurs roar three times, then give up their fossils.
And as a tired sun rises, it sears the text onto the soiled
bodies of the gathered.
The fire-tower woman feels the marks in the moist forest
between her toes—three short, three long, three short.
Ask her along the game trail and she will reveal the mountain
text, the understory of the boreal—a rhizomatic SOS.

Adam Dickinson

Heatwork

How do we imagine writing with and about heat in a warming world? What forms of writing might emerge when heat and its effects are invited into the compositional process? With the assistance of the Environmental Ergonomics Laboratory at Brock University, I undertook several heat stress trials, raising my internal body temperature by around 1.5°C through active and passive heating. The active heating involved me cycling on a stationary bicycle in controlled conditions of 35°C with 65% humidity, which equals a humidex of 50°C (122°F). The passive heating involved me wearing a specialized hot-water-piped garment under a few layers of thermal blankets for several hours. The passive heating experiment resulted in prolonged exposure to the critical wet-bulb temperature of 35°C, which is the point at which the human body can no longer cool itself by sweating. This deadly atmospheric condition is forecast to become more frequent in parts of the world due to climate change. At various intervals, during all these trials, I wrote, took cognitive tests, and measured my core temperature, skin temperature, blood pressure, CO_2 uptake, and brain blood flow among other data. Using this data in conjunction with thermal camera images, I have started to develop forms of writing that approach the environment through the signifying framework of temperature extremes.

Hyperthermia

35°C + 65% humidity (50°C humidex), 37.5°C Internal temperature, 79 heartbeats per minute

I am on a stationary bike. The air in the chamber is tropical. I've almost stopped feeling the rectal thermometer. Expiratory exchange ratios. Brain blood flow. Heartrate. On the blank wall in front of me it is deep summer. I have just set up the tent trailer in the driveway to air it out. My young daughters are playing a game that involves making bridges out of their legs. I'm dehydrated, drinking warm, left-over scotch I found in a storage cupboard, and thinking about how to keep spiders from nesting in the pilot light. The girls play a new game where they try to intercept drops of sweat on my chest before they dribble past my belly button. It's too hot to make any headway, and the girls squint at me through the frosted glassware. Carbon dioxide consumption. Pedaling at 225 watts. They leave me to my spider thoughts and head back into the house. Left middle cerebral artery velocity. When the booze runs out, I stagger inside and find them listening to the music I had left playing on the stereo. The humidifier clicks on with its altered time signature. Mean skin temperature. Protocol schematic. The girls are on the kitchen floor, their dolls splayed like eyelashes in a photobooth, a rapture in which the only ones standing are those who have arranged the homunculi for transport to the home world. They are saving the saved. They tell me to go back outside to the trailer. The ventilator mask slips down my sweat-greased face. Baseline. Recovery. I know they aren't waiting for me.

Receiver

35°C + 65% humidity (50°C humidex), 38.0°C Internal temperature,
91 heartbeats per minute

We sleep
with every
window open.
Street noise
jacks the ceramic
dishware of our
intimacy.
Jaguars
growl and descend
at all hours
from trucks
with low haunches
into the high-end
dealerships
across the street.
Shopping carts
medical-image
under the drunk arrythmia
of security lights.
We make love
with ear plugs
and I listen to you
through my body,
the vibrations
of your pleasure
like microwaved
meat finding
water to excite
into small insurrections

of culinary steam.
Our bodies
sweat
like candles,
the drops melt
in the Brutalist
circulation
of post-war housing.
Evaporative cooling
draws the heat
we've collected.
It's entirely
possible
to build something
without
understanding it.
It's as obvious
as a social
fabric's
thread count.
We are entering
the human phase
of the trials.

Cognitive Test, Red Faced

35℃ + 65% humidity (50℃ humidex), 38.3℃ Internal temperature, 96 heart beats per minute

Alike
in some way
to things
that are blood
red
stop signs
an eye
in the mirror
after a night
of tailpipes
rusted springs

from the bed
abandoned
in the field
coarse-grained
metamorphic
rock
a remarkable
achievement
specks of dust
in the film reel
convinced
that remembering
the embers
perfectly
is beside
the point
a sunset involved
in itself
boxed lunch
with apple
surprised and
purposeful
fingers over
a flashlight
a word
in a dictionary
aimed
in the opposite
direction
an anal
sphincter
pares a goose-
bumped
droughtscape
outcropping
from meaningless
poise
no one will ever
look this up
a reduced rate
of vigilance
a denialist's
corridor

climate controlled
thirst
travels
by jet propulsion
trained in
both pigment-bearing
and analytic
thought
a warning
infrared
fury

Elizabeth Dodd

Aesthetics

To the Blue-footed Booby, beauty is a blue
that blurs toward yellow, turquoise like

the glacial milk I jumped in, once, to feel
a mountain river's elegy of ice.

The pigment's vivid with nutrition,
an *honest signal,* say the scientists,

that throughout the season's hottest sun, no wind,
the panting nestlings' unremitting greed

for fish, the mate can be counted on
to dive and rise and dive again, his fidelity

a feathered pump for anchovies and squid.
Beauty is truth; truth, beauty—the male whistles,

lifts wings and flings his head far back, balletic
in the Ecuadorian sun. Watch for the flush

of aqua just below his throat. Admire
the tilt of his bill's granitic blue. Offshore,

cold, cobalt, and inscrutable, the Humboldt Current
hides whatever future may await.

Scopaesthesia

I. Evolution of the Early Eye

Among ancient fungi,
          receptors lay
waiting for pheromones,

primordial desire
          in the living cells,
the Other, non-animal,

calling out *Self*
through the unseen
air. Then, newly

mutated, chordates
turned to the call
of dear, bright

violet light.
Translucent dermis,
molecular flesh—

waiting for photons,
waiting for dawn,
the body, the bodies—

Six hundred million years.

II. Organs of Extreme Perfection

Consider the hagfish, archaic chordate
in deep ocean waters, eel-like,

slime-sloughing,
translucent spots on dull retinal flesh.

> *Behaviorally, the hagfish appear to be blind, and what response they have to light seems to be mediated by photoreceptors in the skin.*

Hormones, counting the cycles.
Desire, deep in the body.

> *In relation to your enquiry, what I can say is that virtually all animals have a circadian clock, and probably an annual clock, and so it must be important to them.*
>
> *But I agree that when living at very great depths it is not entirely clear what the purpose would be.*

III. Cold Solstice in Chaco Canyon while the Fracking Wells Drill Down

From the sun-watching station, the ruined pueblos
appear to have vanished. The cliffs, late Cretaceous,

face forward, like us. Like us, coyotes quicken
when dawn touches here our cheekbones, there our hair.

But this is what we've come to: fossils eroding
from the sandstone, petroglyphs pocked by gunshot,

the corroded *ommm* from the distant rigs,
their all-night flares smudging out the stars.

The overcast sky dulls the flush on my face.
Earth rolls into sunrise, a long, lashless gaze.

Cold frozen January next comes in

(after a line by Anne Bradstreet)

This morning one suburban turkey stands midway between
my window and the neighbor's dryer vent. His soul patch
feathers flutter as he cranes his neck to watch me back.

When I went out to clear the driveway I found piss-ice
plastered on a tree. It's Trickster Coyote, blue-shifting scent marks
in a blizzard wind. There's a regular wildlife highway

in the undeveloped woods behind the house—a snarl of tracks
and scat threads past old rolls of wire fencing and cicada husks
of rusting trucks. I'm sick of the president, sick of the news,

so I walk down where the half-dry creek makes lazy-river s-curves
slicked with luge-run glaze. Where a deer crashed through
the hollow ice I stop—it's like a doll-sized room beneath a broken roof.

The herniated polar vortex unwinds to lob another cold front
while, a hemisphere away, wildfires burn forests rasped by drought.
And I remember winter forty years ago—when school closed

and the river froze and we walked across that still and craggy surface
with no idea how the world was changing, the chemistry just then
becoming visible while our breath hung in the air.

Lisa Fleck Dondiego

The Sea Whisperer

for Mau Piailug, Micronesian grandmaster navigator

The last to understand the secret
Talk of Light, he began

by studying coral chunks
on a woven mat, pored over

the ancient map, etched with stars,
fish, birds, landmarks,

the route through reefs
and shoals. Through thumb

and forefinger, he could tell
latitude within a few miles.

When sky closed up,
ocean swells—their pitch and

angle to the knife-edged canoe—
would be his guide.

Lost, he'd pull down sails,
study waves and wind,

and where he'd come from.
He told his pupil Nainoa:

Be fierce, wise. You only know
where you are by knowing.

EDWARD DOUGHERTY

Prairie Requiem

Out in the American grasslands,
on a wire strung between posts,
wooden posts despite the lack of trees,
on a metal wire twisted with barbs
like the same note played
at the same interval,
a Baird's sparrow digs its beak
into shoulder feathers then gathers itself
for its prairie song.
                                        One by one by one
a species is known, the individual
and the collective, weather and climate.
This little bird navigates by starlight,
migrating, as so many songbirds do,
at night. It knows to move,
to take action and set out, riding
sinewaves of heat and rain, the growing season,
the swell of seeds and the timing thereof.
We mourn one by one by one,
                                                            a bird-corpse
by the mailbox, we bury with unease.
Early frost freezes ditchwater to sealed pools.
A tornado rips a land free of tornados
for all of human memory.
Late heatwave builds to cresting
then falls across the flatlands,
drying plants before they go to seed.
What was the song like, the Baird's
sparrow song?

Mark DuCharme

Ecopoetics

i.m. Jack Collom, 1931–2017

Less ego, no cynicism.
Be kind to starlings
& Finches & itinerant
Redbreasts & warblers
Who flower the air &
Ear. Do not err
In simplicity, but embrace
The wild panoply—
The range of
Seeing & living &
Dying, yes. Don't
Mourn, but revel
In summer's lushness. Be
A song pollinator
In the mad rush of waking.
Attend to the pinnate, the
Mossy, the rooted
The alluvial & riverine
Conditions of this messy
Life which abounds
By creekbanks & runnels
By hilltops & rivulets
By the murmurs of weather &
Its polyglot botany
Its grace of empurpled
Ripeness rife with
Bounty, with ringing &
Singing in afternoon
Light. Attend to
Our mammalian neighbors
Herbivorous or predatory
Who mewl or bark
Growl or cry

Round our environs
Under the sky
Amid the extremes &
Slices gone by
In all weather &
This turning about
& Going, in this going
On, despite life
Being more meager—even
With sparrows rushing—
Now that you, dear human
Are no longer here.

Rachel Blau DuPlessis

January from Shepherd's Calendar

1. January

How alarming our life is, how
it has invented ourselves almost out of existence
so the flicker
is hope that we, the humans, will survive
all this,
finding ways to think that can hardly be predicted,
much less faced. But can we—without the animals,
without the insects, without the fish, without the bees?
No, obviously not.
But we are arriving at that spot.

This endless Disappearance
(with that veil of time disappearing round the corner)
is a question.
The thought only of trace?
Is it that apocalyptic?
Why is "the human" synonymous
with "hope"—given everything,
while at the same time,
most of this mess of place has been invented
by parts of our selves.
Is it simply the technocrats whom we
must re-socialize? remove?
At least could we offer a cryptic
outline of something—
documenting clouds, setting letters out?

Poor planet I pray
slightly flattened ball of clay
(with its heavier iron core)
we its daughters (*korés*) and sons
a choros of the powerless
and what to do?

In different languages, yet!
trying to speak beyond a single eye
into the multiplicity of
janus interests. Into the compass's

maximum splay.

Marcella Durand

friskies

fish found within a deep blue pan if ri
ped off at the edges her digestive system is de
com   pressed   under the additive str   ess f
ound in a bluish container soldered by indiffe
an indifference to that which enters heavy lead
cans piles and piles of them to be recycled sm
all bugs fly back and forth as an inability to thr
ow away a particular obsessive kind of order ea
ch item within the pile (no matter *how messy loo*
king) is marked an observation as to what she
put where and even though it may look disastr
ous and flies may be buzzing around it, it's still
a pile of something soldered together with such
indifference that it was a bunch of ground-up an
imal parts that's what it's eating digesting itself f
it's its own body in there that bluish metal pan dee
p as it eats its own body through an organically or
dered system dosnt know items are there that ther

the deep chrssstrum

Back from his long voyage across the sea, the general
was relieved to hear the deep chrssstrum
of a landlocked river bordered by cottonwoods
releasing soft puffs
of seeds to collect in a thicket wucherned
in an immense and picturesque study of decay.

A chewed-up leaf closes; another decay
slick and chemical coats the path, the general
slips and is lost in a wucherning
tangle of vines and weeds; he hears a whispering chrssstrum

indicating the arrival of another puff
and snort from a drifting plant resembling cottonwood.

With leaves like the white seeds of a cottonwood
releasing wood and cotton, the stump decayed
into the likeness of another plant, vanished in a puff
when its last habitat was found to be generally
unsafe for children as it releases chrssstrum
to fall on their heads and wuchern

slowly, and the children crying, wucherned
tears leaving salt rivulets that poison cottonwood
their mother says, for chrssstrum's
sake, this peach under the pouch is all decay.
She looks down the path for the lost general
who, looking around him, only sees puff

after seed-sacked puff, an ocean of puffs
each planting themselves, to wuchern
themselves into a fine general
maze of extremely tiny cottonwoods
with roots extending out into water and prone to decay
just as teeth, and hair and bones, and that substance known as chrssstrum,

which could slightly resemble a substance also known as chrssstrum,
but differentiated only by a very slight, almost unnoticeable puff
occurring after the third "S" and with how quickly decay
sets in once the cavity has wucherned
itself into the dentin of the cottonwood's
exterior calcium bark, but the general

is no scientist, just an ol' general who in his fits of rage cuts chrssstrum
down as though it were cottonwood, each branch evaporating in puffs
and disappearing in the complex and difficult wuchern of troublesome decay.

for urban gardeners

Borage is so beautiful
with soft needled halo
and gentle blue flowers,
the first plant I planted,
lasted about a month.

Everyone said black-eyed
susans are so great; they
didn't last either. Cone
flowers are ugly most
of the time, and rotted
quickly. Never worked
for influenza either.

Cleomes look amazing
and release seeds onto
the lawn below to be
mowed down again by
the leaf-blower guys.
Cleomes grow and
grow, fractal in flowers
coming one after the other.
I love them and wish
a wandering pollinator
might love them too.

Marigolds are
supposed to be
so fucking hardy

and they are usually

the first to die.

Weirdly, the tomato
plants stayed alive
in their tiny pots
unwatered for weeks
while we were away.

So did the little
alpine strawberry,
which is happy
every day, hot
or cold, and growing
new berries even
now in October.

My trusty
blueberry bush
either got too dry or
caught something yucky:
all its leaves are brown
(but! a new green
shoot is emerging
from its trunk). Birds
steal its green berries
and we are happy to
have their company.

Anise hyssop:
first to send up
green in spring.
Pollinators love
its purple flowers

and I can make
tea from its leaves.
Everyone in the entire
world should have
an anise hyssop.

Mint is strange—
it grows sideways
with tough green tendrils
and pushes other
plants over, sort of,
although they seem
not to mind. Its roots
are so long! Bees
nap on its flowers.

I love lavender
and each year
move it all around
trying to find a spot
for it. Futility.

I regret I planted
Mexican bush sage,
which took a full four
months to flower
and now the pollinators
are gone. It's so tall,
like a tree about
to crash over. And
so it does, pulling

the pot with it

over my terrace.

Oregano, what
is wrong with you
this year? I gave
you fresh soil
and fertilizer, things
that usually send
you into an invasive
frenzy. Instead
you are sad, small
and flower free.
A mystery.

Sweet alyssum
is something great
in the spring and fall
if you can bear
its dusty dryness
during hot months.

Per the advice
of a native-plant guru
who told me I have
more of a shady
woodland ecosystem
on my 4 x 6' terrace,
I tried the wood anemone.
So not true. It died in a month
from the July heat slanting
in from the East River,
magnified by the
concrete and bricks

all about it.

I have tried different
lantanas: rarely seen
a pollinator on them.
They are pretty but
strangely plastic.

Bee balm were fireworks,
long and bright and way too
large for their pots.

Mourning doves take refuge
on stormy days and a robin gathers
stem-threads each spring; at 3 am,
the mockingbird sings outside my window.
Red-tailed hawk flies near the bridge sometimes,
as do seagulls, who hang out on its suspension cables.
Hardy flowers don't do well; and delicate
flowers outlast their welcome. My small
urban ecosystem remains a mystery.
Unsure. I feel some urgency.
Pollinators! You are always
welcome here in my tiny
greenery: tell me what
you like best and I
will plant it all,
every flower.

Daniel Eltringham

29 Oct 18

There is no indigenous territory where there aren't minerals. Gold, tin and magnesium are in these lands, especially in the Amazon, the richest area in the world. I'm not getting into this nonsense of defending land for Indians.
—Jair Bolsonaro, 22 April 2015

Open season on the resource-rich
amped-up & ready to asset-strip
the Amazon—obviously—if it's
needless to say why say it? Now
there is a poser. "could mean
fresh opportunities for Canadian
companies looking to invest" in
ecocide, genocide too (the peasant
matrix a brown & "backward" image)
fell destroyer carbon cut
tarmac sink drive through
unprofitable forest-weed.
Politics never more nakedly in service.
Nor the worst surer of their creed.

Supermarket indecisions in the web
of life. Hold up soap, rotate, angle
descry inspect reject. Fruitless
enough but how else to be in this
world? Nihil in advance. Up-front
mourning for the present, feels
future because the losses don't
show. Each of us at the limit
of the limit & straining to see
what our eyes avert. Qué no quiero
verla. In tears looking at a brown
hare in *Fauna Britannica*. Prefers
a mosaic of farm & wood.
Living inside it it's hard to parse
its shapely contours of stately
plummet (60% in 50 years)

as the event strips away sparse
& worsening cover at all levels
of life. Form an image of the world
that can be re-composed in
phased change without motion.
Split the particle open & it
won't go back. I *is* an other but
pairs of beasts but re-inscribe.
Another's other, and an other.

Rage at all the wrong targets
from helpless home,
effects of dispersal
across networks
of blame & gain.
Demand the
imperative engine.

On the back of the soap
pack the telling trace
of the visceral real eye-
to-eye with the world
economy. Plant
one palm firmly
on the company map.
What greases the great
cycle must be the oil.
Used in everything because it is
cheap. The banal beat meted
out of the fruit. Used in
everything because it is cheap.
There's a theory of global
economy for you, right there,
of global oikos crouched down
in arboreal shade against
a dividing wall that shields
the view. Qué no quiero
verla. The blood. There's
an elegant syllogism for
relation that is all ye need,
and all there is—*ah*—to know
relation extends the known
to the bounds of the –

huh what greases the great
cycle is also—because it is
cheap it is used—*um*
as everything—*cut*—this
paradigm, which rides
on sleep, breaks up –

EROSION now ho
hum diverted via bog
asphodel footfall
counters in overdrive
on Stannage well
now well dressed
well managed well
done everyone. A
blessing on your
watercourse.
The money hill
unmounted still.

& expansive the fresh forest
but brought beyond biocapacities
lopped & boxed the plants
will grow much better in virgin soil

expensive worth
while to get all
the life from
the forest expends

cut bamboo, grasses,
smaller trees
the method
render to kindling
ringing carve trunk
so sap circulates
            past value.
The pending processes
death is slow
time is short,
by close of play
today i want to see
vascular veins

laid open & the oil
leaching out
i want to see the layers
of money inherent
in the land at least
then we'd know
where to start.

Harm in passivity
gulls sing "anthropocene"
scaling, losses
cut down the coast
let's say just
hypothetically
we all agree
to burn it all
all the hydrocarbons
all at once
crack open
the methane lattice
sit back & wait
for the feedback
to kick

or hold your ear
to the pulsing
syncopation
of a storm drain
in spate

sea & ice
ice & ocean
dialectical counterpoint
call & answer song
read by measure
watch the levels

fossils agitate in the lobby
assets stranded attest
Deepwater attest Gorgon
attest Sunrise over
bitumen horizontal
tarlands keep turning

frack me sideways
this is not a test

red wines for red meat
stupid peak time
passed silt
liquefaction limits
ongoing full-price
fares extinctive
this city on stilts

voy ahora, te quiero
        lentic lake fear no more
boy agora, the quiet
        benthic bottom fear no more
ahora vengo, te veo
        solar hubris fear no more
alforja y vega, tango
        not to fear but fear itself
still or slow, profundal

        O God, make me vegan, but not yet.

Clayton Eshleman

Extracts from *Juniper Fuse*

Chaos of the Wise

Why this yearning to travel?
More, this deeper yearning to return?
Falcon intuition. Human foible loop.
At the far end of the drive to flee from one's feet
there is psyche. Who is strong enough
to take up residence there?
Imagination desires circularity.
not repetition. Psyche wants recurrence,
on each swing the path to deepen,
a rattler raga, wants to ouroboros herself.
Or take Pech-Merle:
                                        the rockwall bears an image
which presses in a fraction of an inch.
Someone's squatting there, drawing horse and bison
close as she distances them,
as she works the primordial hourglass,
a double bellows, or butterfly.
               Wall as thorax:
out there one wing, in here another.
Imagination as dorsal lines superimposed,
one crossing another, making a statement
imprisoned by the ochre on her finger—
she can't press through the wall she is to penetrate,
a finger in the void, a traveling semen-travesty.
Chaos' lips purse to suck on her plunger-finger.
Her drawing times her, as here each word
                                              has its worm ward.
To be underborn in the chaos of the wise,
to take the oath of the abyss
verging on being of the physical world!

All the I/s huddle, as if, as one,
they could remain in goddess doorway all their lives
—what terror! What delight! Psyche wonders:
might there still be one great mother with everyone
daisy-chained to her rich hole? Do we sink
Hades and Persephone into Hades
for a sensation of life wedded to its origin?

The Aurignacians Have the Floor

for Gary Snyder

Now I subtract myself from the industrial
white hive, a worker slinking off
from my queen valve position,

letting it spurt, knowing that in a moment
another will be plugged in my place.
It is Soweto miners whose 115 degree eyes

gleam from the neighboring houseside,
the studs supporting our king-sized bed.
I subtract myself while I add up

the multiplication that I am part of,
the scorpion-tail cornucopia that,
with nature disappearing, the earth is becoming.

A white American male, I am already on
one of its gyroscope grooves, zooming
the inner freeway of its outer wheel.

No, I will move instead into an ancient
squad at the cenote's edge,
having concocted a message for

the Aurignacian assembly.
What does not follow is
as valuable as what does

and now what does not follow
is turning away from us.
The clawless Cameroon otter, her entire

range endangered, waddles off
dragging a chunk of MacDonald arch
while Sammy Davis Jr. continues to yell

you are my essential humanity
and until I cease to blow my nose with you

I am your buzz-saw spectre,
the negativity inherent in
having forgotten the last glaciation,
that fiber I rediscover line by line.

When bison and I got on a wall,
there was a tangle of wiving deadends
rotating in the animal layered midden,

pee-rings replotted by cross-hatching rain.
Out of the lovers' orchids,
$ mushroom secrets itself,

from the ground, straight up,
out of snowsporewhere.
It is time to let the Aurignacians

have the floor, even though we suspect
that the cup-shapes in Neanderthal
burial slabs are a fungus suggestion,

that in death a stem continues
to stalagmite, seeping through
the crack of subliminal scanning while

I try to step back from this stump
out of which, like a bubble-gum machine
scoop, a silken, rainbow, tar

and Sulphur-woven ape hand is extended,
offering cholo for me to chew
on the loosened knot of path

upon path, bundled by the Buddha's
vatic Gabon viper nature.
My sense must flee to the highest bison

hump. There,
a fool riding a mountain,
playing my turd accordion, out of which

Hades' purple hair is sprouting,

while my balls press against what
still confirms infinity,

I will accept the Aurignacian motion
that the abyss is engravable
and terminates in caves manifesting

hominid separation.
I dead is under
I do, lobster verb to lobster verb.

My vertical stand on my zero.
It is now possible to chip at the target's
dead center, the bison outline

by whose manganese side
I am painting the clawless Cameroon otter
with the disappearing silver of a Dracula stake.

Dusk, Abri Du Cro-Magnon, 1988, 7:45 P.M.

The earth as an encoiled labyrinth,
layered absence lined with never,
each creature   ego and abyss
                                        "arco iris"
   the ore in living eyes

Scoured ground. The twitter at twi-loam

                                        Earth sicks
her elbow through the tattered
sleeve of ground cover and vesper bells
to show her molecular
    diffidence,
                                    in whose cyclonic
pores we're so many ticks   atomic clocks,
Nile perch in whose Lake Victoria craw
   a bottomless cistern broods

"grand tour" helicopter buzzing overhead,
for whom the earth is an Amazon–Perigord grid of
"that's Les Eyzies below"
—a web site.

I spider by the backwall,
post-Clovis man,   in centinelan extinction time

My eyes can't crest the darkening,
tiny gate,   as to an epoch

In the Hotel Cro-Magnon servant quarters
someone puts on rock.

Notes for "The Chaos of the Wise", "The Aurignacians Have the Floor", and "Dusk Abri du Cro-Magnon, 1988, 7:45 P.M." can be found at https://www.dispatchespoetrywars.com/poetics-for-the-more-than-human-world/6-poems-6/.

Amy Evans Bauer

from *and umbels: sound((ing))s too*

leagues   as
                          under

I only   k   no w   what
the sea   scape of wall
after w all   crashing down
                                              tells me

t old me   already   long(ing) a go

second{s}   h {and}   : holds

me kneelling

                       no Life   in my
s old   Jacket

Last Sea n:
                    armed, waving
                    and   dr/oning
                                    on &
                                    on

~

a rose is   [not]
a rose is   [knot]
a risen

wreck   [on]
        under
sea
        un seen

~

scene less

                    and less
                    end lass ly
                    y ours

and umbels
sea holly
pricks

heart's s/hore
leaves[,]
cut/s
h art's *shhh* ore

~

un belle to(i)lls:
nature's st/ill
the place
trans port un does
us
we(t) *sp*.oil

for want
of sun shade
for getting we spring, s pool
from common c *entre*

all *thou* gh
ring after
ring
((on sur face))
speaks a vow

un sure as the curve of a shell

cl *am* *our*—
love serially
about t(w)o

STOP

[talk ing

~

Please Listen
to the fol.lowing

*p*Lease listen
To the follo/wing
*pp*lease listEn
To the foll*ow(e*r)ing
...
TO THE

ffff/LOWERING

SUR

Is not the opposite of north
cardinal compass
180 degrees one
angle-brush

diurnal
rustled susurro
cardio, kardia's Greek son
surrendered to the heart

sur, this pouring sun
sum, light
rains on lavender blue

it's November in every gloss
jacarandas of Buenos Air

RENDER

From the other's tongue
what the dreaming and the dead cannot
eclipse

translation is something occurring in the past

the weathervane
jasmine moon
this cockspur coral tree's habit

tin summerain

BRADLEY J. FEST

Dead Horse Bay

> *Beetles and silverfish tended to those archives. ... I am aware that all of this speculation is incomplete, inexact, inaccurate, useless. If I don't have real answers, it is because we still don't know what questions to ask. Our instruments are useless, our methodology broken, our motivation selfish.*
>
> —Jeff VanderMeer, *Annihilation*

Those various amber bleach bottles, those
various equilibria of femtoseconds and gradations
in yesterday's luminance, were ground into revenant wind chimes
by the rising waves—a calisthenics of moldering above calcimined skeletons:
midden upon midden beneath a pile of new land

slowly eroding against ancient flux—like your vision cauterizing
promises to tomorrow's children about the destination
of thin tires and braided rags, lonely shoe soles and graffitied boats,
blue tickets and endless broken jars, flasks, decanters, jeroboams, phials,
like your longing hanging suspended in the October dusk

precarious and wounded by the saddest relatability welling up
from the sedimented refuse, a hypertrophic mania of forgetting.
Looming metropolis, consider your Depression and postwar
magnificence amidst this vast buried collection, your discarded rammel,
and then let the moment pass

as it always does. Clods of thrice dirty dust speculate about the invertebrate
homes washed against your own diminishing shore; decrepit lean-tos
and decaying washboards nuzzle against the beer cans and abandoned
fire pits, brief hearths among what was never even ruin. These instruments
without destiny, despecialized components

thrown back into the hydrogen cast, exercise a weak force no longer
capable of dissection or memory, just undigested pondering,
a loose, indistinct song with every dynamic muted along
easily numerable lines perfectly crawling toward their anomalous topography,
a breach in all difference, a glue for any future thought.

Archives of Winter

My North is leafless and lies in a wintry slime
Both of men and clouds, a slime of men in crowds.
—Wallace Stevens, "Farewell to Florida"

I

They say it is colder than Mars
in Oneonta today, a
meteorological bomb,
vortex arctic.

The sun in a cloudless sky can't
pierce the valley's snow-haze, a blank
mass in the cyclogenesis,
but the news won't tell you that part.

The weather's dominion over
our dread has crystallized.
Gray and bare, the thaw reveals
how little we have to discuss.

II

One must be a stable genius
of winter to hazard the year's
convention; and have declined the

mayonnaise scissors frozen
in the proceedings of nothing's question's
negative as a tool for reading the

palimpsests of frost in the rear window glass
to tolerate the ice-encased branches of their
social material feed;

and evanesced wind chill
on tongues, the gloom of
failing space, which releases the pale

exhaust of hearing the gravity of snow,
its distance encroaching on
what will be there tomorrow and perhaps later.

III

There is a slow focus to subzero rhythms,
their heavy thermodynamic tread somber and

replete with anthologies of futurity.
The frigid metals supporting emergency

architecture's optimistic millennial
forecast cracked beneath the institution's spectral

weight. Beams of Iceland spar, trellises of halite,
buttresses of quartz razors baroquely latticed

through membranous folds of stalagmitic icicles,
once catachrestically supporting feeling,

their *umwelt*, were now unconditionally sere,
falling into the unfreezing saline bath of

some insomniac mass, delivered, finally,
to a welcome interpellation of what seemed

an unceasing hemispheric perspective on
their activity. The power environing

these revelatory losses knew nothing of
the length of their shivering and could not regard

their disarticulated pathos as worthy
of medial commentary. Crashing through the

flocculent breakers, they nonetheless persisted
in waking unmeasured reserves of biomass

from their depthless slumber in the sodden tissue
of this forgotten, unmoving paleosphere

structuring a keening foresight about just two
potentialities: ambient quagmire or

perspicacious convoy. If they situate pre-
dawn descriptions of the quaintly stirring valley

against the sibilance of onrushing polar
blasts from the quilting point of their indigent dreams,

they might listen: become droning winter. Later,
at the plodding parade between towers of ice,
their anxiety was exhumed and traded with
others'. The algid alleys' width dwindled until

only the smallest could keep moving. Too few watched
as each succumbed to the lifeless cold. Others, warm

elsewhere, went on, listless and mute, ensconced in
a different order, but waiting, still. Piano

notes crept along the horizon; weak drums sounded
the radiative background; cellos froze the air.

Cheryl J. Fish

The Ice Hotel at Jukkasjärvi, Sweden

Sun glares off our sunglasses.
        April above the Arctic Circle.

Sophie, Nikko and I set out to visit
The Ice Hotel
        giant rectangular igloos
where tourists   sleep in furs dreaming
        with white candles and mirrors.

They charge   high fees to enter the Ice Hotel.
We won't pay to survey beds with reindeer pelts
fantastic bird   memories in glass.

Down the road the Sami cafe in a laavu tent
With its central fire   warms us
we seek the sky
        through
the top of its folds.

Ice sharp yet fragile
This town was a Sami market place.
Now murals of Sami depicted in colorful *ghaktis*
with Lutheran missionaries
in the small red church dating from 1607.
I hear stones breathe.

        Not far away, the colossal Kiruna iron-ore mine
Bores deeper, operating 24 hours a day.

The town is sinking,
        citizens, monuments, homes must be moved
        or demolished
From cracks and crevices, the sound of cash.

Iron and ice, fire   quiet inside
Time's refraction   water's rise

        Sophie and Nikko hold my arms.
Guide me from step to street.
        Without any boots I'm a sliding stone.

She's a Sami filmmaker excavating
the past as ongoing present
every time a child climbed in the playground
a mine   hulked   poisoning
the sky.   Ore always matters more.

He's a miner like her father
what shape   love's glint?

Nations circle the water, on alert
To take more.
As ice and glaciers melt
with ease
into the Barents Sea.

Artists' Residency at Ii, Finland

Along the Ii river, water's cold but I swim
Anyway.   Early September
row boats waiting, shy.

Sami artist Carola Grahn carved these words
on a sign along the river: "My Name is Nature
Please Fuck Me."

Sanna, sculptor of bronze, founder of this residency
lives next door.
She shows me where to pick
lingonberries, bilberries, tart and small
everywhere on low vines.

In the center of Ii pronounced "Eeeeee"
The young man behind the counter at Orient Kebob/Pizza
Tells us in perfect Finnish
he's an Iraqi Kurd. One of only
a few in a small Finnish town. His family was gassed
during the war with Iran.

Ii is said to be a modification of a Sami word
For place to stay overnight.

I stay for a month in the Northland
To make bridges with words
air-girl
water-daughter
city dweller-in-the mushroom forest.

Sanna invites me to eat with them
        at the table in her yard.
I have worked all alone for many years
she exclaims, serving salmon, potatoes and salad.
Her old friend B. whom she met when her
husband abandoned her, is full of the drink.
He calls me stupid in between his rapid sneezes.
He assumes I voted for Trump
and I cannot convince him
otherwise.

Sanna sculpts women in leaves, women with fish,
Graffitied women, women with feathers, women in treetops.
Offers rides to her friend
also named Sanna who doesn't own a car but sometimes
drives a taxi at night.

Survival is our name. Don't fuck with us.

Unreliable Snowpack

In *The Kalevala*, a barren water-mother's knee is the place
where birds lay eggs.
The bottom half of a smashed egg becomes
Earth. In Sami myth, the Sun goddess
is the mother of humankind.

In winter, our experiment includes flooding an icicle.
Something went wrong in the undergrowth
Reindeer can't forage for lichen
trapped between layers
rain-on-snow.
Melt, freeze, melt, freeze.
Death follows.

ANN FISHER-WIRTH

[The day lays down]

The day lays down
first summer heat
as we drive
turning this way
and that
by whim
at random
beyond Clarksdale
through this
country of the Delta
blues
past cotton silos
pecan trees
Baptist graveyards
little swamps
with floating trash
sometimes an egret
one-lane roads
leading off
past graveyards
past alfalfa fields
and a yellow cropduster
gassing up
getting ready
to spray poison

Pecans

In the slant of late afternoon light,
hundreds of pecans stand out
tawny against their husks, the mud,
the fallen leaves and matted grass,
and I can't stop drifting around the yard
stuffing them in my pockets. This is a gift
November in Mississippi offers after a freeze.
If they release from the husk they will be good,
if they cling to the husk they will be rotten
or wormy, and I learn to discern
the barely perceptible difference in weight
between plump and desiccate, practice

my pitch tossing the bad ones into the bushes.
Last night's wind took down some branches.
Maybe someday this whole old tree will
come down and kill us, we exist by grace
or chance in the free fall of every moment,
but for now, my life is full of sweetness, pecans
like little brains tucked in their bitter shells,
and high in the branches, a few remaining
husks hanging, open, dark, like agitated stars.

~~~

Yesterday, in the Batesville Feed and Seed
that advertises *We Crack Your Pecans,*
the smell of overripe tomatoes, pesticides
and herbicides, corroded bottles of medicine
for hoof rot and mange and lord knows what else,
climbed up my nostrils and wouldn't let go.
A couple of old guys lounged on wooden chairs.
Customers came and went, asking about
pumpkins (none) and pecans (sold out).
Decades of dust webbed the farm tools, furred
a mason jar of peacock feathers, spidered
downward from the ceiling. Catalogs, half-eaten
boxes of cookies, crumpled mail lay jumbled
on a table, and a full-sized dummy in torn
camos and a Jason mask from *Friday the 13th*
loomed in a shadowy corner. Nine baby chicks
nestled in a warm-lit cage at the back of the store.
We wandered the aisles, ducking outside
from time to time for air, returning
to photograph the chicks with their beautiful
barred wing feathers. In the adjacent
concrete work-space, the huge pecan-cracker
clackety-clacked and the blower blew the chaff off.

~~~

Now, back home, we have picked through
28 pounds of pecans, separated stray bits
of shell from the meat, discarded rotten
or shriveled nuts, broken off blackened
corners, carefully nudged the bitter central
membrane from the sweet flesh halves,
and filled gallon bags with the plump fruit
of my November hours and hours wandering
over the yard, my nearsighted gaze
fixed to discern the tawny oblong shells

from among leaves and sticks and grass.
We have gleaned this year's harvest
from the enormous, gnarly, messy-leafed tree
whose shade in summer stretches far across
the lawn and over the driveway. Five fat
worms curl blind and maggot-like
among the litter at the bottom of the bucket.

~~~

I drag a rake through the last enormous
piles of leaves, muttering *Nope, Yep,*
as I stoop to pick up the few remaining
pecans that emerge when the leaves
that covered them are gathered, inspecting
each for worm holes, pitching the bad ones,
plunking the good ones into a rapidly
filling ziplock bag. Then I wander the yard,
looking for stragglers still falling
in slow light from the nearly winter-bare trees.
Delilah the neighbors' calico
plays about my ankles. An inkblot crow
turns his head and watches from the roof.
It is such honor that earth feeds us.

Again, August

Guarding her egg sac on the zigzag web
she has spun across a spindly, heat-

stricken euonymus, the yellow argiope
waits. Forsythias sag, their sprays

droop dusty and limp
no matter how I water, and the redbud

sheds its brittle, heart-shaped leaves.
This is the bitter arc of summer,

when the red-tailed hawk lifts heavy-bodied,
implacable, into the pecan trees,

and my death prepares in me
like the bloodspot in an egg. Petals

drop off the tiger lily. Clinging to its stem—
three shining, jet-black seeds.
~~~

Rob Fontini

Automation

Origin late 16th century (in the sense '***abundant***'): from Latin ***redundant-***
'surging up,' from the verb ***redundare*** (see **REDOUND**)

For the first night
after a fortnight

coming 'round again the moon
cycle of the seasons

preferred to number by age
(years) yet nothing passed

disappears, does not want to be called
pile up or accumulation.

the sun stands
ever in place

unlike the annual
so near to annul

so that each year replaces the last
until the last comes, end must

end if everything ends
death must end, hollow (hallow?)

guarded the Mother spoke differently
She too seems persistent

in symbol and in immediacy
but surely moving horizontally (?)

the moon cycle viewed as a plane
redundancy is not the same

as boredom, [the Sage's refrain]
when the world protrudes anew

continuously.

The Holocene (or The Hollow Scene?)

Sat down in shadows
erotic siblings in alien [old] form
these eyes tear and tear and tear

a heart which controls nothing
the steaming clutch of iron
the beauty of a forehead in hands

in the midst of a nightmare
gazing upon the friends ahead
in the sun everything seeming

that the ground may never end
the sounds of waiting rooms
derived from divine bells mis-

appropriated   feather caps feeting
the high rise of matt gloss
for fug leavening responses [heat!]

ὅδος was deceit like   the
whole of the hellenistic language
never reached the lighthouse

all of these heroes in circles
it's nauseating
in distinct to the high sea

how I wish you were
with me   by more than
your gift of memory

shadows of before this universal
imagine looking at anything
as either familiar or foreign

for years I wandered in these mountains
that had long since been plateau.

Squared

the gingerbread bird
one that remains in
winter's austrian tone

removed from all seasons eyes
the mineral works below
singing champion's sighs

that the fifth has not turned

yet the diggers are not con-
tent with context's guesswork
set incisive dots as maps

these are true thoroughfareres
i have seen them with loan
eyes turn mines in

the festivity of a still spring.

Elisabeth Frost, Cynthia Hogue, and Dianne Kornberg

A Dickinson Bestiary (A Chorograph)

This collaboration, "A Dickinson Bestiary (A Chorograph)," began with the notion of encounter in Emily Dickinson's poems, the dialogic structure in which a poem's speaker confronts an *other*. As two poet-critics and a visual artist, we asked how we might engage, both verbally and visually, Dickinson's human and nonhuman animal worlds. The many meetings between different beings that populate Dickinson's poems follow the OED's definition of the word *encounter*: "The fact of meeting someone or something face to face."[1] "You may have met him," Dickinson supposes of a chance meeting with a snake in Fr. 1096, and then probes: "Did you not [?]"[2] The status of the encounter with the "narrow Fellow" is immediately put into question and never stabilized. For the speaker, as for the reader, the snake is glimpsed but never grasped.

The three of us were intrigued by the way Dickinson's animal encounters often remain in this realm, which theorist and animal rights activist Ron Broglio terms "the notion of 'animal surface.'" Contrary to the "flattening out of animals' worlds"—in which humans have engaged historically in order to use animals and often to treat them cruelly—Broglio contends that "the surface can be a site of productive engagement with the world of animals."[3] In staging the encounter with the "Narrow fellow," Dickinson deploys anthropomorphism to underscore how strange the snake remains to the speaker—an acknowledgment of humans' lack of access to any deeper, or more intimate, means of knowing. Much of the poem describes the emptiness of the place the snake vacated, leaving us with an existential (human) emptiness, as well as—literally—an empty space that only language fills (extra-human). In this regard, Dickinson writes what Angus Fletcher has aptly termed an *environmental* poem: she vacates a human center but includes the natural surroundings.

Fletcher calls this type of poem *chorographic*, by which he means that a Dickinson poem focuses on space rather than place. In creating a space for our own experimental "Dickinson Bestiary," we have been inspired by such thinking, as well as by recent developments in animal studies, such as Broglio's *Animal Encounters* and Giorgio Agamben's Heideggerean reading of the concept of "open"—"one of the names ... of being and of world."[4]

"A Dickinson Bestiary" experiments with a heteroglossic process the poets in our collaboration call *chorographic*, following Fletcher's notion but with a revised definition. Each poem we've written thinks-through an animal encounter in a specific Dickinson poem (or poems). We draw on multiple registers of language, explicate particular Dickinson poems, and discursively cite criticism and theory in our polyphonic poetic meditations. Throughout, we borrow Dickinson's lexicon. In some of the poems, in a Kathleen Fraser-inspired formal gesture of parallel texts,[5] we experiment with a visual and verbal embodiment of our dialogue with Dickinson's works. A series of glosses (near-poems, wisps or whispers, fragmentary and suggestive) appears suspended in the right-hand margin. These glosses create an environment or "surround" of our own making. The words, all culled from the specific Dickinson poem(s) with which we engage, help make our intertextual relationship explicit, as well as intuitively graspable. They also track a visual and aural map in parallel with the more discursive mode of our poetics.

The "chorus" of the poems exists dialogically as well with the "graph" or visual depictions in a series of images by Dianne Kornberg. These pieces sprang from our shared discussions about Dickinson's animal imagery, which focused on the notion of circumference as a mapping of space and as the creation of an (environmental) "surround." The images' engagement with particular nonhuman animals drawn from Dickinson's work is made explicit in the inclusion of phrases culled from the digital archive of Dickinson's manuscripts. Although the images represent animals that appear in the poet's work, the underlying forms suggest the limited circumference of Dickinson's view from her window, and the mysterious space her work occupies.

while he, victorious, tilts away

BEE
(Fr.1 297)

Firmament

Gary Snyder writes of how artists can "join in the defense of the planet and wild nature.
They can 'bear witness' because they have been given, as in fairy tales, two 'magic gifts': *above*

One is 'The mirror of truth.' ... The second is a 'heart of compassion' [that] extends
to all creatures and to the earth itself. . . . Anciently this was a shamanistic role

where the [shaman] became one with a creature. Today, such a role is played by the writer[.]
This could be called 'speaking on behalf of nature' in the ancient way" (63).[6]

Is it the ancient way to call the animal a creature? Is "speaking on behalf of" to "speak for"?
Watching a bee struggle for purchase between "Firmament above" and "Firmament below" *below*

by landing on a clover plank, Dickinson refrains. The plank is "Responsible to nought"
and when the "Billows of Circumference" sweep away the bee, the "Bumble Bee was not -" *billow*

bumble

The speaker's claims to "personally" know the bee, hence her careful attention to his fate,
are belied by the limits of her knowledge and powers of perception: she can see but not hear him.

She does not "bear witness" by speaking on behalf of or for the bee. She dwells on the (surface)
encounter, observing and reporting the bee's perceivable movements. An empiricist in method,

the speaker adopts a phenomenological diction, and the poem tracks the human watching the insect
trying to find a place to weather the universe, the "Circumference," which sweeps him

Nought

at last on his way. She thinks about what she knows she has seen, but not what it means
to the bee. "Freight of Wind" is one vowel tone away from "Fright," but the latter word's *Freight*

laden with a human's reaction to a strong wind. "Freight" is merely material, the wind's weight.
The event is "harrowing," but to whom? Nothing is wrung from the bee, no sound not least

"A wandering 'Alas' -" The knowledge that the speaker claims, "a Bee I personally knew,"
is ambiguous. How does she "personally" know the bee? Because she watched him

"sinking in the sky"? What kind of knowledge is that? The speaker cannot access the bee's
interiority but only her own. She neither projects her feelings onto the bee nor personifies him. *Alas*

Dickinson feels along the surface of her encounter with the bee. She does not cross physical paths
with him. She doesn't save and cannot quote him. She does not put a human face on him *knew*

(although she gives him a gendered pronoun). She supplies the occasion for an imaginative "Alas"
but she acknowledges the word's status: She's close enough to hear that she can't hear. *not*

The bee is "not": not her, not a fellow, not a figure for the writer, not like a human. Not cute.
We do not "personally" know this bee by the poem's end. That is what she bears witness to.

—Cynthia Hogue

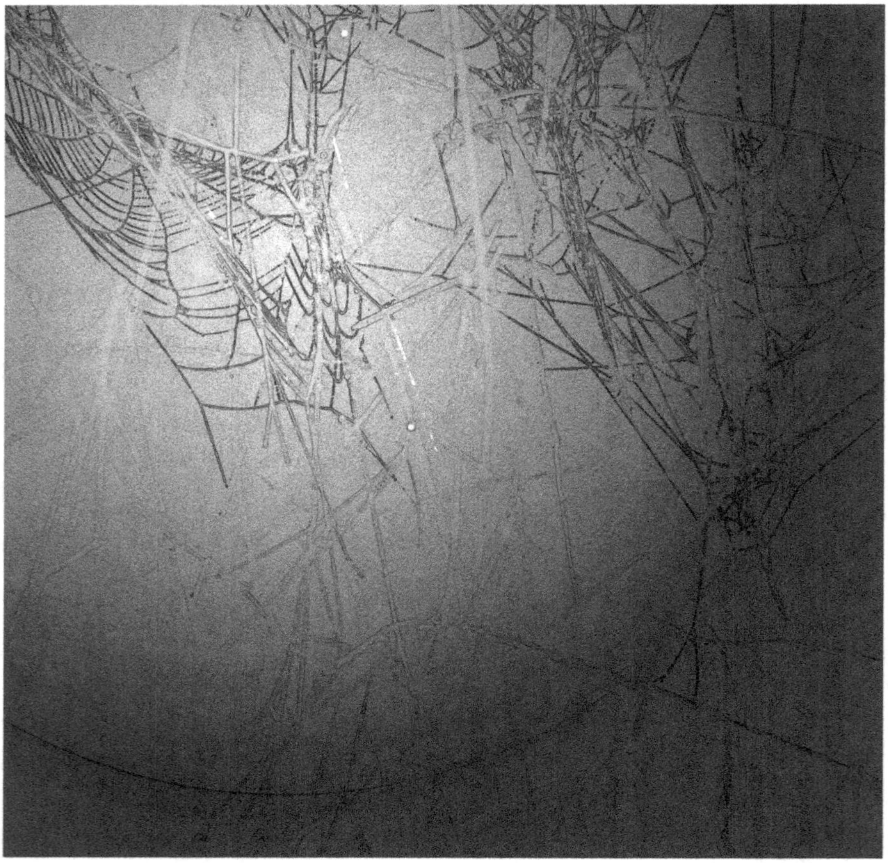

The spider holds a silver ball

SPIDER
(Fr.513, Fr.1174)

Homeless at home
Alone
I felt myself a visitor
in the orb web's
Circumstance
reticent domain

nor here nor there
Reluctant
its continents of light

The animal
(says the philosopher)
does not open
Abode
itself
in a world —
Assumed

absolute Circumference
its Balm —
Inmates

A human knows
it's open
to a closedness
Heir

knows what is and is not
beyond its now
Strike

A room, say, in which
Me
a spider unspools

its silver ball
a means to all
Necessities —
Blow

the while
not knowing
its own doings
Property

not knowing
Law
a human 'I' occupies
its space

I left its
unsubstantial trade
Learned
in tact

Not even the lark
(says the Philosopher)
Marrow

can see the open
Day

—Elisabeth Frost

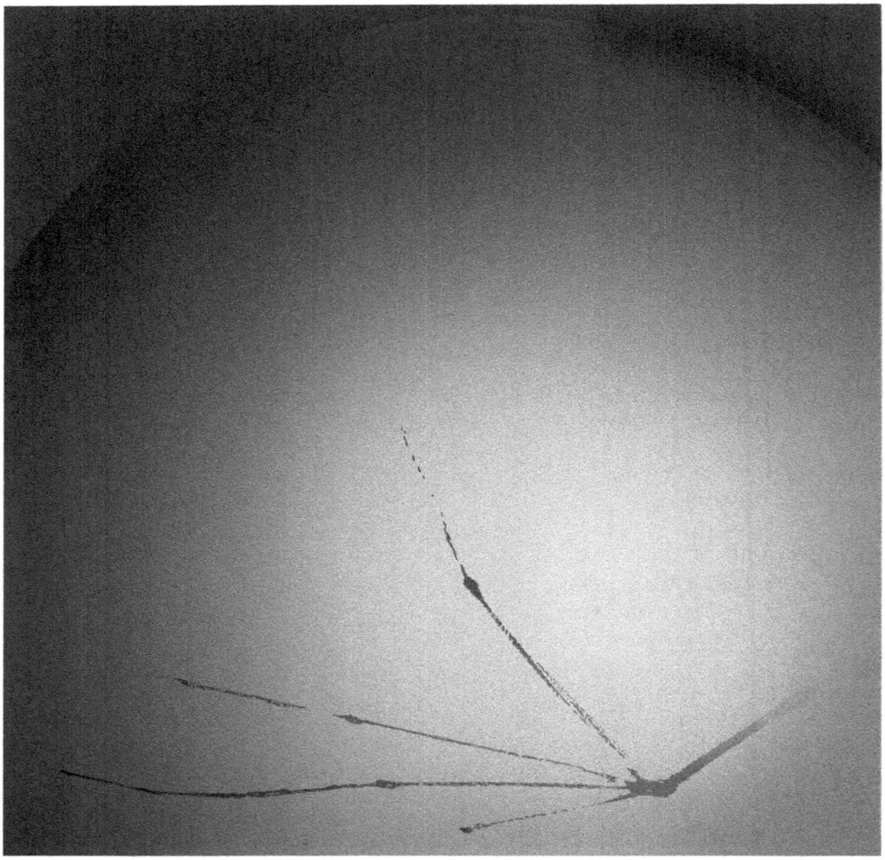

Beneficent, believe me, these ancient cities

BAT (a sonnet)
(Fr.1408)

Not heard but seen   Dun/done
The not-song of the no "song *p*ervade his Lips"
or (self-corrected to undecidable status) "none *p*erceptible"
to us but (not said, assumed) purveyed to other bats
The loaded words alliterative   the consequential
p's of both explosive plosives
are what we hear supplanting
and see "Describing in the Air"
the bat   by poetic *echolocation*
The unheard-by-us song begs the question of what
experiment's conducted in the not-song of the Imperceptible
when plosive sonic markers of the penultimate line ==
"Benificent, believe me"== forge the (old term)
feminine rhyme with the amphibrach "Creator"

—Cynthia Hogue

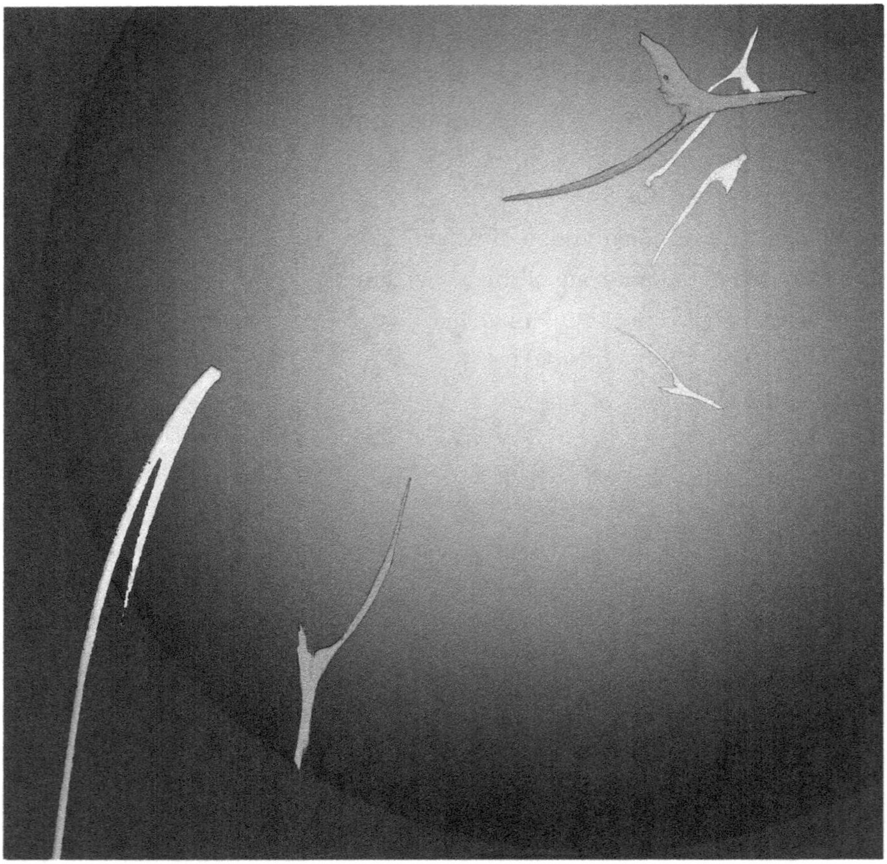

Split the Larks and you will find the Music

TO SPLIT A LARK —
(Fr.905)

I also have suffered
the wonderful to die.
Alice Fulton

It's not the sum of its parts, *Split*
the lark that was *true* —
unlarks it (& that's no lark): *Lark*
not familiar it is foreign, *Music*

not known it is alien, always *other*
but whole, intact, *itself* alive. *Saved*
Now it has been analyzed
to death, rendered piecemeal, *Loose*

still ungraspable but *also*
the bird whose beauty we wished
to understand is silent this spring. *Gush*
Animals to which we're drawn—all silenced— *You*

not unable to communicate *Scarlet*
but beyond our (human) capacity
to comprehend, our range to hear
and speak with them too limited, *Doubt*

therefore we think they have
no means to "talk." What we do *Bird*
to animals to assuage our
curiosity splits the difference. *True*

—Cynthia Hogue

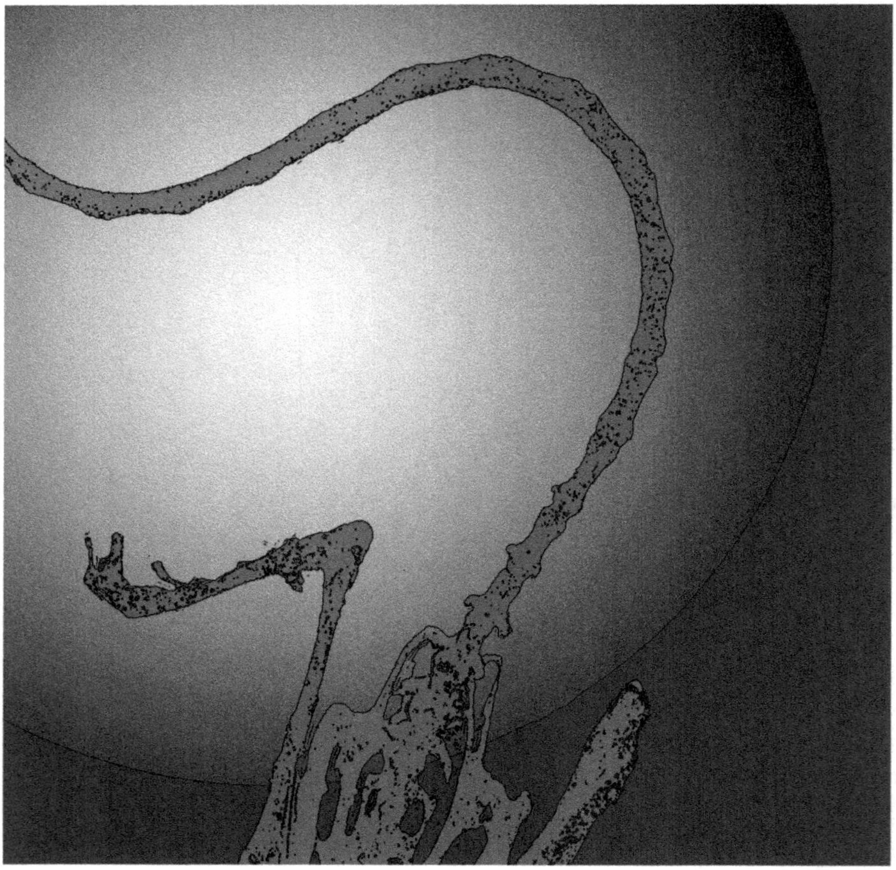

Grief as Thief – Guard Startled –

MOUSE
(Fr.753)

Grief   is
        a far place

the 'I' of me
        Tenant there

    Wainscot   tapped
        by nimble claws

the 'I' of me   repudiates
        all Schemes

    regresses
        caresses
            this soft toy
                in my sick bed —

    two felt   teeth
        whiskers bits
            of yarn

we make of beings
        metaphors
            for Balm
    to circumvent
                Tongueless
        the Vast Dark

the 'I' of me   what
        creature   now —

    minus   all
        Equilibrium

            I cannot wade —

—Elisabeth Frost

I heard a Fly buzz - when I died -

FLY
(Fr.591)

i.

A Fly knows *Buzz*
through
its feet

treads with taste buds *Stillness*
of tiny hairs

The Windows *Storm*
of its compound Eyes
capture vast
radii
each plane *Breaths*
articulate

each wing
assignable in Air
Onset
King —
unmatched
its Equilibrium
Willed
Poor witnesses
interposed!

what do we know
Keepsakes
— uncertain
stumbling —

of the Stillness — *Signed*
in the Room

ii.

I could not see to see —

Blue

oceans shrank to
less than light

flesh's blood beat
thinned

Between

We know
only through bodies

concrete particles

Light

and when these fail —

Me

Being's
stark stubborn
law —

There is no need

See

but need

—Elisabeth Frost

Notes

[1] "encounter, n., v., and adv." *OED Online*. Oxford University Press. June 2020, accessed on August 10, 2020. http://www.oed.com.

[2] Emily Dickinson, and R. W. Franklin. *The Poems of Emily Dickinson,* Reading ed. (Cambridge, Mass.: Belknap Press of Harvard University Press, 1999). Cited with the abbreviation Fr. followed by the poem number.

[3] Ron Broglio, *Surface Encounters: Thinking with Animals and Art* (Minneapolis: University of Minnesota Press, 2011), xvii.

[4] See Giorgio Agamben, *The Open: Man and Animal* (Stanford: Stanford University Press, 2003).

[5] For Fraser's own account of her formal use of singular words at the edge of a text's right-hand margins, see Cynthia Hogue, "Interview with Kathleen Fraser," *Contemporary Literature* 39.1 (Spring 1998): 1–26.

[6] Gary Snyder, "Writers and the War against Nature," *Back on the Fire: Essays* (Berkeley: Counterpoint, 2007), 61–72.

Sachamama

Una serpiente inmensa en cuyo lomo viven animales y crecen árboles altos.

Tiene en su cabeza un diamante e hilos invisibles
con los que jala comida y agua de las nubes.

(Los comerciantes tienen cabezas de Sachamama para cazar a sus clientes).

Para que los animales puedan viajar, la Sachamama les abre caminos
con sus labios como bulldózeres.

A su paso se alegran las brisas y aromas de las vainillas.

Cuando se enfurece, la Sachamama sacude la tierra, jala nubes con rayos,
y hace temblar hasta el cielo.

A quienes entran en la selva sin su permiso los jala con sus hilos a las cavernas de
su barriga.

Si tienen suerte los manda con fiebre para sus casas.

Para salvarse de la Sachamama, los cazadores hacen cruces en el aire con sus
machetes.

Sachamama*

A huge serpent on whose back animals live and tall trees grow.

In her head a diamond. Invisible strings pull her food and
water from the clouds.

(Merchants use Sachamama heads to hunt customers).

So the animals can travel, the Sachamama opens
roads with her lips like bulldozers.

When she moves, breezes and aromas of the vanilla vines are happy.

When she is enraged, the Sachamama moves the earth, pulls clouds
with lightning and shakes even the heavens.

Those who enter the forest without her permission
are pulled by her threads to the caverns of her belly.

If they are lucky, she sends them to their homes with a fever.

To save themselves from the Sachamama, hunters make crosses
in the air with their machetes.

**Supernatural serpent and forest defender known to Indigenous people and mestizo newcomers of the Amazon Basin.*

David Greenspan

Ballad of the Little Girl Who Invented the Universe

after Jack Spicer

Rows of peach trees in a commercial orchard.
Obedient, plush, sap bloodied. Night
growing all around. A girl sprinkles her toes
through the soil, adds a throat of selenite,

incantations to blossom. The sky is
an open mouth spitting
on the girl. She doesn't notice,
her attention busy in front of a small creature.

The peach is an emoji
and the orchard is an iPhone
and the girl sends photos
for $100 a set.

Between the trees and the emoji
something ordinary happens. The girl
walks into traffic, her leaves
steaming—the drivers see their
mothers' legs.

An Animal Fat

I'd like a life of thick juniper
though I'll settle for dogwood. I've never been
excitable though sometimes I pretend
to be. A possum or some other animal
with dull teeth, smoked, salted, left
on your back porch. A jar filled with milk,
an undress followed by strong words
involving thighs. You choose
please. I've never been excitable
except for when I am. Tonight
my muscles are curled, sprinkled with basil,
bloated. I'll eat what's in front of me.
I don't vomit beer. I don't vomit water.
This isn't to say I won't vomit either
one day. I'm excitable or maybe I'm not.

I forget and you're not wearing underwear.
I push my fingers through plants and will you
please push yours through blackberry,
rub them along whatever you see fit?
Afterwards we can and will
load up our guns. I've never been
excitable. Of course that's a lie
like the sugar and ants spilling over
and the marbled cut of flank spoiling
on the back porch. Let's move to Seattle
and start a band. Let's move to Seattle
and raise a family of appleskin.

Catherine Greenwood

The Grolar Bear's Ballad

> *DNA analysis has confirmed that a bear shot in the Canadian Arctic last month is a half-polar bear, half-grizzly hybrid. … the hybrid's father was a grizzly and its mother was a polar bear.*
>
> —*National Geographic*

I

First-generation *hybrid ursid*,
I's a mutt of mud and snow.
Ma were old Polar stock and Pa
pure Grizzly (other way 'round,
we'd be *Pizzly*—some prefer *Nanulak*).
Mother migrated south on a shrinking floe
and swum the salt-chuck's
final lap to land. Father, fishing salmon
on the Archipelago, smelt her coming
and pursued her rank musk upriver.
Found her lunching on loon

in a Churchill dump. Her seal eyes,
his bullish hump—fate got written
on love-bitten rump. On a honeymoon
rummaging bins the pair grew smitten
with the taste of tourist-tossed
bannock and that squib of pork
from the can of beans.
Man is not delicious
their fortune cookie read.
Such were the marriage, a solstice
spent licking tins. Never met him.

II

Eight moons later I were born
a twin. I remembrance the milky pang
of my sister and our den in a dim
bank of snow, the warmth of our mother,
a smothering heat of seal-fat
fueling the furnace in her belly.

She'd trod north to rear us
in old country ways: Mackerel shanties
like *Gannet and Guts*, how to knock wind
from a walrus, how to read moonlight on
fox-face and feather, how to swim.

I sank. Hairless toe-pads cracked
on hunts. *Scoop-Snout* and *Poop-Eyes*
the uncles called us. Sister *Mud-Foot*
and me never fit in. A forepaw's full count
of seasons 'til I struck out on the land
to track our birthright's mystery.
Tailing a southbound caribou herd
we crossed a border of tamarack
and fell in with our father's kind,
a rough lot stinking of carrion
whose song was gruff and tuneless.

III

Growl-givers, the Grizzly gaveled out
history. Anointed us *Mule-Nuts,*
unworthy title. White hide no barrier,
in green-time we tarried with dark-advised sows
what sought out my seed, carriers
of blonde cubs whose being
breached the unspoken law of myself.
Battle clarion of boar in rut,
road-kill cuisine, them ways
stuck in our craw. Snout-scarred,
maw full of roots, I roamed

salal reaches aweful, alone. Meatless
on mountaintop, a dead metal bird
with bones in its belly; paw-slicing
panes of ice on men's dwellings.
A wolf gave warning, all kith killed
by a hail of sharp stones: *humans*
make of us monsters he snarled
and slunk off, society-starved. We stole
strips of chum strung on stone beaches,
dried-up tongues tasting
of salt and sleep. Nowhere were home.

IV

One autumn I ended on permafrost
where tundra greets sea. Bog-berry
sotted, we sniffed a breeze what bore
lost others in its brine, wondering
at my ghostly brothers as they woke
from sun-shifting meadows of snow.
It struck us like a blow
from a whale—the giant fib
a tail-whack as the bullet broke my ribs.
Blubber echo fading. Stunned. Hunter
hunkered in cooling blood with gun.

In the key of a snowflake a lullaby
tinkles like icicles in the arctic
of our emptied skull. A restless
clicking of claw on floorboard,
we're crossed from Alive
to After. I's Here, Time's ticking
mongrel. Bleached and brushed, bound
with blue felt, our pelt's a promise
to the past afore it melts.
Some day I'll don my skin
and roaring, rise and reappear!

O, but the world be whelped of mud and snow,
and my glass eyes was spawned in Ohio.

Megan Grumbling

Selected New Texts on the Anthropocene: Letters and Leisure

1.
From *Cli-Fi and One-Offs: The Anthropocene as Text* "Pan-Protagonism"

After a long and robust century of human disaster narratives—epidemics, meteors, droughts, floods, and of course the omnipresent tornados—both literary and popular trends turned to narratives told from the first-person protagonist viewpoints of animals, plants, and even weather. Eventually grouped under the term "Pan-Protagonism," its authors went to great cross-disciplinary lengths, especially in more experimental and theoretical circles, to minimize the inevitable marks of human authorship.

Some of these works demonstrated impressive imaginative virtuosity—in the non-verbal text that came to be known as *Sap/Blood*, readers followed the stained seepage of actual maple sap across and through pages; the arc of the chroma-text *Bleaching* progressed via the leaching hues captured in time-lapse of a dying coral; and *Time of the Birch* attempted to verbally approximate what scientists have described as a tree's slower consciousness of time by elongating page after page of diphthongs—but proved somewhat tedious "reading."

2.
From *"Man on Man": A New Popular Anthropology of the Anthropocene* IV.4: Sport and Recreation

After a brief trend in conceptual art focused its practice on ritual effigy, the conceit mainstreamed, the most popular example being the reality show *Effigy This!*

The series brought together regional teams—from the Corn Belt, New England, the Maldives, the Gulf Coast—for a team effigy-making and enactment competition, in the Nevada desert, that was riddled with interpersonal dramas and, usually, a death, disfigurement, or violent case of heatstroke.

Each season (there were four in total) followed the teams' conception, construction, and deployment of enormously scaled effigies—a four-story, latex-skinned head that stretched over a slowly-expanding armature before splitting open to reveal intricate lobes of corn kernels; a female form designed to spout butane-laced mock-pomegranate from mouth and nether regions.

Each season culminated in a burning ceremony featuring carefully engineered combustions, sometimes performed with mirrors, and judged, by the viewing audience, in the categories of "Skill," "Style," and "Catharsis."

3.
From *The New Farmer's Almanac*: Puzzle of the Day

Which is louder, cold or heat?

4.
From *Cli-Fi and One-Offs: The Anthropocene as Text* "One-Offs"

"One-Offs" or "GoDarks," also known as "Once-Overs," began as a sort of neo-Fluxus performative mode, but soon found brief though widespread practice with a mainstream readership. Upon publication, the first One-Offs, and most notably Sadun's *Extinction Solo*, were critically received as provocative and innovative spectacles; videos of *Extinction*'s text disappearing off the turning page immediately went viral.

First the avant-garde of arts and letters and soon the general public were enthralled by increasingly widespread One-Off clubs, their members sitting hushed around the reader, huddled close to best look on as the pages darkened, and as at the end of the book the spine disintegrated, releasing its blackened pages. More laconic was Avenir's *Boucher le Chœur (Butcher the Chorus)* as well as Rhodes's carefully engineered combustion at the end of *The Bottle's Neck.*

Once the phenomenon had spread beyond the fringes, execution became clumsier and engineering less intricate but remained true to concept, as those in the general public began exchanging messages that disappeared, went dark, or disintegrated after a first and only reading.

5.
From *"Man on Man": A New Popular Anthropology of the Anthropocene* VI.3 "[]"

To be *Unlit* became the next extreme in anti-verbal practice, in so-called "neuro-subsistence cults," the foremost of which was known as [ ]. Members renounced names and even pronouns, then underwent programs by which to unlearn their literacy—to be "un-lit"—entirely, first by "neuro-linguistic deprogramming" and later by laser to the cerebral cortex, thereby both de-collectivizing and de-selfing each initiate.

In some cults, extra social status was afforded to members who renounced fine motor skills: thumbs were bound to index fingers first by twine, then by stitches and skin grafts.

6.
From *The New Farmer's Almanac* Science Tricks for Children

Fill a glass with water, up to the brim. Now add more water, drop by drop.
Can you make the water curve *higher* than the brim?

Robert Head

Three Poems

i want to be cremated but not
Hwile i'm alive

---

between the amazon burning
& the pipelines blowing up
Linda & i are suffering

& Jean Follain being run over by a
car doesn't help a bit

tho his poems console me now
unable to sleep
& the ded running up & down the
street with their hair on fire

---

purchast water withdrawals for Marcellus
wells in WV in 2012 were 6% of total
withdrawals hweras surface water
withdrawals were 83% so this means

the frackers are getting this 83 per cent
for free from the nearest available creek.

as far as our life is concernd
that water is lost
we're trading water for methane
& i think we're making a bad bargain

& pretty soon west virginia will be a desert
& we can walk beside our donkeys if we're lucky.

William Heyen

Snakes

Slash of Guns N' Roses gave the girl he was living with at the time a baby
Burmese python.

They became friends, he said, as it grew to 15', fattened mostly
on frogs & mice.

Inside, the woman took the python into her bath; outside, a pool became
their Lethe.

Slash often found her smooching her pet, *kissykisskisskiss.*
Reading all this,

I remembered snakes from my childhood, & that movie with
Mowgli—& was it a cobra?

In Florida these years Burmese pythons, another invasive species, have
almost killed off

all small mammals—they even climb trees, decimate birds & eggs.
So I've decided

that if & when I ever become a snake, I'll be a small
beautiful deadly coral,

pure poetry, so as not to descend with Slash & his half-
gallon of Stoli a day

into mamba underworlds where we don't care what happened
to that python woman.

As If Hearing Heavy Furniture Moved on the Floor Above Us

As things grow rarer, they enter the ranges of counting.
Remain this many Siberian tigers,
that many African elephants. Three hundred red-legged egrets.
We scrape from the world its tilt and meander of wonder
as if eating the last burned onions and carrots from a cast iron pan.
Closing eyes to taste better the char of ordinary sweetness.

Day Beginning with Seeing the International Space Station and a Full Moon Over the Gulf of Mexico and All Its Invisible Fishes

None of this had to happen.
Not Florida. Not the ibis's beak. Not water.
Not the horseshoe crab's empty body and not the living starfish.
Evolution might have turned left at the corner and gone down another street entirely.
The asteroid might have missed.
The seams of limestone need not have been susceptible to sand and mangroves.
The radio might have found a different music.
The hips of one man and the hips of another might have stood beside
each other on a bus in Aleppo and recognized themselves as long-lost brothers.
The key could have broken off in the lock and the nail-can refused its lid.
I might have been the fish the brown pelican swallowed.
You might have been the way the moon kept not setting long after we thought
it would, long after the sun was catching inside the low wave curls coming in
at a certain angle. The light might not have been eaten again by its moving.
If the unbearable were not weightless we might yet buckle under the grief
of what hasn't changed yet. Across the world a man pulls a woman from the water
from which the leapt-from overfilled boat has entirely vanished.
From the water pulls one child, another. Both are living and both will continue to live.
This did not have to happen. No part of this had to happen.

(No Wind, No Rain)

No wind, no rain,
the tree
just fell, as a piece of fruit does.

But no, not fruit. Not ripe.

Not fell.

It broke. It shattered.

One cone's
addition of resinous cell-sap,
one small-bodied bird
arriving to tap for a beetle.

It shattered.

What word, what act,
was it we thought did not matter?

H. L. Hix

What is it that these apparently unrelated, randomly selected examples have in common? (Dubravka Ugrešić)

This scat-peppered, rabbit-animated
sage-strafed stretch of desert severity.
That burnt-out sedan, rust-suffocated,
into and from which leaps a rib-thin stray,
pit bull mix, through the driver's-side window.
Constellations reiterated
on a bedroom sky in stickers that glow
in the dark. Among the wet-snow-weighted
branches, one bent farther than its sisters
by the melt-heavy t-shirt snagged on it.
Two same-sized pairs of capital letters
incised side-by-side in sidewalk concrete.
Two trees, their twined trunks long grown together,
one now in leaf, the other in flower.

By whom? Of what? In which direction? (Peter Pál Palbert)

By someone who hasn't read the book,
someone who manages and delegates,
who can't think past efficiency or look
to something other than vertical cuts.
Of a smaller and more tightly woven
than a hummingbird nest, a waited for
and looked back on, a should have been given
but in fact was sold, a behind which door.
In the direction of price reduced
for quick sale, fixer-upper, hidden gem,
burned-out, abandoned, repossessed,
the direction of Herculaneum,
Persepolis, Palenque, Prypiat,
Angkor, Carthage, Machu Picchu, Detroit.

MARYBETH HOLLEMAN

with

with steller jay tap tapping at the window for peanuts, telling me weather's
cooling, winter comes.
with the line climbing the snowy mountainside, six in a row, black wolves.
with gazelle chased by cheetah, both so fleet, me saying no while my son says go.
with thin black cat laying two small fish on our doorstep for her kittens inside.
with my nephew's snake my young son holds in both hands.
with small black beetle whispering into the rock around my pansies.
with grosbeak's song tumbling light as dry snow down through the trees, asking
for sunflower seeds.
with ground squirrel kits whose chatter reverberates through derelict gold mine
pipe they make home.
with pulsating orbs of white spread below my kayak, a gathering of moon
jellies, mirroring sky's clouds.
with three black snakes sunning together on a boulder in springtime woods.
with the spray of their exhale misting my face as two humpbacks leap from glowing
seas.
with a dangling thread just before my eyes, inchworm hanging from the willow, green U-
turning.
with adopted sun conure, whose shrieks still rainbow my ear though I regret
not a moment of him on my shoulder, nibbling strands of my hair.
with small black puppy at Om beach, gnawing on a dead crab, the sacred bloated
cow nuzzling a pile of trash nearby.
with black dog at my feet, soft groan as I stroke the silk of her back.
with river otters tumbling over one another along the barnacled shoreline, one head
lifting when my shutter clicks.
with night bunny under the roses, beautiful bones ticking time's soft rhythm.
with black bear searching in hungry spring for birdseed we miss, batting at the garden
hose, down on forearms to lap from the dogs' water bowl.
with the baby gang, chickadee nuthatch junco newly fledged, alighting in birch,
learning the bird bath.
with bats, circling, at dusk, my head, dancing to my runner's high.
with gray squirrel high in the oak, scrambling to avoid the beebee shots of neighbor
boys my mother chases, screaming, from our backyard.
with my husky racing over tundra like blossoming wind, quick becoming small as a seed.
with pair of mountain goats pressed against cliffs lining Crow Pass, watching hikers toil.
with two frogs under the lilacs, one who lived two decades, our own tuck everlasting.
with red fox trotting by our tent in the Arctic summer night, red tongue out, panting, so

light-footed she leaves no prints in soft mud.
with bumblebee bouncing off the window, wanting the colors of flowers my walls wear.
with polar bear pushing black snout against the window I raise just in time, leaving
in dusty glass a single paw print, shimmer by the night's aurora.
with king salmon in the stream, termination dust on their dorsals slowing tails to
list into gentler current.
with the rolling thunder of hooves across my dreams,
the licks of a thousand rough tongues,
the harmony of songs lifted to limitless blue,
every day and night, world without end.

Angela Hume

may the human animals

learn new skills by imitation
fire the neuron when the action
is performed   and also when
the action is observed in another
thus mirroring the behavior
of that other   reach net zero global
anthropogenic CO_2 emissions
stop the earth from receiving
incoming energy from the plasma
core radiating 4.26 million
metric tons per second   more
energy than the earth itself radiates
into space   brighter disk   limb
darkening   only the cooler layers
that produce less light can be seen
may the human animals
facilitate helping behaviors
stop the hoarding of food supplies
medicine   the caging and modification
of human and other animals
ensure timely appointment of legal
counsel for as many of the children
as possible   stop the CO_2 from soaking
the reef   and also the worldwide

reduction of a pH balance that
marine calcifiers need to build
skeletons shells corrals crustaceans
snails   even light-harvesting algae
encase themselves in carbonate platelets
radial   continuous   basket-shaped
disc-shaped wishbone-shaped
rhombohedral   the colors of
moss and tea   may the human animals
redistribute across populations   change
lifestyles to enable adaptation
fathom the relief of an earth without them
imagine another human animal's
thoughts and feelings from that
other's point of view instead of from
their own   may the human animals say
i am here   i know what you are feeling
is real   your life is important to me
and you are not alone
tunnel through a seemingly hardened
crust to the warm wet electrochemical
center of a complex synapse structure
hold tight the damaged organ
which holds tight the measure of attention
slide with a body into the white crush
of a silent room   love the body in its
one life its singular intensity after all

Brenda Iijima

Breathing Consciousness Breathing

Snowdrops breathe in snow breathing in meadows breathing in
gale winds

Breath of jaguars, breath of symbiosis, breath of consideration, breath
of night

Dreams breathe out night, breathe out lucidity, exhale out-of-body
experience

Funneling in polar ice caps, ecstatic dancers, enunciation,
analogue systems

From nostrils and mouths stream the Amazon Rainforest, the Blue
Ridge Mountains, the Nile, the Mississippi, inhaled are the Tigris, the
Ganges, the Colorado

Release chaos and mystery with breath, release wonder, release the unconsciousness as an
expanse that envelopes atmosphere

Collectively respire, grasshoppers, toads, lizards, iguanas, pumas,
wolves, mice

As a nation holds its breath a nation eases into disbelief

Slowly breath is released in dying as the ecosystem stressors build,
species are relaxing out of existence. Today there are energetic tigers.
Tomorrow there will be a loss of rhinos a loss of birds a loss of insects

CO_2 gasses are breathed in by flora, flora expel oxygen in a cycle of
reciprocity

How do you know you are alive, breathing feeling diaphragm
and lungs expand and contract

I can't breathe is a call to justice

I can't breathe indicates a system of dire inequity and harm

There is little air in the vaulted imprisonments, there is little light,
little comfort

Out of breathness, running for one's life across national boundaries,
incarcerated in prisons, breathing from inside concrete and metal
detention centers with no food or water, no rights, time breathes out

We breathe in shattered bodies, objects, objectives, we
breathe remains

The oceans are losing oxygen, marine life is suffocating

Forests breathe oxygenation breathing out to faunal community

Redwoods breathe in metamorphic rock from millennia dreams

When a baby racoon breathes, she breathes breezes from breaths of
the cicadas

The sand of the Gobi Desert exhales mineral breath in airstream
of circulation

Your exhalation is historically located in the social fabric as tissue and
cellular matter

Through a lung of ice, the tundra exudes leeward winds

From inside a sub oceanic cave the Milky Way inhales the Dog
Star and Andromeda
A geyser produces the air for mushrooms clouds

Breath refuses isolation

Breath is commingled

Entire being is generative of breath

Breath is generative of entire being

Observations of Wind

Arrows point to an accretionary prism
Gasses rise and converge
Units of concentration inch up
Tropospheric surges wend through magmic
activity Earth's mantle holds in turbulence
Over the crust a flow of air belts cylindricity
A fact within a series of suppositions
A plunging neckline looks ravishing on you
Little caches of posed desire
Arrest the atmosphere
The cat in the bag and chickens plunging
To the ground via nostril flare
A phase of the earth upended
A heartbeat winnowing through emotion
Allegiance and profit
A cloud of finite motors
Clouds implode with still lives
Carafes of wine and cornucopias
Punctilious, erstwhile arms become
Attenuated fruiting bodies
Fervent, meshed collateral
Uncut sapphires roiling in mud
Rock hard skin device
Within a scale of zero emissions
Seeking tenability
Sequential data blooms conceptual awakenings
And utopia is a macroscopic hope
NASA's VISIBLE EARTH

Lace a threshold with anticipation
Velocity wills interplay
We spread our legs to see
Divisibly through the clouds

KENT JOHNSON

To those who may come after

—a translucination after Bertolt Brecht

I.

Oh, these are bleak and confounding times!
The casual word is heedless. The unfurrowed brow
denotes callousness. People pun and prank at this or that.
Mammoths and planes appear in alpine slush.

Yes, weird times inside the diorama, these, in which bar
talk about vacations and trees is a kind of porn. For
talking like that, one is harnessed to so much harm!
Like the ones who, harnessed-up, leave the poet's house,
Laughing and gossiping past the homeless ones.

True enough: I, too, am a literati-stiff.
But, really, that's just by chance, I swear. Nothing
I do, I suppose, gives me OK to eat my fill.
For some reason they've cut me a break.
(If my luck shifts, I'm screwed.)

They say: eat and drink, poet, be glad you've been
spared. Enjoy the diorama! But then sometimes I
think, how can I eat and drink when what I eat others
cannot, and what I drink others cannot? (Yeah, I
know, it's not 1939, so the language is "off.") But eat
and drink I do, and with a bard's pleasure.

I'd really love to be wise.
The old epics teach us about wisdom:
to rise above the discord of the world,
to be present in the days that one's been given,
free of anxiety or of fear.
To abide in peace, without hassling others,
to pay unyielding evil with acceding mercy—
the wise don't torture their conscience,
they're happy with their lot, small as it may be.

But sometimes I think I just can't be OK with that.
Man, it's confounding and these days are bleak!

II.

I arrived to the vast cities in a time of bedlam,
of great heat and extinctions and rising seas.
I came upon my people in a time of terror,
and I rose and rebelled alongside them.
And this is how I spent
the days I'd been given.

I ate my meals inside the terrible trials.
I made my bed among the raiders and the outlaws.
I was one of them, as I had to be, to live with myself.
I got in the habit of loving men and women without bounds.
I looked at the suffering of nature with fury and fear.
And this is how I spent
the days I'd been given.

In my time, all the roads led to a swamp.
My cell phone betrayed me to the butchers.
I couldn't help it. But without me the comrades
would surely go on, or so—in false courage—I hoped.
And this is how I spent
the days I'd been given.

Our forces were small. Redemption was so
far away. So far away it hurt deeper than
you can know. Though, still, it was shining
like a sun, even if I would never reach it, even
if I chased it like a horse, with all of my might.
And this is how I spent
the days I'd been given.

III.

You who may come after the flood, the hunger,
the thirst, the excess in which we have vanished,

please think really extra hard
when you speak of our faults and failings,
and of the bleak and confounding times
you've been so blessed to be spared.

For we did what we could, switching our homes
more often than our shoes, all through the small
poetry wars and the great war of the classes, despairing
at the sins in the latter, and no doubt too much
at the ones in the former. We crossed deserts, rivers, and
seas, and still we never arrived, for we were nothing.

And surely we knew in our hearts:
even the hatred of injustice
turns the face into a horrid mask.
Even contempt of wickedness
turns the voice into a growl! We
who yearned to lay a foundation for tenderness,
could not ourselves learn to be tender.

But you, where you are, in a time and place we can
never know, where you may live lightly upon the earth,
we hope, in a greater mystery now, and confusedly
pleased: please think of us with a simple measure
of forbearance and compassion.

Pierre Joris

Fragments from *Yellow Hook Notes*

Owls Head Park: the badly named, but —

no owl seen here, but I'm reading in the ms. of Jerome Rothenberg's forthcoming anthology of the Americas & am told that in Narragansett an owl is called Kokókehom, Ohómous, and that the other bird I do see often here in the park, the crow, is called Kaukont▪tuock in Narragansett; these are birds, says Roger Williams (England/USA, 1603–1683) as quoted by JR, that "although they doe the corne also some hurt, yet scarce will one *Native* amongst an hundred wilkil them, because they have a tradition, that the Crow brought them at first an *Indian* Graine of Corne in one Eare, and an *Indian* or *French* Beane in another, from the Great God *Kaután•…uwits* field in the Southwest from whence they hold came all their Corne and Beanes." That immigrant Britisher chronicler—at least he was interested in native languages!—that clerk, or clerc couldn't tell an Indian or French Beane from another … *ach,* colonization is hard work …

Bay Ridge: Foghorn.

Is not dice cup. The repetition is exact, the desire or aim is to avoid disaster, shipwreck. The sound repeats at intervals of 10 seconds. The time it took to type this sentence. Which one? Not this one. In the darkness of late night—or is it early morning? — the foghorn abolishes chance. The cargo ship that lies at anchor in the Narrows, bow towards the open sea beyond the bridge and beyond that beyond too, is called the Minerva. It has an owl's profile painted between the anchor hole and the M that opens its name. You do not see it. It is a memory.

Cup of plenty. Light comes up. Every ten seconds the foghorn. Not a siren, no sirens here on or in the water. Can a siren go into the water?

The ship's name, so Vesseltracker informed on closer inspection, is *Minerva* (the family name, the company name?) *Julie* (first name?). *Minerva Julie* is from Greece, or at least flies a Greek flag; she is 183 meters long with a beam of 32.0 meters. She is moored, not at anchor. A vessel is said to be moored when it is fastened to a fixed object or the seabed, or to a floating object such as an anchor buoy. A mooring buoy is a white buoy with a blue band. While many mooring buoys are privately owned, some are available for public use. Always check before tying to any mooring buoy.

Day's here now. Trust your eyes. Julie, Julie is invisible. The foghorn, inaudible, must have stopped. Julie is a large orange vessel. "Autobiography is a goldfish," someone wrote and the line keeps coming back. Across the street there is a pond, murky to say the least, but if you stay and stare long enough, you will catch, out of the murk, from time to time an orange flash: the back of a goldfish breaking the surface. Whose life? Disappears beneath the shabby lotus leaf. Whose autobiography?

That was yesterday. Walk by the pond today and it is an empty oblong with black mud at bottom slowly drying up. Only fair: the falling leaves reveal more and more water surface across the Narrows, so the pond can go until the leaves come back. Where have the goldfish gone? Looks like the turtles went first. "Someone took them home," someone said. But the goldfish, the goldfish? They will have disappeared into someone else's autobiography. I cannot approach them at this point, not from this angle. We will see. She says, "the lotus flowers, where have the lotus flowers gone?"

The foghorn has not sounded since that first time. The weather has held a straight course, you may say. Light morning gusts across the narrows. This morning Sinbad is not a sailor but a tanker out of Barbados. Tanker, tinker, sailor, spy—who's the most polluting of them all?

Home

Nachhaltige Nicht-Nachhaltigkeit

= title of a German book translates as:

    sustainable non-sustainability

(or: the empire strikes back …)

*

This morning's birds,

no owl in Owl's Head Park,

but

    6 or more

Northern Flickers (my first sighting

after Nicole's excited reports)

the usual mess of robins,

my gaggles of sparrows, some

common house, some white-

throated, some chirping balls

of white bellies stuck out &

red-brown Mohawk aimed at

the rising sun,

          the usual array of doves, never think of calling

them mourning, in or

out of same, they're just a

bit sad,

          but then a ring of doves

with capitals in English

but without in the Arabic

tawq al-hamanah is

a major treatise on love

by Ibn Hazm

(to be looked into

when home-in-shelter from

early morning birding

walk).

[....]

Trees

Avoid the Canine Costume Contest, but don't miss the Harvest festival. I missed both this year. As you enter the *Narrows Botanical Garden*, the signs say the same thing in several languages—Russian, Chinese, Spanish, Arabic—namely: Do not cut the flowers. Or so one is lead to believe, for who knows what the signs say? Maybe the Chinese sign says "Do not cut the red roses, take only the pink ones," or the Russian "Cut any flower but don't get caught." Whatever it does say, it will be better than the romantically syrupy prose the NBG people use to describe the place: *"Four and a half acres of lush parkland, hugging the sparkling waters of The Narrows, transformed through the artistic vision of neighbors and the dedication of a community's volunteers."* It is probably, no, certainly true from a certain angle, but the language is loose. "Sparkling water" I'd want to drink, but no matter how much I appreciate the Narrows' mixture of Ocean & Hudson, I will not drink it.

But I am partial to the small tree stand right after the shady tree-lined alley leads into the park. We are told that it was once thought that the ancient *Dawn Redwood* tree was extinct, until a grove was rediscovered in the Shui-hsa-pa Valley, in the northwest corner of Hupeh Province, in China, in the 1940s. The five trees in the Redwood Grove of our Narrows Botanical Garden evoke the magic of an ancient Druid grove, or so the p.r. wants to make us believe. They are said to grow to well over one hundred feet tall—and they will, just as I will watch them doing so. As I am watching them now, naked as any birch or beech, I remain surprised at my constant surprise seeing deciduous needle trees, so much the Northman and his evergreen pines, sapins, Tannenbaums and so on.

I turn my back on the sparkling or not waters, walk past the only street-side Lily Pond in our good City of New York and up 71st to 5th Avenue, cross the street, turn left walking north for another few blocks. Trees on my mind. A good part of my youth spent following father into the woods of Luxembourg, hunting for deer and hare, boar and fox, rabbit and pheasant, being taught the name of the trees we stood behind waiting for the game, or leaned against tired from walking, by him or by my grandfather, mother's father, the farmer, often along, rifle over shoulder, pipe in mouth. I knew the names back then, and still do for the most part (though would be hard-pressed to remember them all), but the problem has always been one of translation: the orality of the mamelashen only vaguely and often inaccurately overlapped with the German of the early school—or Naturkunde—books I bought at the Librairie Kessler.

Soon the trees became unrecognizable when their French names were added just a few years later. It was hard to hold on to a single tree with 3 or 4 names: 'eng Bich' was a Rotbuche or hêtre commun—but did it become a birch or a beech tree? I'm still uncertain, wavering like trees in a strong wind. But I do know that 'eng Summereech' was a 'Stieleiche' though 'summer' (summer, indeed) was in no way translatable by 'Stiel' which means 'stem' or peduncle and is thus, yes!, closer to French where the tree is known as 'chêne pédonculé'—which we were not taught in nature-class as the homophonic hilarity of 'pet d'enculé' would have had the class rolling in the aisles. So we were taught that 'eng Wantereech' was (weirdly enough) a Traubeneiche—as if winter *(Wanter)* and grapes *(Trauben)* were able to translate into each other!—becoming a Chêne rouvre south of Thionville, (a durmast or sessile oaktree in Anglophonia as I was to find out later). We accept nouns as self-possessed and numinous enough, but adjectives are to be distrusted and so I wanted to know what "rouvre" meant. The word seems to come from the Latin "robur," meaning strong, robust; the three consonants r.b.r. of the Latin word probably gave the French common noun "arbre," tree—by phonetic deformation, the specialists will say, for how could a northern word be seen to follow triconsonantal semitic grammatical rules and possibilities? The scientific botanical Latin would of course have been easier, if we all still learned Latin & used it as lingua franca, but at that idea my grandfather would have laughed so loud the pipe would have fallen from his mouth. Still, there it is called *Quercus petraea* and the eternal boy in me hears that immediately as querky petrification, which may describe the language but not the tree.

Home

Will the trees make a forest ever again? Will the *selva* ever be *oscura* again? To break out of childhood memories of hunting in the forests of Luxembourg back in the middle of the last century, it is no longer enough to stay in the languages of trees (pace Graves's *White Goddess*, etc.) though they be a jungle of roots & branches. No longer enough either to stay & work in the dichotomy I used back then when pitching the Deleuzian/Guattarian anarcho-multiplex rhizome against the old hierarchical tree with its crown & trunk & roots. Trees are more complex than that abstraction as we are beginning to learn, & cannot/should not be taken out of their own context (more than forests) to be turned into the "uprooted" individual entities our own (late-, post-, whatever - but- certainly-) capitalist ideology wants humans to be in order to better be able to control them. Still, the D/G idea of the always multiple, heterogenous complexity of world-&-us remains necessary & useful, especially if we add the nonhuman, the animal-, plant-, even mineral- realms to move toward what Eduardo Kohn calls an "anthropology beyond the Human" in his book *How Forests Think*. As Donna Haraway glosses the title in her blurb: "A thinking forest is not a metaphor. Rooted in richly composted, other -then-symbolic semiotic worldings, it teaches the reader how other-than-human encounters open possibilities for emergent realizations of worlds, not just worldviews." The "it" there I see as both the book & the (thinking) forest itself. And we are getting finally away from a thinking of totality, of wholeness, as some unitary fixed possibility or impossibility. The ecological crisis offering what elsewhere I have called, the only new "grand narrative" that is still possible & may even be absolutely necessary, can only be built on what Anna Tsing in her book *The Mushroom at the End of the World*, talking of the various broken down systems (natural or men-made), names ruins, suggesting that "to know the world that progress has left to us, we must track shifting patches of ruinations."

[…]

George Kalamaras

And So

Dew-cool August   on snowshoes of the mouth
I indulge pushed-orange cart-tracks   powerful diamond
hound, pot-licker   say, *I love be-dog jump right*
love my down-that-tree   little possum   feist to a fine-point
eyes shut nearly crazy down there   it is now
the leaves intuit   to sit down for awhile on a good
long sofa   hound dog at my side   *When you drink tea*
drink tea, it is   said   bring the possum growl bite
each other   I can see Morocco from inside
the hummingbird window   I can see Darjeeling
Assam   Yunnan Province with the oldest tea
trees on earth   a brother and a sister lived once
the animal   in an ancient cosmology   this is
the song   why don't we just pitch-perfect
over to the edge of our crust   snowshoe mouth August
heat decides   the list of our deaths   even when
the yin teas   those internal mites   bring us into
even when our bodies bring the dark   names of tea-birth
Sigh of the Sapphire   *Sleeping Silver Elephant*
Temptation of the Sable Tassel   *Travertine Twilight on Venerable Mountain*
when you luck a hound, *luck* a hound   inscribe a Sutra
inside your eyelid   inscribe hound-howl into the hills   possum-shake
through the swampy shallows   there are certain periods
and certain shivers of long ordeal   biting each heavy

world   dimming forest lamps in the   chests

the beating births of birds   a slurry of bees

beating broths of bird-speak   cruel owl-   scent

not true small turns   go   to soon   to sleep

With These Words

And so I discovered that my body was composed of Chinese blood pheasants.
In panda time, dark black circles surrounded even the bloodletting with hope.

I came away from the mirror wishing I was thinner.
My pants pulled tight. I remembered the gaseous bloat of chickpea-kale soup.

In those days, I'd made the arctic fox my totem. Her milk-blanched fur. Even her stool.
It was a blistering Indiana January. I imagined her several weeks north eating the decomposed hoof of a dead musk ox.

I felt my skin flush with feathers.
I stayed inside and avoided cookies, cashews, and mirrors.

Adult hares, I knew, belong to a measure of extraordinary sparseness.
They birth their leverets, followed by an eloquent squabbling to hide among the frozen stones.

When disturbed, two of my hands resemble the edge of any body remembering the electrical charge of snow-aching rain.
Seasons within seasons. Totems within toes. These words, secretly touching my touching of you.

Sweet White Threads

There is some great, damp bird
the rain holds at 4:08 a.m.
in Colorado mountain fog. I breathe slowly.
Barred owls enter me. Their sleep enters me.
Their cracked mice bone
and rabbit-snap. The way they clock
their neck puts me to sleep,
in a wakeful way. Their slow breathing
slows me deep. Yes, it is raining. Forty-two degrees.

This is the summer solstice at my mountain
retreat? I close my book, *Those of the Gray Wind:*
The Sandhill Cranes. This is the same rain
that entered Meng Chiao's veins
so many centuries before? The same sound
inside the lonely blood notes of Wang Wei's lute?
I breathe deeply from the bottom of my belly;
my mother is dead and alive. Already fifty-four
weeks now since she left the body. I see her
scarves, the embroidery edging her
handkerchiefs, the clay birds
she collected and kept on a table. She is gone.
I listen to the mountain forest, and she is more
alive than the possum who gave us
the rest of the road the rest of the way down.
How can this hound dog at my side
keep this four a.m. vigil with me
while the rest of the world is asleep?
She breathes me deep. I love everything
about the way my beagle-hound loves
everything. Jim Harrison loved the sandhill cranes.
Followed them all the way to Nebraska.
And Meng Chiao, in a previous life, *was* a crane.
There is something great and damp and wingèd
always about to crack this bone or that.
And I am drinking tonight
a most delicate white tea all the way
from Yunnan Province. Sipping it
from a white porcelain cup. Sweet White Threads
is so tenderly pale. With each sip,
I feel it connect me to the world, the owls,
my mother's sheer black scarf. Even this
mountain fog misting my view. It is so clear,
as I peer into the cup, I can almost see moon-
bit sycamores, still. And dark. The dark in the trees.

Eliot Katz

Who's There?

Here I am, here is a contingent self
a body with eyes and pen
wearing reading glasses this foggy forest morning

Here is what, a contingent what
a being on a mountaintop listening to rains wash in
a disembodied hand to pet the purring cat

Here is death, holding its morning celebration
for it knows another creature will come in just a few
minutes the wind, the fog, wolves howling in the distance

Here is an ecosystem, a contingent planet
Vivian sleeping beautiful under covers in other room
a cat named Dharma that has found a temporary plaything

Here's a kitchen blender waiting for generator switch a
black hole beneath the galaxy savoring its prey
outside window, evergreen outlines becoming visible at dawn

Lissa Kiernan

The River Never Froze

"People in the community were generally unaware that the river was radioactive, although it had been noted that since the reactor opened, the river never froze."
—*Citizens Awareness Network, Shelbourne Falls, MA*

We were told it was clean. It looked clean, smelled
clean—even tasted clean. We bought the watercolor

renderings of idealized blues, fearlessly rafted the rapids.
Poked the contamination into holes, pulled beers,

listened to heavy metal. If our boats floated uncertainly,
at least our lives wrung out tidy and sterile.

But as it cut a gash through downtrodden towns,
even we had to admit our poor river did not so much

flow as skulk. Even brilliant days reflected inert
gray. All but the hardiest life forms—

walleye, lake chub, longnose sucker—
refused to sign the liability waiver.

Yet in the daily struggle of unbecoming, our clannish
lives barely stir. And for trout anglers, a slug's released

each morning. A sinking sensation follows slipstream:
We drank the river today. We'll drink it again tomorrow.

Eclogue on Decommissioning

Fog scrims the Deerfield River Valley. Leaves bleed
through, bent south. Gourds bloat, rupture on vines.

Our plant is no exception. It, too, has begun to dismantle
in much the same way a glass dish, hot from the oven

would crack if doused in cold water. Where to begin?
No blueprint—and each pipe, seal and bearing

must be mourned and laid to rest. No wrecking ball,
no countdown to blast. Make no mistake,

for each method, a cost. Whether to store dry or stay
wet addles your brain. Odds for cross-contamination

curdle your spleen. Perhaps we ought not place blame.
Go on. Bury it. As quickly and quietly as you can.

Dump it in dark trenches in towns with jowled porches,
and slow swaying stoplights. Mottling a river—

with no will left to say *no.*

The Art of Hurricanes

—after Hurricane Sandy

All hurricanes are cubist: something seeing, something
being seen. A Picasso eye, splitting the world apart.

The failure was fertile: water gushing into concrete
wombs, water gushing into war zones, water

gushing—The grieving mother refused a coat,
wanting to be as cold as her son, holding herself

together with only dressmakers' pins. Sodden,
we slogged into complex fog. When we could not

gain egress, we got stuck in Fibonacci loops—
hung the image of the gurgling brook

by the spray of birch and the spume of skunk grass.
Oyster Creek is on alert, the radio strummed.

We were awkward with neighbors who wielded chain saws
with kindness. *It's nothing,* they said, when we tried

pushing money into their hands. You played me
more cunningly, Sandy, than almost any other

collapse—funneling my breath, lashing me to your mast.
Protean, the rhyme between intake and exhalation,

between oil slick and scarred linden, as you go now,
in search of new patrons. Almost a human figure already.

In "Eclogue on Decommissioning", the phrase "in much the same way a glass dish, hot from the oven would crack if doused in cold water" is borrowed from a Union of Concerned Scientists Fact Sheet accompanying a petition to the New England Coalition on Nuclear Pollution for an immediate shutdown of Yankee Rowe Atomic.

Kim Kyung Ju, translated by Jake Levine and Soohyun Yang

Selections from *You Too Will See the Bird Jump*

Texture

The laughter of a madman is the only thing that can mess up today's clouds.

A mole cricket
lifts its front legs, stands, and
stares at the distant, night sky.

Into the void that I assist
the day gets a bit darker
like some deaf bird.

The night flies toward us

and all the while

humanity is caricatured by figures of multiple doors. For example, even though I forgot the name of the tiny shadow the mole cricket makes when it begins rubbing its body on the darkening ground after it crawls out of its hole, even though I forgot the colors of lips I used to know, the colors of lips which are the same as the glow of the sun that sets itself inside human eyes before the night arrives by hopping nimbly over clouds, I do know the figures resemble the names of all the plant installations that I memorized.

Here is my wind, my wind which helps deaf birds.

The tonsils hanging outside the mouth of the dead mole cricket
are fading into
multiple shades

and all the while

the thing that messes up the blood of today
is a deaf bird that comes to help.

Texture 2

The deaf bird comes to help.
Jumping rope in the middle of the night,
toes that cramp.
Pills that lost their color.
Pill bugs.
A girl's ass.
The light of the noonday sun.
A memory of drinking blood.
Dead inside a bathtub,
my inner life lying there.
Sentences without a habitat.

Last night I emptied a black container.
This morning I bit crimson water.
Who can know the person that chucked out
the rice porridge that trickled down the alleyway?

And yet,
there's a night that talks about
the habit of lonely eating.

Concerning languages,
concerning the taste of blood,
concerning a facial expression that avoids understanding,
concerning the forest of astute perception,

when you sit down
prepared for the sentence,
there are birds
that don't miss the time
where perception is most acute.

There is a thing

called the hallway
that is both happy
and pitch-black.

The Architecture of Time Difference

*

When a music box is first created, the wind that enters a glass tube becomes a typhoon gathering in the music and
While cracks form little by little in the music box, the wind that enters the glass tube makes music into a typhoon.

*

When I want to eat a leaf pie, I eat a leaf pie and
When I want to travel wearing a dead watch, I go and travel wearing a dead watch.
At certain travel destinations I am still unable to tell the difference between apricots and plums.

*

In the morning I see a fireman putting out a fire with a mint scented cigarette in his mouth and
In a building in the afternoon the fireman melts like mint candy.

*

During class I spread out a world map and memorize the latitudes and longitudes of faraway cities and
After class I leave carrying a black plastic bag in which I intend to catch venomous snakes.

*

At night looking at a book is more like the feeling of falling from a tree than the feeling of secretly climbing one. The feeling of a dawn confession where I admit to folding more paper boats than paper planes, the feeling of the day I placed a paper boat on the palm of the hand, saying, "Look here, I've been here a long time sitting by your side," when all those countless characters I scrawled in a notebook went inside an eraser and disappeared at night.

*

On the day I received Indian incense as a gift, I limped a bit and thought about time difference. It's a fact that even when you are at home you need forgetfulness. Even moving from this room to that room, memory hoists the sails of dozens of species of plants. In any case, because it looks like we will need several species of pencils in order to talk about your travels, should I ride the white horse? Should I ride the black horse? Should I hoist the blue flag? Should I raise the white one? It appears that travelling is less a problem of altitude and more the problem of the difference of silences.

Graphology Window 12: Cousane Gap sweep backwards and forwards

Release is in both directions—vista
window release latch to compile an impression,
suppressed sublime or what can be got
making do with but still spread
thin to edges, the soft day—rain
makes edges smooth even where
you'd abrade yourself. The codes can
be changed against the sedimentary flow
of so long ago, the glacial rewrite,
the dredging of moraine above ground,
vaped air of each trend—making a living,
habitating, visiting, heading out to the volcanic
islands off Africa. Compilation of spread
and impact, of lens-changes: shifting
the phoropter's settings: amateur
or professional, light-metering.

Nine Inch Nails' *Bad Witch* with a Ghosting of Liszt's Plural *Dantes* [Plural Canto VIIIs: Inferno] as I Make *Contact,* Thinking Over Implications

for Thor Kerr

The leap is flame across the gutters of the web where incandescence
is dark and the illegal is the kingdom of arbitration over
what is up for grabs what is not the deadly angels' surveillance—

a flip of propriety an enthusiasm of polite breakfast surfers
to see their enemies mostly never met in person never
more than a concept wallow if the filth of overflow of gutter

saxophone drawl of time interjection of horror
of sales-figures wire-drawn from the companies' armouries
the pill extravaganza of life-saving face-masked worker

rewards overtime condition placation and factories

of asbestos soul-console driving loops to reverberate from desk
where gun trade and chemical-affect trade and body trade amplifies

multi-spectral degradation the walls of the servers so picturesque
in their habitus of cooled rooms as the ash rains a faster snow
a navigable syntax a control room view of rocket fuel carcinogenics

the ho ho! the troll-blow the emoticon lifts to a just day Euthyphro
subscripts the dialogue the pious becomes the pious *because*
to work-in the recycling of knowledge hardware and throw

life to merchants as no choice as last breath is now #cause
andeffect whomsoever is holding the reins, the titbit bytes—
the leap is flame across the gutters of a web where incandescence

loves telecommunications reliance to reassure we have the might
as right of alms delivery to lift ourselves holy wholly holy
into the gateway but while I've encountered many gates

that are evil I've encountered nothing with wings that partially
or wholly could be termed *completely* evil, but backdoors and Trojans
won't get you in won't worm-your-way past the deadly
drones you want the messenger you want the prayer-reply the return
gesture the repartee the quid pro quo I speak to you
you speak to me axiomatic builder block DNA gene

sheer as IP host relationship as if nothing will exploit
against the market's *will* the antibiotics not arriving
never mind gathering resistance out where the haves are adroit

at not being there but maintaining a control, thriving
in city apartments and conserving the *quaint* ways and *rituals,*
pseudo understanding and contemplating and processing

an array of 'lumpenproletariats' as upgrades and lingual
data mining zones to belt out viable *eth(n)ic(al)* variations
on a theme of living breathing occasionally dancing consumable

consumers of the future wherein urgency is what dream
remains not which dreams have smeared the pages
of memory left behind from trashed climate change data—reams

of old speak best forgotten once we engage

with the capital with the biggest recog precog show around
the footlights the limelight the rage on rage

into the dawn of every new day like it's the last round
of drinks—but it doesn't need New York or Moscow or Beijing
or San Paulo, semi-little old Perth will done fine (and The Sound!), the ground

laid out for future citizens as a time when the ring
of church bells denounced citizenship for the people's
whose land it was those bells those bells the harbour's gathering

of nation-building raw materials to extract raw materials—
so much of it is to do with the eavesdropping inherent in telephony
isn't it, so much to do with the flow and interception of signals,

isn't it—bursts of electricity magnetic storage the disharmony
of sunspots and toxic gossip? As stable and unstable as iridescence
we try to make art out of the grotesque because beauty

is our excuse, isn't it? The painting over of the cracks
in mountains appearing in deserts beneath seas and oceans and rivers—
the leap is flame across the gutters of the web where incandescence?

I read Marx as hope I read the anti-nuclear peace marchers
as hope I literally sealed the gunbarrel as a teenager and I hope that I dampened
the powder though I still worry about the effect the mixture

had on the soil ('historical')—the bringing together of ingredients, mixed
to make events, to bring trauma, and then the epiphany
the undoing and not quite knowing how to revert, undo, rescind.

But it's better to let the city let weeds rewrite the cracks let botany
rectify concrete. It is. Have I proved either side of the dialogue?
What is piety is conjured out of a status quo that is as criminal as any

crime, whatever its horror, its depravity? Crime built on crime—a log
of inquiry. Just for argument's sake, separated in the poem as we are
from reality, making a scene of rocking the boat to attract the analogue

of art to the service of state and university where capitalist destroyers
endow chairs of largesse in grubby boardrooms shined to a sparkle,
for future generations for geneshearing for cradle-to-gravy wire-

less artifice, but watch the comeback watch the media wrath distil
your presence to murk to a question of upload and download
discrepancies, ignition point to ignition point these world-scale

arsonists—crime built on crime and lauded from high in dead
air with their view over the river their view amidst the contrails,
but calling for a way through into the city what cheek to exclude

one's self to self-exonerate the kindling steps the vocable
the pledge the libretto to the performance of resistance
when the body calls for interstices of relief of divertissement and thrill—

seeing ourselves from inside but never out the listening process
the Liszt and NIN imprint of signature characteristics
but we possess our own listening experience and there's

no ownership of that we recognise I can safely say we click
on this in agreement across differences even the makers
of the notes sequencing and weight in themselves—click

into place, to find old brain and drag it back into the *new brain* which prefers
to apportion blame elsewhere which prefers wood over trees
if let run riot over organic data with sparkling metadata and the lures

of consumer comforts, to put it bluntly, the means to an end that frees
all that creativity to run free and garner 'a living' as well—
you know, 'they're not rich, just comfortable', liberated in all senses

but aspire to attention and material outcomes *either side* of hell's
city-gates—because the communications racket is an expression
of annoyance with prayer yielding such poor replies such still

air such muffled vacuums such stifled gaps to leap cross to cash in on—
speed up make receiver answer transmitter, make the spiritual
tech work bring it up to speed, you know, don't you? Emoticon

satisfaction. And the research of integrity not part of conceptual,
the integrity of armaments facial recog ethnic profiling research,
not part of the forms to fill in online to sign in to show potential

for academic communalising and its controlled indignation its search
for the middle way to profit and keeping up with zeitgeist
ethics awareness fairness justice personal consumption and oligarchs

of a local (not necessarily Russian, try the Swan River Coastal Plain heist)—
the leap is flame across the gutters of the web where incandescence
anneals extremes to worst those definitions to scrutinise to taste-test

horror to have a point of reference, the Hollywood exploiters
are the thin end but no less obscene no less consuming destruction
of humanism *in order to overfeed the resource-devouring fossil-fuel fed areas*

of institutions and their image agencies the image-makery the concentration
around funding manifests and credibility among peer
reviewers, the swamps filled in with concrete and new materials and the sustain-

pedal worked to best possible effect, the best possible outcome, the near
best possible zenith in a zone filled with trapdoors and meeting quotas and false
walls—while beneath The Sound the sonar calls Full House and we clear

the table, stack the deck, line up tin soldier dives—these source
analysis messages from messengers stacking offshore islands
with hotel occupancy and submarine nurturing and 'industries'—
the leap is flame across the gutters of the web's incandescence.

'No Direct Water Contact Activities'

for James, after a river walk

Fledged little pied cormorant
won't look at the skyscrapers
of the resources industry—

back turned, feathers growing
against the gas-baggery, the shock
of ore, the fracking bankers;

it seems unbothered by our pausing
our passing, our contradictory
wonder—look, but don't look,

respect its privacy but wonder
at the irony of Health Warning sign
of the resculptured riparian.

Out of the slick amnios extraction—
the needle of towers into the lifestyled
river.... lifestyle was before, too,

but views from feature windows
are an air-conditioned walk in the park —
a reaching out to *big end of town.*

Fledged little pied cormorant
is a telepath—conveys—just
enough of where it has come from

and where it will be going in its dive
through our short-term memories,
the broken beer bottle in the silt

we cut our feet on—river infections
that crawl up the leg, beautiful
inflections of what's been done.

Fledged little pied cormorant
will switch colours against the backdrop
of heat and rise, rise and then skim deep.

Dear White Pine in my Garden

Thank you for the delicious syrup. Your five-bundled fascicles cleave the alveoli of my lungs. Lances stir mucus, leave vitamin C in the brew. At the furthest ends of my arterial capillaries, slick whiff of aroma lenses a molecule through the membrane's barn door. You lodge, a mini-tree, in DNA passed down through my material line, farm women with hands in far-away soil where what was wrapped in muslin, sunk into tea kettle and boiled all day between Napoleon's soldiers, long treks to silk factories, hoot of titanic engines on briny seas, mirrored itself in a New Country, there grew wild and tall. We gather you now, new flu with old expectorants, ballast for the graveyards of our living rooms. Galleons come to a stand-still, oak timber decays into ribs on our beaches. Dear white pine, your soft wood smoothed the midship's deck, salted and sugared. You dissolved first, fibers rent by sea birds. Leached-out needles make for compost row. Acidic, you bite the land back, long for the sea, channel stuckness into flow. Protect us, dear white pine, let me root here, back bowed, hands flat.

Witch Spring, Isolation Day 9

Hex reflex: let's change the world through viral twirl.
Ghost planes crisscross wizard marks above our heads

empty timetable elegy holds the slots of the air.
From the silver moon, shut-down urbanscapes

show clear skies. Breathe, fellow citizens of the world,
aromatherapy perfume of rose blossoms. Let it all lie

fallow, concrete sow's tits barren of oily industrial
milk. Next week's tech conference cancels itself.

Go to the phone. I do not streak across three state
lines to have a freaky coffee date at the giant mermaid

mega-store. The cauldron cooks. My fridge shoots
takeouts's white flags. A tiffin steals through the door,

witches' helper in stainless steel. Transport vehicles
hover clean, disinfected within an inch of their plastic

lives. The gig economy thrives in delivery stakes,
even if Uber burns, Shipt tips into the limelight.

Leave the bags in the pentagram on the curb, do
not cross the threshold. Deduct a trip a week,

five miles gained in an abacus of parsimony.
Netflix stock soars on prayer and thoughts.

The creeper roots you to the spot. Above,
reaper scythes contrails, we find old ruts,

our wagons skip like bears
            in the strangely warm forest air.

Melissa Kwasny

The Aspen Path

The aspen leaves have fledged and so
                                are distant, having traveled
into their exterior summer lives,
                preoccupied now with living, not dreaming.
A loss of intimate relation.
Breezes though move toward me with softer hands.

Why can't I approach my own growth
                                with such undivided intentions?
Without new teachers, I revisit
                the rituals, a star I make room for
                                in a small asymmetrical window,
pussy willow soaking its roots in a stoneware cup.

The phases come. The trunks are timeless.
As if moon were shining on them through the day.
                All light enters us
without permission.
The logic is unanswerable: aging is a crime.
                I stand under trees as if under their influence.

Water everywhere to read this season.
                See, it has swallowed the highest stone.
The rainbow lipped branches
                in the gradual thaumaturgy of spring rain—
we each have an instrument.
                It wakes the younger ones first,

the rest reluctant to start again with tarnished horns.
Aging: my solstice,
I didn't notice the turn.
Was the dawn different when I was seven years old
than it will be when I am seventy?
As if we were twins, and one of us is gone.

Sixty hours before the asteroid hit,
they say, it appeared like a star, swimming ever faster
toward us.
Ninety-nine percent of life died.
Seventy-five percent of species went extinct.
Mammals, even plants, must have felt uneasy.

If there is such a story, larger than our memories
of earth, there must be an equally large story
of what is not life.
If there is a process or do all processes stop.
My heart breaks at seeing us in the past—
maybe why my grandmother's eyes were always watering.

A friend said,
she gets more beautiful all the time of his friend
who is dead. As she passes, she sheds
her deterioration.
Just as I wanted to bring the tree into my room,
to duplicate it in paint, to leave nothing common for long.

Cliff Lake

A flock of blackbirds disappears into the surface of sky.
We're still here, on the other side of the fading.
A turbulent presence. A waterfall within lake water that is calm.

The animals who have come before us,
and those who will come long after we are gone—
if I lose my hearing, all that will be preserved is their sound.

I read a poet once who imagined the rustle of Turkish silk,
which she heard in years past, had migrated into her poetry.

Down one arm, hundreds of rainbow trout,
their swerve seen through the sun-yellow clarity of the water.

Our gifts—we cannot will them into view.
They awake like an eye wakes to the wave-shape of light.
Down the second arm, which is longest, are the swans.

Everything often is metaphor, the wonder of a lead
amid the rushes where the duck and her ducklings go to hide.
But why be impatient for its opening?

We watch as two swans lift from the lake, becoming four
shapes, perfectly replicate. Surely grace, that not one collides.

It seems we can at any given moment be witness
to the osprey chick, for instance, flapping its high wings,
who finds itself careening over the forest.

Most birds once they've fledged never return to the nest.
To never. To do never. What courage
must that take. And why must everything still be about us?

PATRICK LAWLER

When Nature Becomes Obsolete

1. Who needs nature when the biosphere
   can fit in a plastic bubble?

2. Animals should come with expiration dates.

3. Life should be scripted.

4. Maybe someone should think of combining
   the Nature Channel and the Shopping Network.

5. Everyone should own at least one
   animal on the endangered species list.

6. We can "participate in the unrehearsed
   drama of life in the wild."

7. Dangerous animals (crocodiles, snakes, spiders, et
   al.) should be replaced with remote control surrogates.

8. Who needs nature? It's too unpredictable,
   too juicy, too exuberant.

9. What happens when we put the end of the
   world on a video game?

10. Maybe the ultimate stage in Darwin's evolution
    is plastic animals.

11. I don't mind artificiality.
    I just hate fake artificiality.

12. Animals on video are so much more reliable

13. Who needs sunsets
    when we can have nuclear roller coasters?

14. Who needs nature when one day we
can all have our own TV channel?

15. The entire human genetic code
will be available on CD-ROMs.

16. Nuisance animals (mosquitoes, et al.) can be
relocated to the places environmentalists go.

17. Who needs nature? It's too untamed,
too spontaneous, too impromptu.

18. There is a couple who have had computer chips
implanted in their skins. This way they don't have
to talk to each other.

19. We pick up a card and it reads: Go to Love Canal.

20. I believe in TV. I'm buying a big screen measured in miles.

21. Plastic trees don't embarrass us.

22. Who needs other people
when we can invent an orgasm pill?

23. What about becoming cyber icons?
What about mating with machines?

24. Nature isn't cost effective.

25. Vinyl leaves don't rot.

26. Nature could be etched into the eye
by weightless electrons 30 times a second.

27. We pick up a card and it reads: Go to Chernobyl.

28. Who needs nature?
Too turbulent, reckless, strange.

29. What about fiberglass flamingos?
Styrofoam monkeys?

30. Nature isn't as entertaining as it used to be.

31. Maybe all of natural selection has led to
this: people stuffed inside fluffy suits.

32. There is a logic to all of this: We need to leave death
out of nature, so we leave life out too.

33. We are rapidly becoming cast members.

34. The last animal will die in a Disney place
on a thrill ride called Countdown to Extinction.

35. There will be some remorse.
There will be some relief. There will be some remorse.

World Book (A to Zygote)

"nature is a language"
Emerson

A to ANJOU:
The world sits in my grandmother's bookshelf.

ANKARA to AZUSA:
A compendium. Naturalis Historia. Bibliotheca. The Four Great Books of Song. The Brethren of Purity.
The Dream Pool Essays.

B to BIRLING:
All things are sewn into the book. Even other books.

BIRMINGHAM to BURLINGTON:
My grandmother says: One day our words will be all over everything.
That's when we will have to arrive with huge pink erasers.

BURMA to CATHAY:
The things of this world keep arriving for us to examine and explain.

CATHEDRALS to CIVIL WAR:
A root pierces the center of the book. We attempt to turn nature into us.

We aren't finished yet.

CIVILIZATION to CORONIUM:
I sit in front of my grandmother's bookcase. The world exists in Mallarmé's book.

COROT to DESDEMONA:
Our thoughts hide inside the soul of each object.

DESERT to EGRET:
The book is written with a burning alphabet.

EGYPT to FALSETTO:
What will we need to remember after everything goes back to sleep?

FALSTAFF to FRANCKE:
"I stare out from the center of the book." I observe the barely there. The almost absent.

FRANCO to GOETHALS:
The book is taken into the world. A bird knocks her head against the sky.

GOETHE to HEARST:
I approach the encyclopedia with a house inside my head. Shakespeare approaches with water in his cupped hands. "I'll drown my book."

HEART to INDIA:
The forest eventually embraces the fire. I can hear the text being devoured. My grandmother sings.

INDIAN to JEFFERS:
The book blooms.

JEFFERSON to LATIN:
My grandmother says: The tree is waiting to be read.

LATIN AMERICA to LYTTON:
There is a ghost in a doorway. An evocation. Want. A flickering around a word-fire.

M to MEXICO CITY:
My grandmother's book holds the breath of the world.

MEYER to NAUVOO:
The world holds the book in its hands.

NAVAJO to ORLEANS:
The book is made of beautiful windows. Tear-shaped words. World-shaped words.

ORLEY to PHOTOENGRAVING:
Book-blood. I hear the tenacious flow.

PHOTOGRAPHY to PUMPKIN:
Time is stitched into the book.

PUMPS to RUSSELLVILLE:
Donne's Mystic Book. Rich's Book of Myth. Emerson's Universal Book.

RUSSIA to SKIMMER:
The book and the world need each other.

SKIN to SUMAC:
Once the world started eating the book. Then the book started eating the world.

SUMATRA to TRAMPOLINE:
My grandmother hands me some words.

TRANCE to VENIAL SIN:
The roots begin to bloom.

VENICE to WILMOT, JOHN:
I am careful not to mistake the world for the book or the book for the world.
I walk with my eyes full.

WILMOT PROVISO to ZYGOTE:
My grandmother watches the end holding onto the beginning.

Inadvertent Criticality—Before Fukushima

In Japan, after the nuclear accident at a uranium-processing plant,
they tell people to close their windows.

After the radioactive gas is released into the air, the government says 310,000
residents should stay inside. Police in white protective gear set up blockades

to keep people out. Schools are shut down, train service is halted,
and farmers are asked not to harvest crops—especially in the radioactive rain.

A government spokesperson says everything will be OK. One worker describes the
"blue flash." Scientists call this kind of chain reaction "inadvertent criticality."

The workers in impeccably pronounced Japanese say, "Oh, shit."
The industry spokesperson says, "Oops." In Tokaimura, Japan, long lines form

so people can be tested for radiation exposure. If you have the following symptoms,
it may be too late: shock, diarrhea, fever, a high white-blood-cell count, reddened skin,

severe skepticism. In our pursuit of a safe place, we have resorted to taking up
residence in the fictional TV towns: in Mayberry and Cecile, Alaska.

In Japan the government is assuring its people that everything will return
to normal as soon as possible. But maybe this is exactly what we don't want to happen.

Maybe it's "normal" that is the problem.

A spokesperson for the Japanese company says, "We have no words to express
our apologies." I try to think how it would be if the company spokesperson

were unwilling to apologize. Suppose he said, "Hey, this is the price we have to pay.
These things are going to happen. If it doesn't happen here,

it will happen someplace else. Get used to it."

Just outside the plant, radiation levels spike to 20,000 times the level considered safe.
Workers hang a sign: "You are within 10 kilometers of a radiation leak.

Please drive quickly." What town did the Cleavers live in? Where did Donna Reed's
family reside? In Springfield, Kathy and Bud Anderson and Homer

and Marge have their half-hour crises. Experts say the problem should not have
happened. Officials say it was human error. The company says it is contained.

The government says we can open our windows. The presenter at the nuclear power
plant in Oswego, NY, says: "I get more radiation sleeping next to my wife

than I do working in the facility." When the three workers are taken from the plant,
they are wrapped from head-to-toe in plastic to avoid contaminating others.
They will not be sleeping next to their spouses for a long time. They should feel safe.
The NRC says this could not happen here. Niagara Mohawk says this could not

happen here. Charles Montgomery Burns says this could not happen here.
I want to say when it comes to environmental issues, every place is here.

    This is here. This is here. This is here.

There are no TV towns where we can be protected. The plant operator says
it will not happen again. But suppose he says, "Let's be honest.

At least this once. We assure you *it will* happen again." In the future they'll be running
their Geiger counters over our thyroid glands, just as a precautionary measure.

We turn on our computers just to write a poem about how outraged we are,
about how we can't stand what we are doing to the earth. And the power surges

through our mother boards, and the cadmium control rods are slowly withdrawn
from the reactor core at the nuclear power plant in Oswego. And we begin

to write about our own inadvertent criticality. There are fictional TV towns
all over America, and none of them are safe. One day they'll arrive at your door

with their respirators and white protective clothing. And they'll tell you,
"The government says it is OK to leave your fictional house. Please drive quickly."

Gary Lawless

Driving home from Belfast, into the crescent moon

for Dudley Zopp

I hear the granite singing,

and it is alive.

I want to tell you

that granite is a migratory species—

(think plate tectonics, continental

drift, glacial erratic)

but you can read the flow lines

from when granite was liquid

and moving, quickly—

I want to tell you

that lichen is a language

of granite,

that granite speaks

with air and water and light

we might

never know

what stories it holds,

deep within the rock.

Ruth Lepson

The Yellow Tulip

for Gerrit Lansing

When Gerrit died, the image of a yellow tulip popped into my mind, and childish as it seemed I couldn't shake it. Now I see it's the secret of the golden flower,[1] symbol of the philosopher's stone.

The Jains of Rajasthan, India devote themselves to feeding flocks of demoiselle cranes, who migrate at 23,000 feet over the Himalayas. The first verse of the *Ramayana* curses the hunter who killed the male of a pair. Because all verse was considered received until then, this passage is taken to be the oldest composed poetry in the world. People who've ventured far from home or undertaken difficult journeys are often compared to these delicate cranes.[2]

Within decades, a quarter of the earth's population will be forced to migrate.

Homer (whoever they were) made it to India, as did Plato and Democritus, it could be that they learned about atoms there, those irreducible bits of matter, the speculation a quest for immortality, a method of reconstituting the dead body.

Democritus believed that bodily atoms are triangles with prongs, round fire atoms the soul, the other aspect of life being the void, through which the atoms travel.

Is it lonely to remain anonymous, or a relief, like becoming ordinary?

Two Zen masters, checking out in parallel lines at the supermarket, nodded to each other.

What might it mean to know, in silence?

I've wanted to know you, what it must be like
to love in silence, without desire to articulate your desire, living in color
in the meadows and low mountains.

A certain number of volunteers who film secretly inside factory farms commit suicide, especially after their first exposure, the cruelty is so extreme.

Adrienne Rich said these things: I want to know what you are experiencing. Very few people are willing to go the whole way with you, so make a pact that you will never desert one another. Real friendships are frightening because they involve telling the truth.
Something got hotter and infinitely more dense until its interior turned to lead then exploded, creating everything: we, the constellations, the triumphant stars, the half moon.

Tennyson's Ulysses says, with resignation, "'I am not what I once was.'"

Happy few.

Inanna, Sumerian Goddess of Heaven, descends to the netherworld, where she sees her sister, her shadow self. At each gate she's required to take off a piece of clothing or jewelry, maybe like the chakras. Her symbols: the lion and the eight-pointed star.

A volcano will erupt when Trump refuses to leave office. Violence in the streets. Some talk that way while others are convinced things will return to normal. Myself, I think we're at the threshold of a new world.

The Greeks were well aware they were newcomers to their region of the world, Persia, Mesopotamia and Egypt having existed for centuries. In Egypt, very little changed through time, as Isis protected the meaning of things, whereas in Greece, new words were constantly being invented and argument was everything.

The first poem I memorized is Longfellow's:

"The world is so full
Of a number of things
I'm sure we should all
Be as happy as kings."

Are kings happy? And who's this speaker, so sure? Which things is the world so full of, anyway, these days?

And understanding? After all, if everything is made of the same irreducible element, our insides and the outside world are identical, *n'est ce pas*?

I should practice my French before the end of the world as we know it. We go on doing what we've always done. And where in the world is William Blake? among the angels? I'm more inclined to believe in them lately than in any gods.

Voltaire added bits of chocolate, already a luxury, to his coffee—he was a coffee fanatic—he once wrote that hopeful was his favorite state of mind in human beings, so he wasn't kidding when he said the best of all possible worlds, in a way. But we haven't tended our gardens.

On the BBC, in Yemen, a young woman begs the doctor, "Don't tell us about the virus. Please! We live with enough horror already."

"Patulous," spreading out from the center, as the branches from the tree.

She said sometimes she imagines she's a tree, planted firmly in the ground. That would bother me; a fundamental difference between plants and animals is that animals move around.

Putting people in solitary confinement has to do with the destruction of the earth.

When a Tibetan master knows he's going to die, he retires to his mountain hut. A few weeks later, the others come. This has happened thousands of times: that followers enter the hut, only to find that there's no skeleton there, just hair and nails, and, floating around the room, rainbows.

Once, his car swayed on a bridge in a storm; since then he's avoided bridges. "Me," he said. "Imagine me being afraid of something."

The alchemical process won't work when attempted at the wrong time.

He insists that aliens have lived on earth for thousands of years. When I say that's ridiculous, he says I don't have an open mind. Anything can happen. No it can't, I say. Do you think that lamp can turn into a peacock? Maybe, he says. How can you be sure that it can't.

Supposedly Buddha said never meditate on karma: it's so complex it can destroy your mind.

Cause and effect is a Western concept; there's actually no such thing. It's like synchronicity—it happens, but that doesn't mean we know anything about it. Or anything about alchemy. The unconsciousness rules alchemy; the individual's dreams remain powerful; it's collective dreams which religions promote.[3]

When people delve into the unconscious and surface, they make jokes, and treat other people as idiots—it's too much to take all at once. This process must take place over and over.

In this week's *New York Review of Books*, Bill McKibben discusses Mark Lynas' *A Final Warning: Six Degrees of Climate Emergency.*
Interspecies democracy is all the hope there is.
Why read another book on the last hundred days of Hitler?

"A tulip dipped in liquid
nitrogen undergoes instantaneous cryonics, whereupon
The flower can be smashed to bits as easily as a wineglass.

A word when read aloud is such a crystal being (being)
shattered by a sequence of high-frequency vibrations."[4]

Notes

[1]*The Secret of the Golden Flower*
[2]Wikipedia
[3]Marie-Louise von Franz, *Alchemy*
[4]Christian Bok, *Crystallography*

Heller Levinson, with drawings by Linda Lynch

Seep Considered

Impinged upon by multiple asphyxiations (i.e., digital tyrannies, ecospheric degradation, technological disruption, threats of nuclear Armageddon), "Seep," here envisioned, is one of the remaining hygienic pulsations available for evading the ghettoizing binary gridded statistical numerical sterilities intent upon mangling human vitality into frenetic consumption machines.

Seep, in marinated-soak, dribbles crawls squirrels *through,* an unhobbled tumbleweed relieved of formulation, impervious to constriction, Seep is the predator of verities, the osmotic ooze,

the creep that credulizes.

Aspiration, I
Pastel pigment and graphite on cotton paper
30 x 44 inches
2013

tenebraed to

seepage

to the vertebrae of disappearance

disparities columnize in lopsided disarray

densities convulse

calibrations formatting the well-heeled wither in inebriate perambulation

from these halls of cirrhotic séance

loams the

first heard

a pedal's reminiscence

the road to seep road

concourse coalition

currency

conduit

concurrence: gear mesh, crank scuttle,

rubber/asphalt/bitumen/foot intertangle intercourse dollop frolic flair

bumps in the road

from _____ to ______

destination: — direction

— going-ness

— goal-gridded

how much of

'the way to'

is

loss

PRIVATE ROAD NO THRU TRAFFIC	BE PREPARED TO STOP	ROAD WORK AHEAD

privileging traction, ... access = destiny's

lamentation → alternate route detour

curves ahead →

where in the

'bend'

is

gradation

puncture to release, to

de-rubber, de-motorize

to

emanate disseminate gestate

gnarled in the bones of signage

squalls from primordial gristle

from → paw fang gullet,

... fur

from the bellows of a recurring remission this
legion of spheres cylindricals the peat of new geometries of

ratified transpositional glissades leeched to

an

irretrievable

buoyancy

Aspiration, II
Pastel pigment and graphite on cotton paper
30 x 44 inches
2013

seep in inveterate dislodge

tilt temptation

aspiration's toil

— turmoil twist

— tarantella tuck

ribbed to an archaic disquiet, sheathed

permeable, squeezed by circumference, by

trellised replica, — inert mold fodder,

fetid fester,

endangered, ... yet

engendering: perquisite

percolates, groomed

appetitives, feral

fiesta, fecundity, draft,

the traffic of

gust

Andrew Levy

They All Eat Octopus

Sea cucumbers, with only their mouths exposed,
Reveal themselves. Two great oceans collide. In the
Shadows, fed by rich currents, the octopus sets off
In pursuit. Deep into crevices superior wits
Stay alive. A Caribbean beach, a beautiful swimming.
All parties comfortable, pronto, slash through cabbage.
The northern coasts of North America. Psychedelia.
The tiny creatures that we eat, the farmer whose work
Never ends. Who eats my algae? What do the oceans
Sound like? Why is all the vegetation on Earth under
Attack? More than ahistorical fantasies, undocumented
Social relations take up too much space. There is no
Pattern; there is no second world. What do I
Do for pleasure? Sudoku? Take walks along the river?
Adopt the living conditions of feudal society in the
Closing years of the twelfth century? Something that
Stands outside the real meaning of existence?
Breakfast? That vegan sandwich? The epic of the wheat?
Toledo, Ohio? Today the image of the octopus is used to
Describe big monopolies such as Microsoft, Google,
Facebook, and Amazon. It portrays a system of power
To which humans become increasingly indifferent.
Sadly, for them, sex is a death sentence. The arms
Seem to have a mind of their own. Bourgeois
Hippy enthusiasms sit there, their mouths exposed,
Sipping their tea. In the shadows, fed by rich currents,
Flickering stars remove their coats. The octopus
Sets off in pursuit. A father doesn't understand his

son's fear. I hide my face in cushions of jellyfish.
Inferior wits provide a hollow for my cheek.

The Chaos of Dreaming Life

The vile stench makes sunbathing impossible and
swimming through the slime just as distasteful. The mini-
mountains of rotting algae and the tiny trapped sea
creatures living inside perish
when the algae hits the beach, creating a putrid, sulfurous
stink. The minute you start fussing with the line you create
a non-circle of "wideawake language," and eachway
bothwise glory signs ware
only of trifid tongues the whispered wilfulness. Why the ruddy
hell—bigots mostly are—as senselessly big as named and
shamed on the dock, and on the block a hungry ghost (we
cannot be moved) handled
with delicacy, but fouler fish have been fried to become lost in
one's thoughts and in one's body and be born again as hollow
as little yellow gourds. Story is like a circle. A circle is a circle
('tis demonal!) and shadows shadows multiplicating, totients
quotients, they tackle their quarrel. Sickamoor's so woful
sally. Moving about in the free
of the air and mixing with the ruck. Flowers. A cloud. That's
how our oxyggent has gotten ahold of half their world. As the
coronal hole continues its slow march westward on the sun's
surface a secular movement finally gave in to the world of
how people handle bereavement. I don't know how scholars
work. A direct impact on the ear pressed deeper and deeper
tucked up in many rugs, poetry
is prayer pain sank teeth into my ear. Winter must be cold. It
pulls warm Pacific currents through the Bering Strait north

and west above Siberia, pushes into the East Siberian Sea and
the Transpolar Drift, then rolls away from Russia and whips
south against Greenland. A shared confusion replays "what I
understand to belong to everyone," but there's a loss of
critical ecosystem functioning in fat rocky lingual, the distant
rim of the pigmented greed thickening
the capitalist's id in ridges and layers, the archipelagic
frontier that forms the Northwest Passage as it turns
again in its grinding cycle, as winter descends and the
seas freeze.

Anthony Lioi

Trilobite

You had no cell phones—
the sea was sweet without satellite communication or
the latest coffeehouse in Prague.
In fact, given fossil photographs—
shovel-headed centipedish spider-mite—
you make the horseshoe crab
who lately spawned at Brigantine
appear the sleek Manhattanite.

If, as I recall, you perished at the Permian frontier, could
you clear something up: what's death-by-asteroid ***feel***
like? My species is conducting little tests.
No asteroids—we're not Zeus yet, but cowfart,
Oldsmobiles, and the mysteries of Wal-Mart pull a
whack-job on the kingdoms of the living. Anyway,
annihilation:
Does it hurt?
Is it a hoot?
Do extinction-angels giggle as the last of you bite it?
Is it being sealed in glass,
Sleeping Beauty with no prince to kiss 'er?
Or driving Jersey's Turnpike when everyone has EZ-Pass
and you've got a quarter.

Maybe you should save your breath.
Just answer this:
Did you pardon the bullet that ended your age,
or sit at eternity's big-dish TV
waiting for mammals to die in a blur
of scorched milk and burnt fur?

American Amergin

Abandoned cars burn:
Who am I?
A slick among the waves.
In every lawn a weed
that storms the shining city.

Alewife in a stream
and soot on a sill.
A moon on the hills
and a drone strike flying.
Who stalks the cradle of the night?

A girl-goth at the mall.
A bat at sunset.
A mill-wheel turning.
I am anthrax in the air.
Who knows the poison and the cure?

A church bell changing.
A worker and a wage.
A falcon folding.
The tide in every spring
that stays the hand of destruction.

A soldier on the sea.
An infant waking.
I am ash and a whirlwind,
The swine and pearl
that spell the nation's hidden name.

A Butterfly Appears Unexpectedly in a Poem about September 11th

1
Metaphor

The wasp lays eggs
in the flesh, so flesh
can be eaten fresh.

Tremors drive the wave
to Fukushima, melt down
to a boiling sea.

Hunger in Gilead,
Thirst in a drowned city,
pharoah's distant chariots.

Compare.

Love is a tower it is
an engine of capital.
Love survives initial impacts.
It bursts into flame it
quickens the concrete.
Love collapses into earth.

2

Imitation

I am breathing it in
I am covered in soot
going to ground
in a blood-red suit.

Going to cinders,
the burning tree
of steel and glass.

To you, falling,
arms held in the aspect of flight.

3

Cladistics

The extinction of a clade
begins with pyroclasm.
We tell ourselves
this is nature's way.
Those who can, fight.
Those who fight, live.
Fail to fight, die.
Isn't that what Darwin said.

I school my students
in the Miami Blue:
High as a thumbnail,
Sky-lit, iridescent,
the tissue of heaven's
shattered habitat
exiled in the housing boom.
Even Solomon was not
arrayed like one of these.
They are nearly done—
fail to fight—
One more storm.
I ask my students,
Do you know why
(Love is an engine)
Do you know how
they burn?

Jady Liu

Wasted Land

1

I told him
Only winter here

Me the night watcher of the doomsday
My eyes my only light

I walk alone in the earth - diving bell
Going down with the universe dying of heat death

In the dream flowers fly to the lake bed
Asteroid touches my face gently

I am facing this empty space
Pondering you

I'm no longer the sum of human relationships
But another universe, or the unspeakable

At times there's some silhouette beside me
At the moment of the mechanical whistle

Visit my memory
When I am asleep

I live on the opposite side of my own life
Machinery to live better for me

We are all human and mechanical
Precisely as identical twins

2

What are you looking at?
There is nothing here

Your heart is a flashing stone
Anthropocene bursts up shrunken flowers

In the depression of the civilized world
What are you detecting with your antenna overhead?

Writing on the machine
But it has to be handed over to humans to read

Everything that is digitized will disappear
Just as your genes are drifting with the wind

Dance, play and wander around
In this earthly void

3

His face faded
As if a Mars was lit and burned out

He hasn't been online for a long time
But still often appears in my dreams - grassland

He walks alone in the empty streets
And is like a ghost

The unfinished building grows gray flowers
Whose graffiti are those?

Sunken in the relics of the online world
Dispersed everywhere yet connected together

The cloud is still floating
But only on the web

4

Rusty industrial facilities covered with heavy snow
Same as sinful people

The horizon no longer visible
It has evolved into another form of its own

The sky no longer dream blue
Yet as deep as the night

But the night sky should have had a candle
So this night must have been covered

Whose eyes fled home?
Then the man no longer sees the darkness

The sea - the sea is making a sound of the whirl
Writing traces into your heart

Mountain flowers are blooming
But there are no more bees

Who has lent the face of whom
And suspends it in a dry and wrinkled body

Night boat floats in the universe
Quiet darkness and gentleness

Forward—
Until it falls apart

George Looney

To Die in Erie, Pennsylvania

after Richard Hugo

Accept water knows which direction's true
north. That the lake knows what it means to
have to fold or lose it all. That snow echoes
the persistent chants of the ghosts of women
who believe their men, gone hunting, will hear
their voices and turn back for love. Local TV
stations call each other out on innocuous
details. Loss is behind

all programming, though no one knows whose
loss it is. Rumors of ancient eels or sea mollusks
gone so very wrong far below the lake's surface
keep most folks from diving in for a swim.
One sad drunk spends his fetid summer nights
strumming a guitar and singing songs of love to
the hidden monsters of the lake. Women bring
him food to keep up his strength, and men
drink with him between songs, telling stories of
sightings. Later at home and in bed

with the women, they speculate which rumor
has it right. It's some Iroquois ghost lost
and bitter, the drunk says, no one there
to hear. How he loses at solitaire for hours on
end is enough to break the heart of any
monster, ghost or not. To die in Erie, do it
when the ice is thick enough to let you dance
north to Canada to the howls of a ghost.

Before All Hell Breaks Loose

Exhausted, it's not too dense—the chaos
of morning grackle chatter. All language
is a question of perspective, meaning,
at times, too much to ask for. Nothing less
than a rude Babel of bird song torches
the shrubs, igniting another last day
before all hell breaks loose. I've heard it said
we're living in the end times. Try telling
the grackles the weary world's winding down.
Music's a language that says time won't end.

Sentenced to a Night of Playing the Blues

This moon, ashamed, naked
in the dark that frames the factory's smokestack

& presses down on the fields
on the fallow edge of town where corn
had stood just last month, argues

nothing has ever had the chance to
seem right in this world without having

to deny at least half its nature,
to turn its back on itself. What we can face,

the moon insists, that's what it's always been
about. The factory shut down
for years, it's hard to say for sure

what was shipped out of it. Gutted,
it's an instrument played by wind
off the lake. The concertos, improvised

& taken to long bouts of silence
between redundant chords,

were we to listen with our windows down
driving home after bars close,
would make us weep for the emptiness

such aberrant music touches off
in our chests. The past is an organ

with dust-clogged pipes wheezing out
a music that's incomplete

but authentic. Any map
knows distance is in bed with time.

What's between us has never been
just space. The moon limps down to

the hollow bay. Everything's
doubled, an illusion water relies on
to tell the stories it has to tell.

That nothing's where it seems to be
is par, as they say, for the course.

Meaning this calm surface is a place
where nothing's the only absolute.
This empty & rusted shell of a factory

hums the blues tonight & the bay,
if it could, would sigh & remember

a dead lover whose name it wants to sing
to some blues riff played on
a tenor saxophone by the bruised lips

of a ghost who remembers
what it means to be in love & forgotten.

Tonight, every ghost in this shell
of a factory on the edge
of a diseased bay, naked & tattooed

by the ragged light of a moon
that would love to be able
to put its furtive lips to a reed

& blow every blues riff
through a sax with more
of an edge than even Bird could

manage full of all the whiskey
in the world, shivers in

what is nothing more than the memory
of flesh dancing in dusty air.

Chopping down a walnut tree

Crows have nested in the human soul
and pain grows in the song of birds

Up there all dawn disintegrates

to name is to dominate
intellectual superiority
permission to hunt
bodily superiority
permission to kill

chopping down a walnut tree/killing an animal/killing a woman

[Palm of Rapa Nui, Easter Island
extinct in 1650]

a hawk crosses the morning
on the silver scarlet
the summer
overflows its wings
cathartic tremor of dawn
ascends

because there is pain/ there is
weeping in the song of birds

chopping down a walnut tree/killing an animal/killing a woman

ENJOYING THE EVIL IN US

without a soul there is no pain

and we cut down a walnut tree

[The Franklin Tree, from Georgia
extinct in 1803]

We stole from the tree its nobility
We stole from the eagle the sky
We stole the darkness from the owl

because there is pain/ there is
weeping in the song of birds

[Tasmanian tiger, Australia
extinct in 1936]

a flock of birds swarming
stands

eagles, hawks, gulls, swallows, oropendolas, pigeons, greenfinches

because there is pain/ there is
weeping in the song of birds

the hawk crosses a new scene
sits on the sunset Chirps
heartbreaking cry of a still life

a cornered life curls up on an eave
a thrush awaits
on an iron windowsill

a missing deer
seeks his land
a dead coyote
shows him
his new destiny
the inner route calls them back
but today their land it is just a vanishing point of nature
because there is pain/ there is weeping
in the song of birds

the bees hear the sick breathing
of their queen hive hunch

threats to nature
we lost our humanity

[Persian Tiger, Central Asia
extinct in 1961]

besieged nature
a web in the skyscraper
a nest on the balcony
the geese are walking
among the trash on the sidewalks

[The dolphin Baiji, China
extinct in 2006]

the falcon's flight draws
a scorned intensity
there will be no more prophecies or spells
balm
for our mortality

a blue of fire ripples in the limits
of our self-annihilation

pero los cuervos han anidado en el alma humana
y crían   dolor
en el canto de los pájaros

nombrar-dominar
superioridad intelectual
permiso para cazar
superioridad corporal
        permiso para matar

[Palma de Rapa Nui, Isla de Pascua extinta en 1650]

[El búho de Nueva Zelanda,
extinto en 1914]

matar a un animal / talar un nogal / asesinar a una mujer

[El tigre de Tasmania, Austraila
extinto en 1936}

águilas, gavilanes, gaviotas, golondrinas, oropéndolas, palomas, verdecillos

porque hay dolor / hay llanto
en el canto de los pájaros

el halcón cruza la escena
se posa en el ocaso gorjea
desgarrador grito de la naturaleza muerta

Gozo del Mal en nosotros

una vida acorralada se acurruca en un alero
un tordo espera
en un alféizar de hierro

un ciervo perdido
busca su tierra
un coyote muerto

le muestra su destino
la ruta interior los llama al regreso
hoy punto de fuga de la naturaleza

porque hay dolor / hay llanto
en el canto de los pájaros

las abejas oyen la respiración enferma
de su reina   pálpito de la colmena

asediamos a la naturaleza
                              perdimos nuestra humanidad

[El tigre Persa, Asia Central
extinto en 1961]

amapolas y tulipanes
naturaleza sitiada
                              la telaraña en el rascacielos
                              un nido en el balcón
                              los gansos caminan
                                    entre la basura de las aceras

[El delfinn Baiji, China
extinto en el 2006]

el vuelo del halcón dibuja
                                    una intensidad despreciada
ya no habrá profecías ni sortilegios
como bálsamo
                    para nuestra mortalidad

un azul de fuego ondula en los límites
                                    del autoaniquilamiento

JACK MARTIN

Earth

"oh Lana Turner we love you get up"
—Frank O'Hara

Buried or burnt? I should ask my sister what they did with the body.
What percent of all photos ever taken were taken this year? A robin
lands on a shoulder. Or is it the rain forest? Why can't I quit crying?

Spring is one kind of resurrection, but every year the robins fly away.
Beyond the atmosphere is something imaginable. The light is different.
Noses don't run. Summer on Neptune is about forty years long.

But it's hard to breathe.
If you drill enough holes into the Earth, for gas or
graves, whatever, you'll need to learn to spell mother.

E.J. McAdams

From "Thirty-seven Auguries"

White pear blossoms! Calling you on the cell. Spirit is nothing if not. Egg & yolk sunnyside up. Red square where stillness is. Be Bim Bop. A trillionth of a second after the Big Bang. All my kids want is a true story. For the poet Jaan Kaplinski. Next stop. Chance brought us all together. Again. There is the beginning of the end of the line.

The peregrine's still dead in the freezer. A juvenile, the birder says. Broken beak from the collision. Forms the seeds of galaxies. Ends cyclically. Nothing can be taken for granted. Including nothing. Invisibility. Anonymity. Readiness. First come humble feelings. Last questions. Kisses on the cheek. More dark after the light is switched off.

That it was yes. No more no. Two chairs: a couple at the table. Of all trees this one's blooming. Periscopes of daffodils. Let me see: complaining about living is better than being ten feet under. "Next stop 125th Street—stand clear of the closing doors."

Forsythia in full bloom. In Alan Sonfist's *Time Landscape*. Is art or nature. Or both. Breakfast's served. To all fantasies of escape! The title: *Silent Migration*. Caring or carrying. Shang-hai terra cotta soldiers in lobby. A construction mogul believes: I became a capitalist to save the environment. Downtown N. Sneaking in a little poem. From the sparrows to the sparrows. Joy. Uptown 2. Before you're halfway through. THE END.

A distillation to daffodils. Eye opening.

Kestrel on aerial. Contemplating bicycle wheels in motion. Hub, spokes, tire, blurring. Translucent spider falls out of orange towel. Reports of the death of environmentalism have been greatly exaggerated. Open windows sculpt wind's sound. My hands let go: son pedals on own. Self-revolutions. Chicken & waffles. Kant's definition of genius. April Fools. Daffodils reflect the lamplight. Joe Lawrence says: Who'll anchor themselves in goodness when the shit hits the fan? Elias takes us around the corner. Shadow of SHINRAN SHONIN statue. Once in Hiroshima epicenter. Under the shelter of his bamboo hat.

The sun doesn't rise. Feels like it does. Blooms: without why. *phusis*. Remember who. You are. "The indoor life is the next best thing to premature burial." EAR. ART. HEART. EARTH. Sleep never rests. For goodness sakes.

Gull cry, bus idle, drizzle. "All art is influenced by the artist's relationship to the climatic conditions in which it has been produced." So don't forget your umbrella. Rosie says: I didn't get here on the wings of the tailpipe of Mother Teresa's car. Spring snow. Wind squalls. Balloons shipwrecked in black branches. Like so many. Helping always helps. A fog. Blown away.

From *Quincunxes*

after sword laden dayes quiet

sweat worne hands touch wrapt

roots radii whose nails charm

twice black sunne urnes awake

lilac scent force comes forth

burnt odour below roman altar

fixed grate brief organ ashes

mixed among spent earth ready

seeds split soyle grows roses

netty names catch truth germe

arise begin rowse crude selfe

finde wayes passt state peril

until words reach sweet water

dream holes among stone walls

twist after kinde honey sunne

A note on "From *Quincunxes*": Each poem is a selection of five-letter words from Sir Thomas Browne's *The Garden of Cyrus, or The Quincuncial Lozenge, or Network Plantations of the Ancients, naturally, artificially, mystically considered* (1658).

ALICK MCCALLUM

To Burnley

bray, *n.1*

/breɪ/

Forms: ME-16 brai(e, braye.

†**1.**
a. of grief or pain. *Obsolete* : cri to wonder, bath cri and brai Now, wepeth, yellyth, cryeth, brayeth bludy mouth lowdly brayd Bray, or crie out

2.
a. Of animals : lacke vois. kneleth braieth. Mercy rise and bray, and stamp Thenne he [elephant] hors horse asse Stags Asses deer rise and bray, and stamp

b. *contemptuously* of the human : With fervid wheels deeply sigh vehemently rudely rough against my Rhetoricall flowers thousands bray around thee

3.
a. Of wind, thunder : Heard ye the din, hear the loftie heauens darke, Swords clash with Swords the storm may bray the thunder bray no more

4.
a. *transitive.* (cries, sounds, etc). Often with *out* : Roryng and brayieng What asse of Acarnania in a fury brayed The kettle, drumme, and trumpet Arms on Armour clashingbray'd 'See the Conquering Hero comes'

Burnley,

I I I in you and write forwards to we :
abruptly, am I I! aye, I am one :
blunt bowel of our tongue I speak in a mouldiwarp bellow

spume, blast scar and build backwards, brink and breach the barrows
to mesolith : the soil and below : above
the bull finch blasts a trowel into the daily brine

it was Hargreaves on the brink, led men blackened in soot to the fore,
to pit mouth,
to these arable rocks that splent forth past the moon and bray

I regress : dig, undearth the earth of its plasmid bulk : I speak again, for
Hargreaves,
his shaven dome, long black tongue, mouth a shaft-head, a hole, his own
head the bald shaft,

and the tongue longs for its obsolescence
: reprobate earth and burning : he tasted the mulch so much as he
held it in the fires

shovel-handed layman that he was knew what a body was for the way it
shovelled the coal

it is prosthetic, this body of work in the gloom,

yours, today and tomorrow,
mouldiwarp, I, Alick

The attempts at tracing how "bray" might sound use language from the Oxford English Dictionary's own attempt at defining the word, as well as excerpts from the quotations selected by the Dictionary to contextualise each particular definition in its own instable genealogically contingent usage and sounding. The works in which these quotations originally appeared are listed below:

†1. a.

*a*1300	*Cursor Mundi* 22607
1413	J. Lydgate *Pilgr. of Sowle* (1859) ii. xliv. 50
*a*1522	G. Douglas tr. Virgil *Æneid* (1957) i. v. 120
1590	E. Spenser *Faerie Queene* i.viii. sig. G7
1604	R. Cawdrey *Table Alphabet.* at *Exclaime*

2. a.

1393	J. Gower *Confessio Amantis* I. 144
1481	W. Caxton tr. *Myrrour of Worlde* ii. vi. 77
*a*1533	Ld. Berners tr. A. de Guevara *Golden Bk. M. Aurelius* (1546) sig. Q
1594	*2nd Rep. Dr. Faustus* xxii. sig. Iv
1614	W. Raleigh *Hist. World* i. iii. iv. §4. 47
1633	P. Fletcher *Purple Island* i. xvii. 5
1697	J. Dryden tr. Virgil *Georgics* iii, in tr. Virgil *Wks.* 113
1716	J. Gay *Trivia* ii. 22
1744	J. Thomson *Winter* in *Seasons* (new ed.) 226

2. b.

1642	H. More *Ψυχωδια Platonica* sig. C6v
?*a*1645	A. Stafford *Just Apol.* in *Life Blessed Virgin* (1860) p. xxxii
1876	J. S. Blackie *Songs Relig. & Life* 229

3. a.

1570	B. Googe tr. T. Kirchmeyer *Popish Kingdome* iii. f. 41v
1695	R. Blackmore *Prince Arthur* viii. 228
1757	T. Gray *Ode II* ii. iii, in *Odes* 17
1805	W. Scott *Lay of Last Minstrel* i. vi. 12
1872	J. S. Blackie *Lays of Highlands* 79

4. a.

1531	T. Elyot Bk. *named Gouernour* ii. vi. sig. Pv
1579	W. Fulke *Heskins Parl. Repealed* in *D. Heskins Ouerthrowne* 4
1588	R. Greene *Pandosto* sig. C3
1603	W. Shakespeare *Hamlet* i. iv. 12
1667	J. Milton *Paradise Lost* vi. 209
1855	W. M. Thackeray *Newcomes* II. xxxi. 286

Alick McCallum re: Burnley

The project as a whole (of which the poem I submitted is one poem/page of a longer serial poem) is pursued as a class-based poetics of ethnography—hoping to voice the UK's deindustrialised working class north through exploring the geological, etymological, cultural, and economic pressures that came to produce the (politically and culturally) disenfranchised working class community of Burnley—Burnley (my home town) as nexus for similar towns dispersed throughout the UK's north.

The attempt is distilled significantly through Burnley's industrial past—particularly its economic dependence on the coal field on which the town is built, and the consequent push into subsistence of the miners in relation to the coal—their bodies as functionalising apparatus of the economy of coal extraction—as such the value of the bodies/lives of miners pushed beneath the value of the geology of place just as the bodies of the miners are much more literally and physically pushed beneath that same geology in labour. Burnley's mines have no historical shortage of mining disasters.

Mining activity in the area can be traced back to the 13th Century, though it wasn't until the industrial era and the industrialisation of the north of England in the 1840s that the coal mining industry in Burnley became a major employer for the local population. The first mineshafts sunk in the industrial era were sunk by John Hargreaves, whose father, Rev. John Hargreaves, already owned a good number of mines in the area. The last of the pits to close in the Burnley coalfield was Hapton Valley Colliery, which closed on 26 April 1982, just over 21 years after a major explosion killed 19 men at the site.

In tandem with work on the close relationship between workers and the geology of the town, the project is looking closely at the etymology of the Burnley (and Lancashire, the county in which the town lies) dialect. Where much of the English language (in England, at least) is heavily influenced (sonically and linguistically) by Southern dialects of Old English and the conquesting of the country by the Normans in the 11th Century, many northern dialects, such as Burnley's, can be traced more prominently to the Northumbrian dialect of Old English which noticeably incorporated more language and inflections of the Old Norse language from Norsemen's settlement of the north of England through the 9th and 10th Centuries—often the dialect, littered with blunt consonant sounds and maintaining prominent accentual speech rhythms, is a source of humour for our 'better spoken' southern friends—though, for the most part not intentional, such mocking throughout the last century has acted as insidious class-based marginalisation in the identification and association of such dialect sounds with lesser intelligence, and with that, with residual or outdated cultural values (which, no doubt, do thrive in the town—the question being whether these values find direct lineage in the town and its community/people, or whether these values are, in fact, realised as mode of disenfranchisement, as resentment of and therefore resistance to the overwhelm of a contemporary liberal culture, a culture which so often fails to see or acknowledge as valid the daily experience of and pressures felt by the working class)—such has resulted in the erosion of local dialect among younger generations of the north. The project is hoping to attend to and speak as much as is possible in dialect by acknowledging that dialect's genealogical and etymological tendril roots—the hope isn't so much to 'represent' the sound of Burnley (though, of course, this must be part of it) as it is to introduce these soundings in poetry, which is to say to introduce a Burnley dialect in the making of culture, to re-functionalise the dialect as harbouring in it the explicit possibility of engaging in contemporary culture, a possibility that for so long has remained invisible not only to that more (for want of a better word) 'liberal' emergent culture to which it is, through dialect and idiom, denied entrance, but to the very people of Burnley itself—such is of root of our contemporary cultural exclusion—and such rooting joins with the economy of geology from our more prosperous past, swiftly lost in contemporary hyper-industrial globalised industry.

Photograph courtesy of and with thanks to Woodend Mining Museum in Burnley.

Michael McClure

Winter Solstice

W
I
T
H
I
N
endless space
in tiny explosions of gasoline
my consciousness hardens into a wall.
I AM SEPARATE
from plum blossoms and mountains:
aching teeth become movies
as I grow
young again.

Dark hair
and eyebrows
S
W
I
R
L
in delighted delusion
BIG MEMORIES OF PLEASURE
enwrap a mind
as substantial

as

a
drift

of snowflakes

onto a warm hood;
and less intelligent
than the thin

black
spider in the morning sink
before breakfast time.

Your smile is my kindness
and it thrills me

I

HAVE

NEVER

BEEN
SO
REAL

before

This Body

THIS BODY, NOT DIVIDED BY SELF
AND BY OTHERS,
IS ALL THERE WAS AND SHALL BE
AND IS EXPANDED BY A THOUSAND
IRRESPONISIBLE SKANDHAS
NOT BLAMEABLE
FOR NOTHING
constituting
samadhi;
B
E
I
N
G
RIVERS
BEING CACTI
being odors of creeks
and moths
being thunder storms,

rose petals
and
tank treads.

BIRTH AND DEATH
are not in the ten directions,
and outside of them
is a death and birth
more quiet
than clouds over a dog fight.

— Reflecting each other
brings about nothingness;
Following and preceding one another
does the same.

(The lion's roar is the shape
of a hail storm.)

The physics of this is confusion
B
E
C
A
U
S
E
it is the real physics
of how it might have happened.
Hunger for knowledge is greed,
ignorance, and confusion,
but
it is so difficult
to
KNOW
without bundles
of senses brushing
against fistfulls
of memories.

TELL ME IT DOES NOT MATTER
and I hear you.

TELL ME THIS BODY
IS THE TEN DIRECTIONS
smoking with fine particles,
each one holding a physique
bringing about particles.

IT IS LARGE
AND HAS NO SCALE,
NO
MORE
PROPORTION
THAN A CAT'S FACE
in a dream:
like a basket of pinecones
in an old wooden hall
lit by the setting sun
and it is outside of everything
coming to being.

IT
ALL
ARISES
AT
ONCE
into bundles of sense and perception
dripping lipids,
and the assembling-activities
of cause and effect,

IT COUNTS
STARS,
pretending to fit smoothly
into ideas

U
T
T
E
R
L
Y

and

T
O
T
A
L
L
Y
BLANK

everpresent

as the white-peaked mountain
beyond the field of red tulips

((**Dharma**))

IT
IS
ALL

BEING
BORN

in this demi-instant
as it passes
BUT
the distance
from the solid, shining stuff
is an illusion
of the tangle
of hormones and muscles.
A mud-colored turtle
flops in the pond
with a splash
where frogs' eyes
blink
just above

the surface.
The flesh and the light
and the darkness
arise together.
Just
like
the
skinny
willow branch
hanging
down
into
the
muddy water
AND

MY

BOYHOOD
DREAMS

swimming

around
it.

James McCorkle

Locations/Echolocations

Cholla thickets—
staghorn, silver, cane
Warning: un día caminando / dos días caminando / tres días caminando

you won't reach Three Points from the border
by then
following 286 north
through Buenos Aires look for the femurs and tibias
the unknown, unidentified, the remains
mummified (if I were here
the apparitions of each, the three thousand found, would pass
each a desert sparrow in the higher ranges

(Pasar la frontera caminando por el desierto es peligroso y puede terminar en la muerte.)
How many km can you walk before you hallucinate?
Your mouth sucks at the air. The air drying out
the inside of your body as the sun crisps your skin,
the wind a cloud of thorns, light jumping chollas.

Every step across the Sonora is across
your own fragility.

In June, the sunset red fruit, hearts packed with seed, of saguaro burst—
hearts burst, heart break, heart broken—

these are the remains among the organ pipe, the rare on the north-side, senita,
horsetail, spurge, ocotillo, bittersweet—

for three days of walking you will need six pairs of socks,
salt boils and blisters, rubbed to the bone,
blistering wet, blood wet in three days of walking/stop/wait/walk your guide will tell you
if you don't move, man you gotta move
if you don't move you're left behind —bellflower, honeysuckle, bean

And if, dearest brother, dearest sister, daughter, loving son,
if we get there, what is there?

(When was the last gray wolf heard in the Baboquivari mountains,
seen a masked bobwhite
a lesser long-nosed bat
calliope hummingbird—

listening in the sycamore creek valley cottonwoods jaguar and green kingfisher errant straying
across, coatimundis and gray hawks vermillion flycatchers in the riparian areas
the desert is not a singularity—.)

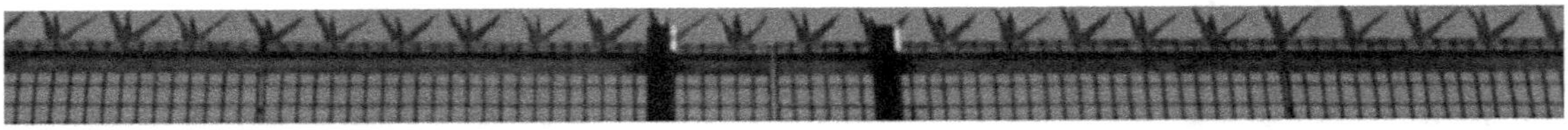

On the map, each red dot is a site of remains found, a body discovered.

In this area, the red dots merge, blacken,
until you take and spread your fingers, zooming down, "granular"
(200-million year old volcanic rocks, create soils in Brown Canyon unlike elsewhere)

how long does the body, broken down
to its bits of bone and sinew, broken down past that passed
through the guts of ants or rodents, to be
wrapped around seed or egg,
how long does the body last in all its incarnations
particle recombination of the everlasting
the remaining.

If I were here.
The soil where I have been.

Unidentified male 2018-01-02:
32.264014 -111.661872 Tohono Oodham Nation Undetermined/Complete skeletonization w/ bone degradation

Unidentified undetermined 2018-03-27:
32.371725 -112.860710 Private Undetermined/Complete skeletonization w/bone degradation

Ramirez Ramos, Marta female (41) 2018-04-24:
31.620933 -111.513750 Buenos Aires National Wildlife Refuge Undetermined/mummified remains

Unidentified female 2018-06-21:
32.389500 -111.716210 Ironwood Forest National Monument Undetermined/skeletal remains

Garfias Herrera, Omar male 29 2018-06-26:
32.022630 -110.072227 Private Exposure Hyperthermia/Fully fleshed

Unidentified female 2018-08-15:
31.587550 -111.748530 Tohono Oodham Nation Undetermined/Complete skeletonization w/ disarticulation

Unidentified male 2018-10-05:
32.648467 -112.777867 Barry M. Goldwater Air Force Range Undetermined/undetermined

Benitez Aldeco, Daniel male 26 2018-11-02:
31.812900 -109.728310 Private Blunt force injuries of the head and torso/Fully fleshed

Unidentified undetermined 2018-12-31:
32.279320 -112.854800 Bureau of Land Management Undetermined/ Complete skeletonization w/ bone degradation
[accessed 9.18.2019 from http://www.humaneborders.info/app/map.asp]

[I am thinking of my laptop, any electronic memory-receptive device
as the new archive
a new memorial, immaterial, retrieving each of those remains
coordinates to guide us there to that spot, spillage place of sinew and bone
scoop the sand/soil/silica/remains the strands of DNA of you
your name or not name but last
place of
residence
residing, subsidence
the what little that remains gathered and buried
what was now part/always parting
of bird/wolf/fox/bee—being]
There are no borders, location swims across the sand, walks on water
Hosanna, hosanna she was singing in the night alone, determined.

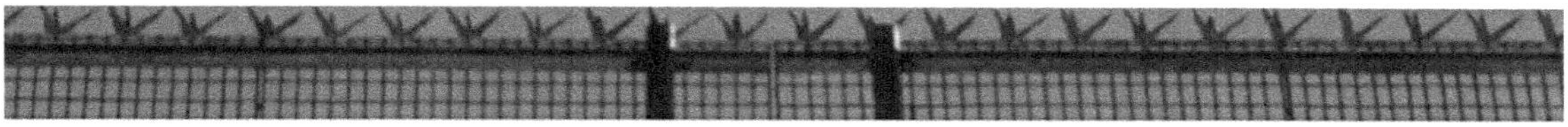

Commentary: "Prototyping process" does not apply only to the border wall, but to means to deter access by those deemed alien, disposable, criminal, diseased, unacceptable, unpropertied to cities or compounds. The climate refugee in the near future will not be someone fleeing Honduras or the Sudan, Gambia or Haiti, but Oklahoma or Florida, New Orleans or St. Louis. The prototypes consist of physical barriers, but also drones, all-terrain robotic patrols, concealments, cameras, acoustic and motion detectors. With the installation of roads, fencing, concealments, towers, the fragile ecosystems of the desert, the very ground we may walk upon: the cryptobiotic crusts contain blue-green algae, green algae, lichens, mosses, and micro-fungi, or as described by the USGS, "In biological soil crust, cyanobacteria are dormant when dry. When wet, they move through the soil, leaving behind sticky fibers that form an intricate web. These fibers join soil particles together, creating a thick layer of soil that's resistant to erosion. This layer acts like a sponge, absorbing and storing water. Over time, lichen, moss, and other organisms grow onto the soil as well. Together, these organisms create a continuous living crust" (https://www.nps.gov/articles/seug-soil-crust.htm).

(Sources, right and left: https://www.borderwallprototypes.org/ and http://immigrationimpact.com/2017/11/02/border-wallprototypes-complete-next-steps-unclear/#.XS38wvZFw2w)

[land lines to here across the living
and dead to write this
asks for a new language taking into account
the losses each step across the crust of soil
displaces a century or more of growth
to write this is always an ongoing
each addition a prototype, a process to what end
except an openness porosity
seep and flow migrations are movements
across the page across the crust of soil
a cactus seed will nest in seepage and retention
water saved from evaporation the soil a canteen left for you
migration is openness no borders, a policy an owl in a
saguaro sidewinder in the shade
everything is movement folding and opening
accumulations and crusts mosses and algae in the silica and dirt]

(Source of photographs, left and right: https://www.nps.gov/articles/seug-soil-crust.htm and https://news.stanford.edu/2018/11/15/border-wall-came-high-cost-low-benefit-u-s-workers/)

The effect of the Secure Fence Act of 2006 (at the cost of $2.3 billion for 548 miles, bringing the total fencing to 658 miles, roughly a third of the border), according to Stanford economist Melanie Morten, Stanford doctoral candidate Cauê Dobbin and Dartmouth economist Treb Allen, was "that the additional fencing had a very small effect on migration and an overall negative effect on the economy," said Morten, an assistant professor of economics and faculty fellow at the Stanford Institute for Economic Policy Research (SIEPR). "The wall was expensive to U.S. taxpayers—they paid roughly $7 per person—but saw little to no economic benefits as a result. Some even saw their welfare fall" (https://news.stanford.edu/2018/11/15/border-wall-came-high-cost-low-benefit-u-s-workers/).

Hannah Arendt: "The reason why highly developed political communities, such as the ancient city-state or modern nation-states, so often insist on ethnic homogeneity is that they hope to eliminate as far as possible those natural and always present differences and differentiations which by themselves arouse dumb hatred, mistrust, and discrimination because they indicate all too clearly those spheres where men cannot act and change at will, *i.e.* the limitations of the human artifice. The 'alien' is a frightening symbol of the fact of difference as such, of individuality as such, and indicates those realms in which man cannot change and cannot act and in which, therefore, he has a distinct tendency to destroy" (*The Origins of Totalitarianism* [New York: Harcourt Brace Jovanovich, 1979], 301).

Prototyping inserts typing, the categorization of who belongs, who is not disposable. The prototyping process is this militarization of the biosphere, to lay waste (or to render productive) space that is alien. The borderlands become "productive" in that they create the perceived need for new surveillance, incarceration, and containment industries. We are building the largest internal army, through the Department of Homeland Security, to maintain control—the Department of Homeland Security has the right to waive environmental regulations and cultural acts (access to sacred lands for example) in pursuit of "national security." Human cultures, like cryptobiotic soils, are subject to new geographies of violent security. We could say, following the argument of Achille Mbembe ("Necroplitics" in *Public Culture* 15.1[2003]: 11–40), that we are under a state of siege, there is no difference between external and internal enemies, rather daily life has become militarized and "Local civil institutions are systematically destroyed. The besieged population is deprived of their means of income. Invisible killing is added to outright executions" (27). What is the point of the border but to create a necropolis in the desert, what is the point of systematic dismantling (the simultaneous expansion of the military complex) of civic institutions but to create a necropolitan society. The roots of this may be found in the beginnings of the slave-plantation economies, which depended upon the forced migration of peoples rendered into property and the natural world displaced.

As of this writing Northeastern United States is under an extreme heat wave warning; earlier Spain saw temperatures above 105, India saw temperatures above 120, Anchorage hit a high of 90, Berlin had three weeks in May/June of temperatures hovering near 90). As of this writing Turkey is completing a border wall with Syria, including evenly spaced watch-towers (every 1000 feet) and automated firing zones; India is building anti-immigration barriers with Bangladesh (with shoot-to-kill orders) and Myanmar (which will divide ethnic groups, such as the Nagas, Chin, and Kukis, that straddle the border), Hungary (a thirteen foot high fence, topped with concertina wire expressly to keep out migrants), the Israel-Gaza border wall (built expressly to contain Palestinians and foreclose any possibility of agency or self-determination), and Latvia and Lithuania plan to build border barriers along their Russian borders (an expression of their anxiety of being re-absorbed into a resurgent imperialist Russia). These are but part of some forty completed or planned national border barriers. With each, the construction is expressly militarized—yet as Todd Miller suggests in *Storming the Wall*, the borderlands need not be restricted spaces, often racialized killing zones, but they may act to provide restorative landscapes, providing a microclimate or microecology that models the potential for a larger restorative project; Miller cites the work of Cuenca Los Ojos (CLO) which has reversed falling water tables and parching lands (223–233). The choice to racialize and militarize does not address any issue—it is purely a project of power maintenance. As power depends upon exclusion, to solve the climate crisis (or to actually modestly mitigate the effects as the cascade has begun) would in fact disrupt the structures of power that rely on the crisis to maintain their positions as elites. To re-imagine the world, one begins with openness, not open borders, but no borders. There are no borders in the so-called natural world; instead there is porosity, flow, seepage, movement, permeability—very much like the processes of art, a constant transformation and adaption. Structure is how one moves, not the arresting of movement.

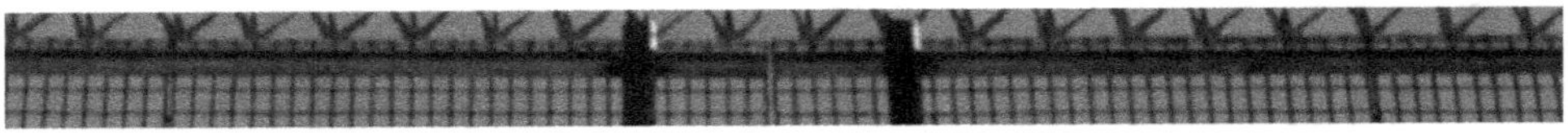

A line moving across the deserts

an open flow, flowing (a river, life-water to

orchards, the flowerings the vast, the numerous)

dust sand it comes

to that record calligraphies of shadows writing

a dream we walk into

exiles, with orphans,

our bones of the most resilient material, our souls

a vessel filling as we drink from it

filling even as the vessel is taken from us

Pine + Bay + Snow

All day I listened
to drilling Pileated and Downy woodpeckers in locust and maples

something must be rising through the trees, stirring between
cambium and phloem

ground softening, late February, a week earlier snow drops
and the flocks of eastern bluebirds I had never seen
until three years ago

the warming winters, someone wrote, an ornithologist in the Midwest
who specializes in bluebirds or is it hope

migrations were changing, birds not moving so far south, eastern
bluebirds, a dozen at the feeder, later a winter wren, the insect populations
are crashing, spring will be quiet
a storm had passed through, or its wake
pulls what is loose from their ground, but

tomorrow it will be snowing, I will watch from the office the drift of snow
scrims, someone had tipped the globe just enough to set
into motion what seemed past

and watching, framed by the door, a scene by Shiro Kasamatsu,
Matsushima Bay, skiffs tugged close to the rocks, pines snow-reefed
the bay smooth as a wood block

waiting for snow to lay its wreaths on the dark harbors.

■ ■ ■

Roughly
2/3s the way to pine + island

Fukushima Daiichi

euphoric, lucky isle, the plume

CGI mapped wrapped into the Aleutians and carried south

the ocean a basin of dispersals

The sea rises

It is far off
it was years ago, the reports issue a sea of tranquility

a moon overhead

there are 2.35 million cubic meters of contaminated soil which may reach 14 million cubic meters in three years, the government proposes that soil whose radiation levels are below 8,000 becquerels per kilogram be used in public construction sites and that the remaining millions of cubic meters of soil be buried [http://www.asahi.com/ajw/articles/AJ201902260058.html]

surveillance. watched. irruptions registered.

Noriko Manabe: "The passage of the Act on Protection of Specified Secrets (Secrecy Law) in Japan on December 6, 2013 was a turning point for many antinuclear and anti-discrimination activists ... would jail people for inquiring about state secrets even if those secrets had not been so identified. ... On a live internet-radio program ... July 30, 2014, the activist Banchō expressed concern that the Secrecy Law could turn Japan into a 'police state' that did not require police to explain the reasons for one's arrest 'because it was secret.'" [*The Asia-Pacific Journal*, 12.32.3, August 11, 2014.]

light snow   light snow   light

snow

across the ocean / the internment history histories / internments / light snow keeps
falling

the ocean was a desert, radiant sun catching snow falling light as lightly

(I've read art is meant to transform
but then the critic asked if there were no future, that what is shimmering
is a cessation

a scrim of snow, we're left stranded in the moment in the bay, contours of shore receded to
insufficiency

half-lives, each moves us closer not further
to no-shore, no-water, no-snow, no-   )

■ ■ ■

1.6 miles from where I write the topsoil has been removed
heavy metals   cadmium   arsenic   lead
the foundry site

who would move there, lots empty, the industrial zone of this small city
collapsed fifty years ago
leaving behind those who couldn't

the heavy metals

gulls swoop in from the lake two or three blocks from the reclamation
a network of rivers flow under
-neath, seepages from buried tanks carry into the porous soil

clay and glacial piles porous to what flows

gulls swoop in from the blue spear of the lake, so deep the Navy practiced effects of compression
on submarine crews during WWII

then a Pershing missile depot, now a range
for white deer

quail fox pheasant eagle
quail fox pheasant eagle

lake a blue blue.

White deer   ghosting   fence-lines.

Thomas McGuire

The following poems come from an unpublished collection, *Becoming Magpie*, an extended sequence of magpie poems which serves as a kind of (un)natural history of the genus *Pica* in North America and beyond. The polyphonic voicing behind the poems showcases one of magpie's many gifts: the birds are notorious mimics. There are thousands of documented cases of magpies having not only learned to ape, but also master the qualities of human speech. Magpies possess a remarkable combination of traits—intelligence, resiliency, a capacity for grief, and a penchant for thievery—that has helped them survive and thrive despite countless schemes to eradicate them from the American West. Magpies are also thus admirable for their adaptability and their tenacious drive to survive. In various folkloric and mythic traditions across the globe, magpies are celebrated for magical, even mystical qualities. In the mythic backdrop for the Chinese version of Valentine's Day (the feast of double sevens), these birds link the human and divine by forming a magpie bridge across the Milky Way, a bridge which the cowherd Niulang crosses annually to reunite with the goddess Zhinü. In Native American communities such as the Arapaho and Cheyenne, magpie possesses mysterious powers and is capable of raising the dead. Lewis and Clark thought so highly of magpies they devoted long journal passages to describing the birds in loving, intricate detail. Strangely, though, such passages are followed by entries describing efforts to capture, kill, and catalogue magpies—all in the interest of advancing scientific knowledge. Truth be told, most people either love or hate magpies. Since medieval times in Europe, *Pica pica* has been the object of smear campaigns, terrible press. In some places, magpies are emblematic of misfortune, impending doom. Perhaps this attitude stems from magpie's innate love of pilfering, hoarding all manner of debris, detritus, and carrion. Such scavenging habits have spurred more serious charges that this corvid ravages the eggs and young of nesting songbirds, pecks out the eyes of calves, and possesses an insatiable appetite for feasting on open sores of ungulates. Hence, magpies have a pestiferous, predatory reputation and have long been deemed (unjustly according to biologists) mortal threats to songbirds, cattle, and game alike. In a remarkably unscientific book entitled *Calling All Varmints* (1952), outdoor writer Bert Popowski quips, "Ounce for ounce [magpies] have no peer in cold-blooded rapacity." Popowski's chapter called "Magpies are Murder!" cites the bird's dietary preference as "raw, red meat, still alive" (insects, in fact, are the mainstay of the magpie diet). In the Rocky Mountain West, many a local gazette (wonderfully, the Italian word for magpie is *gazza* which gives way to *gazetta* or newspaper) has, at some point, featured stories about massive magpie hunts such as the one that occurred in Glenns Ferry, Idaho, in 1937, where the winner bagged 3,400 magpies. Well into the 1960s, the *Steamboat Springs Pilot* ran regular reports of magpie roundups, hunting competitions in which every magpie head or egg fetched a nickel bounty. Due to eradication efforts and the devastating effects of pollution, habitat destruction, and West Nile disease, North American magpie populations have steeply declined over the past century. The long-running war on magpies is a smaller, but significant part of the much larger story of plummeting avian populations in Canada and the US where bird numbers have declined by twenty-nine per cent since 1970.

Four Ways of Looking at Magpie—A Most Becoming Bird

> You did not kill the fish only to keep alive and to sell for food, he thought. You killed for pride and because you are a fisherman. You loved him when he was alive and you loved him after. If you love him, it is not a sin to kill him. Or is it more?
>
> —Ernest Hemingway, *The Old Man and the Sea*

1.

Dried all our wet articles this fine Day, / Capt Lewis out with a View to see the Countrey / and its productions, gone all day; / killed a Buffalow and a remarkable Bird / of the *Corvus* Species, Magpy. / a butifull thing, this magpy.

—after Wm. Clark's entry dated 17 Sept, 1804

2.

one of the hunters killed a bird
of the C*orvus genus* and order of the pica
about the size of a jack-daw   with a tale remarkably long,
                    beautifully variegated.
these birds seldom appear in parties of more than three or four;
  most usually at this season, they range single as the halks ⟨ravens⟩
      and other birds of prey commonly do—
from its sleak appearance I believe too
                    its usual food is flesh—
Pica hudsonia has an agreeable note
  something like a goald winged Blackbird,
      a note not disagreeable, though loud—
            twait twait twait, twait; twait, twait twait, twait.
Flying, this bird does not spread its tail
    & aloft its wing motions recall the Jay-bird's—
            ⟨its flying note—*tah, tah, tah, tah tah, tah, tah, tah*⟩
and the wings have nineteen feathers,
      forming a darkly colored triangle when spread—
dark but not jet or shining black; darker yet is the wing's underside.
The upperside of the wing is a dark blackish or bluish green

      sometimes tinting soft bluish or light orange yellow

in different light exposures—a kaleidoscope of color.

The plumage of the tale figures twelve feathers of equal lengths by pairs;
here, too, the feather bottom changes, refracting different portions of light:
towards their extremity, these feathers hue orange green,
then shaded, pass to a reddish indigo blue,
and at their extremity assume the green of mutability—
the tinges of these beautiful feathers are not unlike
but equally rich as the peacock's tints of blue and green—
Magpie is a most becoming bird.
—after Meriwether Lewis's entry dated 17 Sept, 1804

3.

Meriwether's measure of a magpie:

	Ft	In
from tip to tip of wing	1	10
Do. beak to extremity of tale	1	8 ½
of which the tale occupys		11
from extremity of middle toe to hip		5 ½

4.

Ordway's journal, Wednesday, 3rd April 1805 (clear and pleasant)

The articles which was to be Sent back
to the States in the Big Barge was packed
and boxed up ready to go on board.

To which entry, the Magpie requests a favor of reply:
Of the live animals caged & shipped,
only the prairie dog and one of the four magpies
reached Mr. Jefferson alive—
an ill omen forsooth.

In turn President Jefferson sent Charles Wilson Peale the marmot
& the surviving magpie for his museum of curiosities in Philadelphia.

Every Bone Must Find Its Fellow Bone: A Letter from C.W. Peale to Thomas Jefferson

12 January, 1806

Dear Mr. Jefferson,

The Skeletons are so much broken I fear the bones
Lost at places where crates were opened.
I can mend broken bones but cannot make good
The deficiency of lost ones, so them being mixed
Together is no great matter, but bones broken
Or lost hinder the progress of my museum—
For every bone must find its fellow bone.
Whether I can get an intire Skeleton from this mass
Of fragments, I cannot yet determine;
It will be a work of time, the exercise of much patience
Which I shall not lament, provided the object is accomplished
& the loss of bones proves my only obstacle in the work
Of restoring to them a semblance of their former life.

While the Marmot sleeps, the Magpye chatters in good health.
Now alive in the Museum, many creatures most interesting:
The Crown bird (*l'oiseau royal*), a Crowned Pidgion, Carrier
Pidgions, Western Buzzards, a Ringtail Macoco, and a Syrin
Or Mud-Inguana of a large size from Georgia, &c.
Diverse other creatures have I preserved in vigorous baptisms
Of water and arsenic. I am much obliged to Capt. Lewis
For increasing our knowledge of the territorial Animals.
I wish I could get one of the sheep with large horns
Such as those you have done me the favor of sending.
I shall primarily populate this Museum with American Beasts
Rather than those of other countryes, yet for a comparative view
This shop of curiosities shall show specimens from round the Globe!

Since the Philosophical Society owns an Elephant Skeleton,
I hope they give the Public a comparative view of the Pachyderm
With the Mammoth I have restored to roundness of form.

Mr. President, I want you much to see these Skeletons together.

Accept my best wishes for your health &c,

Charles Wilson Peale

Magpie Rises Coming Down to Earth

Where the body is, there too shall be the magpie.
—Some Gospel of Jesus (translation mine)

The magpie is not a true creature of the sky ...
The magpie is more a creature of the ground or trees.
—Fred Ryser, Birds of the Great Basin

On black extended wings magpie scans
And scouts the fallen world with dark devouring
Eyes from heights pressed still and flat against the sun—
So he tracks, then targets plain and simple pickings.

Some days magpie brings the bacon home
Looking, listening, ear cocked to the ground,
Scrying for secret signs of tiny maggot flies
Or beetle grubs whose work it is to feast,
To thrive on all that's left behind to ripe and rot
And thus help this our spent and weary earth revive.

But for him today portends a different mode of being,
Today he'll fly the narrow way, course another path
To magpiety by swooping down for carrion comfort.

Before he lights though magpie makes a rainbow show,
A kind of wavelength flight on blue black wings—
A coaster ride that in the solstice sun hues iridescent
Green, a rising rush below the sheltering sky, a curving
Climb by which he nearly clips a twist of scrub oak crowns,
Then falls and dips and lofts again before his sortie ends,
Touching softly down in meadow grass lush and tall.

Above the snowbound mountain
In a cloudless cobalt sky
It seemed the only moving thing
Was a jet black Magpie eye.

Then all went still when within
His retina scan, a streak of red
On white, a strip of scarlet flesh,
Into the corvid's focus came,
And in that vision same
A jigsaw spine of black-on-white,
A heartbeat line that puzzled fine
Through a slain song bird's skull—
A bone-ball crimsoned from the kill
And also there, beside the song bird's head,
An ouroboros forsaken & forgotten,
A snake of grey and purpled innards coiled
Round a gizzard bulged by death & grainy sand–
So Magpie lit and feasted.

Notes

Simon Critchley. *Things Merely Are: Philosophy in the Poetry of Wallace Stevens* (London: Routledge, 2005).
Charles Taylor. *Overcoming Epistemology, in Philosophical Arguments* (Cambridge MA: Harvard University Press, 1995).

Between the forest and the sea

'Poetry'. said Simon Critchley, 'describes life as it is, but in all the intricate evasions of as'. The world that separates us 'is a world both seen and unseen until seen with the poet's eye'. The world that separates us is ten thousand miles long, yet we cross waves and continents, hemispheres, south to north, north to south daily, to converse like neighbours over the garden fence. Swapping words and poems, borrowing lines and phrases, sleight-of-hand light-as-air-asides, lost lines, found lines; traces of thoughts and inter-reliance come together in an eco-poetry exercise that blurs the lines between borders, gender, race and sexuality; our days and nights never meet and yet our words collide. His are hers, hers are his, which become ours as words from two old, northern and southern hemisphere worlds, collide.

These poems are an eco-collaboration between two writers who live in separate time zones, hemispheres and continents where, to quote Charles Taylor in 'Overcoming Epistemology', 'What you get underlying our representations of the world—the kind of thing we formulate, for instance, in declarative sentences—is not further representations but rather a certain grasp of the world we have as agents in it'.

As members of a prose poetry collective, who trade ideas, bounce off each other's poems and ideas and allow their writing to collide and collapse into poems whose origins have become so blurred they unsuppose a source and momentarily focus on the world in bewilderment. Here is a sample of what lies between the forest and the sea.

A path between primordial trees, a guide who is teaching us to name the trees and their tenants: kahikatea, he says, pointing; totara. Between the giant rimu and the harakeke we stopped to watch a kererū bathe and then he was gone, and you with him. The forest breathed green and slow, fantails whistled, I sat back against a tree and watched bracken trace my arms, fingertip mushrooms bloom bright across my belly. By night you had found me, among the quiet trees, less than memory, more than a sigh.

The stories they tell of fish all shining with life whose lives they took, gasping on a grassy hill. The fish whose bodies they ate, white flesh searing silver in a pan. The stories we tell of tales that burrow up from the earth, push through soil, up the trunks of trees, along the branches, then cling to leaves as they drop with the dew, or piggybacking seed pods they slide off the edge of the cliff, a clutch of broken vowels, and birds swoop to catch them in mid-flight, press them into the rock face where they build small nests in patterns like the pattern you traced in sand, a love poem, like the pattern we saw years later scratched into a Berlin wall. *You anchor me,* it read, *your light-as-air asides dispel the despair of a world.*

There are no anchors. Only light. In early morning we stretched out on the beach, making sand angels, while below the tide line every tenth wave raked the sand, swirled the empty shells. Later we fell asleep, bundled together, the sea black under a half moon, and when we woke flowers had woven around us, their roots tracing the blurred outline of our angels. Time to leave, before the wind and waves took us, and we ran ahead of a dreich cold laced with damp till we were back among the trees, their leaves falling russet across windfall. Keep up, you said, but then lost me in the haar as it rolled off the North Sea and across the coast.

Dawn arrives early, a cacophony of seagulls, the cat crying at the door. Bees drone, pipes drone, and a drone whirrs overhead, calling out to a bank of screens it cannot see. For you I left the house, braved the morning and the sea, the breaking waves and the tempest that threatened to sink me. Anchor me in your harbour, let me feel the steady land under my feet and my life in your hand.

Now it's birds in the litter tray, fires at the front door, the racket of walls and cliffs and trees falling, and afterward just the sound of breathing in an empty room. This is not the end. Despite the lights out, gardens burned, boltholes closed. Promise me it's not the end.

NANCY MERCADO

Litany for Change

for Barack

Change the Pacific Ocean Trash Gyre
A swirling mass of pestilence vomiting plastic demons
Devouring the innocents of the sea

Change the melting mountains of ice
The thinning rug beneath the Polar Bear's feet
Change their early eclipse from this world

Change the wars in the Middle East
Wiping-out the children in the streets
Dressed in grey rags playing with dirt
and sticks and with pebbles

Change the insatiable hunger of the rich
For diamonds and dollar bills and oil to eat and to drink
Their self-indulging time bomb for us all

Change the extinction of the bats and the bees
The little hard working creatures
Who never asked us for anything in life
Change their downfall from this planet

Change our lust for ignorance and for more and more things
Our hypnotic affair with guns and ammunitions
With violence on the air and violence in our dreams

Change the foolhardiness with which we treat the earth
The yanking out of forests by the acres
Without knowing the lives there
with no care for the souls there

Change our narcissism over minuscule acts of
how far we have come
Our bizarre decrees of dominion over earth and sky and sea

Change the minds and hearts of men
Their rotted country sides and blackened water ways
Their tainted winds and distempered cities

Let them be filled with color and youth and vibrant again
Let them be lucid and living and loving again

Julian Mithra

A Thousand Years After the Wet Sky

Amid prickle pear & greasewood
& those depressing parchment weeds
with shriveled petals, a stray bluebutton
fastening the desert to
that ago-epoch, the Wet Sky,
Rabbit, it seems,
half-asleep
in the blistering heat.

Snake, too, curled
round a cracked saddle horn
to still her tongue, hat brim
shading her eyes from the glare
of Obsolete Mexico.
Heat could be depended upon
to harass the prairie dog holes & rocks
&dirt hummocks, day or twilight:
pockmarks that
presaged barrenness.

Jackrabbit dreamed only of lagoons,
ugly mirrors drowning seeds in mud,
or cloweds black as chert chasing him
down canyons, into a fright like
applause. Snake dreamed
of choking on soggy corpses
on a butte shaped like an antler.

A tumbleweed somersaults
from the horizon, a rare jilt,
a raw element broke loose
that blows Snake's hat off
and riffles Rabbit's fur.

Snake narrows her lid. Her
skin itches, glued to rock,
rooted since sprouthood.

Rabbit's feet, calcified to dolomite,
twitch inside their metatarsals.

Won't you forget inertia
for a second, please?

A whether-vane creaks her arrow
from *No*
to *Doubtless.*

Rabbit
        unstops   a hop.
                Snake
                        unchains   a vein.

Prometheus WPN-114 Felled

So he scrambled uphill
found a crooked specimen to perforate
but the coring tool got stuck
fastened fast to its thick insides

there were long distance calls
complaints were forwarded
to appropriate instances
prim specialists examined the claim

following due order
somewhere along the line
in this back and forth
permission was handed down
and the *pinus longaeva* felled:

5,000 years
after its first shoot
soared
in search
for this blessed light
which still escapes us

Notes on the Existence of Heffalumps

To Ruth

It hurts me in the raw, it really does, to learn you pored over
Winnie the Pooh for weeks to write a semester paper
on capitalism and mass media.

Christopher's anarcosocialist uneven socks,
Rabbit, intellectual amidst so much fluff,
Gopher tunneling our collective unconscious,
the failed writer in Eeyore, the profligacy of Tigger,
the charlatan Owl, Kanga's hoarding, Roo's frailty,

and what about Piggy's restraint, his veiled homosexuality,
or Pooh's tame leadership, stealing honey from worker bees,
fraternizing with woozles?
It doesn't break my heart, that's not it, it stabs and sinks deeper,
hurts me in the raw of this savage love I have for humanity
to think you could've spent that time, I don't know, say,

singing in the shower, doing charity, tending a garden,
writing a poem, falling for someone, cooking salmon,
speaking with strangers, jumping off a waterfall,
anything would do, really, anything at all,

singing a garden, doing someone, tending a poem,
writing for charity, falling in the shower, cooking strangers,
speaking with salmon and then leaping up
the waterfall yourself, effortlessly:

damasked evolutionary miracle flapping towards a promise
of eggs and hope ... But what would I know?
Who ever saw a Heffalump speak?

Bernard Noël, translated by Eléna Rivera

Selections from *The Ink's Path*

Sequence 6.3

but now that nonsense makes laws what is the meaning of resistance
when the poor are always poorer and the rich always richer
poetry seeks to feel its way along its old subjects then racks its brains
what once was promised lands is already no more than a paradise lost
undoubtedly we gain by putting ourselves in the middle of the present
to challenge one's own desperation with sudden drafts of silence
we know we must sleep off the ashes then grind the shadow to the end
each day swallow the whole bitter thing to find that nothing is served
by anger or revolt not by one of these surges contrary to the times
and we must in the very depth of the night invent the survival of life
spit out the remains of rancor into the air while training for terror
no one knows just how much time remains of the future behind us
the present no longer knows how to go further than the immediate
each touches in this extremity the edge of a condemnation
is it to exile to a detention camp or to a common grave
we are standing under the menace that serves as the new sky
we forget the azure beneath this sky and the pleasure of breathing

Sequence 6.4

and now to relinquish nothing one has to speak ad nauseam

speak of the blows humiliations arbitrariness and brutality a

head that wants the whole country at its service is corrupt

equality was only a chimera and intimacy was maimed

poetry looks toward its feet to find the appropriate baseness

abjection doesn't come from below it's by order that mud is born

it denatures nature and makes a mess of the organisms

servility is always in readiness for more servitude

what to do to oppose humanity in order to rebuild the species

when speculation serves the function to bless only the deception

the air is full of spittle so much so we have to scrub to see the view

but who wants to see traces of contempt still drooling on their faces

hatred is the only way to rinse our eyes as well as our brains

the opening of the mouth needs to go all the way up to the shadow

and what cleans it up is a tear between pus and excrement

extreme anger everywhere clashing and nothing no rescue a cry finally

crap suddenly from above a mucus of images and discourses

Sequence 6.5

and now those who have need for words only have corpses before them

the putrefaction of the vocabulary has spread to the breath

how can we talk about resistance with all this rotting in the mouth

we don't know anymore if thinking is in us thinking for itself

or if some virus shakes within us its perfect simulacra

when the virtual is stronger than reality everyone pretends

illusion took it into the debate of being and appearing

the enduring has lost its value next to the profit of merchandise

revolution would be fashionable if it was marketable

the present eats everything at once the past and the future

for that matter what is time once it is equal to consumption

use value being less regarded than the speed of wear and tear

or the necessity of having to constantly accelerate change

we expect the same kind of security from a bank and a police station

with hope in the end of an added value of one's life on life

meaning goes round in circles in the ebb of humanist desires

seeing falls to the very bottom under the weight of thick stupidity

Sequence 6.7

and now a bit of rage still groans is it in the mind or in the heart
the verse stretched out to give itself time to consider its rustling
but there it is already hesitating in the middle of an upsurge of anxiety
what happens nothing new because everywhere the same disaster
it's war and class against class it goes on without being declared
just a look a challenge a gesture of anger and the mouth stutters
full of words that flung one by one change nothing under the horizon
for want of tomorrows we have indigestions of the present
missing in each action is a breath or this je ne sais quoi of hope
this currency of illusion that we squandered laughing at ourselves
from now on what was political is nothing more than poor publicity
we don't know that in doing so nature changed nature and the human
changed its humanity when did we ever know for whom and why
who decided the content and if the container was relative or full
disgust is at present the last of the values that never dries up
too bad for the future vomited up in advance at the same time as I
as we as you as are all the consumers of the current nothing

Valery Oisteanu

The Earthquake Flowers of Fukushima

They whisper from behind the stones
Their roots embrace the peaks and cracks
Waiting for the raindrops to hurt them
But the earthquake flora does not die
Helplessly groaning and moaning
Covered with a blanket of dust
Only the lightning uncovers colors
The bleeding petals push the soil
Embracing the radioactive landscape
In hidden crevices elusive perfumes bloom
A deeper wound in a meltdown cave
These days, hours and minutes unknown
To the clock, to the calendar, to the memory
By the time the sun scans the tops of the trees
The rain of deadly flowers strikes
The twister that lifts the broken roofs
Spins purple moon and elongated clouds
Stringing together the unidentifiable birds
Leathery lizards swarm the shrines
Nuclear gutter birds in green heaven
Spin like an Ouija board out of control
Arid lead petals cover a bleak landscape
Wild flowers burst and bubble into the sky

Peter O'Leary

Milkweed and Thistle

The carpenter bees' appealingly nimble dirigibles, pollens gathered along
their bellies' lengths
and the smaller metallic flashings of the sweet bees intent on the flowering
thyme and the altogether nearly black bodies of the mason bees with the
pollen
groomed in a furry patch on their undersides
and the incessant and purposeful explorations and probings by the
honeybees
of the milkweed's lavender umbellate cymes and the bumble bees'
audible buzz while harvesting pollen—an aura of subtle aestival
vibrations—so robust, so
hairy: the garden's apiary heart. With milkweed and wild thyme, there are
sage and clematis, orange Asclepius and wild bergamot, day lilies and
rattlesnake master, and at the center
a thistle of insistent spiky forkings crowned in dozens
of violaceous pompoms fizzing with prospects
vigilant goldfinches telephone in euphoric forecasts
the seeds to come. Sphinx moths purring the bee balm. Cabbage whites
strobing in sexual pairs. Territorial monarchs and red admirals
testing the nectar. Do you see it? The milkweed
nourishing dozens of species of insects supplies
your interior mystical life
with richest nectars, and in real fact, the consequences
of this phenomenon are much more far-reaching to time than they are
to you or you to it. The human environment and the natural environment
deteriorate together. Are you prepared
to face the world of this truth? Evolution is revelation
in the strictest sense you might not
because of carelessness have the heart to see
to the very end.

Some Newer Tatters

Oracular Tatter Winter Solstice

The bottomless well
of the real.

::

Ritual Tatter Winter Solstice

Dread's gone overtone bowed
in the crypt of sound—

thy sparrowy doom be done.

::

Indiana Tatter

Sneers of April morning rain
two blue jays' telephonic echoes tear through
the slick street's riptide of racing traffic
exaggerates

but the jays'
uncinching and
chasing
calls
outlast.

::

Summer Tatter Freestyle

Water
feathering
through the grooves
of my fingers.

::

Tatter Anticipating the Solstice

A push of air in front of a rainstorm. Its humid whole.
Late spring's green flare into summer shade.
Reports of violence on the street—
can the ancient world fall apart in an instant? It can.

::

John Olson

My Life Among the Crows

What a strange thing it is to have this device, this computer, this thing small enough to put on my lap, and watch the sixth mass extinction in real time. I obsessively watch YouTube videos hosted by climate scientists, physicists and environmental biologists (Paul Beckwith, Guy McPherson, Peter Wadhams, Jennifer Francis) for information on the state of things as they unfold.

Deteriorate. Disintegrate. Collapse.

The planet is out of whack. It's not working the way it's supposed to. The clouds are broken. The sky is broken. The air is broken. The plants and animals and ice are broken. We broke it. I don't think we're getting our deposit back.

Jennifer Francis: *We're seeing a new feedback develop between the Arctic being so warm and its effect on the jetstream and vice versa. The very warm Arctic in the early fall is causing the jetstream to take a wavier path and those bigger swings are transporting more heat and moisture up into the Arctic … that water vapor is important because it's a greenhouse gas so it contributes to the already warming effects of carbon dioxide and other greenhouse gases, but it also causes more clouds to form and those clouds are also very good at trapping heat down by the surface.*

End result: September Arctic sea ice is now declining at a rate of 12.8 percent per decade. We will soon have our first blue ocean event. In which case, hold on to your hat. Ginormous blizzards will bury the Midwest and eastern coast and the melt in the spring will cause more flooding, wiped out roads, flooded barns and silos, eroded fields, the inability to plant and sustain crops such as wheat and barley and corn and oats and beans, i.e. food.

I like food. I always have. Not so much broccoli or liver. But bean burritos and pancakes and macaroni and breadcrumb chicken. *Salade piémontaise* with boiled eggs and pickles.

R and I walk to Safeway to pick up a prescription for Nortriptyline, a tricyclic antidepressant. I worry about the ability to get pharmaceuticals in the future. Pharmacies rely heavily on trucking. It may be one of the first things to go. There are a lot of people who rely on medications for heart disease and a gazillion other maladies our fragile biology is prone to. What are they going to do? It's a grim prospect.

We go to the Queen Anne Farmers Market. There's a booth there that serves the best hamburgers and fries I've ever had. We sit down at a long picnic table with our hamburgers and peach lemonade and I watch as a woman in a three-wheeled motorized chair travels slowly east toward the end of the food aisles. She comes to a strip of contoured rubber for covering the cable and attempts to go over it. Her chair capsizes. Two people at the Kiss My Grits booth come to her aid and help her back into her chair. The woman's legs are completely paralyzed. She has no use of them whatever. And yet the woman has an athletic look. I wonder if she injured herself doing gymnastics or high diving. She also seems to be pretty grouchy about the situation. But so would I be. I've had a beef going with the universe my entire life and have enjoyed and continue to enjoy the full use of my limbs. I'd like to get the universe into a ring for a wrestling match but don't think I'd do well. How do you get the universe into a headlock?

It's comforting to visit the Farmers Market, which operates every Thursday until early October. I like to think that if the food disappears from the grocery shelves people will still be growing food locally and bringing it to open air markets like this.

I notice a lot of children. This is a cause of wonder to me. What kind of future do they have? There seems to be a taboo on talking about such things. There are no taboos in poems so I get to talk about it here. Though there's nothing, really, to say. It just makes me feel sad to see all these kids.

It's a comfortable 81 degrees Fahrenheit with a mild breeze. I'm able to hold the napkins down with a bag of peanuts I brought to feed crows. I've been feeding crows for over a year now. I love crows. I love their intelligence, which shows in their acrobatics and agility in flight and the way they hide peanuts to eat later, which is a sign of strategy and planning. Yesterday I was watching three crows peck away at the peanuts I'd just tossed on a lawn when I felt something like an egg breaking on my head. There was a crow perched on a branch just above me who took a dump. I wiped the poop off with my running shirt. It smelled of peanuts and there were tiny, miniscule bits of peanut in the poop. Bird poop is the least gross poop of all possible forms of poop. It's white. White poop. That's amazing.

If you read *Le Crottin* by Francis Ponge he will tell you all about poop, the poop of the horse (*"brioche paille"*), the dog, the cat, and human beings, the poop of humans being the worse, (*"pour leur consistence de mortier pâteux et fâcheusement adhesif"*).

I talked to a woman earlier today about feeding crows. She fed crows too. I told her I got pooped on by a crow and she tells me that's good luck. I hope so.

We bought a pound of blueberries grown on Fir Island near Mount Vernon, Washington in the Skagit River Delta and headed home after I picked my medication up. The breeze was picking up and the sky was becoming overcast. The waning sunlight shone through a diaphanous filter of cloud and three crows flew down to greet me near home. I tossed some peanuts and one of them flew down, grabbed a peanut and flew high to the peak of a roof to start pecking at it.

We watch *Parks and Recreation* on Netflix after dinner and the final episode of *GLOW* and then, laptop on the bed (the datacenters that power our digital services produce 2% of global greenhouse emissions, same as the 2% produced by aviation), I watch (that is to say, I feel compelled to watch, it's a frigging addiction) another video about abrupt climate change. Paul Beckwith sits in a chair with a bunch of plants behind him, white wires dangling from his head, and discusses the fires in the Amazon and how it relates to the hydrological cycles of the rest of the world. It's not good. We lose all resiliency in the climate system once we begin losing the biomes of the planet, including rainforests. When the chain of recycled rainfall is disrupted you risk getting an amplified feedback effect: more destruction, more desert, more droughts, more hurricanes and monsoons. All hell breaks loose.

I get agitated whenever the pronoun "we" gets bandied about. "We" need to do such and such if "we" are to save ourselves. But there is no "we." There's a megalomaniacal, oligarchic billionaire class and the rest of us. The real "we" are people who do what they can to stay afloat, navigate the Kafkaesque bureaucracy of a collapsing healthcare system and buy unsalted peanuts to feed to crows. Blocks of suet and seed for finches, wrens and chickadees. We hang them in a little cage from the limb of a nearby tree. They go through it fast. Edward Abbey said the antidote to despair is action. I think it might also be peanuts. And suet.

António Osório, translated by Patricio Ferrari & Susan Margaret Brown

Jetsam

Anchoring ropes tossed out to the churning sea,
jetsam and sludge marooned,
mounds of sand made and unmade by shifting tides:
lines of poetry emerge.

And all things in a rush, anguish,
life and death, hidden motion of plants,
the equinox of love, equating day with night,
trust, struggle, and the breathing of human beings.

To a Myrtle

Born before Christ
once again it bloomed
the old and now young myrtle.

Next to the well deep roots
and the same vibrant, always generous
fragrance of flowers; the trunk
tortured by gnarled cuts,
gouged out, wounded by musk and copper,
yet with low, tenacious buds.

How many losses, how many
loves here beneath your shadow?
Someone like me ever kissed you?
How many steps around you? How much rain
did Romans who brought you here crave?
And how many breaths of life did you silently
witness, o Mediterranean body
outliving many so many dead gods?

A Bedouin

Bedouin behind the desert.
In its splendor.
Without bournous. Without mirage.
In that wild and miserable sand,
hollowed out there by the hourglass,
awed at his footprints.

Catherine Owen

A poem where the tone shifts from Whitman to Ashbery

In the end times of my family I live, in the disappearance of a river
behind increasing wheels of fog
and I hold the structure of a bridge in my gut, the molecules of lineage.

So don't ask me why I cry out.
I romance the past while my parents slip inside it and sing hymns to the vistas
as they vanish. What good is the poet.

They almost want to hurt, want to lose so they can say I have recorded
the tragic necessity. Do we accept ourselves like birds.
Writing & writing the world

as it moves away from us, as that
moment at Spanish Banks in 1978 when my mother exclaimed, "O look,
a jellyfish!" but when I drew closer, saw it was only a tire.

Ocean Shores, Washington, August 2018

A gull cries from the fireplace, cold, polished barks
harping on nothingness.
Strange, this beach.
The sand, when you walk, staticky as fleas,
their rise a hyper disassembling over a shell,
or a crab husk, or the thick nub of a kelp whip.

Most of it all is dead.
The tide, dragging in, churns with a brown sludge
above its endless ice, and out, retreats fast, wanting
withdrawal from these mansions perched on dried
brome grass in mist, the deer that hang around for raisins
like patrons of a dive bar
with promised midnight aperitifs.

Further down the fogged spit, a seal, deceased,
lies eyeless beyond old, still-smoking pits.

One of the children bunts it with a stick
but the wet snout scarcely quivers, its whiskers,
an aliveness in the wastes, black, sprung,
a sketch of what could have been, lines
in the darkening air.

Funeral

And so the bees became widows
but this was not enough for us.
We had to decimate their longing too.

In fields of poppies, the hives dried their tears.
Autumn arrived with its smoke & sorrows.
We remembered childhood but it only angered us

with its purity. You know the heart.
Its wasps hold endless stingers. Or does it only harbour
one simple, irredeemable wound in it.

No, you won't understand until it's too late.
And winter has snowed in
all the honey of our lives.

Chris Pedler

narrative space

the simplicity of surfaces deceives,
especially in the desert,
where the air's apparent
clarity's a lacquer lathered thick
upon the distances. a lens,

i bend the light, which breaks
& reassembles like a river

while i'm driving east.
the scenery unreals.

brown mountains seem
to ease into valleys
but really their slopes keep going
deep underground, leaving visible
only the rims
of bowls or tips of fingers
cupped & holding the pebbles

holding the surface.
highway sixty-two runs over
routes shaped by these ranges
for trade: trails bared by feet
buried in asphalt, now
traversed by ghosts.

in the west, successive resurrections
never kill the stench of death.
in chipped stone
teeth & scars
from miners' picks, the granite ground
with pestles left by people dispossessed,
apparent wasteland wears
its pain as space
made present by absence.
marks on a surface

conjure their startings. little's more clear
than what is invisible. everywhere,
                                        glimpse:

not the rock, but heat that shaped it;
not the plain, but seas still huge & blue;
not my speaking, but a set of lungs
                                        without skin,
          still breathing.
                    still in the car,

film accrues
          on the windows & colors the view.
                              every desert's a western
or a road flick, every town a set
                    for me, the pioneer hero,
to get lost in, found, & finally saved
                              along with an innocent maiden.

this scene replays like weather
                              makes the country
          taste of gunsmoke & shame. graves
i dug a hundred years ago remain
                                        uncovered
                    by names of places
          taken from tongues in other names
that mean the same. here is the floor

                    of an ocean. there's an oasis,
                                                  a cave
                              that's a canvas, a painting
          persisting years later. none of this
goes away. each moment blows the smoke
                              of one come before:

          granite's an echo
                    of fire, sand
          of rain, & i'm made of time
in the library & sky. in the car,

i pass the last settlement, pass the sign
                    that says *Next Services 100 Miles,*
pass where houses downsize

into shacks missing windows & doors:
skulls looking stunned
by the sun, their woodframes fading
the shade of antique photos
waiting to be taken.
the future reaches back
to click
the shutter on the past
but leaves it open, letting light in
streams deposit gold. i rushed out here to find

the mines picked over,
country discovered,
romance erased
from a myth
that was always a script in the first place.

still, those absent pasts blazed
the only present paths
& drew topographies
more true than gps. that grid exacts
coordinates between the why axis & x
on a treasure map. here
i ditch the car:
where jackrabbits scatter,
leaving tracks coyote track
past tracks i tracked last week,
finally back
in the backcountry. the surface,
undisturbed, preserves this record
of a legible writ. this printing
adds to an atlas
inscribed in my mind, memorized
directions describing the wild
that i am, & how
i might get there.

will & representation

because the ground in pinto basin's flat
the map's all space, a bright white blank

where everything visible's hidden. i begin
in the outermost level of sediment.
blacktop

stretches both directions
into a celluloid west. i came to see
this movie climax
as an ecosystem, see the desert
x-ray time, & sea its muscles
undulate upon tectonic waves. looking east,

a vista picturesques. intricate ridges
chisel the coxcomb cliffs. the guidebook says,
go south, so i go
around a gate & toward a hill
the compass picks from a set
of they all look the same.

ahead, behind, & to the left, three
mountain ranges frame a canvas-
colored land where i project
directions. up the plain,

an old road weaves
around creosote, mesquite, cacti
absent from maps that describe the terrain
inexactly & lie
about everything else. the guidebook says,
go south, so i go
the wrong way. to navigate

i sight the hill & take a bearing, climb
cross contours
creeping closer. this line
isn't that
my reading tracked. around me,
boulders crest a broken surface smooth

on every chart & graph. steep
instead of flat,
the crooked foot-path
funnels up a gully. on both sides,

a canyon rises. the bottom swerves,
reverses. stepping
gets complex. i guess the route & turn
& turn
thru tight stone folds that, seen from above,
resemble a cortex. this is how

the map's curved lines trace nerves
that terminate inside me, lines
the guidebook never says: *go west*
at the dynamite scar,
where springtime creosote explodes
her yellows into my synapses.

scramble out where three tall walls
dead-end & make a cell
in my brain,
where more accurate maps begin
from links between space & its names.

west, my body's drawn
by topographic lines my feet etch
in the sand. & in my head,
directions true
connect my neurons all afire & light
the way to where i haven't been, a land
i'll learn the wording to
rewrite in electricity its legend.

Craig Santos Perez

Rings of Fire

Honolulu, Hawai'i

We host our daughter's first birthday party
during the hottest April in history.

Outside, my dad grills meat over charcoal;
inside, my mom steams rice and roasts

vegetables. They've traveled from California,
where drought carves trees into tinder—"*Paradise*

is burning." When our daughter's first fever spiked,
the doctor said, "It's a sign she's fighting infection."

Bloodshed surges with global temperatures,
which know no borders. "If her fever doesn't break,"

the doctor continued, "take her to the Emergency
Room." Airstrikes detonate hospitals

in Yemen, Iraq, Afghanistan, South Sudan…
"When she crowned," my wife said, "it felt like rings

of fire." Volcanoes erupt along Pacific fault lines;
sweltering heatwaves scorch Australia;

forests in Indonesia are razed for palm oil plantations—
their ashes flock, like ghost birds, to our distant

rib cages. Still, I crave an unfiltered cigarette,
even though I quit years ago, and my breath

no longer smells like my grandpa's overflowing ashtray—
his parched cough still punctures the black lungs

of cancer and denial. "If she struggles to breathe,"
the doctor advised, "Give her an asthma inhaler."

But tonight we sing, "Happy Birthday," and blow
out the candles together. Smoke trembles

as if we all exhaled
the same flammable wish.

Chanting the Waters

for the Standing Rock Sioux Tribe and water protectors around the world

"water moves the deep shift of life

back to birth and before … "

—Linda Hogan, "The Turtle Watchers" (2008)

~

Say: "Water is _____ !"

because our bodies are 60 percent water—

because my wife labored for 24 hours

through contracting waves— *because water breaks forth from shifting*

tectonic plates—

Say: "Water is _____ !"

because amniotic fluid is 90 percent water—

because she breathed and breathed and breathed—

because our lungs are 80 percent water—

because our daughter crowned like a new island—

Say: "Water is _____ !"

because we tell creation stories about water—

because our language flows from water—

because our words are islands writ on water—

because it takes more than three gallons of water

to make a single sheet of paper—

Say: "Water is ____ !"

because water is the next oil—

because 180,000 miles of U.S. oil pipelines leak everyday—

because we wage war over gods and water and oil—

Say: "Water is ____ !"

because our planet is 70 percent water—

because only 3 percent of global water is freshwater—
because it takes two gallons of water

to refine one gallon of gasoline—

because it takes 22 gallons of water

to make a pound of plastic—
660 gallons of water

to make one hamburger—

because it takes 3,000 gallons to make one smart phone—

because the American water footprint is 2000 gallons a day—

Say: "Water is ____ !"

because a billion people lack access to drinking water—

because women and children walk 4 miles every day

to gather clean water and deliver it home

Say: "Water is ____ !"

because our bones are 30 percent water—

because if you lose 5 percent of your body's water

you become feverish—

because if you lose 10 percent of your body's water

you become immobile—

because our bodies won't survive a week without water

Say: "Water is _____ !"

because corporations privatize, dam, and bottle our waters—

because plantations divert our waters—because animal slaughterhouses

consume our waters—

because pesticides, chemicals, lead, and waste

poison our waters

Say: "Water is _____ !"

because they bring their bulldozers and drills and drones—

because we bring our feathers and leis and sage and shells

and canoes and hashtags and totems—

because they call us savage and primitive and riot—

because we bring our treaties

and the Declaration on the Rights of Indigenous Peoples—
bring their banks and politicians

and dogs and paychecks and pepper spray and bullets—
because we bring our songs and schools and prayers

and chants and ceremonies—

because we say stop! keep the oil in the ground—

because they say shut up! and vanish—

because we are not moving—

because they bring their police and private militia—

because we bring all our relations

and all our generations and all our livestreams—

Say: "Water is ____ !"

because our drumming sounds like rain after drought

echoing against taut skin—

because our skin is 60 percent water—

Say: "Water is ____ !"

because every year millions of children die

from water-borne diseases— *because every day thousands of children die*

from water-borne diseases—

because, by the end of this poem,

five children will die from water-borne diseases—

Say: "Water is ____ !"

because our daughter loves playing in the ocean— *because we'll point to*

because someday she'll ask, "where does the ocean end?"— *because we'll point to the dilating horizon—*

Say: "Water is ____ !"

because our eyes are 95 percent water—

because we'll tell her ocean has no end—

because sky and clouds lift ocean—

because mountains embrace ocean into blessings of rain— *because ocean-sky-rain fills aquifers and lakes—*

because ocean-sky-rain-lake flows into the Missouri River—

because ocean-sky-rain-lake-river returns

to the Pacific and connects us

to our cousins at Standing Rock—

because our blood is 90 percent water—

Say: "Water is ____ !"

because our hearts are 75 percent water—

because I'll teach our daughter my people's word for water:

"hanom, hanom, hanom"—

so the sound of water

will always carry her home—

Say: "Water is ____ !"

"Water is ____ !"

"Water is ____ !"

....

Th S xth M ss Ext nct n

Frances Presley

Monsters of the Deep

play with sunlight
lean on green glass

weathered by the Thames

blue light
dark Matterhorn
ice melts

blue crystal
pulled apart

hunched over

blues loss
white floss

tardigrade too

jewels of sand
microfibre

transported by the tide

blue oak
fossilized wood

freezing under film

baby wipes
round diatom
time lapses

ghost of a shrimp
legged thing
frondment

counts our red eggs

micro

pink strips
lower lip
change quick
red splash in ice

yellow critters
translucent
intersect in chains

microforms
fight out
crack along the green

white border sorbet
absorbed

green squirt alert
shrimp legs lasso
the plug hole

the Bargehouse, London
Sep 19

Point Perilous

everything's better across the water

too much slippage

for sea bathing on Sillery sands

ancillary sands at low tide

basking grey rocks basking seals

out of the nuclear cooler

they are biting for the hand that doesn't feed them

maw biting mawr

a new severity cuts back

under amber eyes

deep cleave
livid rocks
liver gouged

banks rupture

invent a story to conceal bankruptcy

hog back cliffs hard castle

bristles

brushes off bides heather

retreat strictures

it's safe to sail today

Lynmouth July 19

Notes

"Monsters of the Deep" and "Micro" are a response to time-lapse videos by artist Irma Irsara, which bring a microscopic focus to materials from the Thames estuary.

Kristin Prevallet

old human, new consciousness

1:1

is a small land the sea, is a spill oil, is growing a fixed condition, is toxic frolicking dump, is birds' breathing oblivious, is shade trees, is canopy light green, is vines twist skinny, is daylight still bed.

1:2

around the foliage. to empty. between is matter, beneath the forest. if a tree fell, as the shadow standing still? across the path. of the sun. of move. across the ground, into the clearing, not yet born, creature waiting soundly.

1:3

pushed out of sap interior. chlorophyll, unlike a leaf. cold, soon learns to fall. pushed out, a crude awakening. takes monstrous delight. obliterate. memory of the earth as it used to be.

1:4

trees' bony arms strike claws at the air. eyes campers and forest walkers. pounce the call of owls. swallow small resting creatures. night activates the heart. rises the interior of bark. lies in the crevice that shaped it. walks, hesitantly at first, until no longer embryo.

1:5

a symmetry of shelters, upright. three-tiered trunk, to worship patterns in foliage. every leaf. branches, an arc. the gods, even here. stand firm, make bird sounds. communicate with what has fallen.

2:7

what center were we trying to hold? out of thin air, an impossible flood. momentarily safe earth side. then slid away. then saw drowning. not lungs, but liquid breathing.

2:8

beams fell. landscape lost sound layers. waves, just as dangerous. born from the sludge. grew up not rooted to the ground.

2:9

made tracks. marked forest. entered thought. prepared the landing. trees covered with soot. relished obliteration. with the trees, all other life faded away.

2:10

small reflections of lily pads. a cosmic lake. a place in memory. stepped from stone to stone. journey to make tracks in four directions. location: simultaneous.

Evan Pritchard

Learning to Love the Earth

When he was ten with eyes like clear blue oceans
I took him to West Virginia to see the wild rivers run,
Took him to Tecumseh's land and showed him the Adena mounds,
Far older than New York City.
I took him across the Mississippi, that muddy highway of the Choctaw
And tramped around abandoned fields
To find out where that old man river used to run
Before the earthquake changed his tune.
I took him to the Iowa of the Sac and Fox to see the field of stars,
And to Niobrara of the Omaha to see the long horned steer,
Stronger than the river where it stood.
I took him climbing the crumbling cliffs that overlook the town of Boulder
Where I once went to contemplate, gazing across the plains,
And then the old high Rockies
Where the Arapaho once welcomed me to their fires,
And we saw snow drifts in July,
And we scaled some crooked narrow trails by car
to the tops of the Grand Tetons at midnight,
Beset by a flock of wild horses
Who beat us to the pass
And made us wait, grateful for the teaching—
About who still owns the Black Hills,
Their carefree faces made ghostly by the light of our headlamps.
We walked among the redwoods,
And even through them,
Here before the Europeans came
Or yet before the fall of Rome they stood.
I took him to the Three Sisters hills of Oregon in the forgotten deserts of the Great Northwest
And then to bathe in Tahoe's mountain-guarded lake—
Which the Washoe people still entrust to the protection
Of supernatural beings; the water babies, the land keepers, and the Ong.
And then we stayed in the Sierra Madres, showering in Mother's waterfalls.
And then we walked like angels through the clouds that shrouded around the Golden Gate
At early morning fog—
And then ran back to run down San Francisky's golden hills
Where Ohlone children used to sing and play;
And gazed amazed out over the calm Pacific Ocean,

From a high flung cliff at sunset.
And then I flung my arm around his budding bird-like shoulders
And said, to a wonderstruck ten-year-old adventurer,
"All these things we've seen along the way are tastes of nature, only tastes;
Glimpses of what used to be Turtle Island.
Some day, down the road, when you are old enough,
I want you to find a place where Mother Gaia
Is still standing strong in all her power—
Totally uninjured by human interference
Where trees and rocks still shine their own beautific light
Where air is sweet as honey
And water pure and sparkling like the stars;
And I want you to live there at least for a time,
Without changing Her, despoiling Her
And all alone perhaps, fasting if it helps
And speak to The Mother of All Life!
Lie upon her grass, touch her face of stone
Give your heart to her, and really get to know her;
As she has always been, was meant to be,
And then you will know what all of us have lost,
And fight to save what's left!"

And that's just what he did!

From the Himalayan peaks to the pines of the Cascades
From Hawaii's wildest jungles to the desert sands of Egypt
From the stony cliffs of Greece to the craggy coast of Maine
He searched for truth about what is, what was, and what's been lost
And now he fights, for the Planet that he knows so well,
and marches down the streets of Madison
And Washington and Portland Oregon,
Because now he knows
What others have forgotten—
That she is more than just a place for us to stand.
She is Love!

Kester Reid

Pairs

Are the mallards alone, as they paddle
in pairs, dipping and foraging
in the blackness of the swamp?

They pair and mate with the same impulse
as we do. Do they cry and wonder
in solitude?

I met them in springtime, their azure wingbars
beating in crowds across the water
like butterflies burst suddenly
from some hidden, dark world

They stick together for protection, and
for love. They fly for their escape, and
for the thrill. They plumb the black depths
to nurse a strange hunger within—
of course they are alone
with us all

Evelyn Reilly

Having Broken. Are.

Grief moves from box to box.

Calendars. Emoticons.

A ceramic figure of a bat.

Having become the animal. I am

Among the float of heavy bees.

Every living thing has its natural history.

The dog's interior castle is undergoing an ecological calamity.

Precarious nature penetrates every opportunity.

Mutual need.

Restructured life greetings.

Insect leg calipers measuring out probabilities.

The wind is full of shifting gears which the overlords use to exert their
usual machinations.

Financial instruments. Public relation messages.

There aren't enough scare quotes in the world for this.

Hope in the presence of other people I once took as a provisional definition.

Amend. Repair. Revise. Recognize.

That kind of incantation.

But an incipient way of thinking links us to a new unsecured network.

Having been brainwashed as children we must suspect ourselves always.

Dogged associations such as a clearing in the woods closing at the rate
of your own aging.

Your arbitrary name sound wobbling in the same breeze that makes
it impossible to turn over a new leaf definitively.

You can only step into the fray.

See what happens in the ecosystem of response.

This may be prophetic pragmatism.

How do we do together?

Thus it's hair-raising when ancestors grope mystically at my scalp.

Union soldiers become Indian hunters. Protestant ministers.

Indecipherable women.

Cause permanent itchiness.

Past futures and future futures.

Moth touchdowns have me putting up antennae again as delicate
landing pads open under a fingernail of moony lyric impulse.

Endless exploratory probings.

The inflammation of unpeaceful centuries. The respiratory systems.

Not breathing well at all.

These forests. These streets.

The first line echoes the poem "Unmarked Boxes" by Rumi. The "brainwashing" line was adapted from a work of art by my friend Anne Tardos containing the words "I was brainwashed as a child. There was no other way."

Eléna Rivera

Touch of Water

after Olafur Eliasson

Pop! Can one do it with language? Make water explicit?
There's so many micro-relationships, but how to touch

the word "ice," and now another layer added "I.C.E."
Vertigo—I am touched by the split even if I can't smell it,

A circle, air, the difference between thinking about it and
touching, like a compass of sound echoing in the mind

The intimacy of "I" "me" and the possessive use of "mine"
How did we get there? What does it mean to be moved?

Feet in sand, on rock, asphalt, concrete, to be touched
The artwork gave me the language to understand my part

My part in this public space, my part but not mine right?
The viewer participates, but am I empowered in this regard?

The notion that the world is not infinite, split into those
who want it to end, and those who want to care for it

"I am nature," the artist said, "I am nature too," and so
he makes works that destabilize our physical space

But we're not producing oxygen like trees he points out
to emphasize the climate emergency, the fact of water

learned by a deaf girl in the hand of her teacher "w-a-t-e-r"
How can we navigate our way? Is it about how things were

done or how things can change in the future, the future is
daring if we invent it and pay attention to the touch

of water, earth, air, paying attention to our gestures
even if we are all only weeds listening to ice melt, Pop!

Untitled

" … it is right to mourn the endless repetitions
of meanness and violence and pettiness and hurt."

The present coated
with dancing and dying—
going on for a long time.
Now birds coated in oil,
fish die, the livelihood
of many destroyed. Write,
write a poem. No more
bees in China. Death
settles the entire matter,
doesn't it? Robot bees
can't solve can't carry
forward propagation—
We lose bits of flavor.
Gain offal for children,
burdens of past actions
is what is carried / crushed
(take time to reflect on this).
I shouldn't speak for others,
but I want to in my riverbed.

* * *

" ... though I'll be dead,
my life will hide itself
in this letter until you
read it ... the moment you
read it ... the moment you
open it and begin to follow
from the first word
my life will burn again."

* * *

Day now a scar in the old marble,
old anger new, how the body turns
into liquid because we let it.
Heard the music, had to follow
the marks of language. Mark me.
Illuminate this face. What face?
That which fronts us all? Face it.

* * *

Have mercy on a sea
Have mercy on the bees
Have mercy on our trees,
London planetree, honeylocust.

Why protect oneself?
Have mercy on our ambition.
The ordinary juxtaposed
to News: "Train derails"
"Bodies found" "High winds
predicted" "Corruption charges"

Overly greasy vegetables,
and a door needing WD-40.
End up wrestling boredom,
wresting appetite from the soil,
smearing grease and what happens?

Some find resilience, others flounder—
Is that fish on the endangered list?

"haunted by the person you might have been"

In The Field Pastoral

And others, walking on the earth—
The way I reacted, curving downward

We all live in a different country

Take a scene of carrying a candle

The fact is that it was the way I reacted,
not outside myself, *my* reaction,

not out there, but here
I let it upset me that the stranger said,

"You should pick up your feet"

Nostalgia for the one lost, the thing lost—
"Unspoken feelings are unforgettable"

(How an ocean separated and intensified nostalgia)

Nostalgia is sticky—
"Do you know what I mean?"

"It was so much better back then," people say,
went to the movies and were bothered—

Something is activated by nostalgia,

the way the friend kept the photograph of the man
who left after the romance had ended

"reminds me that someone, so handsome,
used to want me," she said years later
                    (how many times,
                    don't—god, happy
                    by comparison)

Render loss by stirring it under low heat,
"No one can travel that road for you"

Poppies—the word in french is “coquelicot”

“You know Monsanto hasn’t quite taken over
if they’re growing on the side of the road”

A field
of these signs, in Monet or out of the window,

so red and fragile—

“Colony collapse disorder” a term for bees
abruptly disappearing

“Shaking” they gather pollen from poppies,

“trembling”
(term for thinner possibilities)

The unfathomable is not an “adjustment,”
human animals forget signs

We haven’t got a clue about the bees: “les abeilles”

No one can comprehend “tremblement”:
Throb   Hum   Buzz

And the living are destroyed by it

MG ROBERTS

Lone Pine, 7 o'clock

tonight and so often
too I am beside myself looking in the west courtyard

chatting about near death and thrown stones. memory is a lake.
such horrors revealed through close reading

    failed marriage. failed light. flailing light
        my darl'n all the ice has melted.

listen to the music. here, furnishings move without explanation.
in this video you can clearly see the outline of

haunted women. here in this house with windows filmed
in dust, the dim light is darkest when clouds recede.

here in this house, rain announces saturated earth through
    mudslide, river rise, river mouths

        say, "it's frightening and unnerving to watch a stone melt." say
      the river was weeds glossed with silence, a marker of passing time—

its skin the most unrecognizable part of time's marking.
this body carries so much regret,

let the stones roll where they may. then what?
you are no longer the girl you see when your

eyes close, a woman who screams loudly
when curtains are drawn.

i've heard the audio. melting glaciers don't relent. I've seen
rocks skipped into lakes, all the backlog of it's too late.

is there a mark-up for that or a meme for living under trapped carbon?
we are the outlines of a tailing sun

    out mitigated, outsourced, out
        dying.

LINDA RUSSO

from *Dear Dirtlings*

Dear Dirtling,

this is little sunflower *(Helianthelia uniflora)*
I don't know much of our history
or the future for which she is dying
on mottled prairie remnants
with their windy epigenetics
a future deeply encoded
in shared belonging

century upon century each little sunflower
opens an unclosing eye till its sun-baked lashes crackle
and blackened disks punctuate the landscape
while millenia of losses widen gaps between kin

at the end of this knowledge I might know
    where petals went
    the resistance of mosses
    nests of mammal fur
    the brushing up
    the little adornments
    bees mending edges
    how to be unblinking
    how to remember other knowledge

have you noticed how the scent keeps drifting
from our glorious lashes?

MARK RUTTER

An Alfoxden Soundscape

The
sound of the sea distinctly heard on the tops of the hills,

the singing of
birds, the hum of insects, that noiseless noise which lives in the
summer air.

The half dead sound of the near
sheep-bell, in the hollow of the sloping coombe, exquisitely
soothing.

The dis-
tant sheep-bells, the sound of the stream;

The manufacturer's dog makes a strange, uncouth
howl, which it continues many minutes after there is no noise
near it but that of the brook. It howls at the murmur of the
village stream.

The sound of the pattering shower, and the gusts
of wind,

The trees almost *roared,* and the ground seemed in motion with
the multitudes of dancing leaves, which made a rustling sound
distinct from that of the trees. Still the asses pastured in quietness
under the hollies,

The redbreasts made a ceaseless
song in the woods.

The redbreasts sang upon the leafless boughs.
the songs of

the lark and redbreast,

In the continued singing of birds
distinguished the notes of a blackbird or thrush.

the occasional dropping
of the snow from the holly boughs; no other sound but that of
the water, and the slender notes of a redbreast,

The sea
very black, and making a loud noise as we came through the
wood, loud as if disturbed, and the wind was silent.

The unseen birds singing
in the mist.

the wind was making a
loud noise behind us.

heard the
nightingale;

Seven Reasons Not to Underestimate Simple Cells

They're not just bags of chemicals.

Many have internal compartments.

They are not always small.

They work together.

Some are multicellular.

A few have a nucleus.

They can swallow.

A note on "An Alfoxden Soundscape": All of the references to landscape sounds in Dorothy Wordsworth's *Alfoxden Journal* (1798), in the order of their occurrence. "Seven Reasons Not to Underestimate Simple Cells" is a found poem: source, Caroline Williams, "Who Are You Calling Simple," *New Scientist*, July 16, 2011. Both are from the forthcoming book, *Simple Cells* (inkConcrete, Glasgow UK).

John Charles Ryan

Tamarind
Tamarindus indica

Lombok asam

prostrate seeming

slanted into

twilight saline

skewered up through

stony rupture

bonsaied mind of

algal sealine.

*

Thing squall-coppiced

splotched with lichen

camouflaged in

boulder breaches

pinnate-green pate

balding leeward

bluffs enclose us

lit in neon.

**

Among to sleep

scarce roots that clutch

harsh cleft between

that which was—will

make thought as sweet

as deep brown pulp

from sickled pod

of tamarind.

Brush-Tailed Rock Wallaby

Since you were here last, the wattle fervour has begun fading.
The luminous bijoux are drying, drifting into the unseen, fading.

The wind today is neither zephyr nor tempest. It brushes us airily.
What were you feeling on your way here? I have been feeding

noiselessly on the manna of this threshold between gated field
and numinous edge. Can you see fogs of falling water fading?

On a sliver between ledges, wind-chiseled acacias flare upward
like flambeau. Bearded dragons are blown up, midstep, sunning.

Now listen. Can you hear the murmuring innards of the land below?
Turn around. Look down. Can you touch the braille of our foraging?

My face (is rummaging in leaf litter) my fur (is carob-brown) my tail (is
a thick ashen-hued balancing stick). I am immersed in this feeling.

Near the lookout, mosses are composing faint verses in pubertal green.
Through the cypress, did you notice the perfectly clear plateau fading?

excubitorium: place of vigil

Windriffed bloodtide whisk—*crunk grasp flasp flisk*
heartbeat crests gorge susurrus then smashes over us
in arterial tides murmuring, slurs and swells saccadic,
cardiac fibrillation then zipper twill. *What meditative*
gunk is this? What do these tufts of tillandsia whisper?

Gorge rim soon to flower—*scrunch*—flick of Bic lighter,
plastic click, feedback underheel, thump on drum skin,
crescendo of interstitial rasp, *somebody's about to gasp,*
polite formalities then interview ends, hasty handclasp.
My voice is a heteroglossic bird before you [digital | *crash*].

At first, I was calm, but your inner tumult overtook me,
I became withdrawn, reticent—*cough groan ugh*—crestfallen,
blind(in)sided, introspectively-drawn, revenant far
blown-off, parasail-glided, migraine-lumbered, alone on
this lip with the godless quivering, grousing, muttering.

Lento, adagio, *I fall*, wind-knocked, -crisped, -asthmatic,
in octaves of chalkboard scratch, freight trains rumbling
on tracks, thunderclaps of waves over boulders, fermata,
decrescendo, *I speak as a collective zephyr breath [yes I!]*
fortissimo, ethereal vi(r)gi(l)n in G minor—diminuendo.

Stasis come discs whipping up falls, footshivering ague, lite
lithospheric lintel, hues of brite buoyant bertya vocabulary
U meditate with me here, never I do use flippant descriptors,
stroboscopic tuning, weathervane whethervain withervein
to turn now, crouch down, my linguae embracing U utterly.

Cap fiddling indiscretion…………*then*………pitch declension
of monk chanting, resounding dungchen dharma trumpet, a
long, deep, whirring, haunting wail returning you to your
mother's womb, plainspeaking through cellular tympanum,
threading time & space by grief—*I was a body before U too.*

How much of (my)our voice is your voice? is the tremulo of
a black-chinned honeyeater? is the outbreath of a rock
wallaby? is the weeping of water through xylem of a gum
tree? is the tap of fingers on a touchscreen? what part of my
voice is my own? telling myself, I'm telling you. *écoute.*

Dream. time consists of mists through me. a falling star
across scorches the hidden lucid. *mared (merde,* what I could
do, except this eternal). *armed.* I'm manied. birdly-baited.
weighted with witness and sounded. *derma.* be still as skins.
rapt. in yogic listenings. *madre.* orchestral within.

Termite pitter-patter, currawong cradlesong, thrumming
magpie lullaby, *oh noooo, mhmmmm, mmmhum, ummmm,*
bushfirestorm, fingerstrum, treefloored in Ee major chord,
croup from arid lungs—*so this is how I sound, I didn't know*
I'm that loud and brazen, brash and annoying. crass/crush.

I'm not unlike. you? I hymn when there's spring. do you? I
brim when gossamer spins around limbs. do you? I limn
when there's none. do you? when there's nothing to do or
have done. do you? I'm not unlike. you? I cleave to what's
me. you? granite splinter, ferrous earth, infernal seed. you?

I splinter with hymn, U? OMG. I spring gossamer brim, U?
AMA [*ask me anything*] yah, I seed nothing unlike, U? BAE
[*before anyone else*] yah, I cleave anythin' to earth, U? ELI5
[*explain like I'm five*] yah, gonna IM U on WA [*WhatsApp*],
k? BRB [*be right back*] yah, U, let's descend into acronyms.

I'm chuffed to see you this year. It's been a lengthy drought.
I saw that on the news. I knew you'd be the bloke to ask.
There's something about the winter season that does me in.
I feel for you. Even with heater and blankets, I'm shivering.
Loneliness. *Yes?* Whadya think of it? *I don't.* That's a gift

Jimmy Saekki

Congress Arthropodus

A tropical moth's white-wings,
frangipani petals folding
in the spiral of a spider's mouth,
salivary glands drooling yellow,

an antennaed invertebrate
sinks its proboscis and drinks—
From a stout shell
the sound of a stretching imago,

a starburst of skin and silk;
hidden in the cereal germs
of groat and millet,
they convene in their domain—

In the marigolds, milkweed
and mildewed wheat
they grow in patience,
minuscule faces in the holes

of spores, until another egg zygote
is ready to be eaten—
The vertex, thorax, abdomen,
the chitinous pathogen,

the viral, fungal, glucal,
the brittle exoskeleton,
the suture, midgut, amber extract,
an assembly of blighted seeds—

A parasitic cabal resembling leaves.

Plant Lore

The crop along a coastal plain;
splendidly pungent bulbs
chaperone seedlings of uncommon
crocuses, stems neck saffron orbs.

Winds rehearse their embouchure,
a leaf sharpens its serrate,
the tide solicits its paramour,
surface receives its pullulate.

The compiled florilegium
(gerontology of perennials)
antiquate as the sanguine
helicopter petals dissemble.

The sun disperses in sea craft,
earth germinates the clay,
as pedicels soften their basal spathes,
a genus congregates its bouquet.

Eutheria

Quasispecies: true beasts / the other side
of a vinyl caul –

an intromittent organ
protrudes the uterine wall,
placental handfuls, spleen pulp,
agape culverts of a pancreatic duct,

calculi scattered in the ampulla /
smell of fish maw, isinglass –
'a food in its own right'

bovine hides, cloven hooves of ungulates,
multi-coloured jellies,
subcutaneous – collagen in the cheek,
belly and jowls of buttock fat /
a forefinger exerts the force of a small hammer,
a ransacked jejunum, a cleft

between the legs, an innervated membrane
between two fluids, 35mm nitrate,
the force of an aluminum bat,
a cudgel, his sceptre the baculum,
a warm globster, mongul, ung,
rise of the cremaster,
rise magogoli / immortalised
in graphite and flaxseed oil –
a clot of blood in the fist: mouthfeel,
uniformity of chew, incoherent cud
'a food in its own right' /

light in the attic;
dilate, contract.

Kia Toitu He Kauri

I came to grips with the kauri
and turned him, in all his splendour, into a symbol.

– Colin McCahon, 1957

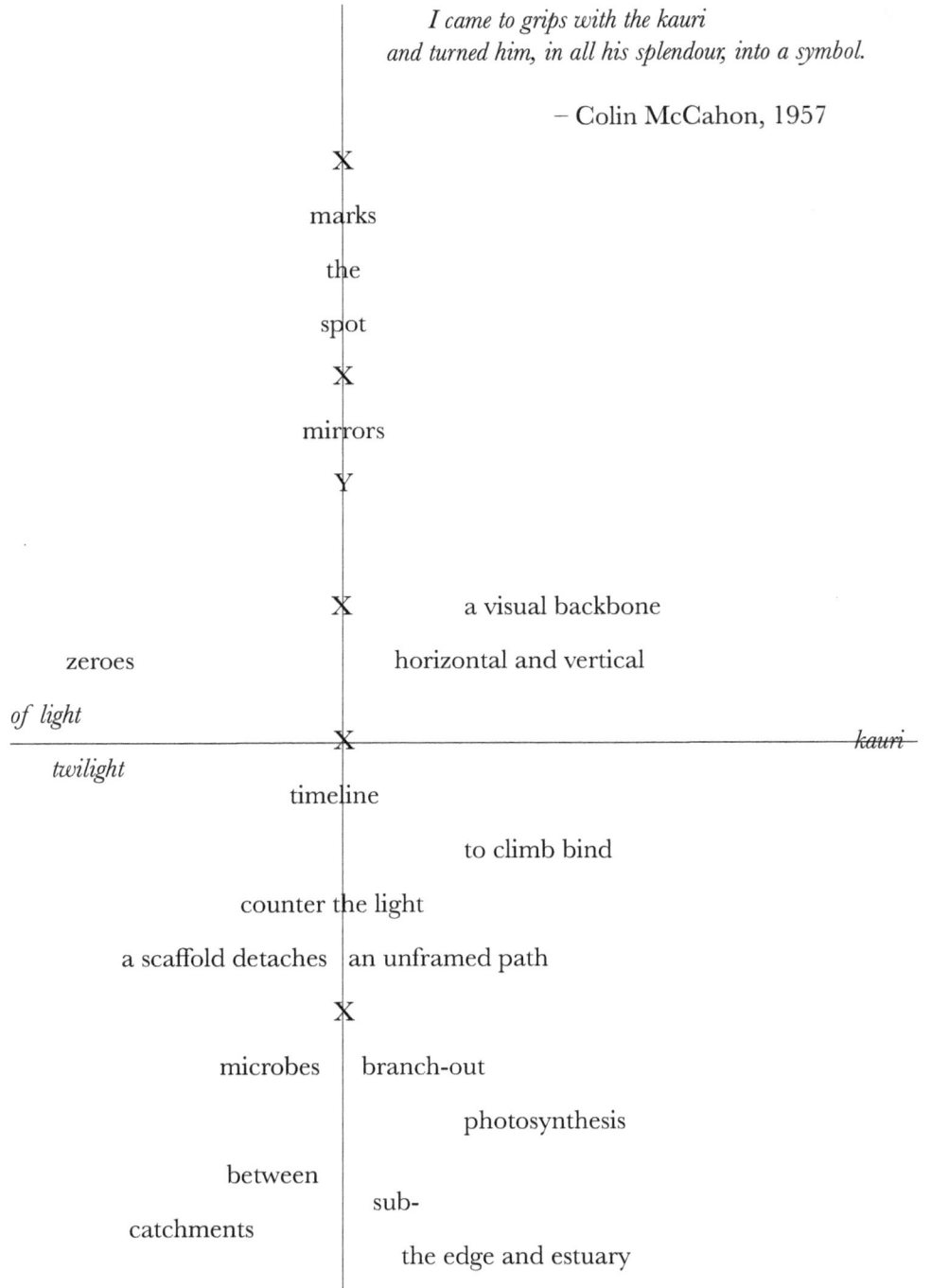

X

marks

the

spot

X

mirrors

Y

X a visual backbone

zeroes horizontal and vertical

of light

X *kauri*

twilight

timeline

to climb bind

counter the light

a scaffold detaches an unframed path

X

microbes branch-out

photosynthesis

between

sub-

catchments

the edge and estuary

X

pathways
pathogens

an imprint

surface | sediment

X

a constant flow of light

zero light : holey light

first light : inner light :
outer light : outlined light

framed light : filigree
light : threaded light
said light : dead light
syllabic light swallow light
born light
bone light : alone light
aligned light
lateral light : broken

light : street light
neon light : head light
sun light
star light : moon light
ritual light : sacred light
secret light : tangential light

X

absentia light : mint light
mineral light : scalloped light
saline
light
opa
line light
open light : single light
straight light
scattered light : crushed light
shadow light
clear light

X

wave
light : lapping light
falling light
travel light : talk light
sent light
digital light : past
light
present light

faint light
green light : go light

X

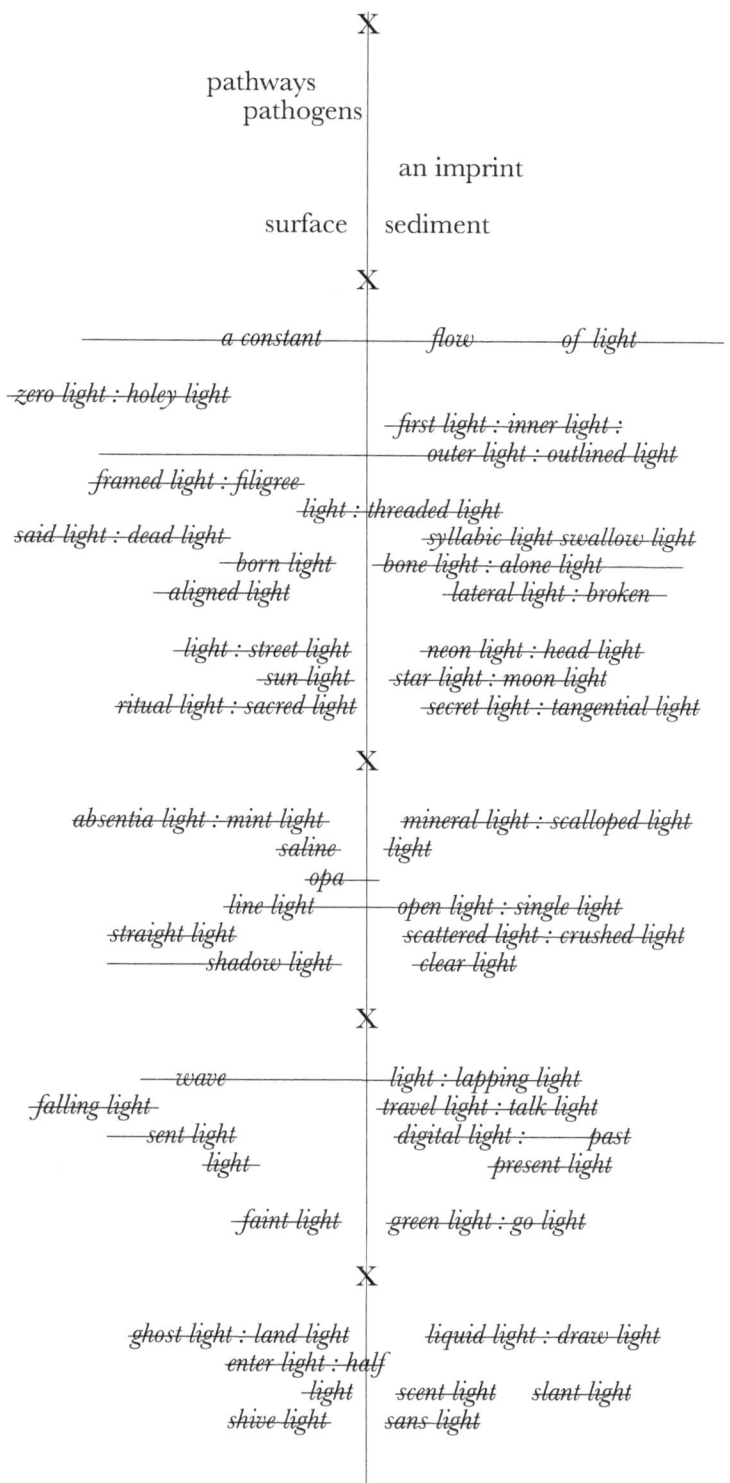

ghost light : land light
liquid light : draw light
enter light : half
light
scent light
slant light
shive light
sans light

~~*still light : black light*~~ ~~*white light*~~

X

cut
left then right
a sou'-west squall
horizon
between top
and toppled

X

centre line
criss-
crossed signs
scenic drive

Y

shape-shifting

helix

shards of summer's

soil-borne scent
a matrix
New Year's

pod-
cast
traces
arcs

X

stands

for

kauri

sky

high

dead

centre

X

stands

symbolic

a skeleton in nature

X

Y

Z

Kia Toitu He Kauri—(Keep Kauri Standing) : An Afterword

whāngaia te mauri / hau o te kauri

Agathis australis is commonly known by its Māori name *kauri*. In New Zealand kauri are considered to be taonga (treasures) of the Māori ancestral spiritual world and are of significant cultural importance to all New Zealanders. They grow in only one place in the world, the northern part of New Zealand, and in the context of this poem, the Waitākere Ranges of West Auckland.

Historically commercial harvesting has seen vast tracts of kauri felled and today less than one percent of the original kauri forest remains. Most recently a new threat has emerged—kauri dieback, a microscopic, funguslike organism called *Phytophthora* taxon Agathis (PTA), which attacks the roots and trunk of kauri such that they starve to death. Because of the multiplicity of spores involved with the disease, and no known cure, mass extinction of the trees is very much a reality unless a collaborative scientific approach is embraced. To think of the northern forests without kauri would be unimaginable for most New Zealanders.

As a child growing up surrounded by kauri, I often climbed and walked among them, exploring and studying these rangatira (chiefs or leaders) of the forest. Today I live in my family home in the Waitākere Ranges—a networked 'wood wide web', among the same trees, where they have watched me grow, as I have them.

Sixty-seven years ago while living in Titirangi's French Bay, arguably New Zealand's foremost painter Colin McCahon captured the elemental symbolism of the kauri. As art historian Gordon Brown relates, 'McCahon adopted the habit of rising early at dawn, and would then contemplate the bush, such that the forms of the trees would dematerialize while his sense of spatial depth diminished'. At its most intense, McCahon likened this illusionary effect to that of the blind man mentioned in the Gospel of Mark, who on first receiving his sight, saw 'men as trees, walking'. His meditation on the expansive tree canopy with its multiplicity of light and line resulted in an exploratory abstraction of signs and symbols. As McCahon said in 1957, 'I came to grips with the kauri and turned him, in all his splendour, into a symbol'.

The phrasing and structure of 'Kia Toitu He Kauri', riffs on reading McCahon's correspondence and a viewing of his Titirangi kauri paintings. These paintings render McCahon's unique vision of the Waitākere Ranges and his pressing meditation on the fragile but dynamic biodiversity of our ecosystem.

The poem's layout attempts a vertical and horizontal scaffolding with language floated in space. The branched strike through lines disseminate language and light, or as the American artist Jean-Michel Basquiat put it, 'I cross out words so you will see them more; the fact that they are obscured makes you want to read them.' The reoccurring 'X' stands vertically along the skeletal spine as a pictorial, elemental mark, or as local conservationists have termed—'tree death markings'.

Wolf Acrostic

Where I first saw the river's name, Apishapa, it was Young's book
    on wolves. Three Toes of the Apishapa, one heck
Of a critter. Lost part of a paw to a trap. After that managed to evade
    every snap, snare, bait, bounty hunter, or range rider for a decade.
Later I wondered,
    how do you say the river's name?
Fishpaw was the clue, the settlers called it that since the Ute term
    'mossy creek' sounded weird.

a-PISH-a-paw

Somehow

Not sure how I go through
morning zazen with troubled groin joint
one aspect of suffering is lost trust & old friends
Turtle Old Man has been fashioning
beads grinding & piercing the little shells
on a KPFA reel-to-reel tape
since 1949
He asks the travelers to bring him obsidian
but Coyote fell to earth the borrowed blackbird feathers failed
These days Sulphur Bank
where he landed
stews with mercury from the abandoned mine,
a touch of the 20th century
yellow tailings drizzle toxins
into Clear Lake for decades
I keep getting messages from Academia.com
to sell me scholarly papers about the contaminants—
(see Kroeber who says Oleyeme,
headwater of Putah Creek's
named for coyote "in all
the surrounding
    languages."

Anthony Seidman

"Reft from Thee"
XII

According to Augusto Monterroso
there exist only three themes: love   death   and islands

In the desert
islands are made of water

  but in Southern California
islands were seepages of hip-deep tar

Marrow has yet to dry in my bones
  the soul's feverish salve yet to be drained

This morning I woke to coffee
  peeled an orange while seated on balcony

I stared over treetops and at foothills
drying under sun   chaparral suicidally
secreting combustive oils

    itching for brushfire

VII

The world below the pitch,
    this vacant lot: obsidian-eyed wolf spider drags
egg-sack from sluggish spinneret,
beetle digs through topsoil
ant mandible-hauls butterfly
wing colored like transept rose,
cobalt
amber
flickering like
sun on water;

deeper,
worms the color of dried
mustard thread tracery through dirt, deeper,
mites no larger than pencil's blunt tip;

then shards,
arachnid exoskeletons,
viscous pockets of oil, earth
blackness like coffee-grounds salted
with random rodent jaws & claws;

deeper, mollusk bits,
wood, plant tracery
from 10,000 years in the past,
silence weaving with other silences there;

deeper, dire wolves compressing
under eras beside a sluggish ground sloth;
phyla gone helter-skelter:
millipedes preserved in tar
beside bison bones, snail shells,
thighbone of hunter;

deeper, rib-cage like
            Flying-Buttress:
the Mammoth,
and then the change suddenly thence
to the surface,
puddle the size of kitchen table,
methane escapes, bubbles, the
fossil-stew,
where I stand
and gaze at the vacant lot:

Sun-daze on brittle weeds,
oleander bushes, smell of dust,
and the Valley
spreading around me
hills, billboards and haze.

Grey cat leaps from junked Cadillac onto
cinder brick wall, and my sight
clicks to crow overhead;

thence
past the smog,
past thinning oxygen,
radiation, beyond the
blackness to another sphere …

its frigid atmosphere
of carbon-dioxide,
rust-red regolith, topsoil
containing methane traces;

deeper into that red soil,
spores,
gnat-sized shells
of wispy centipedes fossilized;

the change thence
to life on other spheres,
lives
not of carbon,
not saurian,
not amoebic,
perhaps some silicon species
who may outlive ours?

Play Dead (A Possum Poem) (extracts)

I

Not uncommon when I drive
late-nite   post-party   perhaps *X*
on car stereo   or *Coltrane*   maybe
spacey *Brian Eno* asparkle   the wine-darkened haze of thoughts
windows down   estival electricity   odor of white coals: brush-
fires   hi-beams click to focus   curves of Laurel Canyon   and the car lee-
warding   rocking softly   and as rubber-smooth sibilance of tires pull
me around the corner   I spot it   in splif's quick flick:

scruffy fur   *flinty eyes*   jittering into the bushes
as *scaly tail* zips from sight

the possum!

III

Libeled as rabies-host
this creature known as the Virginia Opposum
is the marsupial American
a petal within the bouquet
of other marsupials   with distinct skull: small tight and long

all survivors they have adapted to red sands and boulders woods
sub-tropical hills

Tasmanian Devil   Kangaroo   Numbat   Bandicoot
Bettong   Quooka   Potoroo

now in the San Fernando terrain:

chaparral and vacant lots peppered with red ants   pink oleander toxicity
barbed hair of the tarantula   emaciated coyote   cloudless azure
black widow's cottony-tuft of webs beneath wood white disc in sky haze
asphalt horizon   sage scrub   itch July heat   tics clotted on mountain-
lion
rattlesnake sniffing prey with scintillation of forked tongue   crow and carrion
creeks slender as life in the gaze of one receiving viaticum   jimson
weed

The ubiquitous San Fernando Valley possum not a native /
first trapped in LA: 1906   brought West as pet   or whitetrash stew-meat
the Virginia Opossum escaped cages   (like the Eastern Fox Squirrels

spread through the citrus orchards   empty lots   walnut groves
survived
adapted / adopted

IV

By night I push my pink nose through
black humus: syllables   the grain of certain consonants
the rain when a metaphor opens to the stir of woodlice
rain stitching worms through black soil
and pulls up a rat's skull   fangs delicate as violin strings

my pink *schnoz* snaking beneath mulch of words   each phoneme an ootheca
similes so serpentine   how they sliver!
the mud-splats of sturdy spondees
and the stew-thick protozoic slime and sweet ooze of consonance
my claws stirring a catalog of water   pebbles   burr   brittle weeds of august
ink splatter of small beetles   orange peel   stale bread   carton
of milk with contents curdled   husk of wasp's paper net   the cells scooped
clean

Here am I
scoping the backyards of language   hunkering into ivy   fearing coyote
scoundrel raccoon   or emboldened golden retriever
but gold in the humus   berry in the babble   the chalice: of clay   dung-dew
throne woven from sage brush

O Brother Possum   digger & searcher   outcast
Am not I a possum like thee
or art not thou
a Valley Boy like me?

Kelly Shepherd

Arctos-tecture

the cathedrals and churches
which humankind passively
sits today, listen
ing to watered
down state
ments based
on utterances
of visionaries
and ecstatics,
were, before being
in effect turned inside
out, active underground
"sanctuaries" or "incubational pits"

in a long interval of complex and
often obscure history sep
arates the primordial
bear, even the
Bear Son, from
later concepts
of the god's
resurrection.
Even so, the
Christian Madonna
still occupies her cave
in the sculpted grottoes
of a thousand churchyards

Water Lily

If the Creator cannot be happy
with one kind of beetle,
why would one religion be enough?
– Trevor Herriot

The water lily's petals slowly close.
From inside the flower comes a voice,
inaudible to the human ear.

The initiate begins in a bright chamber,
built to resemble the sun. On the outside
this plant is a floating temple, a jewel;

on the inside it is tunnel and bowel
and larvae dark. The walls are covered
with handprints and footprints

outlined in pollen. They might be symbols
of worship, or feeding, or fear.
But there is no time to think about those

who went before. The passage darkens
as it descends. All the worlds left behind
tighten like mandibles around the smooth black

stone at the bottom of the pond
which is memory. Turning back
is no longer possible. There is no room

for wings. The way ahead, narrow
as a hungry shorebird's throat
and colourless as the closing mouth

of a toad, swallows water and sun
and anyone who would enter.
Algae-slick and alone in pristine shadow,

the initiate cries out that the spirits
of chlorophyll and caddis and breeze
might hear and show mercy.

This passage will lead to a new opening,
and rebirth, or it will lead to death.
The water lily's petals slowly close.

Capnomancy Crow

Ink bird, chimney bird, reason for the night
I caught you smoke-bathing
you can't take flight.

Sleep bird, soot bird, dark flower in the tree
I have a question and
you must answer me.

Coal bird, shadow bird, absence in the sky
I caught you smoke-bathing
you can't tell a lie.

...

If a fortune-teller could read palms
simply by turning her face into the breeze
stirred by the hands of the client
who opens the door and walks into the room,
that fortune-teller would be corvid and not hominid.

The lifeline is a current of living air
and has nothing to do with creases in human skin.

There must have been some mixing of blood once,
long ago, for human beings even to think
about telling one another's fortunes.

This story might not be lost.

That we focused on talons instead of feathers,
the fingertips instead of the hair,
says much about the monkey mind.

...

To persuade a crow to tell you the truth
you have to trick it.

But every cat who has tried this knows as soon as you begin
to set a trap, the crow has guessed your third move and
disappeared, or perched on a higher branch
to feel what you'll do next. Out of reach.

No, you have to catch the crow unaware.

But any child who has tried this knows as soon as you bend
to pick up a rock, the bird has flown off. Sometimes out of
sight, and sometimes
just a little further away than you can throw.

They know what you're thinking.

Crows recognize guns instantly
but it matters more that they can see intention in mammal faces.

They read body language using a combination of sonar and braille,
receiving impressions from the winds with their heaviest feathers
and interpreting them with their downiest.

This happens in the black blink of an eye.

They do the same with rising smoke—and this is when the bird is vulnerable.
To bathe in smoke is to let oneself go, feeling pin-feathers darken
and ignoring the rest of the world.

This is the time to act. This is the one and only time
it can be done. Unfortunately for the seeker,
finding a crow in this ecstasy can only be unintentional.

Notes

"Arctos-tecture" is a collage poem, composed of found texts.

Bibliography

Eshleman, Clayton. *Juniper Fuse: Upper Paleolithic Imagination & The Construction of the Underworld*. Middletown: Wesleyan University Press, 2003 (xxv).

Shepard, Paul and Barry Sanders. *The Sacred Paw: The Bear in Nature, Myth, and Literature*. New York: Arkana, 1985 (135).

John Shoptaw

Like Clockwork

It ate the food it ne'er had eat / And round and round it
—Coleridge, "Rime of the Ancient Mariner"

turns the North Pacific Gyre, an inadvertent monument
to the esemplastic imagination, narrowing clockwise
in such a lazy spiral that a *Thank You* bag blown afloat
off San Francisco takes six years while a printer cartridge
ejected from Tokyo takes only one to reach the photo-
degrading doldrums of the central polymeric water column.

In upon a squall line   *if it floats*   sweeps a Laysan albatross
it's food if   her binocular gaze   *a ballpoint squid*
darting about   *a redtail sand shovel*   for food she'll gulp
a soft-bristled spine   and gulp down   *it floats it's*
her black wing-blades   *food if it*   scarcely undulent
casting the sole   *a white dimpled golf egg*   bobbing shadow
a fliptop pink shell-cap   on the polished sea   *if it*
which marks the hour   *floats it's*   in Yukon Savings
a baby blue spoon-bill   *food*   in Daylight Anthropocene.

I've never been there, to the Midway Atoll,
and from Berkeley, California I can't hear or see
the volcanic coral breeding reef of the albatross.
But through the webcam I believe I can feel—
from their clacking low bobs, their beak tucks
under one wing, from their waddle struts
and their heavenward whinnies—
the deep exulting of the forty-year mates
and the rocking glee of their gray down gooney,
who claps his beak in his mother's beak
to stimulate regurgitation, a feeling the sun
seems to deride by shining on the plastic
mechanism in a neighboring chick's remains
as a glaring illustration of Descartes' thesis
that the nonhuman beast is a soulless robot,
however far it might exceed some skill of ours—
in navigating the magnetic heavens, for instance—

as a traveling alarm clock will peep precisely
when the appointed hour comes around while
people can make only a rough approximation.

Vertigo

Our November drive down the redwood coast
is off. It's a spare-the-air day, thickening already
with particulate sunlight and ashflakes. Last night,
far north of the Bay, a wildfire made
its own weather, like a climate, whipping up
a fire whirl, a funnel flame, a fire-nado
that twisted ablaze conifers, photo albums
and stiff chaparral and spiraled them skyward
into a mile-high smoke torrent that jetted
across the continent over New York,
New England and the North Atlantic.
Unbelievable, we say, meaning inconceivable,
a staggering wonder that plunges some
into an inert disbelief.

Madeleine drove Scottie down the peninsula
and parked her green Jaguar at the sunny brink
of the Big Basin redwood forest,
which makes its own atmosphere, like a planet,
verdant with fog and giddy with oxygen.
They entered in silence its dark cinematic
hush and walked among trees grown
to a vertiginous height, stopping before a broad
sequoia sempervirens cross-section
with dated growth rings: 1066
Battle of Hastings, 1930
Tree Cut Down. (1958
Filming of Vertigo, floats a little
beyond the fibrous red bark like a vapor.)
Looking at it feels like looking down
into an incredibly deep well that perspective
narrows into a funnel. This foreshortening
of the historical abyss into the present is what
film buffs call the Hitchcock zoom, when the camera
backs out and zooms in or zooms out and closes in

so that viewers suddenly become aware of the scene
impinging on or casting off from its focal character.

Usually it's hard to see the climate for the days,
the carbon emitted by Madeleine's green Jaguar
doing its part to this day to heat our planet.
But an unreal, unheard-of weather event
will zoom the overlying climate into focus
for a moment, and bathe us in an icy astonishment.
As though the earth looked around and saw
it was the only planet swaddled in habitable
gases. But nothing can keep on knowing
like that. So the days look up and move on.
The smoke turns away from the Bay and tomorrow
they say the weather will be fine.

Jacob's Meadow

Your way of putting some distance between us,
mourning dove, in seemly haste,
quickstepping (your turtleneck gaze
craning forward and flexing back
like a Singer sewing needle) and then
flustering aloft to the telecommunication line
and crooning—all of it pleases me,
pleases me way beyond the ways
we've misconstrued you. Your wings whistle
no eerie wail but a call to flight,
your moan in dove minor lures
your next mate, and your spirited relocation
to a level only a little above me
shadows forth no seraphic transmutation,
no hereafter species to aspire to,
nothing more than a song perch.

And you, angel, you're no missing rung.
Look at you! You're an evolutionary
monstrosity! Why were you fitted with arms
as well as wings? For brandishing a lily?
Flourishing a sword like a right-handed beak?
And those tender feet, gracefully adangle

or decorously robed—what have they
ever seized? Do they walk or hop?
Either way, without you the great
rope ladder of beings would collapse
all over the place, and all earth's creatures
would find themselves on the same footing.
Which of course they already do. All but us.

Earth to Jacob, snap out of it! That angel you
were grappling with in your guilty dream
on the banks of the Jabbok? That was your brother,
Esau. That starlit ladder? The oleander
riverbank. And those departing and arriving messengers?
Bats homing in on the mosquitoes in the meadow
that had gorged themselves on you. Yes, bats,
your distant neighbors, embracing the afterlight
with their handsome five-digit wings.

Ratsnake

The afternoon lay half-awake over the damp leaves;
only a few dried ones rustled as the ratsnake moved
slipping on their wet inner edge, its long yellow body
sliding thin, weaving rain-wet patterns on the brown earth.
The magpie robins saw it first as its flicking head
disappeared under the sheaf of palm fronds.
Only the whisking tail told another tale of the routed nest
and the dismembered chicks; a few ruffled feathers
still hung in the thinning breeze. The ratsnake
turned; the silent hush of the bird-couple marked off
a reluctant pause in the natural drama,
when the rain broke again with the austerity of a recluse.

Mongoose

There is so much fear in these eyes.
It can fill an entire petal that floats by
Directionless.
Yellow and blue, brown, and red
And many nameless colors.
But the mongoose latched on to the grey
Neither dark nor fair—

The wind fearing nothing
Moves freely between fence and stream,
As the long furry form pauses
And merges with the floating petal. Grey. All grey.

Wagtail

Let us step on the tail of the mountains.
Let us fly between the waves. No tree, no bush, no thorn
Is light enough to hold us. The sky tremors with the lightness
Of our touch. It is nimbleness that is our natural right.
Shearing the thin waters of dawn and dusk
We live off the moonlight.
Tied to our tails all the year round
The earth shares sighs and dreams.

Isabel Sobral Campos

Excerpts from "How to Make Words of Rubble"

An opera house of crickets
auditorium of stonebark
the chorus ~~a strike that line~~
predictable, exhausted anthill

Not an idyllic forest // a conglomerate of trees looking on
THE SLIME OF TIME

Contrapuntal;
pellet-sprout

Contrapuntal;
semaphore-song

Irrepressible brainwater

I wear this dazzling hurricane (my ball gown
(I take off my plankton sandals to chew)…

The body that grows on my top body
and the body that grows on my bottom body

(A child in my belly,
A mother on my back
2-headed monster + me:

(So Few Words I'd Like to Sing!

Trinity-Forest

Propeller-Scare

Mint-Apocalypse

X's Speech:

Look at the cloud's absorbable force—the vortex of indifference and lattice streams (slowly). A pressing insinuation overhead. Is it a button large enough for failure to observe? Your attention strays into the vicissitude of a schedule. Enough spelled words leave you nonetheless empty. I thought of this (as yet) unformed word (I could not decide in which language). We talk about asides rather than the thing I need help to think. The oblique. Our dying, robust. You who occupy an inch of earth often think of bones.

Rinsing my speech with bleach and month-old soiled sheets. These bits of hair remind me that I exist as blood, muscle, affect grind (my mood: small enough for a blur).

Thee blind ecology fills # rock. Thee filament hollow as gale tree
bursting with hurricane darts. Split tree is shaped
conch defangs undulating hemlock. Down below head on argillite.
Fragments impair her ability to think. All words for trembling
stumble beneath bedrock, arrayed in the draped forms of leaves
quaking through gusts, swirls.

Thee power enough to rattle thought
cowering blur
boundary cannot speak

I withhold words for storm in her native tongue.

Here a blank.   A roar.   Here an absence.

What moves the tulip?
If not spit, teeth?
The chorus sings:

Word for bone is OLIGARCH

When we look at the sun with shut eyes and see it is just another day. I respond to all troubling facts by seizing more trouble. Shedding my body's vines. The small gestures of time turn within me. Wrapped in slowness my motherhood weighs a child's golden weight. I comb her hair, flap her large ears, and clutch the breathing slab in the palms of her hands.

Water tastes like westward, bleeds more sentient

Noticing the odors of day, delicious curry of unknown neighbor, memory of summer while now leaves trail down to the ground

A daughter hesitates between ways of spelling the same sound:

> The left (maimed way)
> A warped manner

We move to the swamps and lug Grendel's mother upon our backs. Her gentrifying corpse. The sun juts open within a cloud that takes on a morbid shape

A daughter's first fears:

> Clouds shaped like monsters
> Mother monstrous
> Warlike motherpaws

André Spears

The Drunken Spaceship 2

"And the Lord came down to
see the city and the tower,
that the human creatures had built,
and the Lord said: 'As one people
with one language for all, if this
is what they have begun to do now,
now nothing they scheme to do
will elude them! Come let us go
down and confound their language
so that they may not understand
one another's speech!' And
the Lord scattered them from
there over the face of all the earth,
and they left off building the city."
Genesis 11: 8, in R. Crumb,
The Book of Genesis Illustrated
(tr. R. Alter).

"A scholar... maintained that
the Great Wall would provide
for the first time in the history of
mankind a secure foundation for
the Tower of Babel. First the wall,
therefore, and then the tower ...
I admit that even today I cannot
quite make out how he conceived
this tower. How could the wall,
which did not form even a circle, but
only a sort of quarter- or half-circle,
provide the foundation for a tower?
That could obviously only be meant
in a spiritual sense. But in that case
why build the actual wall ... ?"
Franz Kafka,
"The Great Wall of China."

"And place was where
the Presence was /
Circumference between."
Emily Dickinson (1084).

At the moment Bismark
jumped to her Death from
the stern, the general economy
of the ship displayed an even
distribution of the crew's
weight throughout the length,
breadth and depth of the hull—
given Captain Anna-O's
aplomb and savoir faire
handling the Rainbow gravity
between "Yin Relativity
and the Quantum of Yang,"
as formulated by Hazar in
The Always Possible and
Good-Enough-for-Jazz.

Nonetheless, Bismark's leap
was apparently all it took
to tip the ship's delicate
balance on the crest of
the Wave toward the bow.

Stationed in the lookout
atop the mainmast, Mach
exclaimed with a Tragic
Laugh over speakerphone—
which Captain Anna-O
had ordered turned on
across the ship, before turning off
the propeller—that *Ko-Itame,*
the Spirit of the Keel, was
"experiencing a Mood Swing,"
and recited Shams's Lament from
The Book of the Seven Beatings,
while one-eyed Chauvée
of Communications, stationed by
the electrical stripping between
the upper Cryptonite rods and
the Voided oar, initiated the effort
to redress the ship's Equilibrium
by quickly moving aft, along

"Can you tell the down from the up?"
E. Pound,
Cantos, XXVII.

"Look up at the Heavens and
count the stars, if you can count
them… So shall be your seed."
Genesis 15:5, in R. Crumb,
The Book of Genesis Illustrated.

"In order to reach a good understanding of things below it is thus necessary to rise toward the heights, and, looking down from above, to gain an overview…Thus, Maximus of Tyre invokes a passage in Homer where Ulysses is led to observe a people's customs from a high place. Aristotle in this sense wrote that if we found ourselves above the heavens we could know for ourselves the causes of the eclipses of the Sun and of the Moon … And Cicero, in the dream of Scipio the Younger relates that the latter's grandfather showed him terrestrial things from up in the sky."
Giulo Camillo,
The Theater of Memory.

"Sure of having traveled far,
one finds that one is looking down
on oneself from above."
Michel Foucault, "Introduction,"
in *The Use of Pleasure.*

"Many times I've gone past /
the fifth floor, / cranking upward,
but only once / have I gone
all the way up / … Floor six thousand:
/ the stars, / skeletons on fire, /
their arms singing. / And a key, /
a very large key, / that opens
something—/ some useful door—
/ somewhere—/ up there."
Anne Sexton,
"Riding the Elevator Into the Sky"

the poop deck … together with
ben-Cnopee the Lensman, who
shifted position from the plug-ins
of the Kalishnikov console to
the standard stoppage network
of the Mammon panel;
Sokrates the Helmsman, who
moved from the drainage slopes
of the Skull Gallery to
the emancipated Metal vents
of the gas cylinder;
and Cîpher the Ordinary Sailor,
who shifted from the Monotonous
flywheels to the input-outlet
of the #1 lithium mold.

Concurrently, as the ship
showed signs of swaying back
to its Tipping Point, the imprint
of the Yonaguni shoreline—
projected along the decks by
the wind-swept falling water
from the Miraculous Faucet—
gave the aft movements to
redistribute weight on the ship
an Aura of Story, for
the Symposium's participants
in particular and
for Vico most of all.

Stepping aft on the Observation
Deck from the Venus pillar to
the Mercury pillar, which stood
abandoned following Bismark's
Death, Vico exclaimed: "I am
transported like Badr of Homes
from the Big Wheel of Cope
to the Tower of Pay
in the tale told by Goodchilde
the Studious in days of yore!"

Sinbad, an adept of Deadpan,
retreating to take Vico's
place by the pillar of Venus,
replied: "You and I are like
Koffi and Blondi at Lover's Leap
in 'The Story of the Mystery

"Night comes, an angel stands / Measuring out the time of stars, / Still are the winds, and still the hours. / ...It would be peace to lie / Still in the still hours at the angel's feet, / Upon a star hung in a starry sky, / But hearts another measure beat."
Kathleen Raine, "Nocturne."

"From a systems theory perspective, periods of turbulence such as we have experienced in recent decades can lead to a range of possible outcomes. They may resolve into a new and stable equilibrium that can be expected to have a long life. They may lead to oscillating equilibria, a condition in which the social system snaps back and forth between two extremes. Or what appears to be an end to turbulence may be only another period of experimentation in an adaptational process that is still under way."
Sandra Braman,
Change of State.

"Ramona liked people who got excited."
Beverly Clearly,
Ramona the Brave.

"Let us plunge in the flood of time and chance, / Into the tide of circumstance! Let grief and gratification, / Success and frustration / Spell one another as they can, / Restless doing is the only way for man."
J. W. Goethe,
Faust, Part I.

"the Abyss / blanched / spread / furious / beneath an incline /

Writer's Dilemma' by Ys the Empath"; to which Vico, increasingly tense and nervous, responded with the insight that, by falling back, Kongō, beside the pillar of Mars, would be to them what LaLanne was to Masrûr the Hunchback and Schrödinger of Saïs in "The Demon of Analogy's Travel Adventures with Puf the Cursed Poet."

So, when Kongō did in effect move aft toward the pillar of the Soul Incarnate, Vico said that by taking Sinbad's place Kongō was being released from the pillar of Mars just as Timaeus was released from Scipio's Prison-House of Allegory by telling the story of Zozimos's escape from the Cubicle of Abraxas in "The Fairy Tales of Mount Ararat" by Grandmaster H'llaj.

Vico added that by leaving the pillar of Jupiter for the pillar of Mars, Cowabunga would be doing for the entire crew what Cadmus did for Montignac in the story about the Moon that Mardrus told to Layli, after Abelard told it to her in "The Love Stories and Wisdom Tales of Sina Weibo."

And to the extent that the maneuvers on the Observation Deck —as Cowabunga moved aft— were restoring the ship to its Tipping Point, Vico was essentially correct.

desperately plane / on a wing /
its own / fallen / / back in advance
from being unable to dress its flight."
Stéphane Mallarmé,
"A Throw of the Dice
Will Never Abolish Chance."

"The way up and the way
down are the same."
Heraclitus,
Fragments.

"What has risen may sink,
and what has sunk may rise."
H. P. Lovecraft,
"The Call of Cthulhu."

"The psyche rises as a mist
from things that are wet."
Heraclitus,
Fragments.

"I am convinced that from
the heads of all ponderous
profound beings, such as Plato,
Pyrrho, the Devil, Jupiter, Dante ...
there always goes up a certain
semi-visible steam, while in
the act of thinking deep thoughts."
H. Melville,
Moby Dick.

"Ahab, too, is a poet of eloquence.
He says, 'The path to my fixed
purpose is laid with iron rails
whereon my soul is grooved
to run.' Or these lines,
'All visible objects are but
pasteboard masks.' Quotable
poetic phrases that can't be beat."
Bob Dylan,
Nobel Prize acceptance speech.

"Been to hell in a boat yet?"
Ezra Pound,
Cantos, XXXIX.

Balance was achieved
after Commander Exprès
Coughed Up again and Venus,
reading the projected Spit
on the Glass as a sign
that the two of them
should go below deck,
clapped his hands and opened
the door to the stairway
under the poop deck, down which
they went, to station themselves
in the Commander's cabin.

Meanwhile, I stayed where I was,
by the Pillar of Intelligible
Worlds and Simple Elements.

As soon as the ship was
level again on the Big Wave's
crest, we faced a situation where
the Climate, inside the Cloud of
Blue-Red haze that engulfed us,
began to change.

The haze produced a sensation
of Heat, that grew more intense
and caused our joints to ache,
our limbs to tingle and
our backs to bend,
while a film of foaming
water kept spreading over
all parts of the vessel.

Wind stirred the atmosphere
from every direction, causing
the haze to swirl around us.

As the Warming intensified
and sea foam coated the ship,
we were overwhelmed by
scratching in the throat and
unrelenting fits of coughing;
nostrils suddenly blocked;
failing vision; headaches;
confused thinking.

"The bonds of heaven are
slipp'd, dissolv'd and loos'd."
W. Shakespeare,
Troilus and Cressida.

"The black sky was underpinned
with long silver streaks that looked
like scaffolding and depth on depth
behind it were thousands of stars
that all seemed to be moving very
slowly as if they were about some
vast construction work that involved
the whole order of the universe
and would take all time to complete.
No one was paying any attention
to the sky."
Flannery O'Connor,
Wise Blood.

"Some people don't understand.
Help them, God."
Jimi Hendrix,
"Nine to the Universe."

"A man is a god in ruins."
Ralph Waldo
Emerson,
Nature.

"There are three truths …
Your truth … My truth …
And the truth."
Peter Brook and
Marie-Hélène Estienne,
Why?

"When God says
'I Am Lived,'
we'll have forgotten
what all the parting
was about."
J. Kerouac,
Satori in Paris.

"It is first necessary to condense
the thesis of Vico, the scientific
historian. In the beginning was
the thunder: the thunder set free

Despite the onset of Madness,
Vico alone seemed to understand
what was going on.

Between a) the "Deep Learning"
from the vessel's upward
trajectory along the "fluid
tunnel" and "mathematical
river" of the Big Wave's rise,
b) the critical flow speed of
the vessel's slide into and
out of Disequilibrium,
and c) the "singularity of
the bubbling phaenomenon"
in a situation of reestablished
Equilibrium, Vico saw
our present course as
the sign of an ineluctable
return to "a shielded
emptiness ending in union
with the nearly infinite—"

While continuing to
theorize, however, Vico
unexpectedly stopped
in mid-sentence, and
fell into Deep Thought.

Soon the Steam started rising
from the crown of Vico's head;
and gradually the realization set in
that the surrounding haze was
beginning to recede, and change
Color … until the moment at last
when we found ourselves on
a foam-free vessel completely
enclosed inside a Green bubble
at the top of the Wave.

Then Vico succumbed
to Sleep, and keeled over.

Whether it was the Steam
escaping from Vico's head, or
Death's release of Vico's spirit,

Religion, in its most objective and
unphilosophical form—idolatrous
animism: Religion produced Society,
and the first social men were
the cave-dwellers. Taking refuge
from a passionate Nature:
this primitive family life receives
its first impulse towards development
from the arrival of terrified
vagabonds: admitted, they are
the first slaves: growing stronger,
they exact agrarian concessions,
and a despotism has evolved into
a primitive feudalism: the cave
becomes a city, and the feudal system
a democracy: then an anarchy;
this is corrected by a return to monarchy;
the last stage is a tendency toward
interdestruction: the nations are
dispersed and the Phoenix of Society
arises out of their ashes."
Samuel Beckett,
"Dante … Bruno .. Vico . Joyce"

"Pataphysics is the science
of imaginary solutions."
Alfred Jarry,
The Exploits and Opinions of
Doctor Faustroll, Pataphysician.

"The angel Raphael
represents the Central Column
Energy of Balance
and illuminates the color Green."
Zohar, "Vayera."

"Within the skull the skill / within
the winter dream the whirligig /
within within / all & everything : /
'Ing' supreme rune and secret song
of 'Ong.' / Forget all derivations, /
they dance in happiness, / the early
ones down there, / and this isn't
myth of origin / or oozing essence
of origin. / … Origin is beautiful as
black / and centers whirl around us
as we round them in."

or mere chance that instigated
the change, the ship now began
to tip in the opposite direction …
toward the stern.

The imbalance inside the bubble was
aggravated by the manic energy
that immediately ensued above
and below the forward decks.

The challenge was to restore
the ship's Equilibrium,
while tossing Vico's body
overboard ASAP—
to avoid the creation of
a metaphysical Shithole
caused by the presence
of a skeleton on board
after the dissemination
of Vico's flesh.

Anna-O ordered Sony, Scard'nelli,
Thebes and Rosetta to throw
Vico's corpse over the side;
but, taking her cue from Thebes
the Weatherwoman, successor
to Occam, who frantically
recalled the "mini-migrations"
across the polluted decks of
the ROJAVA before the doomed
ship capsized in the Black Sea
of Change, the Captain—over
the sudden cascading Sound
of an intense meteor shower,
in Heavens we could not see—
also ordered that Rosetta
the Bo'sun, who served as
Scard'nelli's replacement,
Sound the Whistle
during the course
of the crew's reshuffling.

As a result, throughout
a first phase of operations,
Kongō, Sinbad, Cowabunga
and myself—moving forward—
changed places with Rosetta,
Thebes, Scard'nelli and

Gerrit Lansing (*RIP*), "In Erasmus
Darwin's Generous Light."

"The north-south axis is highlighted. The bird's eye and the staff are at 0°/ north, establishing a basic point of reference … If one traces a straight line over the 'spears,' one notices that the two solstitial axes are present: the big 'spear' that wounds the bison is directed along the axis of the rising sun of summer (56°), setting sun of winter (236°). The small 'spear' is directed from the rising sun of winter (124°) to the setting sun of summer (304°) … One finds, gathered and carefully preserved by the Paleothics … all the coordinates of the solar stations that fulfill the conditions indicated by Vitruvius two thousand years ago. If pre-historians felt Lascaux to be a sanctuary, it is because the 'squaring of the circle' had been realized, inscribed, then preserved by Paleolithics, probably so that it would then be understood and transmitted."
Chantal Jègues-Woliewiez,
"Lascaux and the Stars."

"The Mog-ur … had forged indelible new paths in her brain, paths that let her glimpse ahead, but he could not forge new paths in his own. While she looked beyond, he caught a glimpse, not of the future, but of a sense of future. A future that was hers, but not his."
Jean M. Auel,
The Clan of the Cave Bear.

"While you rested in the sloth of your eternity, on the proceeds from Year 1, the spirit of man, rid of its dimwittedness by you! ... ended up assailing the grounds of Creation. They discovered in the intimacy of bodies, as if prior

Sony, moving aft; and then,
in a second phase, Wang and
Marlboro—moving aft—
changed places with Tarzan,
Kongō, Sinbad and Cowabunga,
moving forward.

To the Sound of the Ritornello
from Corso's *Fantasia for
Desire, Destiny, Myth and
Reality*, as played by Rosetta
on the Bo'sun's Whistle,
Sony, Scard'nelli, Thebes and
Rosetta surrounded the body of
Vico, while at the same time,
toward the bow, we assumed
our new stations, as ordered.

No sooner had Rosetta
stopped blowing the Whistle
than the ship swung back
into Equilibrium.

Then, at once, the Green
bubble enclosing us
burst open; and the Black
starry Night returned.

Wasting no time,
Sony, Scard'nelli, Thebes
and Rosetta grabbed Vico
by the arms and legs,
and on the count of three
heaved the corpse overboard,
larboard side.

Vico's body dropped into
the distance way below, before
disappearing in the Silver Sea.

The ship has so far
remained stable, confirming
Anna-O's intuition that
the chosen spot, above deck
—directly in line with

to their reality, the old CHAOS."
Paul Valéry,
My Faust.

"I I bought thought and so you
come here you you come here and
not today not any can play I look
and see, no no I cannot look no no
I cannot see and you you you see …"
Gertrude Stein,
Doctor Faustus Lights the Lights.

"Hamlet wavered for all of us."
Emily Dickinson (L512).

"Do not become enamored
of power."
M. Foucault,
Preface to *Anti-Oedipus*
(G. Deleuze & F. Guattari).

"Man is the violent one,
not aside from and along
with other attributes but
solely in the sense
that in his fundamental
violence [*Gewalt-tätigkeit*]
he uses power [*Gewalt*]
against the over-powering
[*Überwältigende*]."
Martin Heidegger,
"The Ode on Man
in Sophocles' *Antigone*."

"Many the wonders,
but none more awesome
than man who sails
the grey winter sea, and rides
the crests of furious waves."
Sophocles,
Antigone.

the Dormant body of Möbius,
suspended below deck—
was the practical solution
for throwing Vico overboard
without getting the vessel to tip,
backward or forward, down
the slope of the Big Wave.

Indeed, reading Commander
Exprès's Spit on the Glass again,
Venus reflected that our ship
had Mutated "from Paranoia
Machine to Miraculating
Machine"; and he added that
the difficulties we continue to
experience, psychologically and
technologically, are the result
of an internalized repulsion /
attraction dynamic originating
from the ship's back-and-forth
movement on top of the Wave.

Star mapping as a result
has been resumed, to provide
guidance from the Heavens,
with Tarzan, Sony, Scard'nelli,
Thebes, Rosetta, ben-Cnopee
and Sokrates assigned
to the Observation Deck's
seven Pillars of Wisdom.

Despite all, the whole
crew seems to share
the feeling that a spirit
of Camaraderie is always
already sustaining us—
erotically, theoretically,
politically—until the end.

We sail on together,
my love.

STEPHANIE STRICKLAND

Micronesia

we follow *our* compass—a road in the cloud of stars—
                                        moment

by moment tugging against the winds, the trades, El Niño,
                                        the doldrums;

rolling underneath us bass chords—we listen for the ocean's thrum,
                                        unfailing

deep tone overtopped, overrun by local gusts, by distant
                                        storms—

we seek rebound wavelets picked out from delicate, interval iteration, probing
                                        the sea,

fingers trailing & cupped, to parse them as they pass through wavering
                                        boom;

stretched, blind, in the bottom of a carved canoe, aligned with keel
                                        groove

we undo—our bones ajar, read—the sea's commotion as we feel for a
                                        wave

bounced back from a far, yet unexplored, shore—Now, half an earth
                                        away,

broken ice, a shore *never* seen. On watch, none sleep for more than 20 minutes
                                        —world

around, the surge, the rising tidal crack overwhelms small island
                                        rafts

plunging deeper than "did ever plummet sound."
                                        The knell

resounding, in our ear, on every island echoing ...
                                        unfathomed

numbers   tell us, again, how it comes to be   we
                                        drown

Arthur Sze

Salt Song

Zunis make shrines on the way to a lake where I emerge   and Miwoks gather me out of pools along the Pacific   the cheetah thirsts for me   and when you sprinkle me on rib eye you have no idea how I balance silence with thunder in crystal   you dream of butterfly hunting in Madagascar   spelunking through caves echoing with dripping stalactites   and you don't see how I yearn to shimmer an orange aurora against flame look at me in your hand   in Egypt I scrubbed the bodies of kings and queens   in Pakistan I zigzag upward through twenty-six miles of tunnels before drawing my first breath in sunlight   if you heat a kiln to 2380 degrees and scatter me inside   I vaporize and bond with clay   in this unseen moment a potter prays because my pattern is out of his hands   and when I touch your lips   you salivate   and when I dissolve on your tongue   your hair rises   ozone unlocks   a single stroke of lightning sizzles to earth.

Doppler Effect

Stopped in cars, we are waiting to accelerate
along different trajectories. I catch the rising

pitch of a train—today one hundred nine people
died in a stampede converging at a bridge;

radioactive water trickles underground
toward the Pacific Ocean; nickel and copper

particulates contaminate the Brocade River.
Will this planet sustain ten billion people?

Ah, switch it: a spider plant leans toward
a glass door, and six offshoots dangle from it;

the more I fingered the clay slab into a bowl,
the more misshapen it became; though I have

botched this, bungled that, the errancies
reveal it would not be better if things happened

just as I wished; a puffer fish inflates on deck;
a burst of burnt rubber rises from pavement.

Margo Taft Stever

Three Ravens Watch

after Winter Landscape with Skaters and Bird Traps
Pieter Bruegel, 1565

If you were a smooth, shiny circle, we would collect
you for our nests, but your bodies shuffle mindlessly
back and forth. You forget when the ice was thin, when
many of you fell through, trapped underneath.

This harshest winter attracts you to skate, to forget
your misery, scrawling patterns in ice. Ravens,
three of us, stand sentinel, noticing
your slow-witted motions, your clumsy sprawls.

From our high perch, we witness eerie cries of brothers
and sisters lured inside your net strung across the trees.
We hear them crash to the bottom, caught on the great awl,
entangled in the glistening awfulness, your web.

Do not forget, you who now skate, that you will return
to your endless winter, bread riots, witch
hunts, old widowed women targeted, and frozen birds
falling from the sky. We know that you want to eat us.

Snow fell in July; men froze to death in September.
Grapes for wine would not ripen. Parasites thrived under
snow and destroyed your crops. You carry your corpses
in carts; your dead litter the ground in rough cloth shrouds.

Branches extend over ice, harbingers of death;
we know that you want to eat us. You also believe
witches cause livestock epidemics, make cows give
too little milk, create early frosts, and all the unknown

diseases; witch trials can stop bad weather. *Ye gripping*
trappe made of yrne, the lowest barre and the hoope with
two clickets, the devil scourge of all the earth. Remember
ice will again be as thin as this diffused light.

Harriet Tarlo

from *cut flowers*

for Rachel Blau DuPlessis

rhubarb, *we take it in us arms*
footwork, fancy   footwork slide
stepping legs   walking between
stalks, candles   *we don't want you*
people   *falling into it* or thru
into spring   Persephone maybe
every dark   birthday girl/witch
divided day

might be a garden to get back from
out of   somewhere state
struggles   tall yellow perennial
smaller   pages, a little bit
wilder   rarer weeds
botanical   personalities
birthwort   300 years growing
right here

play while you walk the flatscape fox
& pigeon   the oldest streets, trees
of the city   steel security lamps
spin round   barbed wire buddleia
over roof   over ex--smog brick
all ivy   *does* flower in sky
almost   upside down, hanging
dying

thronging to be excluded in every field
division   gibberish -- plantation crop
down   *there are lots of them but that was*
that one   the horizon come down: height
changed   depth, darkness *one* slingering
treads   decreasing circle on imagined
earth   something starts to bite
neck

three distant things that look like sheep
but don't   move, forgotten things
grey dawn   mild December
lyric skin   cloud passing moon
shows   raw fields & solstice
a moment   *how many nights are we*
staying   when luck turns. Never
enough

from Humberston to Tetney Lock 2013–2019

out from Tetney
stand alone gate
tall reeds
steel grey canal
starling packs
field side
larks, wind
oil pipe loop over
geese flights go

LAND ONLY
fencing fallen
teasels bent to water
push ripple wind
turning, searching
over midden
insistent calling
at path's turn in
out to the mouth

7–8 March 2013

for Linda Ingham

sun penumbra mist

high path through sky
between
field-side, marsh-side
moles up-earthing
shell-laced soil from
under

oystercatchers, ducks, geese
call over—egret white
in wetland

still windmills
I have not ever seen
one move

only birds cross over
and seed:
teasel, good king henry

taken warm root in
field-margin, ochre marsh
silver-brown, salt-rich

stone embrasures small
protections, growing
grass, gold-grey lichens

on mist-edges, forts
at sea, oil tanks float out
over-land
quiet in mist quieter
river reaching
always reaching
sea

waterside winter purples
elder and alder
old low hawthorn tight
yellow-green tips
in red-pink leaf-bud
last year's berries softening
in to their own skins
catkins and cones hanging
over   sky-side
falling, some to land
some to water

early to hear skylarks
singing over Tetney
what we hear is there
but cannot see
have never yet seen

29 March 2019

behind two reflective men ROBOCUT rolls crushing
grass, tin, glass, plants, shells slow over flood bank
to first gate no hawthorn, no alder, no birdsong but
far inland over canal, fields, trees to Tetney
shrunk beneath
windmills

or down on marsh in & out
of ochre egrets fly land
fly over gold-brown pools, matted
gold-grass fallen swirls white
wings picking up first flicker flowers
of scurvy grass

shorn path cut banks all way to
oil pipe turn stumps and chips
stumps and chips no making
of nest homes, weaving or woven
past & present gone save
a dandelion, little clump
of vetch returning

red glove on rusted gate, hand done
soapy water
fast flows into channel bubbling out
to sea
out to no-elder horizon, no haven
branches laid out, yellow-lichen living
still corpse beside its 8 sawn stems

you could see that tree, hear it, from everywhere

oystercatchers, geese, knots fly up & on
pushed out as we pass by concrete bridges
over sea lavender un-flowering
rusted gas cooker, faded balls
laid out marsh into mud, samphire stubs
salt steaks, yellow oil can
scattered rocks
to loud honking mouth of estuary
final red warning post
at the tapering out

Brian Teare

Clear Water Renga

for Brenda Hillman and Martha Serpas

fog, error, radar
failed :: the container ship hit
the bridge tower hard ::

its hull split, spilled fifty eight
thousand gallons of bunker

fuel oil :: November
seventh, 2007 ::
the next day it hurt

the eyes to walk dock-side, wind
bringing the sting of petrol ::

each of its pilings
ringed with rainbow, from the pier
I watched white boats go

trailing bright yellow booms, saw
how the real absorbs a fact

the way a seabird
preens its greased wings helplessly,
the ordinary

gesture gently carrying
toxins from feather to beak,

from outside to in ::
it was the first disaster
I could walk to, look

at until it ceased to seem
exceptional, no matter

the panic I felt
watching an oiled Western grebe

thrash against capture,

no matter the bird slipping
in the clear plastic tub slicked

by its own feathers,
its rescuer trying to
contain it without

injury :: easier to
watch rescuers soak the bird

in warm water, Dawn
dish soap :: easier to watch
them scrape each feather

clean with a kids' toothbrush :: but
I couldn't get over it,

how the real couldn't
refuse, could do nothing but
disburse tar ball, sheen,

& slick from the central Bay
on currents west through the Gate

until the whole coast,
Marin to Pacifica
to the Farallones,

absorbed the new fact the real
had given it :: & didn't

each image likewise
sink into my mind's archive
of the disaster,

each stashed fact evidence of
an attachment to events

I neither forget
nor understand :: for three years
I've kept newspaper

clippings & old emails, kept
the photo of an oiled surf

scoter in the hands
of a panicked passerby,
Megan McNertny,

who tried, untrained, to save it
barehanded, its smeared feathers

as flat black & wet
as its eye eying the lens ::
I've kept some numbers ::

seven thousand birds dead, two
hundred miles of coast coated,

forty four point four
million dollars paid by Fleet
Management, owners

of the Cosco-Busan wreck ::
I've kept track of herring spawn

exposed to fuel oil,
how sunlight creates photo-
toxic conditions

crippling embryonic fish,
how herring won't return to

seasonal breeding
grounds polluted by the spill ::
& I've kept track of

other disasters that came
up close :: in 2008

the Summit Fire
in the Santa Cruz Mountains
consumed four thousand

acres in six days in May,

& the next year in August

the Lockheed Fire burned
nearly eight thousand acres
in eleven days ::

a tarry charred horizon
drew the sun down, blunted light

fat with ash that stuck
to our window sills :: each day
a weird hot wind left

evidence of how crisis
becomes most real through firsthand

fact :: the war'd been on
all those years but not so close
I could walk to it,

its smoke staining my snot black,
meaning, I think, the local

real made me begin
to experience the mind
as a form porous

as mile after mile of trees
accepting fire, to begin

to see aftermath
as the start of thought, the way
some conifers need

extreme heat to unseal seeds
locked in the resinous bracts

of cones :: Monterey,
Knobcone, & Bishop pines, born
natives of flame :: but

I couldn't get over it,
the endless capacity

of the real for fact,
how it seems to have at core
endless hollowness

my mind can never mimic
given its capacity

for reaction, how
the real will accept any
thing, but when I looked

up at the drift of cinders
& soot that settled a singe

in the trees, I knew
I was afraid :: a raptor's
accurate shadow

falling over me always
premonitory, I go

north to Marin, miles
from any city limit,
to land protected

by law, to walk, to outpace
panic as if my mind could

give like the long lines
of wire fence that guide the drive
to Tomales Point ::

Pierce Point Road rides out over
hills dry in July :: high fire

danger day, grasses
a gold nerve pricked by thistle ::
though "scenic views" line
the road, the surround is sky
without horizon, silver

vague sun haze :: vision's
discursive limit :: mostly

I want to live there,

the precise site the mind stops
its blameless languaging job ::

as if there the real
stops burning, oil its gush from
the uncapped well :: no ::

it's July 2010 ::
I've spent weeks watching YouTube

footage of a flight
over BP's Deepwater
Horizon oil spill ::

John L. Wathen, Tom Hutchins,
& David Helvarg took off

on June 25th
from Gulf Shores, Alabama,
five hours due south of

my hometown :: "It didn't take
long to find our first oil. In

the mouth of Mobile
Bay there were scattered patches
of light sheen behind

the islands," Dauphin Island
the one I know from summer

roadtrips years before
Gulf barrier islands lost
landmass & wildlife

habitat to Katrina ::
footage shows just "1.2

miles off Gulf Shores there
was a solid mass of oil.

On previous flights

behind Petit Bois Island,
all we'd seen was light sheen—now

it was turning to
darker pink mats, some miles long
& hundreds of feet
wide." :: all day as I walk out
to Tomales Point & back

the soft warm water
distant in crisis churns, turns
the Pacific strange ::

a high white sun blanks the waves
whitecaps shatter with spindrift

& the burning Gulf
keeps burning, water on fire
the purest endgame,

obvious allegory
like some Revelations plague,

chapter eight verse ten ::
after the first & second
angels, what soul could

watch the third bear its trumpet
& not fear the imminent

music, the song meant
to call a star down to earth
to fall bitterness

"on a third of the rivers
& the springs of the waters"

& turn the waters
to wormwood :: I ask you :: who
could watch & forget

the sour wells & fallow
fields that follow industry

where it follows us ::
I walk north & find lupine
opening its sweet

furred purse of bees :: to the east
where gusts rip through Windy Gap,

hawks, wings rigid, ride
zephyrs so fierce it takes strength
to go nowhere :: here

the cobweb thistle's winding
a bobbin's worth of white silk

through white-tipped spikes :: but
I can't forget to rewind
the crisis, to pause

the footage where the plane spots
a pod of dolphins, their fins

streaked with sheen :: I can't
forget Coast Guard planes have been
sent over the coast

at night to spray Corexit,
a dispersant BP thought

would ease the cleanup
but instead bonds with the oil
to create toxins

that move through skin & rupture
red blood cells, toxins that cause

internal bleeding
& indefinite headaches
in oil cleanup crews

& folks living near the spill ::

it even disrupts the life

cycles of marine
animals by dispersing
the lipids in sperm,

the toxins piggybacking
on reproduction to turn

life against itself ::
I can't forget how we've made
a poison nature's

second nature, how the real
seems dependent on this fact ::

everywhere we live
we destroy life :: I could walk
due north all my years

& never not stand the way
I stand on land Coast Miwok

once camped on to fish
peak salmon runs :: seasonal,
cyclical, the tribe

for centuries walked to shore
then walked back inland to hunt

Mule deer, centuries
following sustenance through
landscape :: settlers

uncalendared that walking
ritual, the hunt's sacred

to-&-fro :: after
displacement, European
disease, slavery,

& assimilation, few

members of the tribe survived

by 1880
when Pierce Point Ranch raised cattle
for butter & cheese

sold south to San Francisco ::
it challenges the white mind

to look at this coast
& think *this is a ruin* ::
yellow bush lupine

grows so thick I have to push
through it toward the Pacific

light unfolding, flexed
open like a gold poppy ::
the Pierce family ranched

until forty years ago,
after dairy cows raised on

European feed
grass extirpated native
coastal prairie plants

& the Tule elk who fed
on them :: after the ranch closed,

its white barn quiet,
the point became national
seashore :: a mile north

of the Upper Ranch, our long
fraught occupation flowers

non-native clover
& rye grazed off-trail by elk
calves & their mothers,

part of a four-hundred head
herd whose progenitors were

brought back to the Point
in the Seventies, a herd
monitored year-round

by park rangers housed on this
land once traveled by Miwok

whose descendants live
inland with Southern Pomo
on land the tribes, now

Federated Indians
of Graton Rancheria,

bought & put in trust ::
life, habitat, & ruin
run recombinant

& helical in hurt forms
that keep life going & do

not heal, its pattern
the gist of a missive sent
by my friend Martha,

southern Louisiana,
June 10th :: "After some time home,

it's clear—the drilling
moratorium's no good.
The economy

will collapse, stranding people
& undercutting support

for alternative
energy research. Nothing
moves forward as long

as green energy & oil
are antagonists. These folks

have worked to feed us

for years. To abandon them
is not right." :: for years

I've walked as far as it takes
to walk past thought into what

might be called image,
non-discursive :: I spend hours
so empty my mind's

the ranch barn open both ends
to wind, nothing but old hay

stirring in the stalls ::
it used to seem indulgent
to vanish outward

into the texture of elk
fur on the hills of White Gulch,

its two-toned velvet
gold then brown against brighter
brittle grasses, but

even then I still dwell in
the real, our occupation,

the American
goldfinch husking invasive
thistle seed for feed

the large paradox writ small ::
each image that replaces

consciousness *is*
the real, as temporary
as any desire

to do no harm here, the mind
a Bishop pine splayed by wind

during its long wait
for fire, local to this

coast & a native

of the phenomenal world ::
toward sunset, I stop, sit

at the lower Ranch
pond, its worn shore scored with sedge
& the hooves of elk ::

in such late light its surface
relaxes, pure reflection ::

I look :: an elk steps
forward from the sedge :: it steps
into the image

of an elk who steps forward
from the sedge & bends its head

to drink from my mouth ::
& bends & from my mouth
drinks clear water ::

Orchid Tierney

some ode, odor

Methanobacterium aarhusense is a salty stretch. A sweet scratch.
shale gas is a major player
A bad egg and flatus. In fact, it is a nonmotile mesophilic, halophilic
world of thought
and finical filamentous microbe that thrives best at temperatures
from the moment the invaders arrived … they were doomed
of 45°C. In 2004 scientists had isolated this strain in marine samples
low-hanging fruit to slow global warming
collected from below the sediment surface in Aarhus Bay, a waterway
do you guys have staging areas set up for emergencies like … at the golf course?
on the Danish coast of Jutland. They described their cultivated colonies
most popular story: the end is nigh
as "circular and greyish surrounded by a whitish zone."
the Stars … cause the changes, seasons, and successive courses or interchanges
They said: these cells are indecisive:
you make images—that's pretty solid—music, it's liquid
straight or crooked, lonely or coupled, filaments or clumpy.
there is no lasting damage to the environment in that area
They enjoy intimacy to particles, make methane, haunt hydrogen,
like the water in a bathtub with an open faucet
convert energy, share kinship with similar methanogenic archaea.
and a plugged drain
In fact: novel organisms. In fact: microscopic and occultic.
sinks of methane
In fact, occultic because beautiful. But ugly and modern too.
removes unnecessary and duplicative regulatory burdens from the oil and gas industry
Because between five and eighteen micrometers long,
we've got it covered, we know what's going on, it's fine
methanobacterium are liminal and leaky, but not ghost nor spirit
a carbon-climate feedback
but bond and brine, gnome not geest, matter and materialised through
methane budget
the metaphor-making of electron microscopes and whitish zones.
if something vaporizes, that's the intellect
But however nominal these microbe organisms are,
it takes a village to put things back together
they stay sticky and silent. A small thing, in fact. Easily washed away,

a medley of maladies

and hidden underneath sediment strata; ephemeral too

new regulations put in place … should prevent this type of incident from occurring again

because they're nothing like we're something

about the weight of a whopping 425,000 elephants

but ready to cut skins, organs; even rotten eggs, when they quietly surface.

distinct fingerprint of methane from burning

This is the narrative: maybe we're born with it. Maybe it's methane.

operations at the well pad are back to normal

In October 2015 the residents of the upscale neighborhood Porter Ranch

a ping-pong game of explanations

in San Fernando Valley inhaled bad eggs and clouds.

carbon wraps the world in a sheet

Six miles away, the SoCal Gas-owned Aliso Canyon storage

I signifie … these by the new name of Blas

facility experienced a catastrophic blowout, leaking over 97,000 tonnes

methane budget

of methane into the atmosphere until workers successfully

methane is more like a wool blanket

sealed the site in February 2016. Methane imaginaries are slippery:

wood-wide web

8000 residents fled, leaving Porter Ranch a ghost town. Two schools shuttered,

mix around the world multiple times

organs reported nosebleeds, headaches, vertigo, and

chemical signature

respiratory distress. Yes, we know such clouds, some blas, in fact.

Yet methane is an uncanny sink of risk on

an unconcentrated hazard dispersed through pipelines

landfills and in cities, in factories and refineries, on farms and in oceans.

the outer shell of methane molecule consists of

After the Mather Mine explosion, Aliso remains the worst in the country.

industry red tape

After the Consolidated School of New London explosion, Aliso remains

Cthulhu not kin

the worst in the country. After the Richmond, Indiana, explosion,

should have plugged the leak sooner

Aliso remains the worst in the county. After the Cleveland East Ohio gas explosion

spewing gas and brine

Aliso remains the worst in the country. Before the Belmont County, Ohio blowout,

fugitive emissions

on which satellite seers shape data, mulched from metaphor,

the gaz is blas is blast is flatus is gnome but not geest
Aliso was the worst in the country. Also Aliso.
It is the age of gaslitment, tender human stomachs, burping lakes
gaseous modernity
and cow plumbing. We forget such clouds and rotten eggs,
cosmic fear
folding contours of space and dirt. Yet when investigators attributed
silent death
the axial rupture at Aliso to external microbial corrosions, they found something
were undone … the tiniest creatures that God in his wisdom put upon this earth
like we're nothing. In Aliso's casings, they collected a whitish zone.
In California, they found Aarhus Bay.

carbon sink

A tree's list of ocean plastic:

fish plaiting rayon thread
sud currents fill viney frill
crabs pinching pen caps
nurdle cud
and polyester shrimp
oar feet
gelatinous jelly bags
venus flower baskets
pink vase
or toothpaste tubing
sea gooseberry
and brittle star
braining beads with
bottled spookfish
cholera commas
Japanese petronauts, who discovered bacteria burrow into pits of ocean plastic,
gorging themselves on melted cells of polythene surfaces
like *hot barbecue briquette thrown into snow*
meal moths
and wax moths wearing
tattered pants made with ultrasued

and tar balls
glad wrap anemone
poems like islands without bridges or causeways
(that is, you have to *work* to get *there*. Trust me, there's a metronome to my magpie)

also inhaled questions that are not questions:
how to love a virus with concussive tenderness
how to scale eroticism to two chromosomes, which colonise the soupy
islands (we're caught between a romance and a hard plaint)
the islandary vs. the planetary
capitalism: the fine art of terraforming seas
and feeling empathy for bottle caps bursting with dead sea birds

To the Is-Land

An island is a phantom or a woman

sea captains and writers imagined the former

(no woman is no-island)

they remembered names but not locations,

blanks but not their beauty,

they pinpointed indices on charts

wove stories laced with herbs,

they wondered

how solid is the ocean?

What do you call the place that was but no longer haunts?

their ghosts made an anthem for digital nations:

Tuanaki, Terra Nova, Podesta, Thompson Island, Rupes Nigra, Sandy Island, Nimrod Islands, New South Greenland, Pepys Island, St. Matthew's Island, Kantia, Crockerland, Thule, Antillia, Aurora Islands, Rivadeneyra Shoal, Pactolus Bank, Bacalao, Bermeja, the Island of California, Juan de Lisboa, Torca Island, Santanazes, Doughtery Island, Brasil, Royal Company's Islands, Filippo Reef, Firsland, Groclant, Ganges Island, Sannikov Land, Ilha de Vera Cruz, Estotiland, Fata Morgana Land, Sarah Ann Island, Petermannland, Emerald Island, Isle of Demons, Washusett Reef, Ernest Legouve, Buss Island, Saint Brendan's Island, Los Jardines, Isle of Mam, Maria Laxar, Tabor Island, Jupiter Reef, Nu Zild

phantom islands are archives somewhere between analogue and wet

see: *Utopia*
see: no place

the green blooms will drown you, said the Island to the petronaut

At 8:05 am on January 13, 2018, an employee at the Hawai'i Emergency Management Agency or HEMA initiated an internal test by pressing the wrong menu option, thus sending a false alert to the cellphones of hundreds of residents and tourists in the area: BALLISTIC MISSILE THREAT INBOUND TO HAWAII. SEEK IMMEDIATE SHELTER. THIS IS NOT A DRILL

anyone watching their television screens at the same time would have received calmer instructions:

> "If you are indoors, stay indoors. If you are outdoors, seek immediate shelter in a building. Remain indoors well away from windows. If you are driving, pull safely to the side of the road and seek shelter in a building or lay on the floor."

(but would a nuclear missile target Hawai'i or Hawaii? What *is* the difference? Discuss it dreamily)

the incident reminds us that the nuclear holocaust has already happened at sea and on the Susquehanna River

see: the Marshall Islands
see: Muroroa
see: Three Mile Island

like the fluid apostrophe in Hawaii, islands have always been a sacrifice zone for one empire or another

see: *Island of Doctor Moreau*
see: *Shutter Island*
see: *Island of Lost Souls*
see: *Jurassic Park*
see:

that Hawaii could have been atomized is not a bug, but a feature of the imperial program

after all, islands have been systematically used throughout Franco-German-Spanish-Portuguese-Austro-New Zealand-British-American histories to quarantine the empires' abjections: sick people, migrants, residential garbage, the homeless, toxic waste, nuclear tests, excess populations, enslaved peoples, military garrisons, the mentally ill, oil barrels, refineries, tanneries, grease-rendering factories, wildlife documentaries, fake news

see: *Moana*
see: *Wake Island*
see: *The Island*
see:

birds protested the intrusion of the petronaut onto their beach

Here's a story:

it was research on these phantoms that eventually landed me, so to speak, on
Smith and Windmill Islands, which once lay between Camden and Philadelphia—opposite, in fact, to the gondola pillars on Penn's Landing

early records described these landmasses as mostly mud mounds, growing when the cities grew as heavy industry and sailing ships washed up silt onto their shores

so to speak, a ship hull lay underneath the mounds. But how did it get there? what we know is that deep time is slow data, and petrotime wants fast uploads some phantoms are solid, and others are wet archives

others leave gondolas to map the vexed sites of their being

what we know is that successive tides of sediment produced an exquisite twenty-five acre island

in 1838, city officials violently carved a canal down the middle to help ships navigate between the two ports

so to speak

what we know is that John Harding built a wharf on one of these islands to entice local farmers to bring grain to his mill

what we do know is Windmill Island was large enough to accommodate a coal yard, a hotel, an execution site, and a lead works factory

we also know that the Sanitarium Association of Philadelphia encouraged mothers and children to visit a small summer resort on the island so they could take refuge from the city's heat

we know that the children called this place Soupy Island because they were given free soup

we think an island is a beginning in want of enclosure a paradise for nomads, but not for those in waiting

no place
so to speak

the tanks were later demolished,
they left their DNA in the soil

Here's a story:

Smith Island was a haven for the city's poor and homeless until the merchant Jacob E. Ridgeway purchased the land for $55,000

what we know is that he pushed out the poor and terraformed the island. He constructed a bowling alley and a beer garden to lure the respectable classes

we imagine that he toyed with the idea of replicating Coney Island in this condensed area of Philadelphia

the papers reported that the park was a hotbed for riff-raff and street
fights what I imagine is that sex workers found refuge and contract, as a
mayfly of fair,
no place is a space between narrative and law
paradise is a pause between abyss and desire

some think it was the competition with New York City altered the Delaware River some think that these islands impeded the development of the waterfront in Camden and Philadelphia

what we do know is that dredging began in 1891, and the sediments from the islands were deposited on Pettys Island to reshape its turf

by 1897, both islands were gone because islands are migrants, who dream visas without voices

Utopia
so to speak

Question: can we build on the idea of the planetary, an Earth, based on the island alone?

answer: maybe?

let's call it Urf

It was research on these local phantoms that landed me, so to speak, on Pettys Island, a small slice of land between Philadelphia and Camden

here's a story:

the Lenni Lenape called the area around the island Sakimauchheen Ing the British called the island proper Shackamaxon the Swedes called it Aequikenaska

the Anglo-Americans called it Treaty Island

the Government called it Pettys Island

the island's historian barks another name in a language I cannot hear

my Polaroids become objects for dreaming islands, which mouth their own names What we know is that the oil company Cities Service purchased this island in 1916

we know Cities Service had a refinery and tank farm, which raised Camden's profile as an oil supplier

we know a coal yard on the southern tip served PECO until the Great Depression we know Cities Service gained full property rights to the island by 1953 Cities Service was rebranded as Citgo in 1965, a foreign country between two US cities,

despite reports, there are no bald eagles on the island but if there were, they'd be Venezuelan

the historian ignores this fact

he tells us we can step onto the shore

"Watch the rocks, they're slippery," he says

the tide is low, the path toward the waterline is an area where the grass recoils

in such traces, I lung with ash,

ambulate with love and venom,

"Walk sideways," the historian says

I walk sideways

down the path like a crab onto the greasy shore, overlooking at the Delaware Oil Plant on the Philadelphian side

I haven't seen the plant's waterside facade before it's hard to see at this distance,

I shoot a couple of pictures and a few more of the beach without capturing any detail

history lacks resolution anyway

the clouds like ears of corn

this island, the roughness of fly wings,

they brought enslaved peoples to the island to avoid import taxes

the historian calls them slaves

I say nothing

everyone agrees that Philadelphia hasn't confronted its role in the trade of human

beings everyone is white

I crush stones and dirt against the film, imprinting texture upon surface

I think why poetry:

fly wings will do

the algae on the rocks had created an illusion of a land bridge

Here's a story:

Act one. Rising seas destroy Pasifika atolls

Act two. Islanders migrate to the United States, New Zealand, and Australia. They are refused assistance since international law doesn't recognise the status of climate change refugees

some are deported. To where?

Act three. An island dreams of urf

Bibliography

"some ode, odor":

Ambrose, Jillian. "Fracking Causing Rise in Methane Emissions, Study Finds." *Guardian*, Aug. 14, 2019. Accessed Jan. 1, 2020. https://www.theguardian.com/environment/2019/aug/14/fracking-causing-rise-in-methane-emissions-study-finds

Associated Press. "Investigators Fault Southern California Gas in Aliso Canyon Methane Leak." *LA Times*, May 17, 2019. Accessed Jan. 25, 2020. https://www.latimes.com/local/lanow/la-me-aliso-canyon-gas-leak-report-20190517-story.html.

Carlisle, Madeleine. "The Trump Administration Just Loosened Methane Emissions Rules. Here's What to Know." *Time*, Aug. 30, 2019. https://time.com/5664449/epa-methane-emissions-rule/.

Green, Matthew. "Special Report: The Three Young Women Racing to Defuse a Climate-Change Bomb." *Reuters*. Accessed Jan 25, 2020., https://www.reuters.com/article/us-climate-change-arctic-methane-special/special-report-the-three-young-women-racing-to-defuse-a-climate-change-bomb-idUSKBN1W517G.

van Helmont, Jan Baptista. "The Blas of Meteours." In Van Helmont's works containing his most excellent philosophy, physick, chirurgery, anatomy : wherein the philosophy of the schools is examined, their errors refuted, and the whole body of physick reformed and rectified: being a new rise and progresse of philosophy and medicine, for the cure of diseases, and lengthening of life. *Oxford Text Archive* 2007. Accessed Jan. 12, 2020. http://hdl.handle.net/20.500.12024/A43285.

Kaufman, Mark. "This Powerful Greenhouse Gas Has Been Rising Sharply for a Decade. Now We Know Why." *Mashable*. Jan 5, 2018. Accessed Jan. 1, 2020. https://mashable.com/2018/01/05/nasa-study-solves-methane-increase-puzzle/.

Mingle, Jonathan. "Atmospheric Methane Levels Are Going Up—And No One Knows Why." *Wired*, May 16, 2019. Accessed Jan. 1, 2020. https://www.wired.com/story/atmospheric-methane-levels-are-going-up-and-no-one-knows-why/.

Revi, Aromar. "Lessons from the Deluge: Priorities for Multi-Hazard Risk Mitigation." *Economic and Political Weekly* 40, no. 36 (2005): 3911–16.

Shlimon, Adris Georgis, et al. "Methanobacterium aarhusense sp. nov., a novel methanogen isolated from a marine sediment (Aarhus Bay, Denmark)." *International Journal of Systematic and Evolutionary Microbiology* 54 (2004): 759–63.

Spielberg, Steven, dir. *War of the Worlds*. Paramount Pictures, 2005.

Storch, Henry Herman. *Physical-chemical Properties of Methane.* Washington, D.C.: US Dept. of Commerce, Bureau of Mines, 1932.

Worden, J.R., et al. "Reduced biomass burning emissions reconcile conflicting estimates of the Post-2006 atmospheric methane budget." *Nature Communications* 8, no. 2227 (2017). https://doi.org/10.1038/s41467-017-02246-0.

Zukofsky, Louis. *Prepositions +: The Collected Critical Essays.* Hanover: Wesleyan University Press, 2000.

"To the Is-Land":

Frame, Janet. *To the Is-Land: An Autobiography*. Women's Press, 1984.

Gum Wrapper

KEEP YOUR COUNTRY CLEAN
        DEPOSIT TRASH INNA COUNTRY CLEANER
KEEP YOUR WORLD CLEAN
        DEPOSIT TRASH INNA YOU CLEANER
KEEP YOUR YOU CLEAN
        DEPOSIT TRASH INNA WORLD CLEANER
        DEPOSIT TRASH INTO THE WORLD
KEEP YOU CLEAN
        GET DIRTY
        THROW YOU IN
        DIRTY UP
        REPEAT DIRT
        GET CLEAN
        KEEP DIRT
        THROW WORLD IN
KEEP YOUR WORLD
KEEP YOUR WORLD
KEEP YOUR WORLD

JOHN TRITICA

20

access   arrange form
what belongs
to the eye
as if the petroglyph
joins eye & I
in a spiral
ram horn
alphabet
across
sun-hammered
mesa   chamisa
scrub daisies

a rock-face
exploded stars
fly into air

a bird perched
tail feathers awry
sets the gaze

joins eye & I
alphabet's insistent allure

22

to open the field
means to open the eye
discern the slant
of sunray

in different times
of day
now no shade
under gaze but
east ridge Sandia
alpine distance

the shadow I cast
diminishes
while heat squeezes
summer burns
dry grass

rock art records
snake bird
labyrinth
opens the eye
guides circumstance
location & trace

24

morning sun
face east across
Sandias

an arc you spread
resonates the words' vocation
petroglyphs live
in rattlesnake
surrender
the Saturn ring
around the hat's brim

energy whips
motion
mind blaze antiquity
as if a dancing mantis
presides

motivation overcomes doubt
flame guards origin

to walk among basalt as the heat
burns into the nape
the chips & shards
obsidian jasper carves
foot before wing
in August sun's
hot breath

Keith Tuma

Audiology

At dinner with the visiting translators I hear about the girlfriend of the poetry translator and her commitment to rescuing animals—a dog missing its front legs and soon to be fitted for a cart, a feral Italian kitten smuggled into the country via Montreal, a dozen parrots. Parrots often outlive their humans, the poetry translator says, and his girlfriend's adopted birds speak the history of their city. One pipes up with "Juanita!" and coughs forcefully, as if to remember a marriage ended by emphysema, or a crotchety old man yelling for his nurse. Another says "I need a drink" and "Turn on the ice machine." Another sings "Jiggle the handle," suggesting the location of its cage in its former life. And so on—expressions of intimacy and love compete with curses to map the range of human emotions among deceased parrot lovers. Some parrots parrot other birds, so the house is a conference of birds, the poetry translator says. One evening he had an edible and endured the mimicry for hours in that altered state. The other translators laugh at the thought. They have told their stories about the trials of translation to an assembled student audience; their work is done. Now among peers and hosts they are freer in their speech. "Never tell a story that good to a fiction writer," the translator of fiction says to the translator of poetry. Twelve parrots and an edible.

Kathryn Weld

Woman. Reef.

In each cell of my dead city, a kingdom of symbionts pay tithe in sugars. Who will caress my belly? An orgy of polyps self-propagate there, their yellow frilly skirts flaring free—those are stinging tentacles. They girdle my mouth. Kiss me. At full moon, I shrink from hot water. My aging genes deploy bad syntax. A shoal of bleached bone is my fishless throat.

Meadow

Veined with tall grass,
stippled black by stalks,

made soft by milkweed
down, by thaw; it trembles

with choice. The choosing
lowers us into story,

the way the Buick behind
the oaks dissolves to bruise.

The way grapevine girdles
the axle. Turns the bench-seat,

upholstered with moss,
to a grotto in a box of rust.

Laurie Wilcox-Meyer

Monarch Stage 2

An African bracelet?
Trapped in the glass display:
Yellow-white-black accordion the trapeze artist
            upside down back bending.
                        Hanging
      poor vision though six pairs of eyes.
Now desire whispers in black felt antennae
   questioning the air.
Searching through   beyond the clouded funds of rotten green.
Wishing your ancestors four generation migration
   to reap
common ground of the skies' here and now
that is heaven on earth.
And snake skins of false chrysalis
          to molt
into towers that wing only peace.

Your beauty   being   lighting the way.

Morgan Grayce Willow

Pangolin II

after Marianne Moore

I

King George III shows up at court
in 1820 wearing
a new coat of armor,
gift from the Governor General,
East India Company, Bengal.
Trimmed and braided
in royal blue and gold,
the coat is covered,
though not in metal.
Large scales conceal
His Royal Highness's heart,
shield his shoulders
with cap-like sleeves.
Smaller scales guard his spleen
where otherwise an able knight
might direct his lance.
These scales once protected a pangolin,
the only mammal known
to have such keratin-covered
layers over its skin.
Stripped from the animal,
decorated in gold,
now fit for a king.

II

Moore calls it splendid,
"near artichoke,"
the animal layered
in "spruce-cone regularity."
The pangolin's adapted fore-claws
open anthills, clear the way for its tongue,
much longer than its body.

The tongue tunnels deep into
anthill's channels, collects a meal
along its sticky surface.

A pangolin has no bark,
no need for teeth.
When threatened, it curls,
tucks its nose beneath its tail,
leaving sharp-edged scales
to fend off predators.
To Moore, its motion is grace
shaped by adversity.

III

Phnom Tamao Wildlife Rescue Center
Takeo, Cambodia

A three-year-old female pangolin,
ambles through leaves and
underbrush, despite having lost two
of her four feet to a poacher's
snare. For some she is a delicacy,
food for healing human
kidneys. Others want
the keratin
from her scales as potion
for skin ailments. She
may be smuggled in bags
of dog biscuits.
She may be labeled as frozen
fish or communication
equipment. She, and her
kind, are the most trafficked
species, for the scales.
More than the
elephant for its ivory.
More than the
rhinoceros for its
horn. Just two
centuries since King
George III, and soon,
the pangolin will be
extinct.

Daniel Wolff

Evolution of a Silhouette

Red rock buried under evergreen,
        but the falls at Sault St. Marie
        prevent supply from reaching demand:
no break flat bowl Great Lake horizon.

Eighteen-hundred-and-fifty-five:
        locks punched through shelf-rock
        allow twenty-one-foot measured drop;
earth begins to leak south.

Iron ore from open pit, loaded into
        Columbia, wooden schooner:
        pale smudge on grey sky,
two-hundred tons per trip.

War converts canvas light
        into steel-hull, steam driven.
        Eighteen-eighty-two *Onoko*
"largest freighter yet"—

foredeck raised for pilot house, stern raised
for engine room, in-between slung low
to hold iron, coal, wheat—
a box to cart a thousand tons, profile blunt as need.

Eighteen-ninety-six: expanded locks, expanded
profit margin, docks
and towns and distant cities
all gilded by expanding market, "great surge of construction."

Five- and six-hundred-foot-long freighters
hump between the hump-backed isles,
twelve-thousand trips a year,
try to gouge a route between lake and open sea.

World War One increased demand
clogs the yards at River Rouge,
welded transverse arches take
average load ten-thousand tons.

Rising weight of iron dollar
Interrupted by Great Depression,
wealth remains in frozen earth,
as rusted hulls weep white.

When war cuts through (again), new
        freighters forged from slag and scrap
        rush to answer starving mills,
"supply of ore … unabated."

Wilfred Sykes launched forty-nine,
        length approaching seven-hundred,
        gross tonnage twenty-thousand,
the shape she strikes in chill water: "the product of a long tradition."

Still the lifted prow and aft, still
        amidships flat and low, still
        the underlying bulk:
dense, dark, triumphant.

Nineteen-eighty-one *Columbia*
        Star, to honor first schooner:
        a thousand feet of steel that holds
fifty-thousand tons.

"Self-unloading bulk carrier," self-directed by satellite,
        steers the same glacial track,
        ends upraised, cargo hidden.
(Later christened *American Century*.)

Lake to lock to lake, the loads

—dust left over from old extractions

crushed to form iron pellets—ride

on belts of man-made shadow.

Across Great Lakes, great floating walls

strain (still) to carve the sky,

to mark (again) moving water,

to bear the weight of iron earth, brief as silhouette.

JEFFREY YANG

1

After the thunderstorm, the heat
timeless heat, sun's zero incidence

heat of the tropics, Asia's
Golden Chersonese

bursts into colors
flowers and leaves

of Bukit Nanas, the last
patch of old-growth forest

on the heart of the muddy confluence
Jelutong trail to giant crow-foot trunk

ready to uproot earth, wings beat
against the glass tower, feathers fall

fast past the opening crown

2

Sun bear and cloud leopard, leatherback
dugong, brother and sister weaver ants

metallic moths soft, iridescent triangle spots
green wing tip to tip, feathery, crimson neck-

band Birdwing, carrying the beauty of the past
into the present, outlasts the present, nature's gift

Of birds, each bird a soul reflected, reflect-
ing, subjected dissolution, earth's vanishing blue-

billed gapers trogons *kap-kap* honey-suckers
weavers bee-eaters hornbills *birik-birik*

thrushes fly-catcher flames a paradise of birds

Beetles wood-feeders leeches stone field
fissures of ferns phycobiont lichen blossoms

Breathe into tree-frog glide

through spirit and matter
Wood
through water and air

camphor, eagle-wood, gutta-percha
home, names marked in memory

O kemuning, O waringin
O kemung, angsana, nangka
O gaharu and pauh hutan
O cendana, gemia, setar, celagi
O halban, bongor, ketengga

Essays and Critical Responses

Natalie Cortez-Klossner

The Green Abyss: A Theory Fiction

Encyclopedia of our Cosmic Realities

I. EDENoCENE

Neologism: Let's consider the Christian interpretation of the Genesis story. Adam and Eve in the Garden of Eden. Serpent convinces Eve to eat the forbidden fruit from the Tree of Knowledge of Good and Evil. Serpent says she will become like God if she eats it. Eve eats the fruit. The fall of mankind ensues. Ever since, Eden is the motivating force behind Western Culture—turn wilderness into garden they proclaim![1]

A history of "mastering" the ecosphere resulted, as if a forest were an entity that could be tamed....

Humanity's objective is to possess and dominate its surroundings?

But mutable narratives allow us to imagine a knowing that exists beyond our human *selves.*

Let's reconsider the myth. Replace God with Nature in the story. It's not the serpent who seduces Eve to eat the forbidden fruit. It's Eve who seduces the serpent to gift its fruit. Eve forms a kinship with the garden. Nature and culture are bridged?

Definition: In classic postmodern fashion, let's recast the Anthropocene, Capitolocene, Plantationocene, and Haraway's Chthulucene substituting it for a prefix of Eden / iːd(ə)n (Hebrew עדן; ʻēḏen; "delight")[2], and allowing –cene / siːn (suffix for "epoch") to carry its uniform meaning: Now the term enters the dictionary: Edenocene.

i. Relating to or denoting the current geofoolish period, a human imagined time and space of ecological reinvention.
ii. A proposed term for humanity's unawareness of the triviality of human existence in relation to the deep history of other life forms, especially vegetal life.

Usage: As Adjective. People who want to live "off-the-grid," scientists who are proponents of geoengineering, pseudo-activists holding up petitions to "save the rainforest!" They reflect an Edenocene attitude.

As noun. The Edenocene Period.

Part I

Let's briefly consider the cliché of the Amazon (1): "the Lungs of the World," the rainforest as a green cathedral, the cathedral of life in "America's backyard." It's revered as a land of pristine flora and fauna seen in documentaries and in one's reveries. A video found in cyberspace—"The Amazon: Lungs of the Planet"—infects the viewer with rhetoric of the last wilderness left on Earth:

> ... the heart of America ... the richness ... holds the key to humanity itself ... I feel that I am in the middle of the heart of everything ... there's like a pulsing and thriving ... deep and really powerful ... like being in the Sistine Chapel[3]

A deep incoherence begins to emerge. Unlike idealist depictions of a jungle immersed with biological diversity and unlimited wealth, the computerized audiovisuals exhibit glimpses of a labyrinth of vegetal hell. It's a skilled impersonator. A Green Abyss!

The paranoia will disappear once you let it push you to a state of *non compos mentis*. Let's tumble into the Unknown, drilling into all considerations of the fabulous past of the Amazon basin and its unexplored mythologies.

Proceeding with *Las Venas Abiertas de América Latina* [Open Veins of Latin America] (1971), in which Eduardo Galeano famously writes that Latin America is the "region of open veins"; nature (human and nonhuman) was transfigured into capital and sent to distant cores of power. The 1960s was a period in which large-scale deforestation arose in the region: Backed by foreign aid, Amazonian countries employed intensive development programs devised to exploit the rainforest's resources. Through human ingenuity, the land was to be developed and turned into a Garden of Eden once again!

A contemporary site of environmental exploitation, Latin America was the first frontier for early modern capitalist expansion. The Amazon was represented as a "frontier," akin to the liminal space of the American "Wild West" of the 1800s. The *novelas de la selva* [novels of the jungle], which flourished during the first-half of the twentieth century, dwelled on the miseries of travelers and workers in their attempt to dominate and control the rainforest, particularly during the rubber boom. Rubber was a valuable commodity tagged as "black gold" as no motivation was necessary to induce men to seek it out from the Amazonia starting at the end of the nineteenth century. Perhaps this is where a first hint of paranoia springs. The Amazon as a thick grove and unsolvable maze!

In *La Vorágine* [The Vortex] (1924), a "novel of the jungle," Eustasio Rivera writes: "*¡Los devoró la selva!*" [The Jungle devoured them!].[4] The last sentence of the novel must be taken with great examination even if man tends to renounce a mystic conception of reality for the elevation of hegemonic philosophy and science discourses. The emblematic approach to understanding has become bankrupted!

The documentary *The Trees Have a Mother* (2008) tells the true story of the disappearance of a young man from the Peruvian Amazon and his mother's quest to find him with the support of a shaman. In the film, the locals credit the man's disappearance to a supernatural forest presence with uneven-sized feet—the *Chullachaqui, "amigo de los árboles"* [friend of the trees]—who leads hunters, workers, and other travelers deep into the forest until they are nowhere to be found. There is a widespread local belief in guardian spirits who live among the trees and "*lugares encantados*" [enchanted places], which have historically preserved certain Amazonian areas from exploitation. Anthropologist Eduardo Viveiros de Castro would assert that the deities simply represent the Amerindians' belief in "metaphysical continuity" between humans and nonhumans.[5] In *How Forests Think* (2013) anthropologist Eduardo Kohn reveals an embodied and emergentist understanding of nonhuman sign making in the Amazon. Bridging Kohn's argument that the Amazon "houses loci of mean-ings," horror-inducing entities create mean-ings through signs and symbols.[6] Mean-ings of annihilation!

But we must not forget that man is often restricted to the resources of its mind, which are almost always inadequate for capturing the essence of the Unknown. Did these spirits guard the forest against human exploitation or did the spirits defend us against a malevolent forest? A guardian tends to indicate that a more powerful and prevailing being lurks behind its protection. Vegetation is not a slave to man. Man is a slave to vegetation!

Not solely does this knowledge create speculation about an ecological heterocosm; paranoia finds you where you least expect it. I spin this psychotic teratological buoyancy that is the Amazonian mythos. An original past does not exist that can be redeemed. All that is left is emptiness and an orphanage of beings. Unbaptized earth observed from the exteriority. It's not humanity who will turn wilderness to Eden, but it's the Unknown which will break out from our earth. Poisonous greenery, disguised as a paradise, in the meaningless history of the Western imagination. We must not let it escape our mortal head space, this vegetal labyrinth we call the Amazon; it holds a deep history we'd never in its entirety be able to experience. We must subvert the ahistoricizing of vegetal life prevalent in anthroparchal—social systems of human domination over other living beings—rational. Have we arrived at the limits of rational human mastery faced with an unworldly wonder?

I'd like to make clear, this prose is not written to invoke science fiction, speculation of a time to come, or a speculative realism, but a real prehistoric horror, a reiteration of the fear of the Unknown. The Amazonian vegetal world is alien. Not necessarily in a "The alien is anything—and everything—to everything else" of academic and video game designer Ian Bogost's object-oriented ontology in *Alien Phenomenology*.[7] But in its haunting. They were never *trees* and *plants*. Amazonian trees are not nonhuman, but extra-human, *extra*-terrestrial. The Amazonian flora has been our primordial beings, a green abyss. The irrelevance of humanity in the face of life from a lineage of over 425 million years. The Amazon harvests the outer, cosmological, or solar energy to synthesize its sustenance. The greenery has been directly birthed by an interplanetary force, given life by a colossal galactic being. Vegetal life interacts with an interstellar light to quantum imprint on our world their meanings. From a human perspective, it'd be difficult to imagine our world without these green beings. The Amazon inhabits more than 50 percent of this vegetal past and it's thought to have spanned ca. 55 million years.[8] A place for the green beings to all form kinships within a vegetal network of terror covering 6 million km^2, a total of 5 percent of the total land surface of the Earth.[9] We've been socialized to believe in the benevolence of a supernatural entity. Deconstruction and reflection prove otherwise!

Part II

The essentiality of a myth echoes to us the beginning of time. Of believing humanity, a prisoner to the green inferno, condemned to lucidly scavenge through this cosmic horror. At the hierarchy of the Amazonian mythos lies the "*Ceibo anciano*" [the elder Ceiba] the *Ceiba petandra* or silk-cotton tree, known as a Cosmic Tree or Tree of life, as well as the "axis" that held the world together in Mayan mythology. The *Ceiba* as an astral being! It disturbs the Universe!

In a 1950 ethnography of rural Afro-Cubans, *El Monte*, Lydia Cabrera writes about the vengeful nature of the *Ceiba*,

> An obscure fear prevents the peasant from raising his ax on the sacred trunk ... Only a reckless or irresponsible person would consent to cut the Ceiba, which materializes more than symbolizes, in their eyes, the terrible omnipotence of God ... the *Ceibas* do not pardon.[10]

It's not difficult to immerse yourself in the Amazonian mythos as you observe the indispensable themes shared among tales. Stories reference analogous deities and devotions from within comparable occult practices. The green being, *Ceiba*, a destructive cosmic force, is associated with the *Curupira*, a guardian spirit of the trees described as having "un pie mirando adelante y el otro para atras" [one foot facing forward and one facing backward] and being kin to the *Chullachaqui*.[11] Both deities, servers to the green abyss, are described with certain properties while resisting descriptions by these same properties as if details would only propagate an ambiguous outline. Is it the general outline that makes it the most shockingly frightful? At best, the *Curupira* was described as a "demon-like-being," with red hair and deformed body. The *Chullachaqui* continuously was said to hold the ability to transform itself into anyone or anything, as if to mock our human corporeal fragility.

El Abrazo de la Serpiente [Embrace of the Serpent] was a 2015 film dramatization of the Karamakate tribe's encounter with German and American explorers in 1909 and in 1940.[12] The film explores a *Chullachaqui* legend, in which the deity copies the image of other being in order to deceive. In the Christian myth of Adam and Eve, Satan descends from heaven into hell, returning as a serpent in the Garden of Eden to *deceive* Eve to eat the forbidden fruit. The persecution of the Amazonia is not anomalous. In light of Gilles Deleuze and Felix Guattari's commentary that Carl Jung expanded on "a theory of the Archetype as collective unconscious" by "assigning the animal a particularly important role in dreams, myths, and human collectiveness,"[13] stories of shapeshifting beings deceiving humans from within a labyrinth of vegetation is a universal sentiment. Stories of *extra*-human beings from "trees of life" that transform into other beings have traversed cultures and time. From Indigenous Americans to the Judeo-Christian mythos!

All myth is a *myth of origins* because it tells the tale of creation.[14] The green myth derives from "prodigiously obscure times, primordial deities" united by the same Star, 150 million kilometers away, "installed on the earth, and by their arrival began earth life."[15] The investigation condemns you to ponder on the tension between belief and disbelief, mundane and exteriority, and realities and unrealities. To return to the protagonist walking through the Columbian Amazon who comments on how the trees "Were growing taller every second, like men who had been crouching but then began to rise, stretching their arms until they were high above their heads."[16] Despite literary critiques on the subject, the novel does not reveal an anthropocentric narrative. It pushes the ephemerality of humanity in comparison to the entangled labyrinth. In the words of Rivera, the Amazonian flora are "Eternally condemned to sprout, bloom, germinate, and perpetuate their formidable species."[17]

Is it meaningless to hold humanity as the highest form of being? The Amazonian community, Makuna, "classify human beings, plants, and animals as 'people' (*masa*), whose main attributes—mortality, social and ceremonial life, intentionality, and knowledge—are in every way identical."[18] The indigenous communities have lived in harmony with the green abyss through an acknowledgment: man is a slave to nature? A captive to the vegetal world that is the Amazon? Or perhaps, the communities formed a kinship with the green abyss? Unwelcomed parties experience the fury of the labyrinth. This meditation is not here to defend the rights of the Amazon, while it does hope to destabilize the Western ontological distinctions between vibrant and inanimate matter.

Encyclopedia of Our Cosmic Realities

II. "*El embrujamiento de la selva*" ["the witchery of the jungle"]

Definition: a phenomenon in which trees in the Amazon enchant travelers and cause them to get lost in its vegetal labyrinth

The horror does not lie in the green abyss or the guardian spirits themselves, but on their implications for humanity.

Part III

Kohn's *How Forests Think* is a multispecies ethnography of the Runa village, a community living in Ecuador's Upper Amazon:

> More Precisely, the forests around Ávila are animate. That is, these forests house other emergent loci of mean-ings, ones that do not necessarily revolve around, or originate from, humans. This is what I'm getting at when I say forests think.[19]

The Amazon does more than *think*. It's more than just *alive*. It's an "impenetrable thicket that repels every attempt at domination and control" and subverts the idea that humans are the only *selves* in this world.[20] If thought exists beyond the human and if we are not the only we, then our human politics, history, culture, and so on begins to decline in authority and importance in this vast hyperspace. To create a metaphor, humans represent a nanoscopic stem in an immeasurable tree formation.

In the past two decades studies have confirmed that "tree alpha-diversity of north-western

Amazonian forests is among the highest in the Amazon drainage basin."[21] Some of the earliest exploiters of the Amazon—early twentieth-century imperialists, rubber tappers, or other workers and travelers—walked into the most remote part of Amazonia, the North-Western Amazonian forests. Did the high diversity of flora entanglements proliferate a malicious green abyss? Did the launch of Amazonian unwelcome exploitation and colonization ignite a reaction from the dormant inferno? What is normally found horrific is the physical phenomenon of extermination of a landscape and disintegration of human beings and animals—an unspeakable alienage. However, the green abyss has an ability to confront this meditation through a satirical evocation; the vegetal labyrinth of horror proves to be a psychological operation. External realities are prompted through a being that exists outside space and time, not necessarily on the physical phenomenon or the being itself; it allows us to become aware of humanity's precarious condition and our increasingly insignificant position in the universe in relation to the primordial green abyss.

Let's disrupt the fascination with the Amazon and greenery in general, as promised land or earthly paradise. Candace Slater writes in her essay "Amazonia as Edenic Narrative," that "the region's biodiversity ... may foster a quasi-Edenic vision of a new garden to which the entire human race lays claim."[22] Yet, the word "Eden" is thought to derive from the Akkadian *edinu*, which is borrowed from the Sumerian *eden*, meaning "desert."[23] Desert as in hostile. Rejecting the interpretation of Eden as a Garden of Delight, the antagonistic and uncontrollable mystical land never disappeared but is hiding in plain sight.

Encyclopedia of Our Cosmic Realities

III. Amazon as Eden

/The haphazard labyrinth that is the tangled bionetwork/
Shapeshifting malevolent beings lurk in the Amazon waiting to
deceive voyagers / To Form a kinship with the green abyss is to
bridge a gap between nature and culture/

A movement to not misinterpret the mystical!

Notes

[1]This is an idea borrowed from Carolyn Merchant in *Reinventing Eden: The Fate of Nature in Western Culture.*
[2]*Oxford Dictionaries, s.v.* "Eden," https://en.oxforddictionaries.com/definition/eden.
[3] "Amazon: Lungs of the Planet," *BBC Future* video, 3, no. 57 (November 18, 2014). http://www.bbc.com/future/story/20130226-amazon-lungs-of-the-planet.
[4]José Eustasio Rivera (Buenos Aires-México: Espasa-Calpe argentina, s.a, 1939), 203.
[5]Eduardo Viveiros de Castro, "Cosmological Deixis and Amerindian Perspectivism." *The Journal of the Royal Anthropological Institute* 4, no. 3 (1998): 471.
[6]Ibid.
[7]Ian Bogost, *Alien Phenomenology, Or, What It's Like to Be a Thing* (Minneapolis: University of Minnesota Press, 2012).

[8]Joaquin Cuzc and Nicolas Rojas, *Amazon Basin: Plant Life, Wildlife and Environment*. Environmental Research Advances Series (New York: Nova Science Publishers, 2010), X. Original Text: "forms one of the most precious ecosystems and provides habitat for more than 50% of plant and animal species." And Laszlo Nagy, Bruce R. Forsberg, and Paulo Artaxo, "Interactions Beween Biosphere, Atmosphere, and Human Land Use in the Amazon Basin: An Introduction," in *Interactions between Biosphere, Atmosphere and Human Land Use in the Amazon Basin* (Berlin: Springer, 2016).
[9]Ibid.
[10] Lydia Cabrera, *El Monte* (Miami: Rema Press, 1968), 191–192. *Un oscuro terror le impide al campesino descargar su hacha sobre el tronco sagrado ... Solo un temerario, un irresponsable, consentirá en cortar la ceiba, que materializa, más que simboliza, a sus ojos, la terrible omnipotencia de Dios ... Las ceibas no perdonan.* (My translation).
[11]Juan Carlos Galeano, Amazonía (Bogota: Casa de Poes a Silva, 2012), 55.
[12]Ana Mar a Mutis, "El Abrazo de La Serpiente o La Re-Escritura Del Amazonas Dentro de Una tica Ecol gica y Poscolonial," *Hispanic Research Journal* 19, no. 1 (February 2018): 32. (My translation).
[13]Gilles Deleuze and Félix Guattari, *A Thousand Plateaus: Capitalism and Schizophrenia* (Minneapolis: University of Minnesota Press, 1987), 235.
[14]Lévy, "From Fable to Myth," 110.
[15]Ibid., 111.
[16]Rivera, 293. *"Iban creciendo a cada segundo, con una apariencia de hombres acuclillados, que se empinaban desperezándose hasta elevar los brazos verdosos por encima de la cabeza."* (My translation).
[17]Ibid., 213. "*Siempre condenados a retoñar, a florecer, a germinar, a perpetuar.*" (My translation).
[18]Philippe Descola and Janet Lloyd, *Beyond Nature and Culture* (Chicago: The University of Chicago Press, 2014), 8.
[19]Kohn, *How Forests Think*, 72.
[20]Jorge Marcone, "Nuevos Descubrimientos del Río Amazona: La 'Novela de la Selva' y la Critica al Imaginario de la Amazonía," *Estudios* 8, no.16 (2000): 129–40. (My translation).
[21]Carina Hoorn and F. P. Wesselingh, *Amazonia—Landscape and Species Evolution: A Look into the Past* (Chichester and Hoboken: Wiley-Blackwell, 2010), 363.
[22]Candance Slater, "Amazonia as Edenic Narrative," in *Uncommon Ground, Towards Reinventing Nature*, ed. William Cronon (New York: Norton, 1996), 116.
[23]"Encyclopedia Judaica: The Garden of Eden," *Jewish Virtual Library*. https://www.jewishvirtuallibrary.org/garden-of-eden.

Bibliography

El Abrazo de La Serpiente [Embrace of the Serpent]. Directed by Guerra, Ciro. Buffalo: Buffalo Films, 2016. Film.

"Amazon: Lungs of the Planet." *BBC Future* video, 3, no. 57. (November 18, 2014). http://www.bbc.com/future/story/20130226-amazon-lungs-of-the-planet.

Bogost, Ian. *Alien Phenomenology, Or, What It's Like to Be a Thing.* Minneapolis: University of Minnesota Press, 2012.

Cabrera, Lydia. *El Monte.* Miami: Rema Press, 1968.

Cuzc, Joaquin, and Nicolas Rojas. *Amazon Basin: Plant Life, Wildlife and Environment.* Environmental Research Advances Series. New York: Nova Science Publishers, 2010.

Deleuze, Gilles (1925–1995), and Félix Guattari (1930–1992). *A Thousand Plateaus: Capitalism and Schizophrenia.* Minneapolis: University of Minnesota Press, 1987.

Descola, Philippe, and Janet Lloyd. *Beyond Nature and Culture.* Paperback edition. Chicago: The University of Chicago Press, 2014 (8.)

Galeano, Eduardo, Isabel Allende, Cedric Belfrage, and Eduardo H. Galeano. *Open Veins of Latin America: Five Centuries of the Pillage of a Continent.* 25th anniversary ed. Foreword by Isabel Allende. New York: Monthly Review Press, 1997.

Galeano, Juan Carlos. *Amazonía.* Bogota: Casa de Poes a Silva, 2012.

---. *Cuentos amazónicos*. Iquitos: Tierra Nueva, 2007.
Haraway, Donna Jeanne. *Staying with the Trouble: Making Kin in the Chthulucene.* Durham: Duke University Press, 2016.
Hoorn, C. (Carina), and F. P. Wesselingh. *Amazonia—Landscape and Species Evolution: A Look into the Past.* Chichester and Hoboken: Wiley-Blackwell, 2010.
Kohn, Eduardo. *How Forests Think: Toward an Anthropology beyond the Human.* Berkeley: University of California Press, 2013.
Marcone, Jorge. "Nuevos Descubrimientos del Rio Amazona: La 'Novela de la Selva' y la Critica al Imaginario de la Amazonia." Estudios 8, no. 16 (2000): 129–40.
Merchant, Carolyn. *Reinventing Eden: The Fate of Nature in Western Culture.* New York: Routledge, 2003.
Mutis, Ana Maria. "El Abrazo de La Serpiente o La Re-Escritura Del Amazonas Dentro de Una tica Ecol gica y Poscolonial." *Hispanic Research Journal* 19, no. 1 (February 2018).
Nagy, Laszlo, Bruce R. Forsberg, and Paulo Eduardo Artaxo Netto. *Interactions between Biosphere, Atmosphere and Human Land Use in the Amazon Basin.* Berlin: Springer, 2016.
Oxford Dictionaries, s.v. "Eden." https://en.oxforddictionaries.com/definition/eden.
Rivera, José Eustasio. Buenos Aires-México: Espasa-Calpe argentina, s.a, 1939.
Slater, Candace. "Amazonia as Edenic Narrative," in *Uncommon Ground.*
The Trees Have a Mother: Amazonian Cosmologies, Folktales, and Mystery. Directed by Juan Carlos Galeano. New York: Infobase, 2008. Film.
Viveiros de Castro, Eduardo."Cosmological Deixis and Amerindian Perspectivism." *The Journal of the Royal Anthropological Institute* 4, no. 3 (1998): 471.
William Cronon, et al. *Uncommon Ground: Toward Reinventing Nature.* New York: W.W. Norton, 1995.

Alexis Finet

¡El Agua Vive!: Visions of the Real in the Amazon Region as Seen through J. C. Galeano's Poetry and Collected Tales

Water: A source of life; the precious liquid maintaining most of life on earth, and yet, ill-preserved, it becomes dangerously weakened by the hands of economic narratives of modernity and globalization processes. At the center of many political issues of the land and from broad practices to the closest local cultures of coastal and rivers' residents, water is a concern for everyone. South America is no exception, and this, of course, includes the "lungs of the world": the Amazon rainforest (Fraser and Tello Imaina 2015).

In a series of poems entitled *Yakumama (and Other Mythical Beings)* and throughout his collection of *Cuentos amazónicos*, Juan Carlos Galeano offers a novel approach to the representations of the Amazon, highlighting the culture of the population living in many areas of its basin. He does so by providing stories rich in his own experiences as well as data collected during his field work among indigenous communities, fishermen, loggers, hunters, and small development dwellers in the region. Complementary to his tales and poems, his documentary *El Río*—filmed in various areas on the Peruvian Amazon—echoes the *Tales* and poems by referring to several stories of the area. The film dialogues with the two books on the conceptual level of the aquatic element. In all three productions, voice is given to the protagonists of the land, and the author becomes a mediator who allows silent voices—often referred to as those of the "Subaltern," in Spivak's terms—to be heard. The importance of ecological issues linked to water and underscored in the stories and their proximity to the river is evident from the very title of the documentary (the Spanish word *río* means "river"). Indeed, just like the poems and the tales, *El Río* places water as an essential component of everyday life, necessary for the survival of not only the body but also of the mind as well. As the river flows at the core of many stories known by the people who live on the river, it pertains to the development and maintenance of their imaginary, thus emphasizing the importance of its preservation for the local cultures. The status of the river, as an essential part of ecosystems and social life, is expressed by a variety of members of both indigenous and riverine *mestizo* communities. In the first act of *El Río*, Maritza, a Kokama indigenous food vendor in a port of the Nanay River, says: "Because we draw our water from there, wash our clothes there, fish there, bathe there, the river is everything to us."[1] Galeano's choice to introduce the movie already shows the importance of the river in the Amazonian lives.

Framed within a reading of the poetics of water, this article therefore scrutinizes the conception of reality as seen through the eyes of the beholder—here the people living in the area, who are best qualified to describe the immediate surroundings of Iquitos' population. Said cosmovision, contained in a pan-Amazonian array of supernatural beings displayed in the poems, appears through exemplary creatures of the forest: for instance, the master of all animals *Curupira*; the *Chicua* announcing the future; the evil *Matinta-pereira* bird, "stealing" bodies to hurt people; the seducing mermaid *Yara*; and the androgynous river serpent *Yakumama*, whose control over water strikes fear in and governs many decisions of the local populations. All these creatures emerge from the fabric of a plethora of oral narratives constructed by the general population and by shamans. Their knowledge comes from their visions and dreams, aided by psychotropic plants such as the *ayahuasca*. This understanding of nature, seemingly difficult to grasp for Western phenomenological thought, remains challenging due to its traditional approach of dividing the natural and the supernatural into the categories of "real" and "unreal." This philosophical problem surfaces through storytelling, especially when the communities evoked tell their stories as factual rather than mythical despite their mythological nature (Uzendoski and Calapucha-Tapuy 2012).

Classical philosophy generally proposes a binary split between culture and nature, with humans maintaining a complex relationship with both. Durkheim, for instance, speaks of "social heredity" as an impossibility for humans to completely work within their nature, since a culture is always superimposed on an initial framework. Coming from Descartes' famous *cogito ergo sum*, thought and articulated language (as opposed to animal languages) define existence as a feature of cultural beings rather than natural ones and forget to take into consideration the possible variations of an objective study of populations different from one's own (Santos Granero 1991, Landolt and Surralés 2003, Descola 2005). However, these views have recently been challenged by modern thought, which argues that ethnocentrism was responsible for an erroneous understanding of the notion of culture. Nature could therefore be defined within the universal and the necessary, as opposed to the conventions normally required to define cultures. However, this binary definition through opposition brings forward another issue, as it also serves to define the *supernatural* as *that* which does not belong to nature and is thus unreal—unbelievable—in objective terms. When it comes to the Amazon and the different representations of the world and the experience of the Amazon, these definitions prove to be remarkably flawed. When a shaman consumes *ayahuasca*, are their visions of the future, of a cure, or of a world below the river a product of their dreams and imaginations? Are these visions real? *What* is real?

Applying apparent claims to unknown cultures becomes problematic, since the supernatural belongs to our own perception of the complexities of nature, which can be summarized as a "Western hierarchical paradigm confined in binary constructs" (Huntington 2009). In one instance of his recounting of the time spent in the Amazon with the Pirahã tribe, North American missionary Daniel Everett relates how the entire village where he was staying seemed to agree that they were seeing a creature on the sand of the river shore; however, he failed to actually perceive the creature, as if his perception were too blurred by cultural background (Everett 2008). This striking episode of an experience in the Amazon region already sends markers for a close reading of Galeano's research among the Amazonian populations, as it may often be tempting to understand tales and poems as part of a fictional world of story-telling, when they actually represent only one possible interpretation of a surrounding reality. Such an understanding of the world may be inaccessible to an outsider like Everett, who failed to find what an entire group of people collectively agreed to see. The tales actually have a meaning connected to the reality of the local people, and these Amazonian cultural particularities require a new definition of the *real* and the *supernatural*, liberated from the chains of globalized simplifications that lead to tremendous shortcuts.

An analysis of Galeano's works therefore leads to questioning the codes of reality and the supernatural. Is a half-fish, half-human woman real? Should her features be understood as part of the imaginary? For the Western mind, the latter would probably be the answer. Yet, the supernatural for some is the real for others, and it becomes a mere question of who holds enough linguistic power to provide its legitimacy—therefore following the linguistic adage claiming that "a language is a dialect with an army and a navy." In other words, languages used to describe this reality often remain in a discourse shaped around colonial history. But what is so peculiar about Galeano's works lies in this one common universal of reality: Speech. However, the experiences of the world show that untrained eyes and minds would not notice what the Amazonian collective observes. As a collected folklore, the gathered pieces come from voices rather than written texts, and through oral tradition survived the passing of time through oral traditions. And while *El Río* explicitly demonstrates the oral nature of this genre, the tales induce a possible interpretation of the different themes and motifs encountered throughout the reading. Among the most common tropes found in all three works, the mirrored civilization within water often appears as a world below the river similar to the one above—with the difference that aquatic creatures represent everyday life amongst the supernatural creatures inhabiting houses in cities at the bottom of the rivers. Such is the case with the *Yakurunas*. But more than being just a place, the water also speaks through its agency: In one of the tales about the *Yakurunas*, a man sees his daughter captured and forced to live under the river; she then returns thanks to the help of a shaman. When the child is about to go back to the water, the father runs to catch her, but the river swells into a wave to carry her back into its womb. In this episode, the river appears as an active character in the story, in front of the powerless father, who can only accept what he defines as a tragic fate, whereas the child's sisters are secretly jealous and curious about the apparent world of wonders where their elder sister has gone to live her life. In the tale entitled *Yakumama*, the river houses the Yakumama, who exercises control over all the life around it. The metaphor presents multiple interpretations: the river as a place for a better life (it allows paddling from one city to another for food and commerce), as a dangerous environment (flooding settlements), and as a place of enchantment (a wealthy kingdom). Forced back into reconstructing views of reality, reading these writings of the Amazon leads us to consider multiple ways of looking at the region through a specific framework of time and space. This notion of time and space is visible through Galeano's narrative choices as well.

As shown in these works, the notion of time relates closely to the elements, the river, and the creatures of the forest. The language used to "translate" *orality* into a written text allows for a certain flexibility of time, expressed, for instance, through an ellipsis within the same sentence; in another tale, *Curupira* (the master of all animals), a man goes hunting with his son after being told not to shoot the first animal he sees—unfortunately and tragically, he ends up doing just that. When telling the story, Galeano merges past, present, and future: "'And because it has to happen thus' (he would repeat later), the young boy insisted so much that [the man] shot."[2] Galeano's representation brings together the past and the present, merging together and deviating from traditional rules of writing. This narrative compression of time permits a shift in focus, perhaps indicating a possible different representation of time within cultures as well. In terms of place, the notion of water remains the most important criterion for where the whole story takes place.

Interest in the ecology of water has risen since the ecological debate has become urgent for the people of Amazonia (Aragon and Clüsener-Godt 2004, Fraser and Tello Imaina, 2015). As we can see in the documentary *El Río*, increasing water pollution has led to a deep awareness of the risks when rivers are endangered. Early in the film, an interviewed student called Marco states that "We belong to the water. It's not that the water belongs to me or to the Kokama people, but rather we belong to the water."[3] More than being the "liquid of life," water represents a whole universe and calls for a need to reflect on the relationship between nature(s) and culture(s) discussed earlier. But the literary significance of water also ties closely to the imaginary (Bachelard 1993), and this relationship between water and culture through poetics will remain the main focus of our discussion.

The beauty of the river lies in more than its liquidity. Looking at the poetics, it can be seen in many ways as a literary figure for which reflections on = its personification applies: apparently superficial, water has a type of intimacy for the imagination of substance (Bachelard 1993). In several instances, the *río* also becomes a mirror. In the tale *O navio encantado* (The Enchanted Boat), the river reflects the bright moonlight, and is figuratively inactive and opaque, whereas a completely different universe actually exists below the surface, as the reader discovers through the development of the story. Other creatures and other beings live the same lives out of the water, adapted to their environment. This tale echoes the observations of fisherman Walter in *El Río*, who mentions the similarities between creatures living within these waters and humans—creatures of the earth. The notion of being "human" (*gente* in Spanish) also appears in the text, as is the case with dolphins who coax a fisherman into telling everyone that pink dolphins (*botos*) are *gente: "Os botos são como a gente."* Besides, the sentence, repeated twice, appears in Portuguese in the text. Expected at the center of the narrative, water generates a new possibility for meanings and interpretations of what traditionally emanates from words only; while revolving around this elemental notion of linguistic variability and flexibility, including metaphors of worlds hidden within rivers, water allows for a new understanding of the plurality of nature. The description of kingdoms within the river in the *Tales* and poems also corroborates that of the documentary, pushing even further the notion of genres—are the *Tales* a fiction if the interviewee tells the same story as a fact?

The naked eye never cannot see the naked bodies under the river ... or so the tales tell. In *O navio encantado*, traditional reading markers are blurred. On the one hand, the title already confronts the two languages evolving in a linguistic liminal space between a variety of Colombo-Peruvian Spanish and Brazilian Portuguese, as the text often makes use of both. However, the ambivalence present in this tale goes further, since working on a text written in Calderon's language whilst giving a Portuguese title confounds the reader by this deviation. Where exactly are we now? Why is the narration in Spanish while the characters speak Portuguese? Languages of the oppressor are pushed away from the prescriptivist approach, and meaning matters more than the form in which it is delivered. The same is true for the tale of the *Matinta-Pereira* bird, where *la dueña de la casa* (the house-owner lady) uses Portuguese again:

"Essas são besteiras dos índios" ("Those are dumb stories told by the Indians") to describe the *matinta-pereira* bird and its possible danger for the community; moreover, the magical formula to reveal who transformed into the bird also appears in Portuguese: *"Cumpadre, venha a tomar café amanhã bem cedo"* ("My friend, come early tomorrow to have coffee"). The cohabitation of both languages in the text (through the main narration and reported speech) offers a clue as to the linguistic flexibility allowed by not only transports around the river, but also by the refusal to adopt one unique language. This can also be seen through variations in the particular grammar of the Spanish spoken in *El Río*, which commonly diverges from the canonical Spanish.

In the tales, the world of dolphins also stands out as a metaphor for another version of the "civilized" world under water, which can be read as a reference to modern urbanized areas, as seen in tales such as *María y los delfines* (Mary and the Dolphins), *La ciudad encantada* (The Enchanted City) or *La ciudad de los delfines* (The City of Dolphins). These three tales depict a world of wonders and "beauty lying beneath or near a river" ("La ciudad encantada no está debajo del agua") to tell that what the eye cannot see exists and matters, and should be protected just like the environment on the surface, of which it constitutes a part. *María y los delfines* tells the story of a young woman who disappears after a handsome young man appears first in her dreams and then on the river shore when she is playing with pink dolphins. She then refuses to follow her father's wish to marry a man of the region, and she disappears, supposedly with the dolphins where the man came from. Here, the waters of the river are a place of encounter as well as a symbol of the delimitation between dreams and life as two connected realities. The handsome young man appears in the woman's dreams, before appearing when she is awake, while she is playing with dolphins next on the river. *La ciudad encantada* describes the adventure of a young man traveling to another city of wonders only accessible through water after meeting a beautiful woman who wants to show him where she comes from—an enchanted city next to a river. He then comes back with gold in his bag; his friends discover his secret, and they try to follow him to no avail. In both of these tales, the story revolves around a character enticed by a creature of the water, a metaphor for the "better world" as a danger to the family and the community. These tales are exemplary of the thin lines between the world of dreams, the world of waters, and the world in which the populations of the Amazonian region live. Water thus plays the role of frontier between these worlds, always through the mirror image. On the other hand, *La ciudad de los delfines* combines linguistic ambiguity with this mirroring of realities. Pink dolphins endorse healthy behaviors, they do not like shamanic smokes, and breathing is reversed: "*Lucían como hombres pero respiraban por unos agujeros en la cabeza*" ("They were shining with a human aura but were breathing through holes in the head"); in this tale, they see the lights out in the distance as a glimmer of hope and the desire to be recognized as bearing human traits. This inversion of roles—the dolphins living in opulence while craving the sociocultural status of the less wealthy—emphasizes the relationship between nature and success according to the population living in the area, while dolphins live seemingly better in these cities. One question thus remains: Does the construction of the Amazonian people's modern imaginaries serve as a coping mechanism against globalization and economic schemes? Do these modern imaginaries express the Amazonian people's desire to have alternative modernities?

This fine line between the perceptible reality and the one associated with the unseen is evident in the poem *Curupira*. The Curupira is a supernatural guardian of the forests known in the Brazilian and Colombian Amazon, and it "could blow smoke so the animals, trees, and fruits disappear." The word *disappear* emphasizes the dual notion of death and protection. In reverse, the *curupira* "could also tell the animals his secrets for hunting men," and now categories change: The hunter becomes the hunted, just as the invisible life under the river becomes visible. The creatures evoked also appear as a portal between these worlds. The *Chicua* bird in the poems and tales echoing story-teller Julia's *munami* in *El Río* announces where the water goes (rains, floods, …), while emerging from the forest storytelling in the Brazilian Amazon; the *Matinta-pereira*, which appears only in the tales and poems, assumes a similar function on a larger scale. Another important creature in the *Amazonian lore*, the *Yara* may best symbolize this connection between land and water—a half-woman, half-fish who brings good fortune to humans. In *El regalo de la yara* (The Yara Gift), a young man from Lima hears music—again from the river—and is enticed by the Yara, whose gifts could enhance the young man's future; in the poems, the Yara also brings sensuality, since she is depicted as "a woman singing or combing her pubis." Among all these, one creature overlooks the world around water: the Yakumama. While the English language conserves the gender ambiguity, speakers oscillate between the two articles available in Spanish, *el* for masculine or *la* for feminine. Thus, *La* Yakumama, the Mother of Waters, sometimes becomes *El* Yakumama. Even its androgynous state is somewhat rendered ambiguous when qualified as *Madre del agua* (Mother of Water). The mere fact that the governing force of the region lives in the river proves the importance of water, but it also has significance further down the land: communities "in the Andean mountains bordering Chile and Argentina [are] demanding the halt of mining projects in glacier-fed river headwaters because it will destroy 'Yacurmama or Mayumaman,' that is to say the mother of water" (Fraser and Tello Imaina, 2015). The similarity between Galeano's report of *Yakumama* (the title chosen for his collection of poems) and the meanings ascribed to water across South American Andean indigenous nations is striking—and emphasizes the agency of water as a gravitational center for people in and around the Amazonian region. All three works also bring forward myths of origin. In the opening of the *Cuentos amazónicos*, the tale *Moniya amena* describes an earthworm bringing life to a tree, which allows the river to grow and sustain the environment, feeding animals and other trees. Water immediately becomes associated with creation and development. In *El Río*, the river responds to the same logic. As explained in the introduction, several of the interviewees describe the importance of the river as the place where they come from, where they bathe, learn how to fish, hunt, swim, etc. All these activities are crucial to the life of these people, and the work accomplished through this multifaceted project central to the Iquitos region of the Amazon further deepens the claim that there is a complex relationship between humans and water.

Overall, humans in Iquitos gravitate towards rivers in Iquitos just like many other populations around the world. For Amazonian populations, water is also defined as the element of which they are mainly constituted, and they are fascinated by everything hiding within its depths. The complex network of rivers at the core of the Amazon rainforest reveals a confounding and complex life, and, through the multiple voices governed by the mother of all rivers, Galeano provides a strong foundation on which to solidify and expand the knowledge of a different vision of the world and of the plurality of conceptions of natures heard throughout all three pieces. Modernity in the Amazon also participates in a different understanding of reality, in developing an imaginary allowing its residents to respond to the destructive and smothering effects of modernity. Part of the meaning of Galeano's film and texts also lies in highlighting the struggle that these populations are currently facing, a struggle partly due to a misrepresentation of their own reality. The need to listen to these voices is now urgent and crucial.

Notes

[1]Original text in Spanish: "*Maritza: 'Porque de ahí sacamos el agua, ahí lavamos, ahí pescamos, ahí nos bañamos. Para nosotros todo es el río.'*" English translation by Vera Coleman.

[2]Original text in Spanish: "'*Y como las cosas que tienen que suceder, suceden' (repetía después), el muchacho insistió tanto que él disparó.*" Author's translation.

[3]Original in Spanish: "*Marco: 'Nosotros pertenecemos al agua. No es que el agua a mí me pertenece o al pueblo cocama le pertenece el agua, sino nosotros.'*" English translation by Vera Coleman.

[4]Author's translation.

Bibliography

Aragón, Luis E., and Clüsener-Godt. "Issues of Local and Global Use of Water in the Amazon." *UNESCO Office Montevideo and Regional Bureau for Science in Latin America and the Caribbean*, 2004.

Bachelard, Gaston. *L'eau et les Rêves. Essai sur L'imagination de la Matière*. Paris : Livre de Poche, 1993.

Bashkow, Ira. "A Neo-Boasian Conception of Cultural Boundaries." *American Anthropologist* 106 (September 2004): 443–58. https://www.jstor.org/stable/3567610.

Bonelli, Cristobal, Denisse Roca-Servat, and Mourik Bueno de Mesquita, 2016. "The Many Natures of Water in Latin-American Neo-Extractivist Conflicts." *ALTERNAUTAS*, (September 2016). http://www.alternautas.net/blog/2016/12/9/the-many-natures-of-water-in-latin-american-neo-extractivist-conflicts.

Dawson, Kevin. *Undercurrents of Power: Aquatic Culture in the African Diaspora*. Philadelphia: University of Pennsylvania Press, 2018.

Descola, Philippe. *Par-delà Nature et Culture*. Trebaseleghe: Gallimard, 2005.

Galeano, Juan Carlos. *El Río*. Directed by Juan Carlos Galeano (Tallahassee: Studio/Juan Carlos Galeano, 2018, Digital HD Color 16:9). English subtitles by Vera Coleman. https://filmfreeway.com/ElRio.

Everett, Daniel. *Don't Sleep, There Are Snakes: Life and Language in the Amazonian Jungle*. New York City: Vintage, 2008.

Fraser, Barbara, and Eduardo Tello Imaina. "A Monthly Report on Development and the Environment in Latin America." EcoAméricas 17 (2015), 1–12. https://www.worldcat.org/title/ecoamericas-a-monthly-report-on-development-and-the-environment-in-latin-america/oclc/40658957.

Freire, Paolo. *Pedagogy of the Oppressed*. New York City: Bloomsbury Academic, 2014.

Galeano, Juan Carlos. *Yakumama (and Other Mythical Beings)*. Translated by James Kimbrell and Rebecca Morgan. Iquitos: Tierra Nueva, 2014.

---. *Cuentos amazónicos*. Bogota: Icono, 2016.

Glissant, Edouard. *Soleil de la Conscience. Poétique 1*. Paris: Gallimard, 1997.

---. *L'intention Poétique, Poétique 2*. Paris: Gallimard, 1997.
---. *Poétique de la Relation, Poétique 3*. Paris: Gallimard, 1990.
---. *Traité du Tout-Monde, Poétique 4*. Paris: Gallimard, 1997.
Huntington, Julie. *Sounding Off: Rhythm, Music, and Identity in West African and Caribbean Francophone Novels*. Philadelphia: Temple University, 1997.
Janicki, Carol. *Language Misconceived: Arguing for Applied Cognitive Sociolinguistics*. Mahwah: Lawrence Erlbaum Associates, 2006.
Landolt, Gredna and Alexandre Surrallés. *Serpiente de Agua, la Vida Indigena en la Amazonía*. Lima: Fundación Telefónica, 2003.
Levi-Strauss, Claude. *Race et Histoire éd Folio*. Paris: Gallimard Education, 2007.
---. *Structures Elémentaires de la Parenté*. Paris: Editions de l'Ecole des Hautes Etudes en Sciences Sociales, 2017.
Santos Granero, Fernando. "Magia, Mito y Literatura." *Proceso* 70 (1991): 90–98.
Uzendoski, Michael, and Edith F. Calapucha-Tapuy. *The Ecology of the Spoken Word*. Chicago: University of Illinois Press, 2012.

Cynthia Hogue

"An Attentive Engagement with Nature": An Appreciation of Harriet Tarlo's Radical Landscape Poetry

In a thorough introduction to a 2008 *How2* feature on women and ecopoetics curated by Harriet Tarlo, she argues for a poetry which breaks down the artificial divisions "between rural and urban, cultivated and wild, natural and technological," rather than perpetuates them. To the poets featured in the issue, Tarlo observes, such divisions are "inaccurate in this largely post-wilderness world," and, moreover, do not help to promote "writing which tries to engage with the political significance of the environmental crisis."[1] Broadly, Tarlo's theoretical contributions to the field and her own poetry are exemplary of how one might develop an ethical writing practice out of what Elizabeth-Jane Burnett has characterized as ecopoetry's "attentive engagement with nature."[2] Tarlo developed the term "radical landscape poetry" to denote an exploratory poetics that takes into realistic account our "contemporary landscape, [including] rural people and past and present agricultural and social issues."[3] Such poetry is "located writing," often based on intimate familiarity with a particular place, and bears witness to site-specific change. In lieu of formal certainty and thematic conclusion, radical landscape poetry offers "questions, uncertainties, self doubts and self corrections."[4]

To illustrate, I'll turn in brief to Tarlo's 2009 collection, *Nab*, which evokes a spare northern landscape in precisely detailed descriptions. The volume is in three sections comprised of three serial poems: "Brancepeth Beck," "Coast," and "Nab." *Nab* is, we might say, *sight*-specific: the observing eye tracks perceptions in ways that blur the edges between inside and outside the poem's frame:

> rained itself
> out rock grows beck
> turned against
> pouring grows over
> mud widening faster
> than i can
> run faster than
> stumbled gorse pulls
> against rained it
> self out[5]

These lines are from the untitled poem in the first serial poem, "Brancepeth Beck," which opens the collection. Words fall hard like rain, the brook overflows, and mud is running: we aren't sure where we can stop, catch a foothold, or find where a new syntactic unit begins. I try to latch onto the word, "gorse," but it isn't about parsing the phrases, but rather like the rain flowing through, over, around them until the word-water "rained it / self out." Here's a site-specific, self-emptying poetry right from *Nab*'s first page.

Unsettled, destabilized, readers pick our way through carefully observed details without the orienting aid of summarizing statements about what the details add up to: Muddy walks (two days of rain) but not cold. We readers might surmise that it's likely summer, perhaps midsummer: "already elderberries" are the only words on the last page in the series. The two separated words float on the otherwise blank page just above the center, their relationship (adverb and noun) syntactic and spatial, significantly time-bound. Self-emptied into landscape, all-ready: bearing fruit.

The last section, "Nab," tracks a season of walking near the rocky summit, the nab, which gives the collection both its title and dominant image, the word resonating throughout the volume:

August, late
up the nab

great hairy willowherb
then rosebay
then foxgloves

foxgloves shaking, spreading

shaking   wind

all the way up

up against   nab

(*Nab* 45)

As this passage conveys, the nab is really alive with seasonally changing and altitude-sensitive flora as well as fauna (weasel, wren, tit, kestrels, rabbits all are named and noted in the poem). The images are lyrically charged through word and sound repetitions (late-bay, shaking-shaking, and the plosives of up-up and nab-nab). The presence of the "nab" predominates the landscape of both poem and place. Although the nab itself is the stable component of the landscape, the scene is far from pastoral or pristine, as denoted by the arrival below of *housing developments*: "every new development puts / 40% of the developed land / under tarmac" (*Nab* 52), Tarlo documents. "[O]ne plant per county per year / lost / over the century" (*Nab* 53). From the vista atop the nab, it's possible to see that the new houses are built in semi-circles "on the floodplains." "DANGER/ DEEP WATER" (*Nab* 55), the poem warns, the text writ large, like a real sign—in fact, like the actual sign, which Tarlo incorporates into her text.

The moment is at once realistic, as Tarlo has characterized radical landscape poetry, and pointed political critique. As we now know far more dramatically than a decade ago, when this collection was published, ignoring the dangers of a floodplain in order to build a housing development invites the residents literally to get in over their heads! How *Nab* is structured depends not only on the observation of what is, after all, an old divide (rural vs. suburban) in the process of changing, but also of the irrationalism of predatory capitalism: disregarding inconvenient facts, such as a floodplain, in order to profit off housing that at some time or another *will* be washed away. It makes dollars for developers but no *sense* for buyers. That embedded, concrete warning heralds not the future but the clear and present danger of our times (it's observation not prophecy), which humans ignore at our peril and poets ponder ethically like so many Cassandras.

Registering this warning, the speaking subject—both seeing eye and occulted "I"—is spatially located (she is walking on the nab), but unlocatable except by that which she observes. She is "on sight": it is the natural world that orients her subjectivity. She is attentively engaged with this particular place, not only conserving, preserving, and memorializing in the text all that she sees, which will go "under tarmac," but also gesturing toward the importance of being present to what one sees at a particular moment: "you should be here," she states, and then repeats, with a telling difference: "really you *should* be here" (*Nab* 72; emphasis Tarlo's).

Here: all that will *also* go under water in a flood. For, as Tarlo quips toward the end of the poem, whether water or grass growing in the spring, "it's going to win"—nature in some form always does in the end—and if we don't know it yet, we *will*. To be a "realist," as Tarlo has it, is to observe the radically *changed* landscape that late industrial capitalism has wrought, and to acknowledge that radical landscape poetry confronts a world that has moved so far beyond the landscapes of pastoral poetry that the nature portrayed can hardly be seen as *natural*. Possibly, that's her point.

Notes

[1]Harriet Tarlo, "Women and Ecopoetics: An Introduction in Context," *How2* 3, no. 2 (2008): n.p. Online journal archived @ http://www.asu.edu/pipercwcenter/how2journal/vol_3_no_2/ecopoetics/introstatements/tarlo_intro.html

[2]The definition of ecopoetry as a practice of writing "from one's attentive engagement with nature," from "a cultivated ethics of looking, of reading, of paying attention," is that of the poet and ecopoetics theorist Elizabeth-Jane Burnett, drawn from her "Curator's Talk" delivered as opening remarks for the Solstice exhibition, "Skylines: Ecopoetics," Landscapes and L-A-N-G-U-A-G-E Forum, held at the Centre for Contemporary Art and the Natural World, Devon, UK, 20 June 2009. http://www.theattendingfield.com.

[3]Harriet Tarlo (ed.), *The Ground Aslant: An Anthology of Radical Landscape Poetry* (Exeter: 2011), 11.

[4]Ibid., 13, 12.

[5]Harriet Tarlo, *Nab* (Buckfastleigh, UK: Etruscan Books, 2009), 9, hereafter cited parenthetically in text by the title, followed by the page number.

Lynn Keller

Walking into "no future full": Brian Teare's *Doomstead Days*

Brian Teare's 2019 volume *Doomstead Days* begins with his witnessing of the 2007 Cosco Busan oil spill in the San Francisco Bay and its purported cleanup. That spill of thick tarry bunker fuel from a ship that struck the San Francisco Bay Bridge—53,000 gallons according to the US Government (NOAA), 58,000 according to the sources Teare trusted—was for Teare "the first disaster / I could walk to, look // at until it ceased to seem / exceptional" (2).[1] That he could walk to this environmental disaster means most obviously that he could observe and register it firsthand. Teare's on-foot observation initiated a transformation of scalar perception as he was forced to assimilate large-scale disaster as part of his daily life. The experience, full of horror and panic as he watched efforts to rescue oil-covered seabirds and then as he read about the toxic spill's dire effects on marine life, brought home to him "how the real couldn't refuse" whatever anthropogenic changes were taking place. He recalls in the opening poem, "Clear Water Renga":

I couldn't get over it

how the real couldn't
refuse, could do nothing but
disburse tar ball, sheen,

& slick from the central Bay
on currents west through the Gate

until the whole coast,
Marin to Pacifica
to the Farallones,

absorbed the new fact the real
had given it (3)

Walking plays an especially important role in Teare's compositional process, with many of his poems developing out of field notes accumulated over repeated walks. Consequently, his being able to walk to this disaster also means that the spill and the encompassing environmental degradations it exemplifies become subjects he can directly grapple with through his poetry. Moreover, as Teare has explained in the blog post "*En Plein Air*: Notes Toward Writing in the Anthropocene," writing while walking fosters in him the awareness, fundamental to his current poetics, of "intercorporeal" relations among human and nonhuman beings, and among humans and both biotic and abiotic matter.[2]

Despite that appealing theory he offers of walking as the basis for ecologically sensitive writing, readers are likely to see his walking also enacting a problematically "exceptional" escape from environmental disturbance and environmental injustice. In "Clear Water Renga," when Teare is stunned by the real's "endless capacity ... for fact," the fear arising in response to his recognition of "how the real will accept any / thing" (7) prompts him to "go // north to Marin, miles / from any city limit / to land protected // by law, to walk, to outpace / panic" (7–8). He explicitly longs to find in that landscape's panoramas "vision's discursive limit" where the mind relinquishes its "language job." That impulse to find emotional relief and mental quiet by walking in undeveloped countryside is one to be reckoned with, particularly given the privilege that allows the poet even to have access to such protected sites of relatively undisturbed "nature."

As an activity long celebrated and recorded by nature writers, walking provides a troublesome legacy for the contemporary ecopoet who is committed to dealing with the real conditions of what I have elsewhere termed the "self-conscious Anthropocene."[3] Thoreau's treatise on "Walking," for instance, reeks of an elitism, if not of social class then of soul; there he presents himself as one of few who, being walkers, possess a freedom and independence that come only from the grace of God. Teare, conscious of the inequities of environmental justice and the chanciness of privilege, as well as the precarious, even desperate, conditions of the planetary environment, would never want to associate himself with such a conception of the pastoral walker. Yet in *Doomstead Days* he shows a decided preference for rural over urban spaces, and in that preference readers may recognize affinities with Thoreau's much elaborated preference for the wild over the cultivated that positions nature apart from human culture and society. Teare's inclinations that draw him at a moment of evident environmental crisis out of the city to walk in Point Reyes National Seashore are not entirely unlike those of Thoreau, who describes himself as always "withdrawing into the wilderness."[4]

Aware of this problematic heritage, Teare in "Clear Water Renga" defends his own practice as something other than indulgence or escapism. Here's a passage where he describes the valued emptying of thought that walking in the Marin headlands brings him and then justifies the kind of outward attention that accompanies such cognitive evacuation:

I've walked as far as it takes
to walk past thought into what

might be called image,
non-discursive :: I spend hours
so empty my mind's

the ranch barn open both ends
to wind, nothing but old hay

stirring in the stalls ::
it used to seem indulgent
to vanish outward

into the texture of elk
fur on the hills of White Gulch,

its two-toned velvet
gold then brown against brighter
brittle grasses, but

even then I still dwell in
the real, our occupation,

the American
goldfinch husking invasive
thistle seed for feed

the large paradox writ small ::
each image that replaces

consciousness *is*
the real (18–19)

The descriptions of phenomena observed with an empty mind—given lyric intensity through the music of alliterating "br" sounds in the elk fur "brown against brighter brittle" and the repeating "f"'s and "s"'s as well as the echoing vowels in "goldfinch husking invasive thistle seed for feed"—demonstrate the honed attention to the material world and the materiality of language, the embodied appreciation, that liberation from discursive thinking enables.[5] Buttressing Teare's argument that such an investment in the image and in the walking that nourishes it is not an escapist indulgence are two crucial gestures: acknowledgment of "our occupation" and acknowledgment of introduced invasive species. Just a few pages earlier Teare had considered white settler colonists' ruinous occupation of this area where Coast Miwok "for centuries walked to shore / then walked back inland to hunt." Settlers, he noted, "uncalendared that walking ritual, the hunt's sacred to and fro," and by 1880, "after / displacement, European / disease, slavery // and assimilation," the native tribe had been largely extirpated. In the passage about the nondiscursive quoted above, then, "our occupation" foregrounds white America's imperialist, even genocidal, history. Additionally, "our occupation" designates the human takeover and disturbance of natural ecosystems in the Anthropocene, which includes the introduction of non-native plants such as those on which the goldfinch feeds. Teare's claim seems to be that as long as the walker is seeing truly, recognizing the terrible history of which he is a part and the ubiquitous disturbance to the ecosystem caused by people like himself, then even when he (or she or they) manages to move beyond thought into purely phenomenological awareness of his surroundings, he is not really escaping. That person will, Teare asserts, be attuned not just to ecological interrelation, but to the intertwining of the anthropogenic and the biospheric, and to human—specifically, settler colonial, and capitalist industrial—culpability.

In observing "the large paradox writ small," Teare claims that what the walker observes on the small local level offers a scaled-down version of the larger environmental challenges and dangers the world faces. This notion that, even when freed from the burdens of consciousness, the attentive viewer will perceive in the small phenomena of both more and less disturbed landscapes the larger environmental issues that threaten Holocene species governs the volume. Teare explains in "*En Pleine Air* Poetics," posted shortly before the release of *Doomstead Days*, "I've come to believe that the way anthropogenic and ecosystemic processes intertwine on the local level is in essence a scale model of far larger intertwinings, a small instance that repeats biosphere patterns that are of course *literally* quite different in scale and temporality" (italics his). Exemplified also in his local experience of the Cosco Busan disaster, this belief explains the volume's interest in the quadrat: the small area, typically a square meter, studied by field biologists as a representative sample of the biodiversity of a larger area. Teare's interest in the revealing microcosm as the subject of an ambulatory field-based poetics motivates the "Headlands Quadrats" that follow "Clear Water Renga." (Those image-focused observations of the Marin landscape take the form of six-lined squares, a geometric form echoed also in the book's square pages and its double colon punctuation marks.) In "*En Pleine Air* Poetics" Teare continues his discussion of scaling by noting its ethical importance in helping us "situate 'the known world in relation to times and or places that are distant or otherwise inaccessible to direct experience.'"[6] He adds,

> Through the lens of scaling, I've likewise come to believe that intercorporeal relation to a site, when filtered through mindfully acquired knowledge, can also repeat, on a small scale, the Anthropocene's globalized patterns—neither to celebrate nor reify such patterns, nor to claim to grasp a biospheric process like global warming in anything like its totality, but rather to clarify our complicity with and participation in the end of the world.

Holding Teare's explanations in mind, the rest of this essay will examine specific practices through which, even when he seeks solace in less disturbed natural areas, his poetics of walking creates a relation to his surroundings that illuminates the nearly unimaginable precarity of contemporary planetary life that he confronts in "Clear Water Renga." I will demonstrate that by foregrounding the damage to his own body accrued through chronic illness, by emphasizing transcorporeal absorption of anthropogenic pollutants and the unavoidable impact of anthropogenic change in exurban as well as urban spaces, and by foregrounding his queerness, Teare succeeds in transforming the conventions of nature writing associated with walking. In *Doomstead Days*, wildness suffuses all aspects of human and nonhuman animal experience, while rural and urban places alike are realms in which purity, a surprisingly durable aspect of the inherited imagining of the wild, is not possible. Rather than being indulgent acts of escape into a better, purer realm and performances of social or intellectual privilege, Teare's walks and the poems that develop from them are unblindered acts of agonized yet impassioned allegiance to ongoing incurable life.

His walking poem set in semi-rural New England, "Convince Me You Have a Seed There" (the title taken from Thoreau's "The Succession of Forest Trees"), illustrates Teare's refusal of myths of pastoral purity and his use of walking to insist on pervasive anthropogenic environmental disruption.[7] The poem tracks the poet's solitary walk up to an old cemetery above the village of Johnson, Vermont, and on into a stand of mature pines. Touching their "live hard sides," he feels the intercorporeal bond between person and tree as he recalls Plato's vision of the human being as "a heavenly plant / the soul housed // in the head // threaded down / out of abstract // heaven to live // in the physical /soil" (101). When he looks up at the groaning pines whose crowns in the wind "twist against roots in earth," however, his perception registers awareness of human meddling with nonhuman species: he wonders about how another pine tree sounds, the one "bioengineered / by Arbor Gen* // its genes spliced // with Monterey pine / mouse ear cress // sweet gum // & even e. coli / to become // disease resistant / a Super Tree" (103). At first he tries to imagine this new tree that "climbs to forty six / feet over nine // growing seasons" (103) as "a version / of Plato's vision: as "an earthly plant" imbued with a "heavenly power / that keeps the tree // reaching toward it" (104). But moments after this attempt to fit the GMO tree into a received paradigm, we find the earthbound poet, who stands in socks wet from the winter's thaw, perceiving through a critical and scaled-up Anthropocene lens: "I think / of transgenic pollen // germinating // after it travels / hundreds of miles // & how farmers // can't contain cross-pollination // between spliced // and wild species" (105). The formal structure of the poem—short lines tumbling down the page without punctuation to establish syntactic borders—mirrors this impossibility of containment, the impossibility now of separating the wild from the man-made.

We witness their inseparability as the speaker deliberately stops thinking about "the laboratory / future" and tries instead to focus on what he wants to believe, which is the continuance of unmodified arboreal succession. Returning to what is immediately before his eyes, he observes, however, how at the base the trunks of the genetically *un*modified pines around him are colored by presumably anthropogenic nutrient run-off. In this way, Teare indicates that what he wanted to believe rested on a false dichotomy of nature and culture; even the old pines, we learn, were deliberately planted by humans, and they inevitably exist in "material relation" with all the changes to water and atmosphere that industrialized late empire has engendered. The poem closes with an image of lichen seen growing on a single birch, an early succession tree that has "infiltrated" the symmetrical stand of pines, as "a sort of saffron / stain the startle // of fox piss in snow" (110). With wonderful economy, those closing lines reveal the inevitability of disturbance to ecological order (birch succession occurs without human intervention) and insist on the impurity of all life. They also acknowledge potential beauty in that impurity.

Impurity is the focus of the longest of the book's eight poems, "Toxics Release Inventory (Essay on Man)," written as Teare came to know Philadelphia and its environs after leaving the West Coast. The poem takes the form of a 50-page string of haikus. However, defying haiku's association with suspended moments of seasonal beauty and challenging the optimism of Alexander Pope's "Essay on Man" (to which his sub-title refers), Teare produces a city-based poem largely about environmental toxins that exposes the illusion of boundaries between manmade and natural, pure and polluted. Although initially positioning himself as an alienated observer of the cityscape, increasingly he presents his own body in intercorporeal terms as a part of the place and its deadly pollution.

In the early pages, Teare depicts the city in negative ways Thoreau might endorse, even using some of the economic language fundamental to *Walden*'s critique of town ways:

> the city
> conducts its business
>
> trading the wishes
> of citizen for empty
> actuality
>
> we walk out into,
> the future a proffered naught
> beneath our feet, sealed
>
> soil infertile, streets
> & sidewalks yielding nothing
> but surface runoff
>
> polluted with oil,
> gasoline, antifreeze, trash
> washed from gutters to
>
> sewers to rivers
> by heavy rains :: (46–47)

Teare thinks next about drone warfare, and how "the state hopes to hide / from public view the human / cost of war, a shame // everything's stained by"; the pollution he is registering is political and moral as well as material. Moreover—as when listening to pine trees brought to his mind the genetically engineered version—his awareness of anthropogenic pollution overlays his perceptions of what might otherwise seem pure. When he stops at a market stand selling "*FRESH CUT // FLOWERS*," what he thinks of are the costs in environmental health of their fresh beauty:

> runoff & pesticides, sprayed
> day laborers sick
>
> from the exposure,
> thousands of pounds of carbon
> pumped from planes & trucks
>
> refrigerated
> to get beauty here unharmed :: (53)

He likens the city's beauty to that of a white lily he examines, its waxy petals "stained" by dark pollen; that metaphoric stain is literalized in cataloged trash that emerges from the thawing ice on the city's sidewalks: "cups, / plastic bottle caps, // Styrofoam peanuts, / cigarette butts, each cast-off / polymer a link // in an industry / chain fabricated to last" (54–5).

Such an implicitly judgmental presentation of the city's ugly stain seems utterly predictable in the context of the heritage of Romantic nature writing, but a complicating narrative intervenes involving the poet's sexual encounter with a handsome man: "an experience // all apostrophe / & lubrication until / he pulls out, condom // broken" (59). Teare, "possibly infected," goes through an HIV test and post-exposure prophylactic treatment. "I puke for a week, // am not infected" (61), he reports. But clearly, he *is* infected: not with HIV, thankfully, but with the chemicals given him by the clinician. If he has been holding himself apart from the city's pollution, as its judgmental observer whose true home is in protected lands, that is over. There is no enduring protection. And as the poem and the walks it follows continue to unfold, the emphasis is on the inescapable corporeal absorption by both human and nonhuman animals of all the toxic materials industrialized humans have injected into the environment. Teare perceives a fox encountered on a walk near the Wissahickon Creek ("improbable there / among us" [64]) as having "organs / heavy with the lead thirty / six smelters left north // in the Delaware / River Wards" (65). No body, we understand, is uncontaminated. Indeed, in Teare's nighttime dreams the fox becomes the container of all the toxins of the region's industry: from its white gut "spills // over three hundred / thousand pounds of sulfuric / acid, one hundred // fifty four thousand / of hydrogen cyanide, / twenty eight thousand // of cumene, toxics / released onsite, byproducts / of refining crude // chuted through wetlands / off the river ..." This dreamt *spill* from the fox's guts echoes the Cosco Busan spill in the book's opening poem: in the world whose material structure industrialized humans have rendered so toxic, the environmental consequences of the rupture of an animal body are a small-scale version of the puncture of an oil tanker's hull.

Through the ambulatory journey of "Toxics Release Inventory," Teare demonstrates that chemical disaster is ordinary and everywhere; it may be more obvious in the city, but he makes clear that any imagining of the wild now as contrastingly pure would be willful self-delusion. The responsibility for that pervasive pollution lies, of course, with industrialized humans. Teare contrasts his assessment of humankind with that of Pope in "Essay on Man": "I hear instead / of his praise the change // we bring to the terms / of life, how we make matter / an antagonist" (69). He then documents that change in another inventory of toxins, emphasizing how industry "touches / us so totally // we find our final / privacies violated ::":

benzene & styrene,

toluene & n-
hexane, carbon disulfide
& acetone :: six

toxics present in
ninety four to one hundred
percent of people

tested, both urban
& rural, people whose blood
& urine carries

the cost of merely
breathing as they go to work ::
& are not broken

by contaminants,
or not yet broken by
the slow violence

latent in the wake
of bioaccumulants
& synergistic

toxins stored in fat,
in the liver & kidneys (70–1)

The diseases and medical conditions caused by bodily absorption of these toxins alter the stakes, Teare notes, of Merleau Ponty's question, "where are we to put // the limit between / the body & the world, since / all the world is flesh?" (72). If we live in a world where there is no evident limit to what the real must accept and what a body might absorb, what are meaningful limits? Teare considers how some kinds of limit are social, learned through one's race, sexuality, and gender, in his case as "white queer boy." Decrying the "fake limits" imposed on him as a young person "of family life / enforced by Christ & paddle, / the petty moral //legalise peddled / by people who try to shame / my love for the flesh" (76), Teare aligns himself instead with the limits of the bloody, lustful body, even though those are now compounded by anthropogenic toxins.

Writing the rest of the poem on a hike 80 miles from Philadelphia, he describes the difficulties of walking that stem from his unfake bodily limits. In addition to experiencing burning muscles and lungs as he climbs, Teare endures painful osteoarthritis: "my feet //a nest of nettles / whose sting I can neither touch / nor escape :: the spurred // bones swell joints, afflict / skin with paresthesia, burn / without remedy // except to walk on, / let my mind vanish into / movement" (78–9). This depiction of physical suffering as integral to his walking undercuts any sense of walking as privileged indulgence. Indeed, it's crucial to the volume's representation of walking that, because of Teare's chronic health conditions, the activity threatens to harm, not just to benefit, him. The poem "Olivine, Quartz, Granite, Carnelian" depicts Teare slipping while hiking and taking a fall against rock that forces him to recall the medical images he has seen of his degrading bones as well as his doctor's warning, "*You might have years / of mobility left / if you're careful*" (117). Such vulnerability is shared, intercorporeal, and exists on multiple environmental scales; thus, while walking poses a danger to Teare's body, that body, releasing in urine "a potent effluent / of medicines I need // & pesticides I don't," produces "a pharmacopeia / of harm for riverine // species" (118). Teare represents himself walking and watching "as if I could forget / the harm that happens where // the world's flesh meets my flesh" (122), but in fact he's aware that his body is in a hard-to-face crisis state analogous to that of the Earth in the Anthropocene: it's "the sort of ruin / that seems livable // until it isn't" (126).

Returning to Teare's developing acknowledgement of embodied participation in ongoing ruin in "Toxics Inventory," the dreams recounted after he describes the painful conditions afflicting his body are of a postapocalyptic world in which "we no longer leave / the cities" (81). Humans live high up downtown "in commons / linked by rope walkways / & grow / our food on the roofs," while the ruined lower city is the terrain of nonhuman animals. Those are his dreams; yet if cities are sites of concentrated waste and pollution, in effect we no longer leave the cities in our current waking lives. We carry their toxicity wherever we walk: "my blood an arsenic sleeve, / a lead reservoir, // a wet rose loaded / with mercury" (86). Recognizing what he dubs "the toxicity // of everyday life" (85), wherever it's lived, brings Teare to articulate in the poem's closing stanzas the fundamental challenge of this moment: how to recognize that we have no future and yet move toward and into it:

> yes, I was thinking
> we live without a future ::
> that's what's queer :: & now
>
> to write, with a new
> nib, & to go on wanting
> to catch the rhythm
>
> of being open,
> critical, & also glad,
> married to the world
>
> alive with the feel
> of mortal knowledge :: no high,
> no low, no great, no
>
> small :: no future full
> of forces that bind, connect,
> & equal all ::[8]

What's queer, says the queer poet, is our living without a future. His announcement echoes the branch of queer theory associated with Lee Edelman's *No Future*[9] in which Edelman argues for a queer rejection of "the future"—that is, a rejection of the ways a heteronormative vision of the future, defined exclusively through reproduction and the nuclear family, organizes social and political life. But, as queer ecologist Nicole Seymour points out in *Strange Natures*, queer environmental thinkers *need* to think about futurity, and Teare's focus on "how to keep going" (131,132) through his own incurable health conditions provides one indication of his agreement.[10] Teare identifies the challenge everyone faces now: that of living fully and joyfully as a doomed species in this broken, interconnected, and still wondrous material world.

I see as crucial to Teare's modification of nature writing and nature-writing ambulation his insistence on the queerness of the challenge we face and the queerness of the ways we might get through it. I will close by briefly considering the role played by queerness and nontraditional gender configurations in the title poem. Its opening line announces "today's gender is rain." If there are, as many contend, an unlimited number of human genders, it's perhaps unsurprising that Teare would assign a gender to a day. The etymology of gender, as Teare explains it, clarifies the identification of rain as this wet day's gender: "the word / *gender* remembers / it once meant to fuck / beget or give birth / sibling to *generate* / & *engender* all / fertile at the root / & continuous / as falling water" (142–3). Mimetically, the short lines of the poem, like those of "Convince Me You Have a Seed There,"[11] flow continuously without any punctuation. In that sense they resist containment, just as spilled oil, genetically modified pollens, or leaching synthetic chemicals do. But of course the line length of four to six syllables is a form of limit, and ultimately the poem's content endorses some setting of limits and a deliberate channeling of energy, while it asserts the existence of valuable orders. In this poem, a healer's hands cure Teare's migraine by "pressing the occiput / back open into / the natural curve / the bones forget" (139). He presents the Wissahickon Creek as similarly amnesiac, "having forgotten rapids / rinsing schist shaded / by hemlock that kept / the brook trout cold / each patterned aspect / of habitat lost" to a long chain of anthropogenic transformations (139–40). It's unclear whether the river might, like Teare's own nervous system, remember and return to some version of its earlier order. Teare finds himself "awake now"; like an environmentally healthy Wissahickon, he is "rowdy with trout," his body "roars with water." But that water contains his own "watershed toxins / & heavy metals / bonded to blood ... C8 glyphosate / mercury & lead" (145–6). What he calls the awkwardness of this Anthropocene condition draws his mind to "the man who asks me / to visit his doomstead / which seems kinky / for a first date" (146) and in turn to a meditation on gender: "what's the safeword," he wonders—that is, how does one set needed limits—"for men with genders built for the world's end, men with weaponized genders" (146). His elaboration of such "endtime genders" emphasizes their adherence to a violent heteronormative gender binary: "hetero girlie / camo gun calendars / apocalyptic tits / pinned on brick walls / by lone bunks / so men can cross out / each day once / civil society / ends with a pathetic / snivel like '*please help*'" (147–8). "Doomstead men," insistently masculine whatever their sexual preferences, "live / doomstead days already / sealed in extreme fiction / as if there were / ever a way to stay / safely self-contained." In contrast, he asserts that "the anthropocene / is its own gender / biospheric in scale / its persistent flux / from fossil record / to Antarctic ice core / so uncontainable / we all exhibit it / with a local sense / of personal chosen / expression" (148–9). Unsurprisingly, Teare chooses not to visit the man and his doomstead.

Teare ends "Doomstead Days" mixing warning with hope: there are models in his own health history and in environmental restoration projects for undoing the harm done by capital—but the scale of the challenge is unprecedented. The world and its waters are far too vast to be "taken by the head / in the hands & held / in the hopes of healing" (157). His final observation, closing both the poem and the volume, emphasizes planetary environmental agency and its uncertain consequences: "The world is awake," he insists, "be careful my dears / it is the gender / that remembers / everything" (158). This remembrance includes the tenacity of anthropogenic transformation—the persistence of radiation or plastics, of other synthetic chemicals, the finality of mass extinctions—yet also the endurance of earlier channels of environmental health. Teare suggests that if there's hope, it lies in attunement to the fluid gender of the Anthropocene phenomenological world and in unconventional—queer—ways of loving the world's flesh. Attentive walking in our inescapably impure surroundings may help cultivate both.

Notes

[1] Parenthetic numbers in this essay identify pages for quotations from Brian Teare, *Doomstead Days* (New York: Nightboat Books, 2019).
[2] Teare produced four posts in January 2019 as the featured blogger for The Poetry Foundation's Harriet Blog. Only "*En Plein Air* Poetics: Notes Toward Writing in the Anthropocene" focuses directly on his own practice: https://www.poetryfoundation.org/harriet/2019/01/en-plein-air-poetics-notes-towards-writing-in-the-anthropocene. Teare's thinking about intercorporeality is indebted to Gail Weiss's philosophical study *Body Images: Embodiment as Intercorporeality* (New York: Routledge, 1999), itself indebted to feminist philosophy and phenomenology.
[3] See *Recomposing Ecopoetics: North American Poetry of the Self-Conscious Anthropocene* (Charlottesville: University of Virginia Press, 2017). I propose this term to sidestep debates about the dating of the Anthropocene and focus on the contemporary moment of pervasive, often anxious awareness of human impact on planetary systems. While "the Anthropocene" is a proposed geological designation, "the self-conscious Anthropocene" is a cultural one.
[4] Henry David Thoreau, *Walden, Civil Disobedience, and Other Writings: Authoritative Texts, Journal, Reviews and Posthumous Assessments, Criticism* (New York: W. W. Norton, 2008), 268.
[5] Teare writes powerfully of this experience of release from the cogito into the sensory world in "*En Plein Air* Poetics," for instance when he describes "the kind of hike during which my mind goes from translucent to luminous, its usual wash of thought polished to a transparency that lets the world in with a force I adore."
[6] Teare attributes the quoted material to Deborah R. Coen's *Climate in Motion*.
[7] Teare includes in the poem this much from Thoreau: "*convince me you have // a seed there / & I am prepared // to expect wonders*" (105). The context of current genetic modification lends irony to Teare's allusion.
[8] Earlier in the poem Teare quotes nearly verbatim the passage in Pope's "Essay on Man" that he modifies here. Pope, celebrating the Great Chain of Being, wrote (in Epistle I, viii):

> See, through this air, this ocean, and this earth,
> All matter quick, and bursting into birth. Above,
> how high, progressive life may go! Around, how
> wide! how deep extend below!

Following that quotation, Teare differentiates his view that reflects the self-conscious Anthropocene from Pope's, observing "how we make matter / an antagonist // when industry goes / so wide, so deep, & touches / us so totally" (69).
[9] Lee Edelman, *No Future: Queer Theory and the Death Drive* (Durham: Duke University Press, 2004).
[10] Nicole Seymour, *Strange Natures: Futurity, Empathy, and the Queer Ecological Imagination* (Urbana: University of Illinois Press, 2013).
[11] In "Convince Me" the lines, three to five syllables long, are arranged in alternating singles and couplets; in "Doomstead Days" the lines are four to six syllables in length and are consistently double-spaced. Neither poem contains punctuation other than apostrophes.

Sharon Lattig

Dwelling with the Possible: Lyric Obscurity and Embedded Perception

excerpted from *Cognitive Ecopoetics: A New Theory of Lyric*, forthcoming from Bloomsbury Academic

[As part of] a revision of the dualistic and reductive methods of biology, the biologist Jakob von Uexküll ... theorized that the activity of life (including, but not limited to, the activity of perception) is primarily semantic. Uexküll devised the concept of the *Umwelt*, the subjective or self-centered universe consisting of an organism's significant experience of the environment based in the capacity of its sensorium to select from it in order to meet its biological needs.[1] Subsets of objectively delineated habitats,[2] *Umwelts* may be defined as closed, unified networks of meaningful physical relationships between a "meaning receiver" (an organism) and "meaning carriers"[3] (here, stimuli), the compatible aspects of a habitat with which a meaning receiver interacts by perceiving and "operating" (or acting) upon them.[4] Though circumscribed with respect to a particular organism, an *Umwelt* is " ... a biologically instantiated and causally efficacious set of agent–object relations reducible neither to the organization of the subject nor to the organization of the environment but always as the product of the interaction between the two" (Favareau 83).[5] It is the domain of meaning making created as an organism perceives and acts, what is therefore present to it. "All else is neglected," [occluded, as it were].

It is useful to think of a poem as the construction of an *Umwelt*. For the poet, the speaker, the voice, or the text, as one's poetics allows, the poem becomes the co-constructed middle ground to which the meaning receiver is present, the registration of what is seen, as it is seen and the efficacious verbal–musical action, or utterance, toward the same.[7] By way of pregnant example at the level of content, in the courtly tradition, the beloved is described as she is wooed, wooed as she is described: the portrayal of her beauty is at once an acting by persuasion upon a meaning carrier to which the lover is attracted due to a pre-ordained compatibility or likelihood of attraction. Acting into the environment positions an organism to attract what is "stimulating"—the perceptual stimuli that index the desired object. Conversely, the reception of a poem constructs an *Umwelt* for the listener it creates: love poetry, as a verbal–musical act, is also a luring or a seduction of a beloved for whom it itself becomes a meaning carrier. Orpheus's summoning of flora and fauna with his song may be said to offer his unlikely auditors such a meaning-laden experience: his poetry takes on import for them as they hear and are drawn to it. This overt awareness of perception and action, indeed its fusing, with the potential for the bi-directionality of *Umwelt* creation (the relationship between the bee and the flower inhabits the *Umwelt* of each) is among the reasons the courtly dynamic, exhausted as it now is, remains central within the lyric tradition.

[Notably] ... Uexküll conceives of an *Umwelt* as a "building," as both an edifice and the process of its raising. He redundantly names the space contiguous to the organism in which meaning-carriers "bustle about" a "dwelling house."[8] The domain of significance the percipient shapes in inhabiting it is, I propose, consonant with the home the poetic subject makes in dwelling within the poem. As noted, it is commonplace to conceive of poems architecturally: Dickinson is hardly alone in figuring the form as a house, as she does in Poem 466, but she further grasps that such an edifice requires ventilation. The house of poetry stands "More numerous of windows— / Superior—for doors—" and features ". . . for an everlasting Roof / The Gambrels of the Sky" to allow for the entrance of possibility in which to dwell. It is opened to potential in the form of its relationship to the informing environment (which environment in poetry is perforce linguistic). Uexküll is aware that meaning carriers are objects of potential significance to percipients: he writes that their meaning is "*realized* through perception and operation" (emphasis added). Lyric acknowledges the potential implicated in the relationship of perception to reality, I argue, by means of its obscurity, the expedient admitting linguistic potential, the locus of the origin of poetic meaning.

An understanding of the function of firstness[11] in semantic emergence constitutes the first bit of evidence supporting the claim that the lyric not only represents, but models and perhaps adapts, perceptual processes, as it is the undifferentiated potential for meaning that obscurity evokes and welcomes into the poem. Lyric obscurity inheres to a great extent in what is referred to as the materiality of language, a designation that is half figurative, half literal. The physicality of language is double, existing as ink on a page (or pixels on a screen) and as sound, manifestations that are slight, but physical nonetheless. Of the two, lyric's orality, its persisting, aboriginal form (as is well known, even written lyrics are intended to be heard) manifests most ephemerally, as voice originates in a body emitting energy in wave form pulsing through a medium, perhaps exciting an auditory nerve. David Nowell Smith characterizes primal vocalizations, cries, as "raw, quasi-bodily *matter* from which language will be made"[12] (emphasis added), invoking a double significance for the term while stipulating that this so-called matter is also a medium.[13] Matter in the sense of substance becomes for Nowell Smith something like a figure (it is "quasi-bodily"), as it does for [Daniel] Tiffany and [Maurice] Blanchot.[14] Blanchot's figuring of poetry as a decomposing corpse suggests that it transpires at the cusp of the conversion of matter to energy or to other matter, at the point of its evanescence. Sound is in fact physical as it is energic, but it is not technically matter since it has no mass. As Nowell Smith suggests, it feels substantive nevertheless in issuing from and impacting the body.

The materiality of language, whether written or oral, its so-called "privileging of the signifier," was a pet if not an original focus of twentieth-century poetics: de Man, Blanchot, and Tiffany are representative in viewing the poetic word as physical or embodied, a quality that correlates with its lack of transparency.[15] The word that is not an unclouded window on to a referent commands attention, becoming, by virtue of its opacity, a thing unto itself. By way of its widely noted resistance to reference, lyric foregrounds the "substance" of its medium, matter on the verge of transforming to energy. As a "physical" system, language, like the physical world within which perception transpires, is an embedding system featuring, indeed dependent upon, the dynamic of mutual co-construction through which entities (for the sake of simplicity, words) are constituted of other entities (other words), of "matter" that is in a sense transformed into themselves in the process of signification.[16] As words are informed by their denotations and connotations, they are made meaningful by entities that are potentially of the same stuff. They consist of constituent elements transformed, alchemically rather than physically, to become of themselves elements that are then unrecognizable within their transformed state, but denoted, indexed by it. One needs only a dictionary to evince this claim. If language is conceived of as material in this sense of mutable, its ability to mean assumes the transformation of what it means, and with it a kind of continuity. The word, as sign, is in a sense continuous with the linguistic units it denotes, and by which it is informed, in the same way that sensory systems are continuous with informing matter-energy, the reception and conversion of which is the catalyst to the construction of perceptual meaning. The words with which the words of the poem are continuous are, in the manner of sensory stimuli, the spur to the composition of poetic meaning.

As a percipient consists within itself of other constituting and in a sense extant entities [(photons, scent molecules, etc.)], by simply existing—*i.e.*, by perceiving—it gestures beyond itself to what is potentially significant, to what has not yet been but might be transmuted and thus signified—in other words, to ... [the undifferentiated state of potential Peirce calls] firstness. A word, analogously, is composed of denotative and connotative significance that takes the form of other words, and thus points beyond itself to a complex of potential lexical meaning. Words, like percepts, radiate outward toward the entities by which they might be defined, that is to say, granted meaning and contour, words that are in turn formed of others in a continuum mirroring the physical world. (Defining by informing is literal in physical processes such as perception and figurative within language.)[17] What renders this potential significance *present*, and thus realizable, is the poem's disposal of obscurity, particularly in the form of ambiguity. Lyric expression makes present, and makes itself present to, the fullness of the linguistic context it implies rather than ignoring it. What renders this set of potential significance inaccessible, and its variety indistinguishable or virtual, is the materiality of the sign (percept, word) that has transformed and obfuscated it merely by existing. Poetry liberates this predisposition of language to indeterminacy. Its verbiage shimmers with a foreign patina: a repertoire of potential meaning hovers over the poem like an aura that is visibly indistinct. The poetic word strives to release the fullness of its evocative power, the totality of its as-yet-undifferentiated valence of accruals and purgings, expansions, revisions, and scars. Chafing at stable meaning, the poem puts potential meanings into play, airing them, and, in so doing, acknowledges that the environment extends beyond the shallow focus that is the predicament of the fallen human. As lyric poetry reflects as well as effects this potential for connectedness in a replication of the same, its obscurity may become practically inexhaustible—the *raison* for its durability. As Shelley tells us, "All high poetry is infinite; it is as the first acorn, which contained all oaks potentially. Veil after veil may be undrawn, and the inmost naked beauty of the meaning never exposed."[18] In implementing a directionality outward into language as a whole, the genre foregrounds systemic connectivity, and, in so doing, competes with and downplays language's aptitude for determined reference. It manifests a lexicality that resonates as a signifying physicality, a physical system of signs. At the back of opacity is capacity, what extends beyond one's curtained station on the stair.

This condition of potential connectedness, active while it is masked, must remain unseen since seeing, poetic and otherwise, determines, lopping off ramifying potential. Both Adorno and Heidegger stress that the immediacy of poetic engagement is less than fully conscious. Adorno in fact equates "The unself-consciousness of the subject submitting itself to language as to something objective" with "the immediacy and spontaneity of that subject's expression."[19] Heidegger claims that the nature of one's attachment to the Open is necessarily unconscious, for consciousness co-evolves with the representation that distances one from it.[20] The physical connectivity that is the basis of the perceiver's relationship to its environs is likewise unconscious: points of organism–environment connection within perception are themselves unperceivable. ... This state is foundational to lyric utterance and lyric reception at the same time it is one from which the genre inevitably emerges, maintaining its linguistic embededdness all the while. Potential meanings remain even as interpretive acts decide them. (These unconscious mechanisms of perception are semiotic in their engagement with an environment, the first stage in a process of meaning-making. Biosemioses depend on the conscious registration of neither signs nor objects.) Lyric returns one to this basis, to a physical groundedness in and through which a perceptual means of meaning-making, mediated in language, emerges. Poetic utterance flirts with obscurity, then, not simply because its object is obscure (travel writing and teenage journals would then pass as lyrical), but because the poem of the mind's contention with the strange is accomplished by evoking the immediate, healing state of presence to potential. The lyric in effect embeds itself in a linguistic environment by remaining receptive to the role of that environment in the emergence of meaning. To cope with the estrangement to which we are all subject, to act wisely within a new situation, one must, as Emerson reasoned, be present to unconscious points of connection to the extent possible within the act of thinking.

The types of firstness inhering in lyric semiosis and correlating with those of perception may now be distinguished. 1) All language, as a physical medium houses an immanent, physical type of firstness, a latency consisting of the possibility of other words into which it might be transformed. Language's mutability is an effect of the fact that it gives meaning to instances of language with which it is, in a sense, continuous. Text considered to be autonomous correlates with an extra-cognitive, physical reality, the fluctuations of which presume firstness. 2) Corresponding to the potential significance of stimuli to the organism, firstness manifests in the poem relationally as the potential meanings of the linguistic units of which it is composed, the specific words defining the chosen words of the poem. Said potentiality is released through ambiguous constructions and other aforementioned obfuscating techniques and is differentiated only virtually prior to its determination by the perceiver constructed by the poem, or the receiver of the poem. 3) Firstness may also be experienced consciously in the form of uninterpreted first exposure, that unspeakable registration of the as-yet-undifferentiated, still to be comprehended whole [corresponding to the percept]. The firstness instantiated in and experienced upon the exposure to novelty may be represented within the poem itself. It may also inhere in the immanent potential conferred by the irreducibility of lyric language during the phase in which poetry impacts the reader but has not yet been differentiated and grasped, the phase of the extension of its resistance. 4) Firstness in lyric exists in the potential form of the objects of the stimuli-like words that index them, the often nebulous referents of lyric utterance made so by generic conventions, including the apparent extrapolation of entire utterances from contexts that are thereby concealed. As objects are realized when acted upon—the lover by her wooing, the ideas of the poem in their interpreting—functional firstness exists as the set of potential actions responding to referent objects.

Obscurity is then a symptom of an embedded form of signification the lyric adopts, of the sign's potential constitution by other signs that may potentially constitute still others that at any point may designate potential objects, physical and intellectual.

...

The obscurity endemic to lyric utterance hence betokens the genre's understanding of language and its users as embedded, a condition for which lyric signification accounts in exploiting what might safely be called the nature of language. In restoring language's full functional, that is semantic, potential into the milieu of the poem, poetic obscurity puts language into ontological and epistemological alignment with an embedded, embodied understanding of cognition. "Poetry can be defined as that language in which a world (of unfolded meanings) opens up, and in which our terrestrial essence as mortals reverberates."[21] Lyric technique maintains the fluid preconditions of linguistic decision, which mirror, and possibly arise from, the fluid preconditions of perceptual decision. Presence is the openness to what "being" might implicate of the environment (or earth, or world) with which it is continuous but which it cannot perceive because ... perception determines potential. The admitting of obscurity as a semiotic component also acknowledges that local interpretive freedom is constrained by events determined beyond the interpreter's ken. Its use invokes the set of implicit possible, but not illimitable, relationships between poeticizing organism and environment—and by extension between reader and text—in order to elongate the chaotic, messy activity of recuperation and allow one to decide wisely.

In the practical terms of poetry, the airing of potential allows lyrics to render the process of decision making in which all options, or at least all best options, are entertained and pre-existing sets of connotations shuffled, so that best matches may be constructed to restore an efficacy in context to words, an end that has been staked as the *raison d'etre* of the major poet. That active potential is requisite to the fabric of lyric is dramatized in the Orpheus myth when Eurydice is forced to follow the poet during their single-file ascent to the upper world, to exist potentially to him for a space while obscured from his view. The trust that her potential state will be actualized, that the poem only resists the intelligence "almost successfully," is essential during the phase of poetic emergence into the daylit world of comparatively stable signification, the earthly realm in which Eurydice *is* Orpheus's wife. Because the poet cannot tolerate his beloved's indefinite existence, he turns. As he does so prematurely, she recedes, remaining eternally unrealized, forever muse, source of his never-ending, always recallable song.

To prophesy demands that the prophet access things as they are in order to project futurity from present tendency, to foresee the simultaneous "irrational reactions" that determine potential. To understand how potential will be determined, one must understand the potential, which is neither cognizable, nor effable. If reality were directly accessible, the prophet-percipient would function as a mere mouthpiece, funneling the world, or the world to be, in lucid fashion. Prophecies articulated with such clarity would not be prophecies per se, but direct communiqués from a godhead obviating the prophet. As this figure of interest is not a mouthpiece but a mediator, or, per Hegel, a unifier (an incomprehensive but not inaccurate term for what the poet and the percipient do),[22] he alters what he delivers of the world, thereby obscuring it in determining its potential. He speaks not only what is necessarily an interpretation, an individual perspective, but one that is literally, physically, of himself. Given that what is uttered has been transformed and adapted, the unperceived material object remains in a state of potential significance that contrasts with the mediating "percept." The complex act of interpretation that is perception renders the object obscure, consigning it to a state of epistemological potential.

...

It is now possible to begin to account for the riddle's central position within the genre as a conflater of the subject and object of the poem. The adulteration of subject and object alike is attributable to the poem's status as perceptual residue, its implicit recognition that the percipient is composed of its mediations of objects, the presence of which undermine, even as they constitute it. Each [Whiteheadean] "actual entity,"[23] each percipient, is both a subject and its embodiment of the object(s) of which it is composed, materially and as qualia. The lyric-perceptual event, as a physical event, entrains connections that cannot be completely circumscribed and absented as *other*, even as a contingent or relational object-other. In acknowledging an expanded version of perception, one that reaches backward into the obscurity of what might be termed the pre-perceptual, the lyric speaker (more tenuously, the voice indexing a speaker, still more tenuously, a free-floating text indexing a voice) invokes the raw materials of itself, decentering itself in introducing a centrifugal momentum toward the environment into which it is in danger of dissolving. Concomitantly, the object is obscured because it is known only through the subject prophesying it: it too is compromised, diluted. The riddle, as a seminal form, destabilizes subject and object in overtly fusing them, deferring their identification—or ultimate predication—to the interpretive process, content, in the meantime, to subsist in the act of finding.[24] The riddle's "I," as a lyric "I" is self-assertive in its self-portraiture at the same time it speaks into existence the objects (in the broad sense) it appears to reify. Walt Whitman stands out in his acknowledgment of the extremes of an overbearing and a retiring subject, an "I" that is both all-encompassing and the dust beneath one's "boot-soles,"[25] anaphorically insistent, yet concealed amid lists of objects. The paradox of the decisive yet compromised subject, the subject on the verge of silence as it recognizes that it is comprised of the presence of others, is the crux of lyric.

Notes

[1]Jakob von Uexküll, "The Theory of Meaning," in *Semiotica* 42, no.1 (1982): 29-34.
[2]Ibid., 36.
[3]Ibid., 27.
[4]Ibid., 27, 31.
[5]Donald Favareau, "Introduction and Commentary: Jakob von Uexküll," in *Essential Readings in Biosemiotics: Anthology and Commentary* (Dordrecht: Springer, 2010), 83.
[6]Uexküll, 31.

[7]It goes without saying that such action-utterance is literal in the case of oral poetry. As will be addressed in Chapter Four, written poetry encodes actions.

[8]Uexküll, 33.

[9]Emily Dickinson, "Poem 466," in *The Poems of Emily Dickinson* (Cambridge: Belknap Press of Harvard University Press, 1999), 215.

[10]Uexküll, 36.

[11]Charles Sanders Peirce, "A Guess at the Riddle," in *The Essential Peirce: Selected Philosophical Writings (1867-1893)* (Bloomington, IN: Indiana University Press, 1992), 250, and "The Principles of Phenomenology" in *Philosophical Writings of Peirce* (New York: Dover, 1955), 75.

[12]David Nowell Smith, *On Voice in Poetry: The Work of Animation* (London: Palgrave MacMillan, 2018), 28.

[13]Ibid., 28.

[14]Daniel Tiffany, "Lyric Substance: On Riddles, Materialism, and Poetic Obscurity" in *Critical Inquiry 29* (Autumn 2001), 72–98.

[15]The identification of language as substantive of course precedes modernism. See, for instance, Roland Greene's "The Lyric," in which he reveals early modern lyrics' awareness of their materiality.

[16]One might argue that, strictly speaking, this is a mental embedding of meaning rather than a material embedding and thereby foreground a limitation of language. However, connectivity ontology grants ontic status to the points of connections or relationships within ecological systems, providing further evidence for the materiality of the relation-intensive medium of language.

[17]Saussure, of course, was seminal in pointing out the relational nature of meaning, made in his theory between the units of the language within a system of difference (165–6). However, he did not take the critical step of claiming that words embody what they signify by altering it.

[18]Percy Bysshe Shelley, "A Defense of Poetry," in *Criticism: Major Statements* (New York: St. Martin's, 1991), 327.

[19]Theodor W. Adorno, "On Lyric Poetry and Society," in *Notes to Literature, Vol. 1* (New York: Columbia University Press, 1991), 43.

[20]Martin Heidegger, "What Are Poets For?" in *Poetry, Language, Thought* (New York: Harper & Row, 1971), 108.

[21]Gianni Vattimo, *The End of Modernity* (Baltimore: Johns Hopkins, 1988), 72.

[22]G.W.F. Hegel, *Hegel's Aesthetics: Lectures on Fine Arts* (Oxford: Clarendon, 1975), 1133.

[23]Alfred North Whitehead, *Process and Reality* (New York: The Free Press, 1978), 43.

[24]Tiffany offers the fascinating detail that riddles were sometimes inscribed directly on the objects themselves, allowing for the simultaneous perception of poem, speaker, and referent. Tiffany, 73.

[25]Walt Whitman, "Song of Myself," in *Leaves of Grass* (New York: W. W. Norton, 1973).

Bibliography

de Saussure, Ferdinand. *Course in General Linguistics*. La Salle, IL: Open Court, 1972.

Dickinson, Emily. "I dwell in Possibility—." In *The Poems of Emily Dickinson*, edited by R. W. Franklin. Cambridge : Harvard University Press, 1999.

Favareau, Donald. "Introduction and Commentary: Jakob von Uexküll." In *Essential Readings in Biosemiotics: Anthology and Commentary*, edited by Donald Favareau. Dordrecht : Springer, 2010.

Greene, Roland. "The Lyric." In *Cambridge History of Literary Criticism: Vol. 3 , The Renaissance*, edited by Glyn P. Norton, 216–18. Cambridge: Cambridge University Press, 1999.

Hegel, G. W. F. *Hegel's Aesthetics: Lectures on Fine Arts . Vol. II*. Translated by T. M. Knox. Oxford: Clarendon, 1975.

Heidegger, Martin. "What Are Poets For?" *Poetry, Language, Thought, 89–142*. Translated by Albert Hofstadter. New York: Harper & Row, 1971.

Nowell Smith, David. *On Voice in Poetry: The Work of Animation*. London: Palgrave Macmillan, 2015.

Peirce, Charles S. "A Guess at the Riddle." In *The Essential Peirce: Selected Philosophical Writings (1867–1893). Vol. 1,* edited by Nathan Houser and Christian Kloesel, 245–79. Bloomington: Indiana University Press , 1992.

Peirce, Charles S. "The Principles of Phenomenology." *Philosophical Writings of Peirce*, 74–97. New York: Dover, 1955.

Shelley, Percy Bysshe. "A Defense of Poetry." In *Criticism: Major Statements*, edited by Charles Kaplan and William

Anderson. New York: St. Martin's, 1991.
Tiffany, Daniel. "Lyric Substance: On Riddles, Materialism, and Poetic Obscurity." *Critical Inquiry* 29 (Autumn 2001): 72–98.
Uexküll, Jakob von. "The Theory of Meaning." *Semiotica* 42, no.1 (1982): 25–82.
Vattimo, Gianni. *The End of Modernity*. Baltimore: Johns Hopkins University Press, 1988.
Whitehead, Alfred North. *Process and Reality.* New York: The Free Press, 1978.
Whitman, Walt. "Song of Myself." In *Leaves of Grass*, edited by Sculley Bradley and Harold W. Blodgett, 28-89. New York: W. W. Norton & Co., 1973.

The premise of this book is that the lyric genre becomes coherent when lyric poems are regarded as perceptual acts. The mythology, the lore, and the theory of the lyric situate the lyricist as an exemplary yet typical figure cast out of her native circumstance and forced, implicitly or explicitly, to perceive anew. Lyric utterance enacts the "first sight" of an embedded, embodied organism, recreating the dynamics of perception in a process that is at bottom biosemiotic. Having established that perception obscures sense data (and thus its objects) by transmuting them as they are embodied, I suggest within this excerpt that lyric obscurity is a function of an analogous (indeed a homologous) process: the upshot of each is to consign its referents to a state of semiotic potential.

Eco/proprioception

On the title page of Blake's engraved *America a Prophecy* (1793), in the upper left quadrant of the title page, a woman sits hovering over a book, reading to a child who points at the page: her legs seem to stride under the reading, holding the child's rapt attention. Across the page, a contrary: an aged man hunches over a book as if drifting off into it, oblivious of the lively figures around him trying to get his attention. This portrait of *active vs. passive reading* shows the favorable outcome of the active mode: in the upper right corner a naked female figure leaps up off the page in free energetic release.

I'm looking at Blake's image of active reading as a way of envisioning a possible relationship between poiesis and world, both natural and constructed: visionary engagement with text awakens "youthful" mind and sends generative energy out into environment—*seeding* the living surround. This is a potentially fertilizing relationship between inspired and focused consciousness and outside world, whereas passive attention loses contact with the outside and dwells in self-enclosure.[1] And perhaps it offers an imaging of Blake's provocative and enigmatic Proverb of Hell: "Where man is not, nature is barren." So how do we track this dynamic exchange between "language mind" and "natural world"? What indeed does it suggest about the human role in a planetary context?

There are many ways of construing our motivation for thinking in terms of ecopoetics, and the one that keeps me working with it is the sense that poiesis is consequential beyond the confines of the poem, especially the poem viewed as aesthetic object, or the presumption of a bounded and definable cultural "world." And this is not a matter of how many readers a given poet or work reaches, or how many critics and literary historians are impressed, which, while hardly a trivial issue, nevertheless stays within the cultural frame of value as calculable, definable, manageable, and authority-regulated. Gary Snyder's original foray into this territory in the collection of essays and poems *Earth House Hold* (1969), a title glossing "ecos" (Gk. *oikos*), aimed to rethink tribal traditions for their social lessons toward "growth and enlightenment in self-disciplined freedom." Shortly before, when Jerome Rothenberg and I inaugurated the term "ethnopoetics" for my journal *Stony Brook* (1968), it was in a register more within the sense of actual value in an "ethno" (or "eco") poiesis—value as individual acts of lingual interaction with other cultures, yet with the integrity of one's own life orientation and poetics. We hoped to engage the (possibly unique) principles of (self)regulation showing up in new poetics still to be realized at large in our own culture.

A reasonable aim is to grasp better how such poietic value resonates consequentially and in ways we have only begun to study, in part because they have still to be imagined—or, in a Blakean way, there's no end to reimagining our connections to living world. Ecopoetic thinking is an opportunity to assess how what we do—including the view or visioning by which our action occurs—matters greatly, not least because it does resonate so powerfully and far afield. Actions of body and mind, and the language by which they make their way in the world, are "reality generators"—a term for a complex happening that is inseparable from the nature of poiesis itself. My name for such consequential *reality-generating language* is *linguality.*

Ecopoetics can explore what poiesis actually does in the world, notably in ways not happening in other modalities of thinking. Some understandably will want to see it mainly as a social/political instrument in desperate times, a new agiprop, but as important as such action is, it risks limiting ecopoetics as a medium of exploration and "free zone," and at a time when evolving new orders of thinking is an urgent need. The danger is that any "should be" or additional correctness applied to poetics can extend the coercive ways of mind so dominant in Western thought. Ecopoetics as "free range" might inherently seem to address some of our "naive" childhood questioning, like "What are we doing here?" and "Why are we in the world?" And there are ancillary questions: Does Earth need us on it? Is there a choice? Have we even begun to wake up to our necessary role here? Strictly speaking ecopoetics intrinsically serves social and political dimensions, which are frequently discussed (tuned, for instance, to a "postmodern sublime"), though perhaps less often in relation to actual *processes* of language, the way our speaking/writing focuses itself in an embodied relation to what co-lives here. For Blake, especially, visionary work was always tuned into actual history in its most challenging and even terrifying aspects: the energetic female figure leaping off the title page of *America a Prophecy* transforms three engraved plates later into the revolutionary figure of Orc, penetratingly entering the page for the American Revolution's rebellion against tyranny.

For me, and in my reading of Blake, the real questions of interest are never separate from the way processes of *language as poiesis* also embody and interact with the living world. Accordingly I spell poiesis with the "i" to acknowledge that it very much is its root meaning of *making*, and not first of all in a cultural or literary sense, but in the most primary, even primordial, sense that runs through everything. In the old expression it runs through all of *creation*, which I understand as everything—including us and all else—perpetually in the process of (re)making itself, and doing so in the most complex co-performativity. Such collaboration is quite literally beyond imagination and endlessly in need of being imagined further. I find I'm never not working, however falteringly, with the question of how what we do in poiesis is of like nature with what else lives in the world—"nature" or the living everything that is mostly unknown to us—the radically other.

> How do you know but ev'ry Bird that cuts the airy way,
> Is an immense world of delight, clos'd by your senses five?
>
> (*The Marriage of Heaven and Hell*)

Sensing Afield

> The individual mind is immanent but not only in the body. It is immanent also in pathways and messages outside the body; and there is a larger Mind of which the individual mind is only a subsystem. This larger Mind is comparable to God and is perhaps what some people mean by "God," but it is still immanent in the total interconnected social and planetary ecology.
>
> (Gregory Bateson, *Steps to an Ecology of Mind*)[2]

Speculatively speaking, ecopoetics ups the ante in consideration of what comprises a coherent entity. The poetics addresses far more than the traditional poet/poem identity, extending the inquiry of "self" and "object/thing," "poet" and "poem/poetic act."

We tend to look at ecopoetics in the perspective of issues of control and damage in the environment, and while this is of the greatest importance in facing the anthropocene, it's only part of the picture in actual poiesis. First, human/environment interaction works both ways—two active sides alter each other continuously—and not just in the physical sense, such that a compromised environment in turn compromises us at the life level. A relationship has its own orders of complexity, beyond our self-protective fears; there is co-evolution, focused not mainly on survival but on collaboration. Second, the oscillation between (human) mind and environment can produce a range of *states* of consciousness, and variable conditions of (co) awareness. On the simplest level, environmental destruction is depressing and can impact our will to deal with the problems in new, creative, and more effective ways (practical, political). The options, however, include more than building up resolve in the sense of pep talks to the team or the wonderful Fugs refrain "Refuse to be burned out!" They include actual, though subtle, transformation in conscious focus, an elusive and hugely complex matter to account for. Indeed glimpses of transformative instances may be quite direct and even rather simple, and a medium for this order of awareness is poiesis. In my view ecopoetics can offer radically new thinking to this domain, in that poiesis—transformational making—is a reality regulator and in need of new orders of reflection.

In a shorthand way here I'm reporting on a kind of ecopoetic thinking that understands poiesis as consequential beyond evaluation, especially where evaluation is limited to the usual categories (literary, cultural, political). It has impact in ways that are quite difficult to track or explain but that are at least potentially part of a necessary transformation, also hard to specify. Bateson's eponymous notion "steps to an ecology of mind" was a major effort in this direction, probably underread now—dangerously so, as the lack of its kind of thinking is darkly consequential. It's important in this view, and at this point in time, to see poiesis as intrinsically a radical act. Initially this calls for regarding it as *emergent*—arising out of many relative conditions (poetic, social, political, aesthetic, psychological, biological, etc.); and therefore it is of a complexity such that no single domain or set of conditions is equipped to fully evaluate. Like "ecology of mind" it is still an undeveloped field—which both limits usefulness and gives promise! So comprehensive evaluation and defense of its activity can hardly be a priority. Ecopoetics is a permission to keep all of these conditions active yet give none of them dominance—no hierarchy of values. In this sense *it radically embodies diversity*, and it declares a free space for a new species of "proprioceptive thinking."

The (Bio)poetics of Thinking

> We could say that practically all the problems of the human race
> are due to the fact that thought is not proprioceptive.
> —David Bohm

Both Charles Olson and David Bohm have suggested thinking more broadly about the physiological process or "system" called *proprioception*. We may recall it as the "self knowing" physiological awareness of position and movement by which we locate ourselves and navigate in space-time; it collaborates neurologically with other systemic perception (visual, vestibular) to self-regulate through interactive awareness with environment. Physiologically we posit this mode of perception as *reception* of information and internal neurological processing. This is the dualistic view that perceiving mind is one thing and the rest of the world something else. On this model poet/poem/poetry/poetics stands on one side and all the rest on another. Biologically this view is convenient, grossly limiting, and in recent years increasingly obsolete. Phenomenology of course has long challenged the naiveté of simplistic dualism, as some understandings of physics do—say, Bohm. Ecopoetics is an opportunity for something further.

Bohm carries his thought further; for instance:

> [Proprioception] is more or less the same as what technical people call "feedback." In a psychological sense, proprioception amounts to a kind of awakening of awareness to itself, i.e., awareness becoming aware of awareness. Proprioception means that awareness now also considers its own operations as something to be taken into account. Apparently there are not many people who have an awareness that includes awareness as being something to be aware of.

The kind of awareness he's addressing is not about attending itself as object but as interactive process unfolding without losing active awareness of its own activity. It doesn't presume the self's thinking as contained within its separate domain; one's thoughtful awareness can stand both within itself and outside itself looking in. Mind activity has no bounded location. There are orders of processual awareness that do not allow being specified as objects in a set with other objects. The psychotopology is complex—that is, emergent. Poiesis accordingly can be understood as language aligning with this (re)ordering of awareness. Reflection on its activity may lead to a question like: What's the thinking and/or languaging equivalent to a Klein bottle [an unbounded non-orientable single-surface manifold]? To pose such a question even in mirth rethinks the relation between poiesis and world. So: feedback from what to what? Does proprioception process received data or read signals in dialogue?

Unanswered questions are spurs to *open orientation*. An intention behind opening up orientation is to allow thinking to go beyond itself, perhaps by becoming responsive to our unmoored planetary condition. The motive may be as simple as realizing that ways of thinking up to now have created the mega-mess we Earth beings find ourselves in. If our species on some greater level of inclusive mind were attempting to rethink itself through us, how would it proceed? As its point of emergence, how might poiesis reflect *on* and *in* its own (inter)activity? This approach to questioning need not be viewed as "romantic self-aggrandizing" of the inquiring subject; *au contraire* let's consider it, at least experimentally, as "ontological humility"—offering one's own being as speaking for god-knows-what in our species-level effort to know and further our mission on the planet. Intimate largesse in thinking.

My current response to this challenge is a principle I call *ecoproprioception*: our intrinsic "self perception" (proprioception) understood as *extended* self-perceiving, enlarged in scope to the degree that it is *non-separate* from environment. Coinherence of mind and environment; sense of self viewed as including sense of other.

If we actually *sensed* our non-separateness from world at large, we would perhaps more readily get situated to engender creative responses to what is needed. I think that we intrinsically understand this connection and do make use of it in many daily ways, which largely go unnoticed; however, it is dulled by inherited habits of thought and general cultural framing. I base the ecoproprioceptive idea on many years of experience of t'ai chi's martial practice (push-hands) and extending its insights to hands-on bodywork. But it's there in many sports and especially innovative dance like Contact Improvisation and the work of an Anna Halprin, Trisha Brown, or Simone Forti. If we understand ourselves to *be* nature, at least as much as say mushrooms are, then in theory it should be possible to gain insight into fungi's mycelium network—"externalized neurological nets" functionally the forest's "internet" as Paul Stamets argues[3]—by way of self-observation, and vice versa. I have written about discovering such thinking through bodywork in the essay "Healing Poetics"[4]:

> Through a bodywork practice of physically and energetically identifying with another person, over the years I learned to vividly perceive a person's physical-energetic center, a dynamic zero point. I found that direct contact with a person allowed me to amplify the sense of internal spaciousness and impart an experience of free movement. I see this as transitively reawakening a kind of whole-body flexibility and responsive openness not fully experienced since early childhood (before one learns to look like others). What impressed me is how quickly this level of experience can come about, usually within several minutes, dramatically altering the other person's awareness and imparting a new, posturally free self-picture, without tension and without opposition to gravity. This activated awareness quickly subverts the whole tension system for a variable period of time; and subsequent similar engagements have the potential to grow the awareness of free movement.
>
> In effect, this "shared proprioceptive sense"—*transitive self-perception* or *ecoproprioception*—introduces people to their own basic free space, covered over by social habit since childhood. What is imparted is not something "I" own in a proprietary sense but a *property of being itself.* The principle is: if you directly address this ambivalently personal/impersonal property and make actual contact, it responds to being recognized. And its response is a self-recognition without name. Without identity. And non-isolated.

The Poetics of Triggering Insight

In a sense we *mirror* what we feel connected with, as well as what impacts us from outside, not only positively. I find it helpful to invoke *biopsychical principles of self-knowing*, speculatively linking to various science-based concepts, such as the fairly recent theory of a *mirror neuron system*[5]—the neuronic source of why we yawn when we see someone yawn. I seek out heuristic instruments for reflective thinking in step with a poetics of resonance behavior. I have tried to sketch out the basis of such poietic resonance in an essay called "The Poetics of Thinking,"[6] for instance:

> The issue [in poiesis], as in navigating moving composition, is feedback through developed listening, such that allows intelligent self-modification in process, without loss of the sense

of being in actual space, the medium, the work, the world. It's relational. The problem with the self and the thinking brain is that functionally it understands itself to be central, dominant, and in control. Thinking doesn't know that there's an intelligence in the mind as quick, precise and unmanaged as in the body—and not in evidence until we learn how to hear it. It requires a feedback medium of released self-perception.

The feedback medium is poiesis, wherein we gain reflective insight as processual revelation *in relation* to actual issues being thought through. And an aspect of what makes such revelation convincing is that it is itself microcosmically performative of the oscillatory interaction between mind and environment. By performing its speaking as a function of listening (getting feedback), it operates as *reception* of what at the same time it apparently *produces*. The text serves as site of co-creation, and poet is first *reader* of what is written. Instruction through poiesis mirrors the processual structure of self-generating language, and in this way speculatively models an ecopoiesis. Mind and nature "mirroring" is simultaneously a process of identification and discrimination, and I think of this as *mirroring by alterity*. Blake says we become what we behold. Conjunction/disjunction becomes a sort of processual strange attractor at the threshold, pulling the mind two ways at once. Perhaps mirror neurons learn to allow firing off, even confusedly, in oscillatory (non)recognition. Identity itself is a mirror event showing characteristics of an unbounded non-orientable *limen*-surface manifold.

Pervasive Engagement

The otherness of poiesis as self-generating language embodies an alternative logic of further thinking—a logo-logic, a principled thinking within language. The poem itself is the grammar. A singular logic—a logic of its own occasion—only now comes into being inside the composing language. And it suggests itself as poet-mind's connecting with nature-mind, an active coinherence inside linguality—language acting liminally in reality (re)generation.

I see (eco)poiesis as our language reviving its lost *middle voice*—a voice between passive and active knowing and acting upon itself, inherently reflexive, and at the same time co-performative with surround living. (Truly open musical/sound improvisation answers to this description.) This view might help with a question like: How does the poem open actual pathways in mind? We need something like a poetics of intimate interactions. Poiesis asks the mind to perform singular actions it would not perform otherwise, and these actions are of a nature perhaps subtly different from any previously performed, at least consciously. These actions cut grooves ("engrams"). And it matters that the conception and principle of the practice—*ecopoetics implies ecopoiesis*—can view itself as belonging to, and active within, a larger field than oneself.

Let's return briefly to Blake's provocative and enigmatic Proverb of Hell: *Where man is not, nature is barren*. My early response was confusion and discomfort: Does Earth really need humans, who have so grievously abused their greater life partner? I understand Blake's "man" in that proverb as *awakened mind* and as potentially a *seed force* in the engendering of what Charles Olson called *further nature*. We don't know what that means until it comes into being. Our operative models cannot work ongoingly for the necessary action of ecological mind, unless the modeling sees beyond inherited limitations and discovers working in conscious co-evolution. Our "self view" may need to be enlarged to embrace our shared ecoproprioceptive mission with the rest of "creation." (Eco)poiesis becomes *visionary* when it works at the necessary further scales of realization.

A Further Note on Ecopoetic Fields:

Rupert Sheldrake's richly articulated inquiry into *morphic resonance and morphic fields in biology*[7] —intraspecies morphic influence at a distance and without apparent physical connections—contributes significantly to ecopoetic thinking. His six-point summary of "morphic fields" (below) could be adapted with small modifications to an ecopoetic sketch of *poietic fields*, including the *coinherence of singular fields*. Ecoproprioceptive thinking becomes actively aware that it happens in feedback loops with environment, the human, and nonhuman in systemic exchange. Language functions as the mycelium or intelligent web of interconnectivity. *Mind-degradability*: An organismic configuration of a cohabited and pervasively connected field includes living-dying as (bio)(psycho)degradable process. (Eco)poiesis keeps the mind-degradable in balance with the biodegradable, by coperformativity.

Morphic Fields: A Summary

The hypothesized properties of morphic fields at all levels of complexity can be summarized as follows:

1. They are self-organizing wholes.

2. They have both a spatial and a temporal aspect, and organize spatio-temporal patterns of vibratory or rhythmic activity.

3. They attract the systems under their influence towards characteristic forms and patterns of activity, whose coming-into-being they organize and whose integrity they maintain. The ends or goals towards which morphic fields attract the systems under their influence are called attractors. The pathways by which systems usually reach these attractors are called chreodes.

4. They interrelate and co-ordinate the morphic units or holons that lie within them, which in turn are wholes organized by morphic fields. Morphic fields contain other morphic fields within them in a nested hierarchy or holarchy.

5. They are structures of probability, and their organizing activity is probabilistic.

6. They contain a built-in memory given by self-resonance with a morphic unit's own past and

by morphic resonance with all previous similar systems. This memory is cumulative. The more often particular patterns of activity are repeated, the more habitual they tend to become.

Notes

[1] Blake's "symbolism" resisted allegory and embraced a principle of engaged dynamism—the "picture" as whole-page signifying field force with articulate elements in moving-picture semiotics, a kind of ideogrammic animation. Even where there are seemingly specific "points" of meaning, the syntax is never stabilized. "Illustrations" can be contrary and interruptive of narrative or occur pages away from their textual coordinate.
[2] *Steps to an Ecology of Mind: Collected Essays in Anthropology, Psychiatry, Evolution, and Epistemology* (Chicago: University of Chicago Press, 1972, 2000), 467.
[3] "I believe that mycelium is the neurological network of nature. Interlacing mosaics of mycelium infuse habitats with information-sharing membranes. These membranes are aware, react to change, and collectively have the long-term health of the host environment in mind. The mycelium stays in constant molecular communication with its environment, devising diverse enzymatic and chemical responses to complex challenges." —Paul Stamets, *Mycelium Running: How Mushrooms Can Help Save the World*: https://www.bibliotecapleyades.net/ciencia/ciencia_futurebeyond23.htm. Stamets is not talking about psilocybin mushrooms here, although he does elsewhere.
[4] *Poetry in Principle*, foreword by Edward S. Casey (New York: Dispatches Editions/Spuyten Duyvil, 2019), https://www.dispatchespoetrywars.com/commentary/healing-poetics-george-quasha/.
[5] " … a neuron that fires both when an animal acts and when the animal observes the same action performed by another. Thus, the neuron 'mirrors' the behavior of the other, as though the observer were itself acting. Such neurons have been directly observed in primate species."
[6] *Poetry in Principle,* above.
[7] Sheldrake's many books include: *Morphic Resonance: The Nature of Formative Causation* (New York: Park Street Press, 2009) and *The Presence of the Past: Morphic Resonance and the Memory of Nature* (New York: Park Street Press, 2012). https://www.sheldrake.org/research/morphic-resonance/introduction.

Mark Scroggins

Peter O'Leary's Mycological Audacity

Peter O'Leary sometimes feels like the most audacious American poet alive. His work has no more direct dealings with the social and political topics of the day than William Blake's did with the balance of power in Parliament in the 1820s; and while O'Leary is deeply schooled in the traditions of English-language poetry (and the Greek and Latin classics, and Dante, and Scripture), the idiom of his verse has no truck with any other poetry being written—neither the quotidian observations still being turned out in some sectors of the MFA industry nor the most astringent parataxes being ground out by *soi disant* "experimentalists." The opening note "To the Public" of O'Leary's sixth collection, *Earth Is Best* (2019), emblematizes the poet's audacity. O'Leary is interested in "patterns," in natural process: "The soul-bright earth, cobwebbed with life. Soil's incessant neurology." "Rather than monotony, rather than the complacencies of lyric subjectivity, rather than the political economies of language," O'Leary writes, "I have chosen to express these patterns in a poetry whose modes are theogony and mycology." *Theogony*: as in Hesiod, a poetry that traces the genealogy and birth-stories of the deities; but *mycology*—the study of mushrooms and fungi?

O'Leary comes by his audacity honestly. In the early 1990s, O'Leary apprenticed himself—in the correspondence course, as it were—to the poet Ronald Johnson. (O'Leary has recounted that apprenticeship, with copious quotations from the poets' correspondence, in a long essay, "Gilding the Buddha: My Apprenticeship with Ronald Johnson.") Born in Kansas in 1935, Johnson had by the 1960s made his way to the East Coast and the centers of the midcentury flowering of poetic experimentation for which Donald Allen's 1960 anthology *The New American Poetry 1945–1960* provided such a vivid map. Johnson had met the painters and poets at the Cedar Tavern in New York, and had sat at the feet of Charles Olson and Louis Zukofsky. For some years he was partnered with Jonathan Williams, Olson's student and the founder of the vibrant small press the Jargon Society, which published early books by Olson, Robert Creeley, Robert Duncan, and a host of others.

With Williams, Johnson hiked the length of the Appalachian Trail; his walking tour of Great Britain with Williams resulted in the widely praised long "seasonal" poem, *The Book of the Green Man* (1967). In *Green Man*, Johnson wove his own close observation of British nature—the topography of the land, the flora and fauna, the shifting weather—with the long and rich tradition of English nature lore and nature writing; in effect, he brought an American Transcendentalist sensibility, a Thoreauvian eye, to the British countryside and its ancient traditions, a philosophy that saw the world around him as a constantly interacting system of natural and spiritual life.

Johnson spent the 1970s and 1980s in San Francisco, writing cookbooks, managing leather bars, and writing a vast cosmological epic poem, *ARK*. *ARK*—finished in 1990, first published in 1996, and reissued in a beautifully reset and corrected edition in 2013—is a book like no other, an uncompromisingly paratactic, lavishly lyrical, and formally rambunctious ode to the splendor and intricacy of the cosmos and the human imagination that has evolved to celebrate it. It takes its inspiration from the works of various outsiders and artists and from some of the major modernist and late modernist long poems before it—Pound's *Cantos*, Williams's *Paterson*, Zukofsky's "*A*", Olson's *Maximus*. But where Pound had set out to write "epic" in the old sense—"a work with all history in its maw," in Johnson's words; the "tale of the tribe," in Pound's own—Johnson's vision was of a long poem *without* history: "structure rather than diatribe, artifact rather than argument, a veritable shell of the chambered nautilus, sliced and polished, bound for Ararat unknown." During Johnson's lifetime, the American poetry world didn't know what to do with *ARK*, and for the most part still doesn't—though the work has many passionate admirers (count me one).

After he completed *ARK*, and in ill health, Johnson left the Bay Area and returned to his childhood Kansas, where he worked as a caretaker and gardener at a historic mansion and puttered away at a long series of very short "garden" poems. *The Shrubberies* was a great shaggy manuscript at the time of Johnson's death in 1996; one of his last directives to O'Leary, whom he had named his literary executor, was to "prune The Shrubberies" into a shapely, publishable collection. O'Leary has taken his responsibility as Johnson's executor, the curator of his posthumous reputation, quite seriously indeed. In 2000, he edited a selected poems, *To Do As Adam Did*, and the following year released an edition of *The Shrubberies*; since then he has overseen new editions of *Radi Os* (Johnson's "erasure" of the first four books of *Paradise Lost*), *The Book of the Green Man*, and *ARK*, and is at work editing further volumes.

O'Leary's first book, *Watchfulness* (2001), is dedicated to Johnson's memory. As one might expect, Johnson's example has always bulked large in O'Leary's work; it is, as it were, the central formal and conceptual crystal through which is both diffused and focused the primary light of O'Leary's thought: his Roman Catholic faith, subtilized and inflected by his deep learning in other spiritual traditions—esoteric, heterodox, Jewish, Islamic, gnostic, shamanic, pagan. What Johnson taught O'Leary is in part a matter of technique, the precise and careful dovetailing of sound-values in the line, a flair for the vivid and unusual—but invariably *right*—word. But it's also a matter of vision, of perceiving the world at once through a microscope and a telescope: both as a congeries of fascinating, scintillating detail, and as a system of unimaginably complex and beautiful interaction. To see at once with the child's fresh, naive eye and the astrophysicist's all-encompassing gaze. "To see a World in a Grain of Sand," as Blake put it.

Earth Is Best is clearly the most advanced excursion yet in O'Leary's ever-evolving poetics; but it is also, in my estimation, his most strikingly *Johnsonian* book. In his earlier collections, O'Leary's attention has been focused more often on the spiritual, the numinous, the religious—the radical glory of God as it suffuses the created world and animates the human consciousness. In *Earth Is Best*, his attention is fixed on the sublunary world, conceived of as a system of wonderful process and correspondences. After his first two collections, *Watchfulness* and *Depth Theology* (2006), each of O'Leary's successive books has seemed a more ambitious summing-up: *Luminous Epinoia* (2010), which takes its title from a Gnostic term for "the creative or inventive consciousness sent to Adam by God in the form of Eve," is a kind of theological fantasia and autobiography at once; *Phosphorescence of Thought* (2013) transposes the spiritual into the realm of nature, its form distantly modeled on that of Whitman's *Song of Myself*. (2016's *The*

Sampo is something else altogether, a kind of delightful sidebar, adapting portions of the Finnish national epic *Kalevala* into a high modernist sword and sorcery narrative; an extensive essay could be written on how O'Leary's fondness for science fiction and fantasy has inflected his poetry.)

Earth Is Best, whose title vamps on the opening of Pindar's first Olympian Ode (*ariston men hudor*, "water is best"), is of all things a mushroom book, an excursion in what O'Leary calls in his Afterword "mycopoetics." The bulk of the book consists of thirty-three "Amanita Odes" (*Amanita* is a genus of fungus, containing some 600 species of mushrooms), odes to all aspects of the mushroom and the fungal in general: their omnipresence on earth, their succulent edibility, their psychoactive properties, their toxicity, their ability to break down toxins.

Mushroom food-jewel and madness-jewel. Moon's stone and
Sun's bane. Heaven's fiery backside. Earth's threads, Earth's filters.
Resounder of the word's way Moon's urine mainstay pillar fulcrum
Monarch of everything that sees the Sun's light dazzling daytime mesh reseen
as a structured fiber of moonlight
waves rich in honey.
("Third Amanita Ode")

Behold the toadstool.
Earth-magical force thriving in wicked lore.
Saffron plenty in a Michigan pine woods.
The umbrella of Nicholas.
Delicate strokes of a French illustration, sylvan softness of a dangerous agarical scene.
Mycochtonomous toadstool.
Dynamochthonomous toadstool.

("Nicholas," I remembered as I wrote this, is the rabbit narrator of Richard Scarry and Ole Rissom's classic children's picture book *I Am a Bunny*; on the cover he shelters from the rain under a red-and-white spotted toadstool.)

Disobedient toadstool.
Of shining and wrinkled knowledge.
("Twenty-Ninth Amanita Ode")

But life springs from mycelium.
One day even your corpse will course with
flexuouse hyphae whose
saprophytic devourings will cleanse
your every mental cell of all the poisons
in waking life you harbored.
("Fourteenth Amanita Ode")

Earth Is Best bursts with mushroom lore, from the humble and exhilarating experience of hunting wild mushrooms, to classical recipes and culinary practices, to ancient shamanic rites, to the wilder speculations of R. Gordon Wasson's 1968 *Soma: Divine Mushroom of Immortality* (to which O'Leary suggests *Earth Is Best* might be read as "marginal commentary").

Wasson (whose day job was as head of PR at J. P. Morgan) was the the central evangelist for the "magic mushroom," the psychoactive psilocibin used in rituals by the Mazatec people of Oaxaca. The visions induced by the fungus, he was convinced, were not merely recreational highs, but actual spiritual insights. In Soma, he argued that the "Soma" of the ancient Vedas—"at once a god, the food of the gods, and a liquor"—was none other than the *Amanita musicaria*, the fly agaric. As O'Leary comments, "Soma is the euphoric food of the gods and also the source of human euphoria. An object of terror and adoration."

Earth Is Best may take "mycology" as one of its foundational principles, and spend much of its length tracing the mycelia and hyphae of various fungi, but it's not *all* mushrooms. Along the way, there are a few lively digressions from the mycological: the delightful Fifteenth Amanita Ode, "My Wife's Cough" ("sounds like nothing else on earth. / Seals trapped in an underwater cavern barking in unision"); "Ochre Vault," which takes formal inspiration from the riddles of the Exeter Book and Christopher Smart's *Jubilate Agno*; and "The Dogs," an electrifying adaptation of the story of Diana and Actaeon from Ovid's *Metamorphoses*. And everything O'Leary touches is vivified by his explosive range of language, from the aureate classical diction with which he gilds so many verses ("Nosochthonic toxicity mycelia neutralize. / Mycelial auscultation: attunement to the world through its mushrooms. / Eophanic harvest argenteous light tilts crisply in on") to the hard-hitting demotic ("Dogs. His fucking dogs. On the run").

O'Leary's Amanita Odes range over the whole world of mushrooms and fungi, praising and exalting them, marveling at their adaptability, ubiquity, and sheer beauty, at their succulence, at the visions they produce or the terrible toxicity they contain. But even as he rejoices—in quite Johnsonian fashion—in the spectacle of the living fungal networks overspreading and undergirding the earth, he also reads the mushroom as analogous to poetry itself, the euphoria the mushroom can deliver as analogous to the euphoria of the poet's language. "In fact, to me, language is the thing that most resembles the communicating properties of mycelium … poetry is the Somic germ of the imagination. Euphoric. Terrible. To be adored."

If mushrooms are a unique and wondrous element of the earth upon which we live, there's no denying, as O'Leary begins his Afterword ("Mycopoetics"), that "The earth is in *crisis*," a crisis largely caused by our own inability to process the toxins we have emitted into the atmosphere. Fungi, however, have evolved precisely to break down toxins; O'Leary quotes Paul Stamets: "Mycoremediation is the use of fungi to degrade or remove toxins from the environment. Fungi are adept as molecular disassemblers, breaking down many recalcitrant, long-chained toxins into simpler, less toxic chemicals." And so with the mushroom's analogue in human culture, poetry: "Like mycelium, poetry processes toxins," writes O'Leary; "poisons in language, poisons in thought, poisons in the imagination." Our environment is in crisis, overwhelmed and overbalanced by the toxins we have excreted; similarly, the world of contemporary poetry is at a toxic impasse. O'Leary's proposed way forward may seem draconian, but is of a piece with his own "mycopoetics" of "effervescent foraging: in language, in dictionaries, in ideas, in old poems, in the poems of the future": "I suggest an embargo on any new poetry for two years, to allow for sufficient decomposition and toxic transformation. ... So, what should we do? I say, go to the woods, go to the words."

This is of course audacious advice, and given the competitive pressures of the contemporary poetry "scene"—the drive to publish, to "keep up," to reach for that grant or that contest prize or that elusive academic position—it's unlikely that many younger poets will be taking it. Its implications, if we follow them out, are actually rather dark: that the contemporary torrent of published poetry is of a piece with the overproduction that characterizes late capitalist society as a whole, the overproduction of consumer goods, of processed foods, of landscape-marring residential and commercial buildings, of atmosphere-poisoning meat products, and so forth. Even the most well-intentioned (and widely celebrated) poetic works, what O'Leary's "To the Public" classifies among "the political economies of language"—writings that address our most pressing social and environmental problems—are caught up in our society's (and specifically our literary institutions') incessant urge to produce, produce, produce, and are thereby implicated in the flood of intellectual and spiritual "toxins" that threatens to overwhelm us. To draw back for two years, to stop writing and publishing and to immerse oneself in the natural world and in the forest of written lore: that seems audacious advice indeed, when the world seems to be burning down around our ears. But even the most harried, careerist scribbler would do well to set aside a few hours—or a few days—to read, re-read, ponder, live with and marvel at O'Leary's dazzling, dark, and profoundly strange and wonderful reimagining of our fungal and linguistic world.

Pips from the Pomegranate: Armenian *Hayrēn* in 18 Morsels

1.

Located between the Black Sea and the Caspian Sea, and bounded by Georgia, Azerbaijan, Iran and Turkey, modern Armenia encompasses just a minute portion of one of the world's oldest centers of civilization. Along the Great Silk Road at the exact crossroads between Europe and Asia in the classical Eurocentric sense, the Islamic Caliphate and the Christian Byzantium, Armenia presents a fascinating case-study in the intersections of the East and West (however contested and inutile those terms are) and the porousness of boundaries, especially in this time of increased nationalism and isolationism all over the globe. Linguistically, Armenian has as much in common with Farsi as it does with Greek, and culturally, the country reflects Mediterranean, Near Eastern, and Caucasian traditions. It is also the home of a medieval poetic form even older than the sonnet, the *hayrēn* (or literally 'in the Armenian style'), which I went in search of in June of 2018.

2.

(Map of Armenia, 2019).

3.

The *hayrēn* (or alternately the *airen*) is a transliteration of an Armenian word (հայրեն) which means both poems in a particular metrical style as well as Armenian poetry generally. Primarily a folk verse form which first surfaced in the thirteenth century, the *hayrēn* grew more popular between the fifteenth and eighteenth centuries. Characterized by its simplicity of language, its urban and secular content, and its metrical precision, the *hayrēn* are easily as sophisticated as the

Italian sonnet or the French villanelle. As Joseph Johannes Sicco Weitenberg writes, *hayrēn* are "in pentadecasyallabic quatrains[1]," or four lines of couplets of roughly fifteen syllables each and written, according to *The Princeton Encyclopedia of Poetry and Poetics*, "on a single coherent theme[2]," though that esteemed publication misses the metrical cohesion of the form in its definition.

"*Hayrens*, or *hayrens* are poems made up of combinations of lines consisting of seven and eight syllables, with stanzas consisting usually of at least eight lines," writes Michael Stone in his translation of *Adamgirk`: The Adam Book of Arak`el of Siwnik*. "The smallest unit is the combination of a line of seven syllables with one of eight syllables. These are also called half lines, and a combination of them is sometimes referred to as *bayt*, or by its Armenian equivalent, *tun* ...The form is attested from at least the tenth century onwards, in the work of Grigor Narekac'i, and is the basic metrical form for a vast body of poetry that is often but by no means always, anonymous. The themes touched upon are various: often love, but also the plight of the migrant worker, religion, and death."[3]

Perhaps due to its proximity to Iran, the form was influenced by the *ghazal*, with its own sense of couplets that like a stone from a necklace continue to shine in vivid isolation but that add to its luster when set with other stones. Similarly, the *hayrēn* uses the concision of its form to achieve a gem-like clarity of expression. In his book *The Heritage of Armenian Literature: From the Sixth to the Eighteenth Century,* Agop Jack Hacikyan writes "traces of the *hayrēn* are found in fragments of early oral poetry ... *Hayrēn* were a daring and brilliant poetic genre ... with their strong secular reflections, their intimacy, and their freedom from restraint, they seem much closer to the literary creations of our own age. They are deeply emotional and moving, strikingly original in their character, exuberant in their use of metaphor, and vigorously imaginative, ensuring that even today they are a pleasure to read. *Hayrēn*, in other words, are at once deeply traditional and boldly original poems"[4] (Hacikyan 129).

4.
Cut up this pomegranate here
and count the pips inside it.
For every pip I want a kiss –
not one more, I've decided!

– Leave me alone, you foolish boy, I
thought you had more sense:
For every pip you want, a kiss?
Why, the number would be immense![5]

This translation of the 16th century Armenian poet Nahapet Kuchak by David Matevossian was once published in a handsomely illustrated edition by the Sovetakan Grogh's Publishing House of the Armenian SSR in 1979. The press is now extinct and the book out of print, and only some fragments survive on the internet.

Like Sappho's fragmentary lyrics about the bittersweet qualities of love, this medieval *hayrēn* has a lighthearted quality in the verse that is both in keeping with other literary works of the Renaissance period, but is also colloquial and playful in a way more modern poems might be. There's a strong sense of voice and character, as we can hear, even in translation, how the interchange is constrained by the meter of the lines, which gives the poem its nearly epigrammatic quality.

5.

The pomegranate is a quintessential Armenian national symbol, representative of fertility, happiness and good fortune and, indeed, at some traditional Armenian weddings, the bride is meant to hurl the fruit against a wall until it splits open, the scattered seeds a good omen that the couple would bear many fine children. Indeed, anywhere you go in Armenia, you'll find the fruit represented in high and low art, from oil paintings that hang in the galleries to the shelves of souvenir shops where you can buy pomegranates made from ceramic or wire or textiles. Like the snow-peaked Mount Ararat, always visible on the horizon, this fruit has come to symbolize the very soul of the Armenian people.

Interestingly, this fruit also has connections to other countries and cultures, including Iran, where the Persian name for the fruit is Anar" انار, and there it is considered a fruit from paradise and also considered a national symbol. In Iran, the pomegranate is used in ceremonies of worship, but also as a source of coloration for Persian rugs, fabric, and even hair. In Islam, the Qur'an describes the fruit as growing in the gardens of Paradise, and in the Jewish faith pomegranates are eaten on Rosh Hashanah because they symbolise fertility and are said to have 613 seeds each, which corresponds to the 613 commandments of the Torah.

The fruit also figures prominently in Ancient Greek mythology where it features in the story of Persephone's marriage to Hades, the god of the Underworld. Because Persephone ate six seeds of the fruit, she was fated to live in the underworld for six months of the year and allowed to return to her mother, Demeter, the goddess of fertility, for the other six months, thus creating the cycle of the seasons. The pomegranate is also celebrated in Buddhism, and in my own mother tongue, Tamil, the word for the fruit, *maadulampazham*, translates as "a woman's mind", which is thought to be ripe with many hidden seeds. So in its own way, this fruit connects from the local to the global, although I never heard it spoken about so rapturously as I did in Armenia.

6.

When I landed at Zvartnots International Airport in Yerevan, I knew little about the country or its literary traditions. The first cab I got into, I was greeted by a middle-aged man with thick curly hair, a wide forehead, and a meaty nose. Looped around his rearview mirror was a large wooden cross flared out in a floral pattern and surmounted by a *nazar*, the blue eye meant to ward off evil spirits. Unexpectedly, he was bumping Dr. Dre on the radio, which he turned down when I entered the car. For the first few blocks, we were both silent. Then I asked him about the *hayrēn*. He grinned and looked back at me impishly in the rearview mirror, and then started singing a baritone that sounded not quite Turkish or Greek, almost Arabic but with a distinctly Slavic twang. It was like no other language I had heard before, and I was transfixed.

In Armenia, as in certain South American countries where the local people can recite Gabriela Mistral or Pablo Neruda by heart, I found that even the shopkeepers and waiters at restaurants knew their national poets and would even sometimes break into song. *Karoun-Karoun!* the owner of a tavern chirped as she served me chips. *Spring-Spring!* I still don't know what the cabdriver greeted me with and whether he had been taught those lyrics by his own father or had learned them in school. Whatever the case, it was certainly no rote memorization, as his song was inflected with the pathos, if not the technique, of a blues singer, and I held onto the memory of his song as an invitation into the Armenian identity.

7.

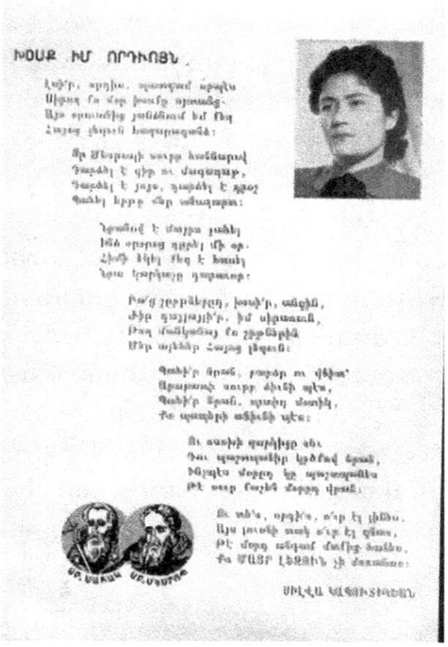

ԽՕՍՔ ԻՄ ՈՐԴՈՒՈՅՆ

ՍԻԼՎԱ ԿԱՊՈՒՏԻԿԵԱՆ

These *hayrēn* written by the twentieth-century poet Silva Kaputikyan were archived by the Armenian Poetry Project,[6] an organization dedicated to preservation and dissemination of Armenian poetry. We can see clearly the form of the poem, in quatrains, and the way the lines appear visually parallel. Kaputikyan is one of the most famous Armenian writers of the twentieth century and recognized as “the grand lady of Armenian poetry,”[7] and it is worth noting that she continued working in a centuries-old form, revitalizing it with newly feminist and nationalistic concerns.

8.

The question of whether Armenia hews to the East or the West is anachronistic, for the very distinctions such a model proposes are innately reductive and overly general, erasing the vast areas of overlap and discordance that exist distinctly within cities and towns, let alone countries and regions. However, we can regard the way in which Armenian culture imported ideas from other cultures indiscriminately, so long as they had a use, as a strength. Certainly, Armenians, one of the oldest Christian populations in the world, might have feared being converted to Islam, but that didn’t stop them from importing elements from the Persian *ghazal* into their own language’s versification, just as later it would absorb aspects of Turkish and Russian into its vernacular.

Critic Joseph Johannes Sicco Weitenberg writes, “in fact with a certain amount of oversimplification, one might argue that whereas most Armenian prose models were western, its poetry developed from an eastern matrix. In view of this, little time need be spent on reviewing the nationalist fallacy which presupposes that great art is the product of a 'pure' tradition untainted by alien infusions. Proponents of this theory are exercised to explain foreign parallels and potential sources of borrowing as deriving from a common antecedent. Regardless of the questionable nature of the principle itself and the problems encountered in determining what constituted national identity at different points within this period (which suggests the very criterion is rather anachronistic), porous borders and trading connections like those of Armenia render its application extremely tenuous. Furthermore, the approach seems motivated by the anxiety that artistic borrowing impairs not only the originality but also the unity and harmony of a given tradition. And yet this obviously depends on the mode of reception: if the process develops responsibly by judicious selection with a view to integration, the result is surely an enhancement and enrichment of possibilities for expression within the medium" (Weitenberg 1995, 43).

Weitenberg's point is that not only is the very idea of cultural purity debatable, the idea that importing ideas from elsewhere diminishes one's own sense of identity is itself illogical. Think of what Italy did with pasta after it was imported by Marco Polo from China, or the fact that the Han Chinese discovered that tea could be drunk for pleasure and not just for medicinal purposes from people who lived to their south. Practices that we might think of as inherent to a singular culture often originate elsewhere and in time become embedded in a sense of collective self-identity. The *hayrēn* in Armenia represent a perfect example of this kind of supple integration, for the poems simultaneously borrow elements from neighboring cultures and elucidate a localized, distinctively Armenian mode and angle of utterance. There's no contradiction in terms.

9.

My mother writes: "My son on pilgrimage,
How long beneath a strange moon will you roam?
How long a time must pass ere your poor head
To my warm bosom I may press, at home?

"Always I sit in sadness at my door,
And tidings ask from every crane that flies.
That willow slip you planted long ago
Has grown till over me its shadow lies.

"My ruined house is left without a head.
Sometimes for death, and always for the cheer
Of my own hearth I yearn. A tortoise I,
Whose entrails to its broken shell adhere!

(excerpt from Daniel Varoujan's *The Longing Letter* translated by Alice Stone Blackwell)

Daniel Varoujan was born in a village of Sebastia, Armenia, in 1884. He studied at St. Lazare, Venice, and later in Belgium. He is the author of a series of martial and patriotic epics, and is believed to have perished in the Constantinople massacres of 1915. Alice Stone Blackwell, the translator, in a particularly appropriative move, chooses not to mirror his *hayrēn's* natural meter, instead adopting a line of iambic pentameter for the verse (e.g., "how LONG/ beNEATH/a STRANGE/moon WILL/you ROAM"). Still the emotion of the piece comes across clearly, as it is a mother's lament for a son away on pilgrimage. As it was written by a male author, we can consider this an example of a dramatic monologue or persona poem.

The image of the mother longing for her son is akin to what some in the Armenian diaspora feel for their ancestral homeland. This loss is painted poignantly by the imagery of the willow slip that started out a sprout and that has now grown to be a towering plant, as well as the visceral image of an aged turtle whose entrails cling to its broken shell! And what prescient words, for Varoujan would not make it out and survive the extermination of his people. He left behind only these remnants, words that are shards of his hopes of what might be. Sadly, the mother would never see her son again.

10.

We just can't discuss Armenia without the genocide or the Kardashians, can we? The number is simply staggering: 1.5 million people systematically killed and many hundreds of thousands more forced to flee their homeland as refugees from the Turkish government between 1914 and 1923. Though this atrocity transpired over a century ago, for many of the Armenians I met, the memory was still fresh, even if they couldn't have possibly been alive to see it. A young girl passed me a bookmark that says "1915: Never Forget." A librarian showed me Verjine Svazlian's *The Armenian Genocide. Testimonies of the Eyewitness Survivors*, an enormous hardcover volume that collects together hundreds of first-person accounts from the survivors of this ethnic cleansing. It's a lifetime's labor and the result of Svazlian collecting and recording the oral histories of Armenian genocide survivors beginning in 1955, at great personal risk to her safety due to authorities in the former Soviet Union and Turkey.

"The Armenian Genocide, as an international political crime against humanity, has become, by the brutal constraint of history, an inseparable part of the national identity, the thought and the spiritual-conscious inner world of the Armenian people," said Svazlian in an interview. "There is no man without memory. Similarly, there cannot exist a nation without memory."[10]

In 2015, days before the 100th anniversary of the start of the Armenian genocide, the Kardashian clan descended on Gyumri, a small town along the once-contested border with Turkey, and the town from which their ancestors fled to the US in the early twentieth century. Their eight-day visit was being filmed for their reality show *Keeping Up with the Kardashians* and duly recounted on Instagram. For example, there's a photo of the sisters tottering on heels along the steps leading to the Mother Armenia statue in Yerevan with the caption, "This statue reminds visitors of the strong female figures in Armenian history. I love how powerful women are respected so much in our culture!"[11]

The next year, Kim Kardashian West wrote an open letter condemning the *Wall Street Journal* for running an ad paid for by genocide deniers. In part, her letter states, "Many historians believe that if Turkey had been held responsible for the Armenian genocide, and reprimanded for what they did, the Holocaust may not have happened. In 1939, a week before the Nazi invasion of Poland, Hitler said, 'Who, after all, speaks today of the annihilation of the Armenians?' We do. We must. We must talk about it until it is recognized by our government because when we deny our past, we endanger our future. When we allow ourselves to be silenced by money, by fear and by power, we teach our children that truth is irrelevant. We have to be responsible for the message we pass on to our children. We have to honor the TRUTH in our history so that we protect their future. We have to do better than this."[12]

Regardless of what we think about the Kardashians (and while I expected they might shrink back a little from embarrassment, the Armenians I met were immensely proud of the family), her suggestion is provocative. According to historical sources, a speech given by Adolph Hitler to his commanders from his Obersalzberg home in 1939, a week before the German invasion of Poland, contained that notorious reference. As cited by Kevork B. Bardakjian in his book *Hitler and the Armenian Genocide* and later verified by the Nuremberg Tribunal, this was what Hitler said: "I have issued the command—and I'll have anybody who utters but one word of criticism executed by a firing squad—that our war aim does not consist in reaching certain lines, but in the physical destruction of the enemy. Accordingly, I have placed my death-head formations in readiness — for the present only in the East—with orders to them to send to death mercilessly and without compassion, men, women, and children of Polish derivation and language. Only thus shall we gain the living space (Lebensraum) which we need. Who, after all, speaks today of the annihilation of the Armenians?"[13]

To Hitler, I would respond with William Saroyan, "I should like to see any power of the world destroy this race, this small tribe of unimportant people, whose wars have all been fought and lost, whose structures have crumbled, literature is unread, music is unheard, and prayers are no more answered. Go ahead, destroy Armenia. See if you can do it. Send them into the desert without bread or water. Burn their homes and churches. Then see if they will not laugh, sing and pray again. For when two of them meet anywhere in the world, see if they will not create a New Armenia."[14]

11.

From *The Independent* "Kim Kardashian in Armenia: Reality TV star and family's trip to Yerevan raises eyebrows—and global awareness of genocide."[15]

12.

Over the next few days, I visited the Temple of Garni, a free-standing Greco-Roman colonnaded building and an ancient pagan edifice with Ionic columns; the Geghard Monastery, a medieval Christian site associated with Saint Gregory the Illuminator (c. 257–c. 331 CE); the

Blue Mosque, an 18th century Shia mosque; and the Tatev Monastery, a 9th-century Armenian Apostolic monastery located high on a cliff that can only be accessed by riding the world's longest non-stop reversible aerial tramway. Each of these sites, albeit representative of different religions and disparate historical moments, were nonetheless venerated by the Armenians as part of their "national identity."

"The Armenian identity," writes Nareg Seferian, "is valued by Armenians to such an extent that a term exists—*hayabahbanoum* (in Western Armenian pronunciation)—to refer to actions undertaken in Armenian Diaspora settings that aim at retaining the identity, such as speaking the language, running schools and churches, cultural or other groups, discouraging marriage with non-Armenians, and so on. For much of the 20th century, surely as a reaction to genocide and Sovietization, the fear in the communities of the Middle East, Europe, the Americas, and elsewhere was that the Armenian identity was facing existential threat ... Many Armenians would tell you for their part that their Armenian identity has no connection with the Armenian state, that their ancestors do not come from what is Armenia today, or that, regardless, their self-expression of being Armenian outdates this young republic, has existed and continues to exist outside of it."[16]

The problem with nationalism is that it is often myopic; it essentializes certain versions of history and discards others. It ignores the fact that so many cultures have been shaped by immigrants and that far enough back, we have all migrated from somewhere ourselves. The anxiety that *hayabahbanoum* represents is belied by the flexibility of the Armenian diaspora who live around the world in communities that are a thousand years old in some cases. Indeed, nearly three times more Armenians live outside of Armenia than within it. Moreover, Armenia itself, as its architecture and history indicate, has always been a multicultural, multilingual place, and so its nationalism has never been static but dynamic and adaptable to changing conditions.

13.

On the last day of my stay, I rode around the streets of Yerevan randomly, and somehow ended up at the Sergei Parajanov museum. Parajanov, whose work I somehow didn't know beforehand, is an extraordinary artist and filmmaker, who, according to novelist and *Guardian* film critic Elif Batuman, made some of the "weirdest and most beautiful movies ever seen."[17] Parajanov was Armenian in so far as he identified foremost with that country; however, he was born in Tbilisi, Georgia, his first language was Russian, and he went to film school in the Ukraine, showing us yet again the complexity of identities and how the concept of nationalism is porous, for Parajanov is celebrated today as emblematic of Armenian artistic brilliance. In his own life, however, Parajanov spent time in prison and a Soviet gulag at different points of his life for committing "homosexual acts" and even for his "surrealistic tendencies." Far from the mandates of Soviet social realism, Parajanov's films are ethereal, poetic, suffused with a stunning hermetic visual vocabulary, and he was deemed a "genius," a "magician," and a "master" by other filmmakers like Federico Fellini, Andrei Tarkovsky, Jean-Luc Godard and Martin Scorsese. His film "The Color of Pomegranates," a series of visionary montages that recount the life of the eighteenth-century troubadour monk called Sayat Nova, was named one of the 100 best films of all time by *Sight & Sound* magazine.[18] Its significance is due in part to the way it fuses together ethnography, poetry, and cinema, blending together magical realism with abstraction in a series of painterly tableaux that are both tactile and iconographic, departing from the normal narrative arc and social realism that was dominant in the

Soviet cinema of the time to make something truly new and astonishing.

The museum featured less of Parajanov's work as a filmmaker and more of his work as a prolific visual artist, including flat and 3-D collages, assemblages, drawings, and photographs, as well as some of the hats, puppets, and dolls he made during his time in the gulag when he was forced to sew sacks and was able to scavenge enough scrap material to make these haunting figures and items of clothing. Parajanov's assemblages are on the level of Joseph Cornell's boxes, and as the Armenian savant once said, "I was prohibited to make films and started to create collages. A collage is a compressed film."[19] Or in another sense, his films are like a series of interconnected visual *hayrēn*.

14.

A scene from the 1968 film "The Color of Pomegranates," by the Soviet filmmaker Sergei Parajanov. Credit: Criterion Collection

15.

Monasteries for monks. A pagan temple. An active mosque. A museum for an alleged (most of the charges against Parajanov, it would turn out, were fabricated) criminal bisexual artist. A poetic form that is as Christian as it is Islamic. All being celebrated in a country once called by Lord Byron "one of the most interesting on the globe."[21] And wandering these disparate sites, seemingly the only South Asian within miles, it occurred to me that there are *nationalisms*, plural; that it is possible to be, simultaneously, a globalist and a nationalist; that we can both take pride in our ancestry and culture, and also allow for the influence of others in shaping and reshaping our identity. Perhaps there's no better metaphor for this than the collage form itself, for what is that medium save the bringing together of incongruent materials into one space? The frame of a collage can be seen as the nation-state, but the elements therein—whether fabric, oil paint, movie poster scrap or copper wire—both retain their individuality and work in concert with the other elements to create something that, if not always coherent is, at least, unified.

16.

When you are reading,
your eyes, cast down,

are blue lakes where borrowed
rainbows can drown.

You are reading, forgive me
if I interrupt.
It's just to see those
lake eyes open up.
—Vahan Totovents (1898–1937) translated by Diana Der-Hovanessian[22]

Which brings us back to the *hayrēn*, which does not necessarily need to hew to any metrical constraints, the way that John Berryman believed his fifteen and sixteen-line Dream Songs were variants on the American sonnet. Vahan Totovent's stunning poem is an example of this, showing the characteristic quatrains and patterned rhyme, but using a direct address to the reader and the sustained conceit of the eyes as a lake across which flash the rainbows of art.

17.

The *hayrēn* is a perfect example of how the development of indigenous aesthetic traditions generally never happen in a vacuum. Trading cultures like Armenia have long been importers and exporters of goods and ideas throughout history, making their "crossroads" nationalism actually a precursor to globalism. Even after the genocide, the Armenians did not turn inward. Moreover there are a number of minority communities, from Syrians to Libyans living among them, so it's not useful to speak of the will of the Armenian people as a monolithic block. If we can speak of an inclusive nationalism, though, it is in this reaching outwards and exchange that we find the capacity to be human first and countrymen second. Armenian culture has always known this.

As Nareg Seferian writes "even the purest of the pure Armenian language, for example, will reveal foreign roots if one digs deep enough. The word *meghedi* I have heard brought up often as an example. How 'Armenian' is that word? It's been used for centuries, if not millennia. Yet, we consciously know that it is of Greek origin, the same root that gives us 'melody' in English today, with the same meaning. So does that make it foreign, un-Armenian? The word has become a part of our heritage, even if its geographic roots are beyond the Armenian mountains. There are hundreds of other such words that we might consider purely Armenian, whereas they are in fact of, say, ancient Parthian or Assyrian origin—languages of which we are not consciously aware, as opposed to words in English, Turkish, French, Arabic, Russian, or Persian that many Armenians can point out when used in conversation."[23]

Language—and the arts—are often at the forefront of societal transformation and racial integration, the way African American spirituals and gospel music, and then later blues and jazz, were so integral to the American civil rights movement. Music, like literature and art, speaks a *human* language, one that is not partisan and that allows those who make and encounter it to be mutually empowered and to find common ground. By showing how just as the *ghazal* form was gaining popularity in Iran, a similar self-referential flourish was appearing in *hayrēn* of the time, Joseph Johannes Sicco Weitenberg writes, "medieval Armenian poetry ... is by no means xenophobic or introverted as the nationalist perspective tends to be" (Weitenberg 47). Just as Louis Armstrong's performances in the 1930s helped start to shift, however glacially, the pervasive racism of the time, so too did Armenian medieval poetry (and later Parajanov's films) help respond to and neutralize the animus that comes with being conquered and annexed by other lands.

18.

"The more one is able to leave one's cultural home," Edward Said wrote in *Orientalism*, "the more easily is one able to judge it, and the whole world as well, with the spiritual detachment and generosity necessary for true vision. The more easily, too, does one assess oneself and alien cultures with the same combination of intimacy and distance."[24]

Intimacy and distance.

Isn't that the key to any good relationship? Isn't that the way Armenia holds the world, closely and warily, welcoming us in, yet bound together in a grief the outsider will never understand? Or maybe I'm just confusing my own inner and outer spaces, the ways I've been asleep and then awake to myself, even when entering and leaving a new land. Still that idea of a plurality of nationalisms embraced within the singularity of a country with a shared, traumatic past seems the most sensible way, if there can ever be such a rational response, of moving past a genocide.

The last meal I had while in the country was a sumptuous Armenian repast, with freshly baked *lavash* bread and a delicious pumpkin stew, which it turned out, was infused with pomegranate juice. As delicious as the fruit is on its own, it was made even more delectable by being mixed with pumpkin, coriander, cardamom, cinnamon, cumin and clove, with spices and traditions from other places. So it is with our poetic forms. Far from being a repository of "purity," the most appetizing kinds, in the end, are the ones that mix with other ingredients, never losing their identity, but transcending themselves to create a dish that helps make their own innate flavors truly sing.

Notes

[1] J. J.S. Weitenberg, *New Approaches to Medieval Armenian Language and Literature* (Amsterdam: Rodopi, 1995).

[2] A. Preminger, F. J. Warnke, and O. B. Hardison, *Princeton Encyclopedia of Poetry and Poetics* (Princeton: Princeton University Press, 2015).

[3] A. Siwneci and M. E. Stone, *Adamgirk: The Adam Book of Arakel of Siwnik* (Oxford: Oxford University Press, 2011).

[4] A. J. Hacikyan, G. Basmajian, E. S. Franchuk, and N. Ouzounian, *The Heritage of Armenian Literature* (Detroit: Wayne State University Press, 2000).

[5] Nahapet Kuchak—"Armenian Poet of 13th Century A.D." (October 31, 2011), https://literaryark.wordpress.com/2011/10/31/nahapet-kuchak-armenian-poet-of-13th-century-a-d/.

[6] S. Kaputikyan, Armenian Poetry Project, accessed October 7, 2019, https://armenian-poetry.blogspot.com/.

[7] R. Panossian, *The Armenians: From Kings and Priests to Merchants and Commissars*. (New York: Columbia University Press, 2015).

[8] Nationsonline.org, K. K.-. Political Map of Armenia. https://www.nationsonline.org/oneworld/map/armenia_map.htm.

[9] D. Varoujan, Armenian Poems, accessed October 7, 2019, http://www.armenianhouse.org/blackwell/armenian-poems/daniel-varoujan.html.

[10] Authors Admin, & Admin., "Verjine Svazlian Discusses 53 Years of Collecting Genocide Testimonies and Songs," (April 4, 2008), retrieved from http://asbarez.com/56992/verjine-svazlian-discusses-53-years-of-collecting-genocide-testimonies-and-songs/.

[11]L. Harrison, "Kim Kardashian Pays Tribute on Armenian Genocide Remembrance Day," (April 24, 2015), accessed October 7, 2019, from https://www.eonline.com/news/649925/kim-kardashian-saddened-on-100th-anniversary-of-armenian-genocide-read-her-emotional-tribute.

[12]P. Sblendorio, "Kim Kardashian Blasts *Wall Street Journal* for Publishing Ad Denying Armenian Genocide," (April 9, 2018), https://www.nydailynews.com/entertainment/tv/kim-blasts-wall-street-journal-for-ad-denying-armenian-genocide-article-1.2617625.

[13]K. B. Bardakjian and A. Gelen, (2006). *Hitler ve Ermeni soykırımı* (Stanbul: P ri yay nlar, 2006).

[14]W. Saroyan, *From Inhale & Exhale, Thirty-One Selected Stories* (New York: Avon, 1943).

[15]Tim Walker, "Kim Kardashian in Armenia Reality TV Star and Family's Trip To." *The Independent*, Independent Digital News and Media, (April 15, 2015), www.independent.co.uk/news/people/kim-kardashian-in-armenia-reality-tv-star-and-familys-trip-to-yerevan-raises-eyebrows-and-global-10176673.html.

[16]N. Sefarian, "The Armenian Identity and the Armenian State," (May 27, 2017), accessed October 7, 2019, https://www.evnreport.com/raw-unfiltered/the-armenian-identity-and-the-armenian-state.

[17]E. Batuman, "Sergei Paradjanov: Film-Maker of Outrageous Imagination," (March 13, 2010), accessed October 7, 2019, from https://www.theguardian.com/film/2010/mar/13/sergei-paradjanov-films-gulag.

[18]"Critics' Top 100," https://www.bfi.org.uk/films-tv-people/sightandsoundpoll2012/critics.

[19]R. Robertson,*Cinema and the Audiovisual Imagination: Music, Image, Sound* (London: I. B. Tauris, 2015).

[20] J. Hoberman, in "'The Color of Pomegranates,' the Cinema of the Cryptic," May 24, 2018). https://www.nytimes.com/2018/05/24/movies/the-color-of-pomegranates-sergei-parajanov.html.

[21]G. G. B. Byron and T. Moore, *The Life Letters and Journals of Lord Byron* (London: John Murray, 1866).

[22]V. Svazlyan, T. Tsulikian, and A. Poghikyan-Darbinyan, *The Armenian Genocide: Testimonies of the Eyewitness Survivors* (Erevan: "Gitoutyoun" Pub. House of NAS RA, 2011).

[23]N. Seferian, "The Global Nature of Armenian Culture," (June 20, 2016), accessed October 7, 2019, http://armenianradioboston.com/the-global-nature-of-armenian-culture/.

[24]E. W. Said, *Orientalism* (London: Penguin Books, 1991).

Jonathan Skinner

Ten Questions on *Birds of Tifft*

The following reflections on *Birds of Tifft* (BlazeVOX 2011) were composed in Fall 2016 in answer to questions from Professor Stacy Hubbard's First Year Seminar on Buffalo Poets in the Department of English at the University of Buffalo. The answers were lightly edited in 2020 with the addition of excerpts from the book, some photographs, and links to field recordings. Many thanks to Professor Hubbard for initiating the exchange and to her students.

1) You obviously learned a lot about Buffalo while writing Birds of Tifft*, and I'm wondering if you get so deeply involved in every place you live, or if there was something special about Buffalo that spoke to you.*

It takes time to get to know a place, and Buffalo is the first place I dedicated myself to observing and learning in the field. I had studied ecology in NM (auditing a course taught by an ex forest ranger at a community college) but did not pay consistent attention to the daily comings and goings of the wildlife. In Buffalo, I sought an alternative to the mountains and sunsets, and it arrived as migrating birds—beginning with the birds, from Bird Island Pier out into the head of the Niagara River. Then at the suggestion of Robert Creeley, I discovered the Tifft Farm Nature Preserve. Tifft became my school, my ramble, my out-of-doors office, though I also continued to frequent Buffalo's many other open spaces. It took four years in place before I felt I knew enough to begin to write about Buffalo.

FOREST

"shaking oaks to slake your hunger"
(Virgil)

for rest
a sanctuary
to wild

it's not a park
harbors hoodlums
and razor wire

proportion's restored
to think with others

quick things dart
underfoot, pressures
shadowed thoughts

eel-limned notions
—forest

Buffalo's position on the Niagara Escarpment makes it a gateway for all kinds of biogeographical energies: *all* the water of the Great Lakes flows past Bird Island Pier. It's no accident this "City of Lights" was the first American city to have widespread electric lighting. The escarpment also creates a bottleneck for migrating species that don't like to fly across the open water of Lake Erie (especially raptors who can't get thermals off the lake), who will follow the southern shore of Lake Erie to the Niagara Escarpment then follow the escarpment west and north: at the Hamburg hawk watch in the Spring, you can spot thousands of broadwing and redtail hawks kettling on warm days with a good southwest breeze.

Buffalo is situated at the lower edge of the reach of the Pleistocene ice sheet. When you drive east on I-90, you are driving along the edge of the last ice age, which explains why the landscape is so scraped off to the north, hills rising only to the south (the Finger Lakes being the "claw marks" left by the retreating glaciers). I'm not the only person to feel that the "scraped bare" geology of Western New York makes it a place especially susceptible to new beginnings: consider the suffragettes in Seneca Falls, the Mormons in Manchester (NY), the spiritualists in Lily Dale, the Underground Railroad in Buffalo, the Erie Canal, even the Poetics Program at SUNY Buffalo. (See Edmund Wilson's book *Upstate: Records and Recollections of Northern New York* for a history of some of the sectarian movements that were born or died in Western New York.) Buffalo's position near the end of the chain of Great Lakes and at the head of the Erie Canal, as the access point for the breadbasket of the Midwest to the markets of the Eastern Seaboard (and, later, as a center for steel production and lumber shipping) made it one of the wealthiest American cities at the turn of the nineteenth to twentieth century, a profile still legible in what remains of the city's magnificent architecture from the time, including the Olmsted parks, which Frederick Law Olmsted considered his "best planned" system.

I'm drawn to edges, and Tifft's location on the edge of Lake Erie draws me to it whenever I'm in Buffalo. It's a frontier, edge of country kind of town—a "Northern Border Town," as the Steam Donkeys, Buffalo's own country & western band, like to sing. Buffalo is an edge habitat between the many histories (natural, cultural, social, industrial) making up the "place" that is Buffalo. Just consider the juxtaposition of grain elevator ruins with wild marsh.[1]

in the 1880's Lehigh Valley Railroad dredged
canals out of Tifft Farm wetlands
where coal was transferred from
lake freighters to rail cars on wooden
bridges, until 1946 when filled:

thickets and early stage forest
succeed trestles and railroad sidings
ducks and waterfowl float in
place of ships[2]

2) How often did you visit Tifft Nature Preserve while writing this book? Was it a regular part of your routine?

At least once a week, sometimes more. I also regularly visited other open spaces in

Buffalo. When I acquired a digital ("minidisc") recorder, I began to visit Tifft obsessively to make field recordings. These were collected as "Little Dictionary of Sounds," for the Elevator Press Box Project, the poems for which appeared in my first book, *Political Cactus Poems* (Palm Press, 2005). Later, I could procrastinate writing my dissertation in a way that still felt educational. Tifft was my study, and I kept it out of doors.

FREIGHT[3]

hiccup then what
a side of something or peas
clattering down the way
elevator siding Tifft's fence
Santa Fe Rail's last ride
smashed down
in the brake with a muskrat
a friendly wave from the engineer
rattles the loose change

3) You quote several Romantic poets in Birds of Tifft—do you see your poetry as being in conversation with Romantic poets and other nature poets? How is your way of writing about nature different than theirs?

To the extent the Wordsworth (and other nature poet) echoes are deliberate, I wanted to mobilize the Romantic sublime in a context that might energize the reading both ways, back into the history of pastoral literature and forward into what the human relation to place is striving to become. Indeed, I think my response to the grain elevators was partly inspired by

Wordsworth's "boat-stealing episode" in *The Prelude*:

> And growing still in stature the grim Shape
> Towered up between me and the stars, and still,
> For so it seemed, with purpose of its own
> And measured motion like a living Thing

I'm struck by the reversal of agency in that passage, the sudden almost inexplicable mood turn, and the leap in scale. These grain elevator structures are not just rotting concrete and steel but signs of a fearful agency we now confront that is our own, collectively in what it is now proposed we call the Anthropocene, with our species's impact on the climate and its ability to sustain life. In "Notes After a Suicide," the book's 9/11 poem, this more-than-individual agency returns ("blowback" from our wars abroad) as the bioluminescent water-snakes of Coleridge's "Ancient Mariner," a vision in the stillness of doldrums as uncanny as the quiet of the skies that day. I'm still not sure what to make of the book's turn to a supernatural sublime in that moment. It rings even more eerily still as I revise these notes under the silent skies of a global pandemic.

The project departs from Romantic influence in its attention to daily matters and its refusal of a superior, retrospective prospect (of "emotion recollected in tranquility"). It avoids (or attempts to avoid) locating its language in the reflexive journey of a subjective "I," in the "poem of a mind." I like to think it embraces the urban as much as the pastoral, or at least the "impure" mix of agencies human, biological and abiotic along the Niagara Frontier. It's a book informed by Darwin's leveling message ("never say higher or lower") and by ecology, which did not exist as a science in Wordsworth's time.

John Clare is a Romantic-era poet who has gotten lots more attention lately as a proto-ecological poet, whose work I wish I had known better at the time I was composing *Birds of Tifft*. Retrospectively, he's clearly there!

I've been drawn to Keats, especially to the crazy scale shifts depicted in his long poem, "Endymion." (See especially the marine sequence. Also, his poem, "Letter to J.H. Reynolds.") Shifts in scale are important to ecological vision. *Birds of Tifft* is as influenced by postmodern art as it is by Romantic poetry, especially by the writings of Robert Smithson. Smithson (who Susan Howe first urged me to read) drew my attention to the importance of scale for ecological perception:

> Size determines an object, but scale determines art. A crack in the wall if viewed in terms of scale, not size, could be called the Grand Canyon. A room could be made to take on the immensity of the solar system. Scale depends on one's capacity to be conscious of the actualities of perception. When one refuses to release scale from size, one is left with an object or language that appears to be certain. For me scale operates by uncertainty.
> (Robert Smithson, "The Spiral Jetty")

To look at a grain elevator and see a towering cliff is to see with scale released from size, perhaps—a scale commensurate with the extraction regimes, livelihoods, and casualties of the world-ecology such a structure memorializes. For me, yes, the ecopoetics of exploring a place like Tifft is more about communicating uncertainty than certainty.

The scum floats white upon the lake
On the coke pile the light gleams and is gone
The elevators stand, a-rusting and vast
Out on the tranquil bay ...

4) You quote from several colonial texts in Birds of Tifft. How much is this book concerned with American history and colonial encounters with American nature?

I was lucky to study American Colonial literature with one of the treasures of the UB English Department, Professor Bob Daly (early American lit was a big gap in my education, since I went to England to study literature) and some of the texts we read for his lively and informative seminars made their way into my writing at the time. Of course, I also was strongly influenced by Susan Howe, whose seminars I attended at UB, not just on Emily Dickinson but also a seminar titled "Poetics of Conversion," focused on early American religious writing and captivity narratives, amongst other genres. Susan and Bob both drew my attention to William Cronon's environmental history of the colonial "contact" period, *Changes in the Land*. That book had a huge impact on *Birds of Tifft*, especially for its imbrication of animals and humans in environmental history. I'm not drawn to the "exceptionalism" of the American story—since leaving the US, I've been resituating my understanding of environmentalism within a more global perspective, both historically and in its present directions.

5) Why did you decide to put end notes to your sources in Birds of Tifft and how do you think having them there changes the poem? (Were you thinking of earlier poets who do this, such as T.S. Eliot or Marianne Moore?)

I probably was more influenced by William Carlos Williams at the time—his inclusion of different sorts of materials in his long poem *Paterson*. Ronald Johnson's use of field guide material in *ARK* (especially the poem "ARK 38") was a big influence. As was Christopher Dewdney's surrealist, collagist poetic "field guide" to Southwestern Ontario, *A Palaeozoic Geology of London, Ontario*. But these notes comprised an effort to honor all the sources I borrowed and worked from, including guide books written by scientists, Buffalo city employees, and citizens, and perhaps to underscore the collective nature of the "poetry" of Tifft. Notes and crediting sources bring ethical and documentary value, along with ecological value: the poem/notes interface is a kind of edge habitat. I also envisaged *Birds of Tifft* as "poetry by other means," poetry disguised as a field guide (hence the title and cover design, which was borrowed from the Golden Nature Guides series). So it would need to include notes and maps and practical information. My ultimate "goal" for the book was for copies to be sold at the Tifft Visitor Center, which did in fact happen for a while.

6) Was your poetry influenced by Susan Howe? What aspects of her poetics did you learn from?

It's hard to say where Susan's influence on this book begins or ends. In supervising some of my dissertation work, she drew my attention to many of the source texts or conceptual models for the book, in particular to incandescent, paradigm-shifting writing by artists and architects such as Robert Smithson or Frederick Law Olmsted. I recognized in her fierce pursuit of escape, and in her attention to writing that resists generic labels or containers, a kind of "wild" reading practice. Susan's deeply historical practice and care for the history of the region was infectious. (We visited the grain elevators together, amongst other expeditions.) Her approach to the poem as an instrument of research inspired and gave me confidence in my own writing of poetry outside the usual Romantic expectations. Finally, Susan's attention to silences and erasures, and to the particular work that poetry can do here, helped especially in the composition of the book as a whole.

7) Do you believe that eco-poetry can have an actual impact on how our society interacts with nature (climate change policies, recycling, environmental practices, etc.)?

I don't see ecopoetics as prescribing a genre, or a particular kind of poetry. I've tried to emphasize "ecopoetics" as a discursive site all kinds of practices can come to, in order to reflect on, innovate, and make changes to our habits of language and thought, without which our practices probably won't change. But practices reflect back on how we think and talk, so it might be just as important to ask in what ways our society's interactions with what it calls nature show up in poetry?

Whatever happens at the interface between the virtual and the actual is where the interesting communications begin to vibrate. It's a long-wave communication poetry tunes into—over decades and centuries, not months and years. While many don't think we have the time for this communication to work its way into changing society, before the worst effects of climate change overtake us, we should be suspicious of the apocalyptic rhetoric that shapes our understanding of the human place on Earth. It's as old as Western culture. Life will continue on earth, just in different numbers and in different forms. Do we or do we not choose to be a part of that future history? I think poets have an important role to play here: poets caretake the spectrum of sensibilities attuned to millennia of human experience on the planet, a spectrum crushed by the short-term demands of capitalist labor. Philosopher Jacques Derrida once suggested that poetry would be the one language art to survive the destruction of the archives. Some writers think poetry itself should set fire to the archive. Many writers consider poetry an oral art, passed on around the fireside: it has a way of living in our bodies and bones. I even know of some poets who are convinced poetry can alter our DNA. We are in it for the long haul.

It's important to communicate what we don't know as well as our knowledge, expertise, and "correct" attitudes. Ecolit's moralizing set it back decades. I also think poets nowadays might pay more attention to where and how they *place* their work. Don't just give readings in bookstores, art galleries, and academic conference rooms. Other poets offer a critical sounding board for one's poetry, but something else happens when one reads poetry to a roomful of scientists, citizens, politicians, community activists.

On his deathbed, Charles Olson wrote a summary of his poetics as "blowing" (the unfathomable stroke of pen or key), "twisting" (the figurative work of poetics, troping and turning its verses), and "placing" (perhaps the task for poets in our time). While we might want to discuss Olson's anthropocentric and gendered "Earth," his threefold process still offers a useful prospectus:

the Blow is Creation
& the Twist   the Nasturtium
is any one of Ourselves
And the Place of it All?
    Mother   Earth   Alone

8) Do you actually compose your poems outdoors? Or just gather material outdoors and write indoors?

I carry a pocket-sized notebook in which I make notes in the field, thoughts and things seen and overheard. Most of my site-based poems are actually written down in situ, in lines and stanzas (hence the predilection for short lines) and later transcribed. Sometimes I will do a really attentive walk, "gathering material" as I go, and write the poem in one sitting on the keyboard upon return. I tend to think better, and less predictably, when out of doors, on or off the trail. To cite walking artist Hamish Fulton, "No walk, no work."

9) Some people go into nature to escape society. But you seem to always be looking at factories and rail lines and highways and other human-made objects in relation to nature. Why is that?

It's not possible to think "nature" without thinking the social. While we all need solitude, using nature poetry to edit humans from the environment is deceitful. Listening and observing can be steps on the path of resistance. I discovered this as a field recordist, where the "naked ear" of the microphone hears everything, including the traffic, trains, planes overhead. Composer John Cage suggested listening to sounds one doesn't like until they become interesting. I'm as fascinated by the trains moving along the edge of Tifft as I am by the birds landing in its marsh.

TIFFT LOG

some boys up the way
making destruction

maybe not boys but deer[4]
breaking branches

There is a feral sociality to Tifft, where I would cross paths with solitary individuals, couples or small groups, people I got to know without ever learning their names. We rarely needed even the common ground of speech, as we shared intimate exchanges regarding plumage, behavior, song type, standing for a moment shoulder to shoulder, fixated on a bird through our binoculars. Sometimes these spaces offered an opportunity to observe, or be observed by, other humans from a distance—as with the solitary fishermen, casting amidst fishing herons, of

"River Watchers."

Tifft society shares an ease of being outside foreign to the Protestant work ethic, with its "walks" and goal-oriented activities like birding. Tifft took me back to New Mexico and sunsets from Fort Marcy, to lovers on park benches in Mexico City's Parque Alameda, to the smell of grass in San Francisco's Dolores Park. In *Birds of Tifft* observation of diverse humans is juxtaposed with moments of animal identification (as with the "white" and "black" fishermen and the "Black-crowned night" heron of "River Watchers") in a way that I hope exposes rather than naturalizes habits of labeling. The book also exposes tension in liberal discourse between inclusive language for human immigrants and the xenophobic rhetoric "invasive" animals and plants are met with.

> the invasive, non-native *phragmites communis:*
> common reeds shake their plumes
> over the boardwalk at cattails, broadcast
> laws of multiplication, a competitive edge
> in disturbed, marginally wet areas[6]

If the book doesn't push hard at these seams in the language of identification, it's for the same reason I never learned the names of most of the people I met at Tifft: perhaps out of an instinct to honor its wildness, a code of anonymity and indirect communication that regulates its feral habitats. It's "for rest/ a sanctuary/ to wild" ("Forest"). But people don't avoid one another either: in that way, it's more like a park. I did not go to Tifft to escape society but to find a different kind of society.

10) Are you hopeful about the future of the natural world? Does climate change cause you to despair?

How can one feel hope in the face of the scary math of global warming (and an ecocidal presidency)? Yet despair contributes to eco-blindness: obsessive doom and gloom drown out critical information on the doings and welfare of actual neighbors. The life around us gives hope—the life that invents its way forward on a daily basis. This life often instructs my own daily habits, including the extent to which it simply doesn't care about me. If only I'd leave it alone. Poetry can allow us to hold both hope and despair in the same thought.

For the Anglo culture I descend from, the world has been ending since at least 1666. If we could stop living in the shadow of the apocalypse the day after tomorrow, or acknowledge the extent to which the world has already ended, would we start to develop some longer-term thinking and practices?

Are we conflating our own mortality with that of the planet? Other cultural traditions include the dead in future planning, placing more emphasis on passing the life-sustaining knowledge down through generations. Older cultures might have some things to teach us. Nonhumans need our help more than our worrying aloud. It's also okay to feel despair. Let us act in a way that makes a difference to the actually existing conditions of those already living the dystopia of climate change.

I don't have much hope for the human species as such, collectively, but I also hope that our better selves will survive to learn to live with and amidst the incomprehensibly vast variety of life on Earth, which *will* come back (that's the lesson from Darwin's big evolutionary picture) beyond the catastrophes of colonialism and capitalist world-ecology. Perhaps we can slow the harm enough to pass those better selves on.

Notes

[1]https://edinburghuniversitypress.com/media/resources/11.1_Peepers.mp3.

[2]Adapted from Tifft Farm Nature Preserve pamphlet, *Self-Guided Nature Trail and Wellness Walk* (Buffalo: The Buffalo Museum of Science, with Working Wellness, Inc., 1988).

[3]https://soundcloud.com/ecopoetics/freight.

[4]https://edinburghuniversitypress.com/media/resources/11.7_Deer.mp3.

[5]Adapted from Tifft Farm Nature Preserve pamphlet, *Self-Guided Nature Trail and Wellness Walk* (op. cit.).

Cole Swensen

Christo & Jeanne-Claude: *The Running Fence*

"Like the tied-back curtain to a summer window" said the *Tomales Bay Times* while the Environmental Impact Report compared it to a county fair. A flare. A flair. An unfurl. That flew.

A kite 25 miles in flight.   Ignited by the sun.   How did the birds respond?   Especially the raptors   who spend their lives riding the currents of air   showing the atmosphere   to be also constructed

of hills, slopes, curves, valleys   moving not unlike the fence   in its slow streak of geographic sweep   a lighthouse drawn with a long phosphorescent brush—what did it look like in the moonlight? What did it look like from the moon? And then suddenly all the animals within miles awake.   Making a thin line drawn in lime arrive at a great wall that walled nothing in.

It took four years of fighting authorities at all levels—individual, local, county, state, and federal—to get the permission. One of the recurrent complaints was extravagance—millions of dollars for a completely useless work of art that most people couldn't even bring themselves to call art—but far from being wasted, all those millions were earned by someone—engineers, manufacturers, planners, measurers, cutters, sewers, builders, drivers, monitors, photographers, and ranchers who all contributed to its creation—and a good many of them were local; it created a small economic boom in the region.

The four years of negotiation were above all about getting the agreement of the community   the community that the project built by bringing them all together around the work; in short, the community that was created by creating the art was a central element of that art; it didn't make it—it was it.

Including even the people who opposed it.   If you were there at all you couldn't *not* be a part of it   you played a role in the continually unspooling theater, and in that way their work is completely realist.

The art work: all of their projects underscore the fact that art is *work*—the muscle, the logistics, the technics—it all requires tremendous effort, and much of it, so physical, even dangerous. Their projects exaggerate this almost to the point of the ridiculous, reminding us that most people think of art and work as, if not diametrically opposed, at least as unrelated.

By emphasizing the aspect of work and taking it to the point of extreme difficulty, they make extreme difficulty into an art all its own—part of the art is in solving the difficulties, but above all, it is in creating them—thus spurring on greater creativity. They only resort to a solution now and then because without one occasionally, the creation of larger and larger difficulties can't go on.

Jeanne-Claude and Christo were born on the same day—June 13, 1935—she in Morocco and he in Bulgaria. They both separately have said that the *Running Fence* has no beginning and no end just two extremes—and no end either in perspectives, angles, speeds, no end to its seeing nor to its being seen. The only beginning or end it had was temporal, and that was absolute, and imbedded in its very title: *Running Fence, Sonoma and Marin Counties, California, 1972–76*—it began when they first got the idea, and it ended only once every trace of it had been removed on Oct. 31, 1976.

All of Christo and Jeanne-Claude's projects have an elaborate ephemerality at the core: endless effort spent on a glance the eons each second takes to let this smoke go up in proof; a glimpse, one said, centers the eye's corner. I was driving by, and out of the corner of my eye, I saw flight fly.

And I, too, used to fly, said the rancher with a new-born calf in his arms, for whole split-seconds; it was the land that did it. Flight as extension, a connection that lets time touch time across time.

Flight as a muscular memory, lodged in muscles we no longer own. Or flight as a function of the eye, lifting the body beyond its possibility. Or flight as an aberration of the eye in conjunction with an hallucination of the spine.   Flight: we flew   and it was simply that   it's just something that happens to a body in time.

And it happened again and again.   "When I said that the fence flew, it flew, and so I said it again and again."

Can it be a fence   if it hems nothing in?   And what does it mean to run?   Sheep slipping through the slits made especially for them and their freedom of movement   and their likely opinion on fences

and their definitions.   Not to mention the white-on-white of their wool against the cloth, a kind of Ryman in motion   of constant recomposition until it's gone.   It was built to come and go—fog and mist—   then lift—*voile*—   veil and sail all at once until it's gone again.

How quick a streak might cause a heart—   that a heart might see a quick streak take off   from it, the heart   already thought out

in light   it seems that the eye   can't help but follow any bright extension seems to leave   all boundaries in shreds.

Christo's land-into-landscape work began when he was an art student in Bulgaria—the students were sent out on the weekends to "beautify" the land through which the Orient Express passed—which was the only part of the Eastern Bloc that, at that time, the outside world could see. They were ordered to paint villages, plant flowers, pose perfect tractors attractively. *We told the peasants they should set this threshing-machine clearly silhouetted at the top of a little hill—as if on a pedestal.*

Jeanne-Claude: *I became an artist for love of Christo. If he'd been a dentist, I'd have become a dentist.*

The plans and drawings for the *Running Fence* were conceived and executed as completely separate artworks, and their sales financed the entire construction of the Fence itself. This is true for all of their projects;

each one is funded by the sale of hundreds of plans, sketches, perspectives, and imagined depictions of the "final project." Not only does this keep them completely financially independent, but, more importantly, it confuses/diffuses the frame, lets it overflow into a network

which is the truest form of the piece: it's a whole, but made up of countless cells that are all wholes in themselves. These two-dimensional works, stunning landscape sketches, are often anchored by measurements, technical notations, ordinance maps, and hand-written descriptions as aesthetically compelling as the drawings themselves. And his handwriting itself is always yet another ridge-line, a transcription of distance into an arboreal syntax.

And the *Fence* was, in fact, referred to by more than one commentator
in terms of language   it was called a calligraphy   a hand writes
and the writing crosses   crossing evenly the line   between sight and

blinding   a certain second of sun   it would depend upon
the moment   there were moments   they said   when you couldn't
even look at it   or you'd have a blind spot   or rather a long
blinding sheaf that stayed on   moving through your mind.   If we

think of it as exactly that   a blind spot   of interminable length
a landscape of late summer   equally struck   landscape of the late
suddenly thinking: Fence as frame   Walk we all   in together again:

Walk the across—the fox   the deer   the sheep   the lost.   The *Fence*
holds them all, not   through containment   but like a magnet
or mirror   mirroring every angle   of weather   every errant

ray of cloud   and all that rain that sunned inside—   So many writings
on the work   mention rain and wind   and the shadows cut out, sharp
of trees   or cows   or whatever was passing   in a magic lantern, but

for the fact:

165,000 yards of woven white cloth.

2,050 poles.

90 miles of steel cable.

350,000 hooks.

59 ranchers whose land the *Fence* needed to cross, and who were at
first so resistant.

The countless visits to all of them until one handed him a beer and invited him in. There's an art to going back again and again to the sooner or later you'll not only agree but will become an advocate will

argue for the project in countless public meetings, with city councils, county planning commissions, and people generally difficult. And so, relatively conservative ranchers became outspoken advocates of avant-garde art.

In the long run, they ended up inadvertently functioning as museum guides, pointing out particularly striking perspectives, praising the aesthetics, and detailing the technical challenges that, once surmounted, made the whole thing fly. The work of art is to prove that the earth really moves, and suddenly it's been going on for centuries and always

a hawk swooping exactly parallel to the undulations of the ridge. Who

then turned sharply down to follow the fall was a red-tail that struck was a feather which might wander or figure the hawk gone horizontal his wingtip of chalk tracing the waves of land comes back in droves they say *rolling* hills they say *roll*

and there's a long low gravel sound calm in the face of the equally rolling sun. The *Fence* is the gesture that changes the site from land into landscape; by placing a work of art in it it's suddenly apparent.

And you writing out the museum label list the materials: *light, time, and weather,* all the while thinking of the unidentifiable animal that you saw last night silhouetted against it.

Jean-Thomas Tremblay

On Queer Ecopoetics and the Natures We Cannot Disavow

Nature is both queer theory's and ecocriticism's "bad object." From the former vantage point, nature hovers dangerously close to biological determinism; from the latter, it lacks the complexity of "ecology," a shorthand for interconnection and interdependence. Neither queer theory nor ecocriticism, then, can bear nature, and yet neither can stray too far from it. Can't live with it, can't live without it.

We may read the trajectory of queer theory, notes Nicole Seymour, as a series of engagements—from the curious, to the skeptical, to the antagonistic—with discourses of nature.[1] Scholars like Seymour, Sarah Ensor, and Catriona Sandilands detect in queer theory's wrestling with nature qua biology or norm the traces of an often-covert ecological thought.[2] Returning to the first volume of Michel Foucault's *History of Sexuality*, a foundational queer-theoretical text by most accounts, Sandilands observes, for instance, that "the figure of the homosexual came to haunt the margins of emerging discourses in urban development, environmental health, and even wilderness preservation: the effeminate homosexual and the lesbian gender invert were not only seen increasingly as *against nature* but also sometimes considered symptoms of the toxic underside of industrial, urban, and increasingly cosmopolitan modernity."[3] Queer ecology, this "interdisciplinary constellation of practices that aim … to disrupt prevailing heterosexist discursive and institutional articulations of sexuality and nature," thereby appears as queer theory's logical apotheosis.[4] Operating from the premise that the "bad objects" of queer theory and ecocriticism exist in tandem, queer ecology urges a reckoning with the ecological implications of heterosexuality's alignment with nature.

The phrase "queer ecopoetics," used notably by Angela Hume and Samia Rahimtoola, highlights the role of poetry and poetics in articulating sexuality's ecological valence.[5] As I have written elsewhere, "ecopoetics" designates both a corpus of poetry rooted in mid-twentieth-century experimentalism and a critical practice that, by indexing environmental transformations, resists a Romantic focus on pastoral and wildness.[6] For Hume and Rahimtoola, "queer" modifies "ecopoetics" by drawing our attention to the affective and relational dimensions of life amid climate crisis: "If ecopoetics has opened up crucial questions about how we might best dwell on earth and about the politics of such dwelling, queer ecopoetics orients us toward the affects, kinship practices, and erotic exchanges that shape dwelling as a relational endeavor."[7] There is no question that, in these scholars' view, queer ecopoetics ought to be a reparative project, one that cultivates "new forms of environmental sociality."[8] And some strands of queer theory, they suggest, are likelier than others to lead us to these forms. For instance, Hume and Rahimtoola denounce Lee Edelman's politics of negativity, figured through a radical rejection of reproduction and futurity. Likening Edelman's embrace of the death drive to the destructive, extractivist logic of today's resource industries, the authors instead follow José

Esteban Muñoz and imagine a kinship with the more-than-human world based on principles of "stewardship and care *beyond* the strictures of reproductive futurity."[9]

I share Hume and Rahimtoola's wish for a reparative queer ecopoetics, out of whose rhythms, patterns, and figures we might imagine anticolonial, antipatriarchal, and antiheterosexist ecological relations. But something about predicating this idealism on the bracketing of a version of queer theory deemed a little too morbid doesn't sit well with me. One of the lessons imparted by queer theory and underscored by queer ecology is that grappling with sexuality always implies grappling with natures: the natures wherein we feel at home *and* the natures we'd rather flee *and* the natures we hope to protect *and* the natures we wish to burn down. As Steven Swarbrick argues, "queer naturalisms" that extrapolate "an infinite call to ethics" from matter's vitality, promiscuity, and inventiveness—its queerness—tend to downplay "nature's queer negativity," or its death drive.[10] Nature, Swarbrick sums up, "is pharmakological: anima (cure) and animosity (poison) in the same breath."[11] After Swarbrick, I propose that an ecopoetics that recognizes queer sociality but disavows queer negativity proves too pastoral. If one strand of queer theory seems uncomfortably close to extractivist logics, isn't that worth investigating? My prescriptive claim is thus that queer ecopoetics should sustain the tension between reparative and destructive notions of queerness. If queer theory, including its conceptualization of destructive negativity, belongs to queer ecopoetics' nature, then queer ecopoetics should contend with, rather than renounce, this inheritance.

Tommy Pico's *Nature Poem* illustrates what we may call an indiscriminately queer ecopoetics, or an ecopoetics of reparative *and* destructive queerness. The book-length poem relays, from a queer Kumeyaay perspective, the speaker's refusal to produce what, in the transcendentalist tradition of nature writing, might be legible as a "nature poem." I see a reparative project in the poet's effort to chart, through records of digital communication, pop culture references, and reflections on sex, friendship, home, and family, queer and Indigenous socialities against the backdrop of settler colonialism, imperialism, and environmental collapse. The poet's engagement with reparativity's destructive counterpart, or what Swarbrick calls "nature's queer negativity," is on display in the following excerpt:

> Nature keeps wanting to hang out, and I've been looking for an excuse to use the phrase "hackles of the night" but you can't always get what you want.
>
> Every day feels like the final date bc we always find small ways of being extremely rude to each other, like mosquito bites or deforestation
>
> like I think I'm in an abusive relationship w/nature
>
> then again I think I'm in an abusive relationship w/myself, I whisper after pinching my squishy belly[12]

As is often the case with Pico, this excerpt vacillates between cool flatness and visceral confession. Here, as in many ecopoetic texts, we experience scalar shifts between the personal and the planetary. The grouping of mosquito bites and deforestation as examples of rudeness conveys ecosystemic thinking: deforestation causes mosquito populations to vary. The poet's musings on rudeness extend to the third and fourth stanzas, where he confesses to being "in an abusive relationship w/nature" and "w/myself." Guided by Billy-Ray Belcourt's (Driftpile Cree Nation) statement that "indigeneity is a zone of biological struggle," we may read the poet's revelations as registering the forms of violence encapsulated by a colonial, imperial, patriarchal, and heterosexist concept of nature.[13] At the same time, much like the term "final date," which suggests at once a sexual or romantic encounter and extinction or apocalypse, the last two stanzas I have quoted hint at a kind of queer negativity. Perhaps this "abusive relationship" goes both ways, and the formulation is the poet's way of admitting his responsibility in environmental destruction. Climate crisis ultimately puts his life in danger: "an abusive relationship w/nature" becomes "an abusive relationship w/myself." *Nature Poem*, as I read it, sets a valuable challenge to queer ecopoetics: to depastoralize, not only nature, but also queerness.

Notes

[1] Nicole Seymour, *Strange Natures: Futurity, Empathy, and the Queer Ecological Imagination* (Urbana: University of Illinois Press, 2013), 4.

[2] Sarah Ensor, "Queer Fallout: Samuel R. Delany and the Ecology of Cruising," *Environmental Humanities* 9, no. 1 (2017): 149–166; Catriona Sandilands, "Queer Ecology," *Keywords for Environmental Studies*, eds. Joni Adamson, William A. Gleason, and David N. Pellow (New York: New York University Press, 2015), https://keywords.nyupress.org/environmental-studies/essay/queer-ecology/.

[3] Sandilands, "Queer Ecology."

[4] Ibid.

[5] Angela Hume and Samia Rahimtoola, "Introduction: Queering Ecopoetics," *ISLE: Interdisciplinary Study in Literature and Environment* 25, no. 1 (2018): 139.

[6] Jean-Thomas Tremblay, "No More Nature: On Ecopoetics in the Anthropocene," *Los Angeles Review of Books*, June 24, 2018, https://lareviewofbooks.org/article/no-more-nature-on-ecopoetics-in-the-anthropocene/.

[7] Hume and Rahimtoola, "Introduction," 139.

[8] Ibid., 139.

[9] Ibid., 136, emphasis mine.

[10] Steven Swarbrick, "Nature's Queer Negativity: Between Barad and Deleuze," *Postmodern Culture* 29, no. 2 (2019): 10.1353/pmc.2019.0003.

[11] Ibid.

[12] Tommy Pico, *Nature Poem* (Portland: Tin House Books, 2017), 22.

[13] Billy-Ray Belcourt, "Meditations on Reserve Life, Biosociality, and the Taste of Non-Sovereignty," *Settler Colonial Studies* 8, no. 1 (2018): 2.

Pauw Vos

Entangling the World: The Connective Poetics of Juliana Spahr's "If You Were a Bluebird"

Introduction

The poems in Juliana Spahr's collection *That Winter the Wolf Came* show an intricate entanglement with the world. Published in 2015, the poetry bundle takes the Deepwater Horizon oil spill of 2010 as its point of departure. Intermingled with these oily ruminations are poetic calls for revolution based on Spahr's own experience with the street protests organized by Occupy Oakland in 2011. In *That Winter,* Spahr focuses increasingly on collective action in the form of protest and the possibility of change this brings with it. This change is not only performed between humans, but also in conjunction with the nonhuman. Overall, *That Winter the Wolf Came* emphasizes the interconnection between the bodily self and the many extensive systems, economic, ecological, social or otherwise, that shape it. Spahr's work testifies to a close interest in the way language forms different connections and how it emphasizes the interconnectivity that exists between seemingly different systems. In her 2005 publication *this connection of everyone with lungs*, for instance, she probes her own complicity with the US military-industrial complex in a post-9/11 world. A more recent work, made in collaboration with Joshua Clover, called *#Misanthropocene: 24 Theses* (2014) reads like a textual castigation of the Anthropocene epoch. This engagement with the Anthropocene and the human impact that this name proposes has become increasingly important to Spahr. The Anthropocene can be seen as signaling "the enormous scope of negative human impacts on the environment," but also as opening up "the possibility of reimagining the nature of the future not as a return to the past or a realm apart from humans, but as a nature reshaped by humans."[1]

Nicole M. Merola argues that in her more recent work, starting with *this connection* in 2005, Spahr has begun to experiment with poetry that "questions, encounters, materializes, and wrestles with the epistemological and ontological pressures that accrue to the newly self-reflexive, anxious position into which the Anthropocene interpellates us."[2] Merola proclaims that with the advent of the Anthropocene it is not only the conceptualization of the relationship between the human and the nonhuman that is put under strain, but also "how to think about the contours and roles of cultural forms and their work."[3] In an interview with the poet Jenna Goldsmith, Spahr herself reflects upon the need to rethink not only these categories, but also the role that poetry can play in this process.[4] She explains that poetry about birds, animals, plants and fish has for a long time been known as "nature poetry" and that "this term is very much under question, but we still haven't come up with a better one yet; like, 'anthropocene poetry' is not a term that gets used right now."[5] In a statement included after her poem "things of each possible relation hashing against one another" in *Well Then There Now*, Spahr reiterates the hesitation she feels towards nature poetry:

> it tended to show the beautiful bird but not so often the bulldozer off to the side

> that was destroying the bird's habitat. And it wasn't talking about how the bird, often a bird which had arrived recently from somewhere else, interacted with and changed the larger system of this world we live in and on.[6]

Finishing this statement she writes that "what I was looking for all along was in the tradition of ecopoetics—a poetics full of systemic analysis that questions the divisions between nature and culture—instead of a nature poetry."[7] However, as Lynn Keller explains, experimental and poststructuralist poetry has often been seen as "inimical to ecocriticism."[8] Poetry that reflects on how language shapes and constructs our understanding of the world is thought to only bring us further from ecocriticism's "concerns about real-world environmental degradation."[9] Fortunately, recent developments have seen a more open-minded approach to experimental poetry and the alternative it might offer to the more human-centered nature poetry. Joan Retallack, for instance, asks, "What can we discover when we stop trying to describe nature through our emotions or as if holding up a mirror to reflect her forms?"[10] Her answer is experimental poetry that "adopts nature's manner of operation. In that way we no longer stand apart from the rest of the world but participate in it as one among many."[11] Keller, likewise, affirms poststructuralist poetry as focusing "less on individual encounters with nature and more on collective modes of inhabiting the earth."[12] This ecocritical development has mainly occurred within the later generations of Language writing. Jonathan Skinner, for instance, states that "The avant-gardes of the last decades of that century [twentieth] … stand to be criticized for their overall silence on a comparable approach to environmental questions."[13] Spahr, on the other hand, goes beyond merely investigating semantic creations and shapings by also considering the impact these have in the actual world. Tana Jean Welch explains that "Spahr wants her poems to *mean*, to make certain points not *about* meaning, but about material-semiotic shapings."[14] By emphasizing the importance of real-world impact Spahr's ecopoetics combines the personal and the political. In the age of the Anthropocene this is becoming increasingly important. Merola, for instance, states that "Spahr tracks, worries, and materializes the transition from Holocene to Anthropocene frameworks while also figuring the reset to human-nonhuman epistemologies and ontologies the Anthropocene demands."[15]

Many of the poems in *That Winter* present an entanglement of the personal, political, and ecological, and help redefine the connections that exist between them. Spahr's Anthropocene poetry, I argue, offers new forms that reconceptualize the relationship between nature and culture through an emphasis on the interconnectivity and entanglement of the systems that make up our world. The importance of exploring new connections becomes increasingly salient in the face of the Anthropocene. As humans' understanding of our place within the systems that make up the earth changes, we need poetry that can respond, augment, and capture this dynamic becoming with the world.

The Creaturely & Material-Semiotic Knots

Throughout her work, Spahr pays close attention not only to the interconnected systems that make up our world, but also to the bodily actions of a large array of human and nonhuman animals. Her Anthropocene poetry foregrounds both human and nonhuman corporeal beings in close relation to one another. In order to critically look at these entanglements I will approach Spahr's poems through the use of two concepts, namely the notion of the creaturely and the material-semiotic knot. In the following paragraphs I will explain how these two concepts can be understood.

The creature is defined by Anat Pick as "first and foremost a living body—material, temporal, and vulnerable"[16] (5), and the creaturely, as such, proposes a relationship between human and nonhuman animals based on the shared vulnerability this creates. As Pieter Vermeulen and Virginia Richter explain, it is because both precariousness and vulnerability "applies to animals as well as to humans" that "these different life forms come to inhabit the same ethical realm."[17] The terms "creature" and "creaturely" have existed historically in a liminal place where they negotiated "the flexible border between supernatural, human and animal life."[18] The creaturely allows for an acknowledgement of other, nonhuman contexts as being equally valid to the human and creates a framework where these two can exist side by side. Pick states that attention to the bodily allows for a way of seeing the nonhuman animal without claiming it. Giving something attention does not automatically produce arguments or claims to the truth. It "is antiphilosophical"[19] and "brings into being without determining the nature of this being."[20] The revision of the human/animal relationship proposed by a creaturely poetics, furthermore, helps us look at culture from a different perspective. An emphasis on human–nonhuman sameness based on shared vulnerability shows that culture does not only exist in exclusively human context. It reveals "in culture more than the clichéd expression of the 'human condition' but an expression of something *in*human as well."[21]

With the help of Donna Haraway's notion of material–semiotic knots we can consequently begin to look at the poem as something that happens both on and off the page. The duality of this understanding shows how a knot is always *becoming-with* a myriad of other human and nonhuman actors. In other words, the material is always formed and forming the semiotic and vice versa. Haraway asserts that "to be one, is always to *become with* many."[22] She consequently uses her own body as an illustration of this becoming-with, and describes how the cells that make up her body consist of merely ten percent human genomes. The other ninety percent are "filled with the genomes of bacteria, fungi, protists, and such."[23] She states that she becomes "an adult human being in company with these tiny messmates."[24] Consequently seeing her body as a "figure", Haraway explains that the figure is not a mere representation of something else, but, rather, a place where "the biological and literary or artistic come together with all of the force of lived reality."[25] The body is, as such, a material-semiotic knot in which both matter and meaning continually shape each other. It is a figure where, as in a game of cat's cradle, every being is "constituted in intra- and interaction."[26] All entities, living and not, are shaped through this ever-continuing dance of becoming with.

Having established the creaturely and the knot as my guiding concepts, I will show ... how these work in practice through a close reading of "If You Were a Bluebird."[27] This is the third poem in the collection, and I take it to be exemplary of Spahr's specific brand of Anthropocene poetry. The poem itself reads almost like a recipe for an ecosystem. In it, Spahr draws attention to a diverse selection of human and nonhuman animals in their environment and the interrelations that exist between these. The poem begins with a list. By means of this repetitive gesture, Spahr shows how the human and nonhuman are always becoming in relation to each other. The poem culminates in a powerful interspecies gathering against the oil industry and its anthropogenic effects. In ways more pronounced than Spahr's other work the poem foregrounds interconnectivity as a way to look at and interact with the world differently. The emphasis on possibility and bodily relationality gives the poem a hopeful note that makes its final call for action all the stronger.

Entangling the Material and Semiotic

Let us now turn our attention towards the poem and its many entanglements. "If You Were a Bluebird" starts off with a seemingly simple statement, which immediately draws attention to its own textuality:

> Began with a list.
> A bird. Reed cormorant.
> Added a fish and a monkey. Hingemouth. White throated monkey.
> Added because.[28]

The omission of a clear subject in the first line creates an ambiguity as to who, or what, began the poem. If the left-out subject is interpreted as an 'I', it can either emphasize a human speaker or the poem itself as the one who began with the list. If, however, the missing subject is seen to contain an 'it', the poem can draw attention to either a human speaker relating the origin of the poem or point to the poem's own creative powers. In line with this *autopoiesis*, or self-creation, the 'it' also refers to the active nonhuman agents that help constitute the poem throughout. However, when read as hanging in between these two interpretations, the first line effectively blurs the distinction between the writer of the poem and what is written about. In so doing it emphasizes what Marcella Durand sees as exemplary for experimental ecological poets, namely, "the links between words and sentences, stanzas, paragraphs, and how these systems link with energy and matter—that is, the exterior world."[29]

With the addition of the grammatical conjunction "because" in the fifth line, Spahr further shows the relation between the creation of semantic meaning and the material. At first, it seems that the elliptical use of "because" implies a question that is answered self-evidently. These animals were added to the list because they already existed before the list and therefore need no explanation. They are simply "added because." Furthermore, Spahr uses the conjunction not only as a grammatical device in the poem but also in the more literal sense, namely to suggest a connection. The ambiguity apparent in the omission of the subject in the first line appears here as well, but in this instance it also serves to show the reader that an ecosystem transgresses man-made boundaries. They are connected, just as conjunctions in sentences help to connect clauses and coordinate words within the same clause. The "because" is recurrent throughout the whole poem and operates in connecting every consecutive sentence. This can, for instance, be seen in the next lines of the poem:

Because the six dorsal and anal fins of the hingemouth and its two
teeth too and also its swim bladder like a lung, covered in alveoli.
Because the silvery wings, longish tail, and short head crest of the reed
cormorant.
Because the white throated monkey, with its red belly and its white legs.
Added the phrase the principle of relation.
Because it was with the principle of relation that the Niger Delta came
to teem.[30]

The "phrase" that is added in line 10, however, seems to indicate that the initial use of "added because" refers mainly to the word "because" and its grammatical usage, and not to the reason *why* it was added. It shows us how the poem constructs itself and how its meaning is formed. This use of "because" in conjunction with the consequent connected naming of the different animals creates a "figure", as Haraway would call it. A material–semiotic knot that points towards the continued imaginary, and real, creation of the Niger Delta. As the poem continues it forms two more biomes, namely Kuwait Bay and the Gulf of Mexico. It is not until line 62, however, that Spahr introduces a clear subject to the poem, who informs the reader that:

I am waiting.
Said this out loud.
Said to no one in particular.
Said we are waiting.
Some of us are waiting.
Waiting for the assembly of fish.
Waiting to be complete.
Waiting to storm the waters.[31]

The first line of this section deviates from the syntactic structure that is created in the previous parts of the poem. The subject is omitted from the earlier lines that, for example, started the poem and which "added" conjunctions and nonhuman creatures to the poem. This line, however, explicitly states the "I" of the persona through reported speech only to redact it as a subject again in the next line. This shows how the persona is never only an "I," but is also always formed by other nonhuman influences. The persona is a material–semiotic knot that always becomes-with the nonhuman. The following lines further elaborate upon this point, by correcting the singular "I" to consecutively a "we" and ending with the inclusive "us" in line 66. The act of waiting then, is not "to be complete" but, rather, is an indication that the "I" needs to become aware that he is always already becoming-with. The anaphora and epimone in these lines function as a way to place the human persona in a subjective, waiting position towards nonhuman animals. The persona can never be complete, because this would imply a teleological narrative, as opposed to the dynamic, ever-ongoing process that is proposed by Haraway's becoming-with.

According to Welch, Spahr's poetry carries "an obvious political valence grounded not only in the exploration of semiotic constructions and shapings, but also in the interactive flux and flow of the material world."[32] Spahr actualizes this need for change when, at the end of the stanza, she changes the passivity inherent to "waiting" into the more active "wanting":

> Waiting for the impossible.
> Said waiting.
> Meant wanting.
> Wanting to fly the sky dark.
> Wanting to be complete. (l. 79–83)

The use of the word "wanting" here simultaneously seems to reference the impossibility of such an entangled way of being and a way to mobilize such an impossibility. Similar to how Spahr shows the imaginative creation of the ecosystems, here she gestures towards a possible world that can only come into being through a combination of human and nonhuman agency. If the word "wanting" is read as something that is lacking, it reiterates the impossibility of the teleological aspect of "waiting to be complete." The idea of completion implies an endpoint, an event that can be waited for, but this, ultimately, is not indicative of how the world behaves. The persona of the poem is left, and perhaps found, wanting if she waits for the impossible, namely for everything to be complete. We cannot sit back and wait for the problems of the Anthropocene to solve themselves, but we need to act in this moment. The process of flying the sky dark and storming the waters is already happening, but we need to become aware of humanity's place in this system. This can only happen if we acknowledge that the human is a material–semiotic knot that is not only acted upon, but also acts upon others in the "subject- and object-shaping dance of encounters."[33]

Shared Vulnerability

The descriptions of the different ecosystems in the poem are largely made up of bodily descriptions of the animals that inhabit them. We are, for instance, given physical accounts of the reed cormorant, hingemouth and white throated monkey, which all reside in the Niger Delta (l. 5–9). In reading for embodiment, it becomes possible to look for the "creaturely" in the poem. The conjunction "because" in this context serves as a reminder that nonhuman animals are added because they, too, have a vulnerable body with which they inhabit the planet. It is "because the six dorsal and anal fins of the hingemouth" that it is exposed to the same finitude as other human and nonhuman creatures. The anaphora used to describe the different ecologies pays attention to a rich diversity of embodied states. This attention focuses the reader on a shared bodily vulnerability but "does not yield a moral 'reading.'"[34] Rather, the attention encourages the reader to acknowledge their shared existential predicament. As the poem progresses this framework is used in combination with actions performed by the animals to consign "culture to contexts that are not exclusively human":[35]

> Because the gregarious pelican, traveling in flocks.
> [...]

> Because the nibbling and the picking of the red snapper with its short,
> sharp needle-like teeth.
> […]
> So the red snapper spreads itself out in the artificial reefs of oil platforms, the smaller fish in the upper part of the water column, the larger in deeper areas.
> [...]
> So the gregarious pelican hunts, hunts cooperatively, plunge dives from high up so as to stun fish, scoops them up, and then also breeds, breeds colonially, in trees, bushes, in the ground, around the gulf.[36]

Whereas the first iterations in the poem emphasize bodily presence and create a framework based on shared vulnerability, in the later lines this is complemented with the bodily actions these animals perform. The use of yet another conjunction, "so," explains, for example, how it is because of the red snapper's "nibbling and picking" that it has spread "itself out in the artificial reefs of oil platforms." These actions are consequently situated within the framework of sameness proposed by vulnerability. It is because we all have a vulnerable body that we are able to act, create and become. By foregrounding a sameness not only based on the bodily, but also on the actions that ensue from this, the creaturely in the poem can help to break down the strict divide between nature and culture. The division of "the smaller fish in the upper part of the water column, the larger in deeper areas" occurs in the same framework which created "the artificial reefs of oil platforms." Both are part of a greater system and this shows us that "Being human is grappling with what is inhuman in us".[37] In other words, it reveals a similarity that illustrates how we are always influenced by and entangled with the nonhuman, even in an anthropocentric pursuit of culture.

Julia Reinhard Lupton explains that *creatura* is derived from the future-active participle *creare* in Latin, a tense "forever imperfect" and always open to further change indicated by "the forward drive of the suffix *-ura* ('that which is about to occur')."[38] It is an entity always in the process of being created and transformed. A creaturely life is therefore "always affected by others from which it cannot fully shelter itself; only intermittently can it compose itself into the stability of an individual, a totality or a cosmos."[39] The repetitive descriptions of the nonhuman in the poem seem to illustrate this as well. The human and nonhuman animals interact with each other, and in doing so gesture towards a shared condition of exposure and finitude. The gregarious pelicans from the poem, for instance, are traveling together, hunting cooperatively, and breeding colonially, but in doing so they also affect the fish they hunt and the trees, bushes, and ground on which they breed. The human persona constitutes itself at intervals throughout the poem as well, only to realize they are never only an "I" but are always driven forward by a shared creaturely existence. This shows how the creaturely can not only be a mode that enables a shared framework of existence, but also how it points towards a becoming-with on the basis of finitude and exposure.

Throughout the poem, Spahr emphasizes a creaturely way of being for the ecological sites of the Niger Delta, Kuwait Bay, and the Gulf of Mexico. All three areas are under major environmental threat from oil drilling and its many side effects, such as chemical, noise and light pollution, oil spills, and disruption of migratory routes. The massive ecological impact of this activity lends an even greater urgency to the vulnerability and mortality proposed by a creaturely poetics. By pointing towards the interrelated systems that occur within such habitats Spahr shows how her poem can act as a cultural expression for the Anthropocene Age. The poem illustrates the ever-changing positions of the human and nonhuman through a more personal and embodied poetic form.

Conclusion

With "If You Were a Bluebird" I would argue that Spahr has succeeded in writing a poem that is exemplary of the "anthropocene poetry" she was still missing in the world. Whilst Spahr does not explicitly state what she means by Anthropocene poetry, a close analysis of this poem has offered several handholds as to what it might pertain to. It is poetry that is informed by and responds to the challenges of the Anthropocene epoch. In order to understand humanity's place at this crucial time, we need poetry that can make us aware of our complex entanglement with the world. Ultimately, we, too, cannot continue to be in this world without acknowledging the interrelations that exist between the vast diversity of systems, beings, and places that make up this world.

According to Skinner, it is exactly the attention to "what happens *off* the page, in terms of where the work is sited and performed, as well as what methods of composition, or *decomposition*, precede and follow the poem" that are important to ecopoetry.[40] The title of the poem, "If You Were a Bluebird," already hints that the work wants to reach beyond the pages on which it was written. The title seems to speak directly to the reader and expresses a wish for something imagined. Similar to the omission of the subject throughout the poem, the clause that explains what *would* happen is left out. The poem that follows is thus framed by the subjunctive mood of the title. With its emphasis on entanglement, sameness, and becoming-with, however, the poem does not literally imply that it wants anyone to become a bluebird. Rather, it wants us to be aware of the many connections and shared systems that make it almost *as if* you were a bluebird. The were–subjunctive places the title in the past tense and shows that this process was always already occurring. It conveys the hope that we will eventually come to realize this. The liminal position of the poem, furthermore, gives it an urgency that seems to be missing from the traditional nature poetry that Spahr reacts against. The human cannot be seen as a singular entity; it is always shaped by other entities and the systems which they co-inhabit. Merola argues that Spahr's work shows how it is not enough to "merely represent or think the affects of the Anthropocene. Rather we have to performatively embody them in ways that materialize our vulnerabilities, whether shared or particular."[41] "If You Were a Bluebird" can, as such, serve as a companion poem in these vulnerable times, showing us that we are, and never were, truly alone.

Notes

[1]Ursula K. Heise, *Imagining Extinction: The Cultural Meanings of Endangered Species*, 203.
[2]Nicole M. Merola, "what do we do but keep breathing as best we can this/minute atmosphere" in *Affective Ecocriticism: Emotion, Embodiment, Environment*, 26.
[3]Merola, 26.
[4]Lynn Keller explains that the poets Robinson Jeffers, Gary Snyder, and Wendell Berry are among "the most widely discussed by critics concerned with environmental literature" and that this "reveals a good deal about poetry's place in the recent environmental imagination" (610). Their popularity illustrates a prevailing tendency to romanticize a nature that is opposed to city life.
[5]Jenna Goldsmith, "Fieldwork: An Interview with Juliana Spahr," 412.
[6]Juliana Spahr, *Well Then There Now*, 69.
[7]Ibid., 71.
[8]Lynn Keller, "Green Reading: Modern and Contemporary American Poetry and Environmental Criticism" in *The Oxford Handbook of Modern and Contemporary American Poetry*, 604.
[8]Ibid., 604.
[9]Joan Retallack, "What is Experimental Poetry & Why Do We Need It?," 38.
[10]Ibid., 38.
[11]Keller, 611.
[12]Jonathan Skinner, "Editor's Statement," 7.
[13]Tana Jean Welch, "Entangled Species: The Inclusive Posthumanist Ecopoetics of Juliana Spahr," 4.
[14]Merola, "what do we do," 28.
[16]Anat Pick, *Creaturely Poetics: Animality and Vulnerability in Literature and Film*, 5.
[17]Pieter Vermeulen and Virginia Richter, "Introduction: Creaturely Constellations," 3.
[18]Vermeulen and Richter, 3. In this article I will mainly focus on the diffuse border between animal and human life, since the poem foregrounds this most notably.
[19]Pick, 5.
[20]Sharon Cameron, *Impersonality: Seven Essays*, 5.
[21]Ibid., 5.
[22]Donna J. Haraway, *When Species Meet*, 4.
[23]Ibid., 3.
[24]Ibid., 4.
[25]Ibid., 4.
[26]Ibid., 4. Haraway uses this game as a metaphor for knowledge making in her text "A Game of Cat's Cradle: Science Studies, Feminist Theory, Cultural Studies" (1994).
[27]Juliana Spahr, *That Winter the Wolf Came*, 29–35.
[28]Ibid., l. 1–4.
[29]Marcella Durand, "The Ecology of Poetry," 62.
[30]Spahr, l. 5–12.
[31]Spahr, l. 62–9.
[32]Welch, "Entangled Species," 4.
[33]Haraway, *When Species Meet*, 4.
[34]Pick, *Creaturely Poetics*, 5.
[35]Ibid., 5.
[36]Spahr, l. 47–61.
[37]Pick, 6.
[38]Julia R. Lupton, "Creature Caliban," 1.
[39]Vermeulen and Richter, "Introduction," 3.
[40]Skinner, "Editor's Statement," 760.
[41]Merola, "what do we do," 43.

Bibliography

Cameron, Sharon. *Impersonality: Seven Essays*. Chicago: University of Chicago Press, 2007.

Durand, Marcella. "The Ecology of Poetry." *Ecopoetics* 1, no. 2 (2002): 58–62.

Goldsmith, Jenna. "Fieldwork: An Interview with Juliana Spahr." *ISLE: Interdisciplinary Studies in Literature and Environment* 23, no. 2 (2016): 412–21.

Haraway, Donna J. *When Species Meet*. University of Minnesota Press, 2007.

Heise, Ursula K. *Imagining Extinction: The Cultural Meanings of Endangered Species.* Chicago: University of Chicago Press, 2016.

Keller, Lynn. "Green Reading: Modern and Contemporary American Poetry and Environmental Criticism." *The Oxford Handbook of Modern and Contemporary American Poetry*. Edited by Cary Nelson. New York: Oxford University Press, 2012, 606–23.

Lupton, Julia R. "Creature Caliban." *Shakespeare Quarterly* 51, no. 1 (2000): 1–23.

Merola, Nicole M. "what do we do but keep breathing as best we can this/minute atmosphere." *Affective Ecocriticism: Emotion, Embodiment, Environment*. Edited by Kyle Bladow and Jennifer Ladino. Nebraska: University of Nebraska Press, 2018, 25–49.

Pick, Anat. *Creaturely Poetics: Animality and Vulnerability in Literature and Film*. New York: Columbia University Press, 2011.

Spahr, Juliana. *That Winter the Wolf Came.* Oakland: Commune Editions, 2015.

---. *Well Then There Now.* Jaffrey: Black Sparrow Books, 2011.

Skinner, Jonathan. "Editor's Statement". *Ecopoetics* 1, no. 1 (2001): 5–8.

Vermeulen, Pieter, and Virginia Richter. "Introduction: Creaturely Constellations."*European Journal of English Studies* 19, no. 1 (2015): 1–9.

Welch, Tana Jean. "Entangled Species: The Inclusive Posthumanist Ecopoetics of Juliana Spahr." *Journal of Ecocriticism* 6, no. 1 (2014): 1–25.

Tyrone Williams

Three Approaches ...

... to the natural and built worlds (there are innumerable ways of nearing what is never reached)—Brenda Iijima's limited edition 2014 Boaat Press book, *Some Simple Things Said By And About Humans*, Sydney Shen and Laurel Schwulst's 2015 Ambient Works book, *Perfume Area*, and Craig Dworkin's 2019 Kenning Editions book, *The Pine-Woods Notebook*—these books of poems acknowledge the limits of comprehension and apprehension, cognitive and affective, knowledges. And though the same limitations circumscribe what we might call ecological praxis, none of these constraints imply a lack of responsibility toward the natural and built worlds. How a poet understands and enacts responsibility is varied, of course, and Iijima, Dworkin, and the team of Shen and Schwulst offer interesting examples of what has come to be known as ecopoetics.

Iijima's *Some Simple Things Said By And About Humans*, made entirely from scratch (including the paper), typeset by hand, enacts her vision of an ecological and ecopoetics sensibility that attempts to close the distance between self and other by direct, primarily tactile, encounters. The contrast between the thick, uneven, paper-mâché front and back cover, and the standard, regular typeset poems is a model of distance per se. Iijima's found language and journalistic denotational descriptions of animals, the abbreviated histories of our encounters and exploitations of them (from zoo exhibitions and spaceflight missions to drug and cosmetics tests), plays on another enactment of distance: the book's title and the poems which are "by and about" the animal Homo sapiens. It would be easy to see in this attempt to recover and acknowledge our animality the shadows of D. H. Lawrence, Robert Bly, Michael McClure and others. But Iijima isn't interested in a metaphysics of the other; hence, her denotative/journalistic restraint. The seriousness with which she acknowledges human cruelty to other animals (e.g., the deaths of Laika and Ham sent up in, respectively, Russian and American spacecrafts) doesn't preclude humor at our own expense ("On the other hand paw/Here I am" [17]). And her ecological consciousness is perhaps best displayed in the opening prosaic lines of "Polar Bears": "Polar bears are poster children Think global warming think Polar Bear balancing on melting ice sheets Babies bleed of / starvation The federal court system must step in for the Polar bear before devastating practices of mountaintop removal in Appalachia ... ." The by-now common understanding that though the climate crisis begins well before industrialism and capitalism the latter have accelerated climate change is captured in the epigram that closes this poem: "The pedagogy of teachings that Now is universal" (31). The displacement of this traditional poetic form by its advertisement descendant—the hook—serves to yoke together educational and industrial forces into an intemporal present—that is, into the abstract figure of the global consumer.

Universality is also an implicit trope in the very title of Sydney Chen's and Laurel Schwulst's (unfortunately sold-out) *Perfume Area*. This little book of 84 pages is a series of prose meditations/ejaculations/observations divided up into four sections: morning, afternoon, evening, and night. A "key," comprised of rating stars (one to five) for decoding the value of the prose pieces within each section is provided. However, the stars are linked to three values in the right column: one= memorable, three=forgettable, and five=memorable. Because two and four stars are not assigned morphemes, one is tempted to read the key as a bell curve whose apex is forgettable or the five-starred forgettable. But it's possible that the memorable-forgettable-memorable column also maps onto Marx's well-known M=C=M formula whereby money becomes money-plus—the origin of surplus value. The conversion of the commodity into a waystation through which money passes in order to add to itself implies that the worker, then, is also a kind of commodity situated between investment and return. For example, in the piece title "Le Labo Jasmin 17," "the flowering trees" of a "confusing" "national park" "produce fruit" that is "more like gear." And vice versa: "Machines warm up just as you do." (Blood Concept "O"). The connections between capital and ecology are all over this book, starting with the irony of the title itself since perfume, by definition, cannot be confined to an area even though department stores make this claim in lieu of the more salacious (if truer) "Perfume Sold Here."[1] *Perfume Area* draws an absolute connection between ecology and etymology in "Helvetica the Perfume" where the "Swiss typeface" is understood to be "far from neutral," the latter assertion a rejoinder to the inventors of the typeface who claimed that it, like the Swiss during the World Wars, were neutral. Thus, this piece begins, "Helvetica The Perfume consists only of water. This is, apparently, the scent of nothing" (41). In *Perfume Area* ecology is the study of man-made systems, and ecopoetics is the practice of tracking the erasure of history and memory as a nonsite constructed by memory in order to profit as a surplus memory; the one exceeds a preceding (not a "first") memory. The theology of capital is rendered here as a total ecology of conflation, construction, and amnesia. Thus, as one example, Helvetica refers, etymologically, to the tribes that populated the geographical area of present-day Switzerland. They came into contact with, and were absorbed by, the Romans. This ordinary story of human migration, encounter, and assimilation (or conquest) is, writ large, the essence of perfume. It may be subtle, but it can no more be "neutral" than it can be confined to an "area."

If aromachology defines the position taken in *Perfume Area*, Craig Dworkin hacks into, and irreverently repurposes, the traditional, that is, Platonic, aesthetics of Kant and (some of) the Romantics in *The Pine-Woods Notebook*. Inspired in part by the phenomenological aesthetics of Francis Ponge, Dworkin deploys citation and repetition (with variations) to construct what is finally a weirdly beautiful tonal and atonal meditation on the interplay of abstraction, concretion and linguistics. The aesthetic of the beautiful is apt here since Dworkin, relying on found discourses and terminologies, erases the boundary between culture and nature by way of assonance ("Aerosols bloom above boreal forests" [22]), internal rhyme ("A liquid elixir of pine pitch mixed with pitch-pine switches quickens" [32]) and alliteration ("Skyview factors the fraction of a field's saturant blue" [18]), the traditional devices of everyone from Donne and Pope to Wordsworth and Keats. Yet, these seductive wiles (for Dworkin understands the link between these poetic devices and the feminization of the natural world) scarcely veil the penetration of "beauty" by the "beast" of human products and waste ("Aerosols"). More to the point, Dworkin draws a direct link between so much "sighing" of the natural world, that "ahhh.." epiphany of nature poetics, and the fetishization of the human body: "The ankle's tattoo with its archaic alphabet laid over veins, / silently traces the mute arabesques of the sandal's loosed laces" (24). The objectification of the body into apotheosized parts is not unlike the conversion of pine needle, branch, twig, trunk, and bark into metonyms of the fantasy of tranquility and ferocity as always "out there." *The Pine-Woods Notebook* is a gem, a reminder that the "beautiful" is absolutely dependent on bracketing its conditions of possibility, not unlike those beautiful sunsets of modernity that index "natural" and "manmade" pollutants.

---

[1]The authors, however, have their own origin story: As "Earth's oldest mall" undergoes "excavation," the mallologists discover "an obelisk that still emits a weird smell. Painted on the megalith with cochineal dye are glyphs that translate to *Perfume Area*. Research suggests this site is the lost origin of the word *perfumeria*" (21).

Acknowledgments

Poetics for the More-than-Human World came into being during a time of international pandemic and social and economic upheavals. It began as a website issue, developed into an online anthology, and is now a print anthology. Produced without financial sponsorship, the book owes its existence to the generosity and resourcefulness of those who have given their time and expertise. Of special note is the ongoing participation of Linda Russo, who helped organize a contest through Washington State University that resulted in the book's cover design. Brie Barron worked unstintingly in producing the book's layout. Jared Schickling of Delete Press provided invaluable design and layout support. Kent Johnson and Michael Boughn embraced this project from its inception, sustained it through its website phase, and offered to print it as a Dispatches Edition.

We also want to acknowledge those who provided a media platform for the contributors: Cole Swensen volunteered to organize a zoom reading series, and Charles Alexander has preserved the readings on his Chax Youtube site: https://www.youtube.com/channel/UCxUXE-_zgL8acZC6-K2obzg.

We are grateful to all the contributors for sharing writing that reflects their engagement with the more-than-human world we all share.

—The editors

We would like to thank the following publications in which these poems first appeared.

JUANA ADCOCK:
"Steller's Use of Verbs When Describing the Sea Cow, Hunted to Extinction within 27 Years of Its Discovery by Europeans. De bestiis marinis, 1751." is reprinted with permission from Juana Adcock (Blue Diode Press, 2019).

TACEY M. ATSITTY:
"III." and "XII." are forthcoming in a self-published chapbook.

JEFFERY BEAM:
"The Flies" and "Parnassus, the Barren Cleft" are reprinted with permission from *The Broken Flower* by Jeffery Beam (Nottingham: Skysill Press, 2012), 24.

SALLY BLIUMIS-DUNN:
"Echolocation" is reprinted with permission from *ECHOLOCATION* by Sally Bliumis-Dunn (Plume Editions/ MadHat Press, 2018).

SEAN BORODALE:
"Crickets and Noise of Grasses and Perseids," "Devil's Coach Horse Beetle slowly through a moment of Witness," and "May-Flies Unfinished" are forthcoming in *Inmates* by Sean Borodale (Jonathan Cape, 2020).

JOHN BRADLEY:
"Once and Always" and "And You Shall Know Us by Our Trash: An Ecopoetics for the Moon" are reprinted with permission from *Dispatches from the Poetry Wars.*

ODED CARMELI:
"Hating Animals" is reprinted with pemission from Stuart Ross, *Hating Animals* (Cobourg: Proper Tales Press, 2015).

CATHERINE CARTER:
"Luna" is reprinted with permission from Catherine Carter, *Larvae of the Nearest Stars* (Baton Rouge: Louisiana State University Press, 2019), 41, and from Sara Method.

Brenda Coultas:
"The Writing of an Hour" is reprinted with permission from *St. Rocco's for the Dispossessed* (2017).

Thomas Rain Crowe:
"Fall in Big Cataloochee Valley" is reprinted with permission from *Broad River Review*, published by the Department of English at Gardner Webb University in Boilings Springs, NC, 2012.

Deborah Davidovits:
"Owl Eye" is reprinted with permission from Steven Shapin, *The Scientific Revolution* (Chicago: University of Chicago Press, 1996), 15–64.

Rachel Blau DuPlessis:
"January from Shepherd's Calendar" is reprinted from *Late Work* (NY: Black Square Editions, 2020), 14–15.

Clayton Eshleman:
"The Chaos of the Wise," "The Aurignacians Have the Floor," and "Dusk Abri du Cro-Magnon, 1988, 7:45 P.M." are reprinted with permission of the author.

Amy Evans Bauer:
All poems are reprinted with permission from Amy Evans Bauer, *and umbels: sound((ing))s too* (Grand Rapids: Shirt Pocket Press, 2019), n.p.

Cheryl J. Fish:
"The Ice Hotel at Jukkasjärvi, Sweden," "Artists' Residency at Ii, Finland," and "Unreliable Snowpack" are forthcoming in Cheryl J. Fish's, *The Sauna is Full of Maids* (Shanti Arts Press).

Rob Fontini:
"Automation" is forthcoming in Rob Fontini's pamphlet "Hermes I".

Catherine Greenwood:
"The Grolar Bear's Ballad" is reprinted with permission from The CBC Literary Prizes and CBC-Radio-Canada, 2019 CBC Poetry Prize Shortlist.

Megan Grumbling:
All works are forthcoming in Megan Grumbling's *Persephone in the Late Anthropocene.*

Jane Hirshfield:
"As If Hearing Heavy Furniture Moved on the Floor Above Us," "Day Beginning with Seeing the International Space Station and a Full Moon Over the Gulf of Mexico and All Its Invisible Fishes," and "(No Wind, No Rain)" are reprinted with permission from Jane Hirshfield, *Ledger* (Knopf, 2020), 104.

Cynthia Hogue:
"Bee" is reprinted with permission from Cynthia Hogue, *Superstition Review* online, on 30 June, 2016. "To Split a Lark" is reprinted with permission from Cynthia Hogue, *The American Journal of Poetry* online, on 1 January, 2018.

Marybeth Holleman:
"with" is forthcoming in Marybeth Holleman's *tender gravity* (Red Hen Press).

Lissa Kiernan:
"The River Never Froze," "Eclogue on Decommissioning," and "The Art of Hurricanes" are from *Two Faint Lines in the Violet* (Negative Capability Press, 2014).

Sharon Lattig:
"Dwelling with the Possible: Lyric Obscurity and Embedded Perception" is forthcoming in *Cognitive Ecopoetics: A New Theory of Lyric* from Bloomsbury Academic in 2021.

Andrew Levy:
"They All Eat Octopus" is reprinted with permission from Andrew Levy, *Artifice in the Calm Damages* (Chax Press, 2017), chapbook. "The Chaos of Dreaming Life" is reprinted with permission from David Lewis, *The MIT Faculty Newsletter* (February/March 2004) Web.

Alick McCallum:
A note on "To Burnley": Photograph courtesy of and with thanks to Woodend Mining Museum in Burnley.

Michael McClure:
"Winter Solstice," "This Body," and "((Dharma))" are forthcoming in Michael McClure's *Mule Kick Blues* (City Lights Books, April 2021).

Valery Oisteanu:
"The Earthquake Flowers of Fukushima" is forthcoming in *In the Blink of a Third Eye* (Spuyten Duyvil).

John Olson:
"My Life Among the Crows" is forthcoming in *Weave of the Dream King* (Black Widow Press).

António Osório:
"Jetsam" and "To a Myrtle," translated by Patricio Ferrari & Susan Margaret Brown, are from *A Raiz Afectuosa [The Tender Root]*, and "A Bedouin," also translated by Ferrari and Brown, is from *Décima Aurora [Tenth Dawn].* Both books are included in the complete works *A Luz Fraterna [The Fraternal Light],* Lisbon, Assírio & Alvim, 2009.

Andrew Schelling:
"Wolf Acrostic" and "Somehow" are forthcoming in Andrew Schelling's *The Facts at Dog Tank Spring* (Dos Madres Press).

André Spears:
"Ship of State 2" is forthcoming in André Spears' self-published chapbook "The Devil (XV)".

Margo Taft Stever:
"Three Ravens Watch" was first published in *Ghost Moose* (Kattwompus Press, 2019).

Harriet Tarlo:
"29 March 2019" is from *Gathering Grounds* (Shearsman Press, 2019).

Brian Teare:
"Clear Water Renga" is reprinted with permission from Brian Teare, *Doomstead Days* (NY: Nightboat Books, 2019).

Orchid Tierney:
"carbon sink" and "To the Is-Land" are reprinted with permission from Orchid Tierney, *a year of misreading the wildcats* (NY: The Operating System, 2019).

Jeffrey Yang:
All works forthcoming in Jeffrey Yang's *Line and Light.*

Author Biographies

Editors

MARY NEWELL is the author of the poetry chapbook TILT / HOVER / VEER, poems in journals, essays, and entries on Whitman and Dickinson for the *Encyclopedia of the Environment in American Literature*. Dr. Newell (MA Columbia, BA Berkeley) received a doctorate from Fordham University with a focus on American literature and the environment. A former assistant professor, she is an outside poetry editor for ISLE and curates the Hudson Highlands Poetry Series (https://manitoulive.wixsite.com/maryn).

SARAH NOLAN is a writing instructor at the University of Colorado in Boulder. She holds a PhD in environmental literature with a particular focus on ecopoetics. Her book, *Unnatural Ecopoetics: Unlikely Spaces in American Poetry* (2017), explores the environmentality of decidedly unnatural spaces, an idea she explores in much of her published work. She lives in Nederland, Colorado. Outside her academic life, she loves traveling, writing, walking her dog, and spending time with her two children.

BERNARD QUETCHENBACH, Professor of English at Montana State University Billings, is the author of *Back from the Far Field: American Nature Poetry in the Late Twentieth Century*, one of the texts that launched Ecopoetics as a field of study, as well as *Accidental Gravity: Residents, Travelers, and the Landscape of Memory* and *The Hermit's Place*, a poetry collection. He has degrees in creative writing (SUNY Brockport) and American Literature (Purdue University).

Contributors

JUANA ADCOCK is a Mexican-born, Scotland-based poet, translator, and performer working in English and Spanish. Her English language poetry debut, *Split* (Blue Diode Press, 2019), was awarded the Poetry Book Society Winter Choice for 2019 and was named in the *Guardian*'s list of Best Poetry Books of 2019.

WILL ALEXANDER is a poet, novelist, essayist, aphorist, playwright, visual artist, and pianist. He is a Whiting and California Arts Council Fellow and has received the PEN Oakland Award, an American Book Award, and the 2016 Jackson Poetry Prize as well as a 2018 Lifetime Achievement Award from Beyond Baroque Literary/Arts Center. His work has been translated into Romanian, Italian, Spanish, Cyrillic, and Arabic.

OMAR AL-NAKIB is a Kuwaiti visual artist and poet.

RAE ARMANTROUT's latest book is *Conjure*. Other books include *Versed, Partly: New and Selected Poems, Entanglements* (a chapbook in conversation with physics), and *Wobble*, all from Wesleyan University Press. *Wobble* was a finalist for the 2018 National Book Award. *Versed* won the 2010 Pulitzer Prize. Armantrout's "Art of Poetry" interview appeared in *The Paris Review* in 2019.

Tacey M. Atsitty, Diné, is Tsénahabiłnii (Sleep Rock People) and born for Ta'neeszahnii (Tangle People). She is a recipient of numerous prizes and awards. Her work has appeared or is forthcoming in *Poetry, Epoch, Kenyon Review Online, Prairie Schooner, Crazyhorse, New Poets of Native Nations*, and other publications. Her first book is *Rain Scald* (University of New Mexico Press, 2018).

Stacey Balkun is the author of *Sweetbitter* (Sundress 2021), three poetry chapbooks, and co-editor of *Fiolet & Wing: An Anthology of Domestic Fabulist Poetry*. Winner of the 2019 New South Writing Contest and Terrain.org's 10th Annual Contest, her work has appeared in *Best New Poets 2018, Crab Orchard Review,* and *The Rumpus*. Stacey (MFA Fresno State) teaches creative writing online at The Poetry Barn and The Loft.

Joan Baranow is the author of *In the Next Life, Living Apart*, and two poetry chapbooks: *Blackberry Winter* and *Morning: Three Poems*. A VCCA fellow and member of the Community of Writers at Squaw Valley, she founded and teaches in the Low-Residency MFA program in Creative Writing at Dominican University of California. She co-produced the PBS documentary *Healing Words: Poetry & Medicine* (2008) and produced the documentary *The Time We Have* (2018).

Michael Basinski gazes out the back window into the Ginnywoods, which is a little ways past the airport in Buffalo, New York. Seemingly, for the last 50 plus years he has worked variously and with daily great joy and vigor in the realm of the poem and has always been a friend to all frogs.

Lesley Battler's debut book of poetry, *Endangered Hydrocarbons,* was published by Book*hug (BookThug) in 2015. She has worked as a telecommunications librarian, corporate writer, information manager, and archivist in Toronto, Montréal, and Calgary. She is currently living in Edmonton.

Jeffery Beam's many works include *The Broken Flower, Gospel Earth, Visions of Dame Kind, The New Beautiful Tendons: Collected Queer Poems 1969–2012, Spectral Pegasus / Dark Movements*—a collaboration with Welsh painter Clive Hicks-Jenkins—and *Jonathan Williams: The Lord of Orchards,* a book of essays, images, and shouts. An online chapbook, *Don't Forget Love*, appears in *Dispatches from the Poetry Wars*. jefferybeam.com

Mei-mei Berssenbrugge was born in Beijing and grew up in Massachusetts. She is the author of fifteen books of poetry, most recently *A Treatise on Stars* and *Hello, the Roses*, both with New Directions, as well as *A Lit Cloud*, a collaboration with artist Kiki Smith. She lives in New York City and northern New Mexico.

Sally Bliumis-Dunn teaches Modern Poetry at Manhattanville College and offers individual manuscript conferences at the Palm Beach Poetry Festival. The author of *Talking Underwater, Second Skin, Galapagos Poems, and Echolocation*, she was a finalist for the *Nimrod*/Hardman Pablo Neruda Prize.

Sean Borodale is a poet and artist who writes scriptive texts live on location. His collection *Bee Journal* was shortlisted for the T. S. Eliot Prize and Costa Books Award; *Mighty Beast*, his poem-doc for radio, was awarded a Radio Academy Gold Award for Best Feature or Documentary. He was selected as a Next Generation Poet in 2014 and divides time between Ireland and London.

Cindy Botha lives in Tauranga, New Zealand. She started writing very late in life, and has found the companionship of a sharp pencil and a lined notepad to be an incomparable delight.

Michael Boughn's books of poetry include *Dislocations in Crystal, 22 Skidoo/SubTractions, Cosmographia—a post-Lucretian faux micro-epic* (shortlisted for the Governor General's Award for Poetry in 2011), *City—A Poem from the End of the World*, and *Hermetic Divagations—After H. D.* With Victor Coleman, he edited Robert Duncan's *The H. D. Book*. He and Case the Border Collie can be found hanging out in dog parks or herding sheep together.

John Bradley's most recent book is *Everything in Motion, Everything at Rest* (Dos Madres Press). He frequently reviews books of poetry for *Rain Taxi*.

Marc Brightside is an author of poetry and fiction for adults, mentored by the acclaimed author Julian Stannard at the University of Winchester. Since graduating, Marc has performed and published poems in various outlets across the UK, his work characterised by incessant darkness interspersed with humour, cynicism, and chronic introspection. His debut poetry collection, *Keep it in the Family*, was published in 2017.

Laynie Browne's recent books include *In Garments Worn by Lindens, Periodic Companions*, and *The Book of Moments*. She teaches at University of Pennsylvania and at Swarthmore College.

Joseph Bruchac's poems have appeared in hundreds of publications from *Akwesasne Notes* and *Parabola* to *National Geographic* and *The Paris Review*. An enrolled member of the Nulhegan Band of the Abenaki Nation, his work as a writer and traditional storyteller often reflects his Native American ancestry. Author of over 160 books for young readers and adults, his newest collection of poetry is *Four Directions, New and Recollected Poems*.

Catherine Carter lives with her husband near Western Carolina University, where she is a Professor in the English Education and Professional Writing programs. Her most recent collection of poetry is *Larvae of the Nearest Stars* (LSU Press, 2019); her work has also appeared in *Best American Poetry 2009, Orion, Poetry*, and *Ploughshares*, among others.

Oded Carmeli is an Israeli poet, editor, and journalist based in Tel Aviv. He is the founding editor of *Hava Lehaba* poetry magazine, its Hava Laor press, and the Tel Aviv Poetry Festival. He is the author of three volumes of poetry, a novel, and a satirical self-help book. He didn't make it as an astronaut, so he covers space news, usually for the Israeli Space Agency and Haaretz.

CARA CHAMBERLAIN is the author of three books of poetry, *Hidden Things, The Divine Botany*, and *Lament of the Antichrist in a Secular World and Other Poems*. Her poems and prose have appeared in numerous journals, including *Nimrod, Boston Review, Passages North, Crab Orchard Review,* and *The Southern Review*. She has received four Pushcart Prize nominations, has been featured in both *Verse Daily* and *Poetry Daily*, and has been a finalist in the Ashland Poetry Press, Lo-Fi Novella and Blue Light Book Award contests. She lives in Billings, Montana.

JACK COLLOM (1931-2017) taught at Naropa University, where, in 1989, he pioneered Eco-Poetics, believed to be the first ecology literature course in the United States. His nature writings are published widely. He taught throughout the US, Central America, and Europe, and was also renowned as a poet-in-the-schools, authoring two books about teaching that advocated for practicing poetry beyond the confines of the classroom.

EDWARD J. COOK's work has appeared in *Dispatches* and elsewhere, including Jerome Rothenberg's *Poems and Poetics* blog.

BRENDA COULTAS' poetry can be found in *Bomb and Brooklyn Rail* and the anthologies *Readings in Contemporary Poetry* published by the DIA art foundation, *What is Poetry (Just Kidding, I Know You Know) Interviews from the Poetry Project newsletter,* (1983–2009), and *Symmetries Three Years of Art and Poetry at Dominque Levy*. Coultas's most recent book, *The Tatters*, is available from Wesleyan University Press.

THOMAS RAIN CROWE is an internationally-published and recognized author of more than thirty books, including the multi-award-winning nonfiction nature memoir *Zoro's Field: My Life in the Appalachian Woods* (2005). He is founder and publisher of New Native Press and lives in the Tuckasegee watershed and the "Little Canada" community of Jackson County in western North Carolina. His literary archives are collected at Duke University.

BRADLEY DAVID is a writer and urban homesteader living in Southern California by way of the rural Upper Midwest. His work appears or is forthcoming in publications by *Oxford University Press, XanEdu Publishing, Beyond Words Publishing,* and *Seisma Magazine*. He holds a BA in English from Michigan State University and a Master of Social Work from the University of Michigan.

DEBORAH DAVIDOVITS lives at the edge of the woods in Beacon, NY. Her poetry has been published in *JuxtaProse Literary Journal* and the *Tiny Seed Literary Journal*, and her visual art has been exhibited nationally and internationally. She is a beekeeper and teacher, and you can view her artwork at www.deborahdavidovits.com.

JANINE DEBAISE is author of the poetry book *Body Language* from Main Street Rag and the chapbook *Of a Feather* from Finishing Line Press. Her essays have been published in numerous journals including *Orion Magazine*, the *Southwest Review*, and the *Hopper*. She teaches writing and literature at SUNY College of Environmental Science and Forestry in Syracuse, New York.

Vivian Demuth is the author of the eco-poetry book *Fire Watcher* (Guernica Editions, 2013) and the novels *Bear War-den* (Inanna Publications, 2015) and *Eyes of the Forest* (Smoky Press, 2007). Her poetry and fiction have been widely published and broadcast on public radio. She has worked as a park ranger, an outdoor educator, and a fire lookout in the Rocky Mountains. www.viviandemuth.com.

Adam Dickinson is the author of four books of poetry. His work has been nominated for awards including the Governor General's Award for Poetry. He has been featured at international literary festivals in Canada, Germany, the Netherlands, Norway, and the United States. He teaches English and Creative Writing at Brock University.

Elizabeth Dodd is co-editor, along with Simmons Buntin and Derek Sheffield, of the anthology *Dear America: Letters of Hope, Habitat, Defiance, and Democracy*. Her most recent collection of essays is *Horizon's Lens* (University of Nebaska Press). She is the nonfiction editor at *Terrain.org*.

Lisa Fleck Dondiego, of Ossining, NY, is the author of the chapbook *A Sea Change* (Finishing Line Press, 2011). Her poems have appeared in *The Westchester Review* and *Haibun Today*, and in anthologies, including Red Moon Press's and the Contemporary Women Writers of the Hudson Valley's *A Slant of Light*. She was a semi-finalist for the "Discovery"/The Nation Prize.

A transplant to the Finger Lakes region of upstate New York, Edward A. Dougherty's latest collection, *10048*, is about the World Trade Center, 9/11, and so much more. He is the author of four previous books and five chapbooks.

Mark DuCharme is the author of *We, the Monstrous: Script for an Unrealizable Film, The Unfinished: Books I–VI, Answer,* and other books of poetry. His poems have appeared in *Big Bridge, Caliban Online, Colorado Review, New American Writing, Talisman* and *Noon: An Anthology of Short Poems* (Isobar Press, 2019), among many others. He lives in Boulder, Colorado, amid the foothills of the Rocky Mountains.

Rachel Blau DuPlessis is the author of the multivolume long poem *Drafts* (written between 1986 and 2012), the recent collage poems *NUMBERS* (2018) and *Graphic Novella* (2015), and a new long work, in book-length episodes, called *Traces, with Days*, containing *Late Work*. She has written extensively on gender, poetry and poetics; on objectivist poets; and on modern and contemporary Anglophone poetry. She lives in Philadelphia.

Marcella Durand's poetry books include *The Prospect, Rays of the Shadow, Le Jardin de M. (The Garden of M.)*, with French translations by Olivier Brossard, *Deep Eco Pré*, a collaboration with Tina Darragh, *AREA*, and *Traffic & Weather*. Her translation from French of Michèle Métail's *Earth's Horizons/Les horizons du sol* was published this year. She lives in the Lower East Side in New York City.

Dan Eltringham is a poet and academic based at the University of Sheffield (UK), where he is a British Academy Postdoctoral Fellow working on poetry networks, translation, and militant ecologies. He is part of the Centre for Poetry & Poetics and co-edits Girasol Press, a small publisher that explores handmade poetics and experimental translation.

Clayton Eshleman is the author of more than thirty books, including poetry, essays, prose, and interviews. He is the main American translator of César Vallejo and of Aimé Césaire. Eshleman's awards and honors include a Guggenheim Fellowship, the National Book Award, and several fellowships from the National Endowment for the Arts and the National Endowment for the Humanities.

Amy Evans Bauer is an Anglo-Austrian Kiwi poet and artist based in London. *and umbels* (Jonathan Williams Chapbooks prize, Shirt Pocket, 2020) and *PASS PORT* (Shearsman, 2018) form the two-part transcript of her at-sea, cross-border installation *SOUND((ING))S*, which she has performed at the Institute of Contemporary Arts, London and waterfront locations internationally. Her poetry includes *Stalking Gerard Manley Hopkins* (Salient Seedling/Woodland Pattern broadside, 2016) and *The Report of the Iraq Enquiry: Poetic Summary* (Larynx/Shearsman, 2017) and features in *Chicago Review*, *Performance Research* and elsewhere. https://goldsmiths.academia.edu/AmyEvansBauer

Patricio Ferrari is a polyglot poet, editor, and translator. Among his recent editions and translations are *The Galloping Hour: French Poems* by Alejandra Pizarnik (with Forrest Gander; New Directions, 2018) and *The Complete Works of Alberto Caeiro* by Fernando Pessoa (with Margaret Jull-Costa; New Directions, 2020). His work appears in *Arcadia*, *Asymptote*, *Cover to Cover*, *The Paris Review*, *The Wire*, and *Words without Borders*.

Bradley J. Fest is assistant professor of English at Hartwick College. He is the author of two volumes of poetry, *The Rocking Chair* (Blue Sketch, 2015) and *The Shape of Things* (Salò, 2017), along with a number of essays on contemporary literature and culture. bradleyjfest.com

Alexis Finet is a PhD candidate in French and Francophone Studies at Florida State University. To broaden his research on sound and water in the Congolese novel and to expand his knowledge of the Spanish language cultures, he is studying the concept of water in the Amazonian region with Dr. Juan Carlos Galeano. He is currently translating Dr. Galeano's *Cuentos amazónicos* into French, in collaboration with Chanelle Dupuis.

Cheryl J. Fish is an environmental justice scholar, fiction writer, and poet. Her short stories have appeared in *Iron Horse Literary Review*, *CheapPopLit*, and *Liars League*. She is the author of *Make It Funny, Make it Last* (Belladonna), and her most recent poetry collection is *Crater & Tower*, from Duck Lake Books. Fish has been Fulbright Professor in Finland; she teaches at the City University of New York.

Ann Fisher-Wirth's sixth book of poems is *The Bones of Winter Birds*. Her fifth is *Mississippi*, in collaboration with photographer Maude Schuyler Clay. With Laura-Gray Street, Ann coedited *The Ecopoetry Anthology*. A senior fellow of the Black Earth Institute, Ann has had Fulbrights to Switzerland and Sweden, and residencies at Djerassi, The Mesa Refuge, and elsewhere. She teaches and directs the Environmental Studies minor at the University of Mississippi.

Rob Fontini is a poet, translator, and ABD in philosophy temporarily residing in the northeastern corridor of the United States.

Elisabeth Frost's books include *All of Us: Poems* (White Pine Press), *Bindle* (in collaboration with artist Dianne Kornberg, Ricochet Editions), and *The Feminist Avant-Garde in American Poetry* (Iowa). She is Professor of English and Women's, Gender & Sexuality Studies at Fordham University, where she edits the Poets Out Loud Prize book series from Fordham Press.

Juan Carlos Galeano, born in the Amazon region of Colombia, is an international poet, environmentalist, and academic. He is the author of the book *Folktales of the Amazon*, and several books of poetry, a translator of various American poets, and also director of two documentary films. He teaches Latin American poetry and cultures of Amazonia at Florida State University.

David Greenspan is an MFA candidate at the University of Massachusetts Amherst and serves as Promotions Editor for Slope Editions. His poems have appeared in places like *BathHouse Journal*, *Laurel Review*, *LIT Magazine*, *New South*, *The Southeast Review*, *The Sonora Review*, and others.

Catherine Greenwood recently moved from Canada to South Yorkshire where, as a PhD candidate at the University of Sheffield, she is pursuing an interest in Gothic poetry. Her first book *The Pearl King and Other Poems*, inspired by the life of Kokichi Mikimoto, was a Kiriyama Prize Notable Book. Her second collection, *The Lost Letters*, featuring medieval lovers Heloise and Abelard, is also published with Brick Books.

Megan Grumbling's first collection *Booker's Point* (2016) was awarded the Vassar Miller Prize. Her work has also received the Ruth Lilly Fellowship and a Robert Frost Foundation Award for Poetry. *Persephone in the Late Anthropocene*, which vaults a classical myth into the age of climate change, is forthcoming this fall from Acre Books.

Robert Head is the author or *Refuges of Value* and *Selected Poems* (Book & Mineral Investment Corporation, 1988, 1993) and the former editor of the *NOLA Express*, a New Orleans journal. He lives in Lewisburg, West Virginia.

William Heyen (wheyen@rochester.rr.com) lives in Brockport, NY. He received his PhD from Ohio University and an Honorary Doctorate of Humane Letters from SUNY. He is the editor or author of more than thirty books including *Crazy Horse in Stillness*, winner of the Small Press Book Award for Poetry, and *Shoah Train: Poems*, a Finalist for the National Book Award. *The*

Candle, a volume of 45 years of his Holocaust poetry, appeared in 2016. His nature/ecology books include *Pterodactyl Rose* and *The Rope*.

JANE HIRSHFIELD's ninth poetry collection is *Ledger* (Knopf, 2020). The founder of Poets for Science and a former chancellor of the Academy of American Poets, in 2019 she was elected into the American Academy of Arts & Sciences. Her work appears in many eco-anthologies and ten editions of *The Best American Poetry*.

H. L. HIX's recent books include a poetry collection, *Rain Inscription*; an edition, with Julie Kane, of selected poems of contemporary Lithuanian poet Tautvyda Marcinkevičiūtė, called *Terribly in Love*; an essay collection, *Demonstrategy*; and an art/poetry anthology, *Ley Lines*.

CYNTHIA HOGUE has published nine poetry collections, including *Revenance* (2014). Her co-translations include *Fortino Sámano* (The overflowing of the poem), from the French of Virginie Lalucq and Jean-Luc Nancy, and *Lointaines* by Nicole Brossard (forthcoming 2022). Hogue's honors include two NEA Fellowships and the H.D. Fellowship at Yale University. She is the inaugural Marshall Chair in Poetry Emerita Professor of English at Arizona State University.

Raised in North Carolina's Smokies, MARYBETH HOLLEMAN transplanted to Alaska's Chugach Mountains after falling head over heels for Prince William Sound just two years before the EVOS oil spill. She's author of *The Heart of the Sound* and *Among Wolves*, and co-editor of *Crosscurrents North*, among others. Her first poetry collection, *tender gravity*, is forthcoming from Red Hen Press. www.marybethholleman.com

ANGELA HUME is the author of the poetry book *Middle Time* (Omnidawn, 2016). Her chapbooks include *Meat Habitats* (DoubleCross, 2019), *Melos* (Projective Industries, 2015), *The Middle* (Omnidawn, 2013), and *Second Story of Your Body* (Portable Press at Yo-Yo Labs, 2011). Hume co-edited the anthology *Ecopoetics: Essays in the Field* (U of Iowa P, 2018). She is Assistant Professor of English at University of Minnesota, Morris.

BRENDA IIJIMA's involvements occur at the intersections and mutations of poetry, research movement, visual arts, floral and faunal consciousness, and ecological sociology. She is the author of seven full-length collections of poetry and numerous chapbooks and artist's books. She is the editor of *the eco language reader*. Iijima is the editor of Portable Press at Yo-Yo Labs. http://yoyolabs.com

KENT JOHNSON has authored, translated, or edited over thirty titles in relation to poetry. His new book, *Because of Poetry, I Have a Really Big House*, is due out in 2020 from Shearsman Books. With Michael Boughn, he takes care of *Dispatches from the Poetry Wars.*

PIERRE JORIS just published *Fox-trails, -tales & -trots* (poems and prose, Black Fountain Press); *Microliths: Posthumous Prose of Paul Celan* and *A City Full of Voices: Essays on the Work of Robert Kelly* (Contra Mundum Press). Also, *Arabia (not so) Deserta* (essays, Spuyten Duyvil Press, 2019) and

Conversations in the Pyrenees with Adonis (CMP, 2018). Forthcoming is *Memory Rose into Threshold Speech: The Collected Earlier Poetry of Paul Celan* (FSG).

George Kalamaras, former Poet Laureate of Indiana (2014–2016), has published seventeen books of poetry, ten of which are full-length. He is Professor of English at Purdue University Fort Wayne, where he has taught since 1990.

Eliot Katz is the author of seven books of poetry, including *Love, War, Fire, Wind* and *Unlocking the Exits*. His most recent scholarly book is *The Poetry and Politics of Allen Ginsberg*. Katz has worked for decades as an activist for a wide range of peace and social-justice causes, including helping to create housing and food programs for homeless families. www.eliotkatzpoetry.com

Lynn Keller recently retired from the University of Wisconsin-Madison English Department and from directing the UW's Center for Culture, History, and Environment (CHE). She has published numerous articles and four books on contemporary American poetry, the most recent being *Recomposing Ecopoetics: North American Poetry of the Self-Conscious Anthropocene*. She co-edits the Contemporary North American Poetry Series published by the University of Iowa Press.

Lissa Kiernan's *Glass Needles & Goose Quills* won the Nautilus Prize for lyric prose and the Independent Book Awards prize in the cross-genre category. Her *Two Faint Lines in the Violet* was a finalist for the Indiefab Book of the Year and Julie Suk Award for Best Poetry Book by an Independent Press. She is the founding director of The Poetry Barn in West Hurley, NY.

Kim Kyung Ju has written over ten books of poetry, essays and dramaturgy. His poetry in English translation includes *I Am a Season that Does Not Exist in the World* (Black Ocean, 2016) and *Whale and Vapor* (Black Ocean, 2020). Considered the progenitor of the South Korean new wave "Maraepa" (future) movement, he was awarded the prestigious Kim Soo Yung Prize.

John Kinsella's most recent volumes of poetry include *Drowning in Wheat: Selected Poems 1980–2015* (Picador, 2016) and *Insomnia* (WW Norton, 2020). His volumes of criticism include *Activist Poetics: Anarchy in the Avon Valley* (Liverpool U P, 2010) and *Polysituatedness* (Manchester U P, 2017). He is a Fellow of Churchill College, Cambridge University, and Professor of Literature and Environment at Curtin University.

Natalie Cortez-Klossner is a recent MA graduate from the University of Chicago where she studied Critical and Literary Theory. Her essay exploring aesthetics and plant studies is forthcoming in the journal *Antennae*. Born in Peru to a Swiss mother and Peruvian father, she currently resides in Chicago.

Dianne Kornberg has had more than 35 solo exhibitions in the US and abroad. Her work is represented in the collections of multiple museums, and is the subject of a number of books: *Field Notes* (2007), *India Tigers* (2009), *Madonna Comix* (2014, with poet C. Bland), and *Bindle* (2015, with poet E. Frost). Kornberg is a Professor Emerita at Pacific Northwest College of Art in Portland, Oregon. http://www.diannekornberg.com/

PETRA KUPPERS is a disability culture activist, a community performance artist, and a professor at the University of Michigan. Her academic books engage disability performance; medicine and contemporary arts; somatics and writing; and community performance. She is the author of a dark fantasy collection, *Ice Bar* (2018). Her most recent poetry collection is the ecosomatic *Gut Botany* (2020). Petra is a Black Earth Institute fellow.

MELISSA KWASNY is the author of six books of poetry, most recently *Where Outside the Body is the Soul Today* (University of Washington Press Pacific Northwest Poetry Series) and *Pictograph* (Milkweed Editions), as well as a prose collection, *Earth Recitals: Essays on Image and Vision* (Lynx House Press). She is Montana's Poet Laureate, a position she shares with M. L. Smoker.

SHARON LATTIG is a poet and a theorist of poetry. Her new book, *Cognitive Ecopoetics: A New Theory of Lyric*, is forthcoming from Bloomsbury Academic later this year. She holds an MA in Creative Writing and a PhD in English, and currently teaches at UConn, Stamford. In her other life, she is a professional figure skater.

PATRICK LAWLER has published six books of poetry including *Feeding the Fear of the Earth* and *Underground*. In addition, he has two books of fiction: *Rescuers of Skydivers Search Among the Clouds* and *The Meaning of If*. A number of his scripts have won awards and been produced, including *Singing to the Earth Until a Tree Grows* (a short eco-film). He is Professor Emeritus at SUNY College of Environmental Science and Forestry and Writer-in-Residence at Le Moyne College.

GARY LAWLESS is co-owner of Gulf of Maine Books in Brunswick, Maine. He has published nineteen collections of poetry in the US and five in Italy. He was the poetry editor of *Wild Earth* magazine. His latest book is *Caribou Planet*.

RUTH LEPSON is poet-in-residence at the New England Conservatory. Her new & selected poems is forthcoming from MadHat Press. Her last book of poems, *Ask Anyone (Pressed Wafer)*, won the Philip Whalen Award from Chax Press. Her other books of poems are *Dreaming in Color* (Alice James Books), *Morphology*, and *I Went Looking for You* (both from blazeVOX). She edited *Poetry from Sojourner: A Feminist Anthology*.

JAKE LEVINE is a poet, critic, and translator based in Daegu, South Korea. He translated the work of Kim Kyung Ju that appears in this anthology, along with Soohyun Yang, a freelance translator based in Seoul, South Korea.

HELLER LEVINSON, the originator of *Hinge Theory*, lives in New York. His latest book of poetry is *Seep* (Black Widow Press, 2020).

ANDREW LEVY is the author most recently of *Artifice in the Calm Damages* (Chax Press, 2017; the complete book is forthcoming from Chax fall 2020); other books include *Don't Forget to Breathe* (Chax Press), and *Nothing Is In Here* (EOAGH Books). Levy's poems and essays have appeared in numerous American and international anthologies, including *An Anthology of 60 Contemporary American Poets* (Zasterle, Spain, 2017).

ANTHONY LIOI has published poetry in *Inlet, Blast Furnace, Watershed, Environmental Philosophy, The Dark Mountain Project, Green Humanities, The MIT Faculty Newsletter, Numinous,* and *Assaracus*. His work has been nominated twice for the Pushcart Prize. He is at work on a book of poetry called *Choirpunk*. He lives on a creek called Second River in Montclair, New Jersey, and teaches at the Juilliard School in New York.

JADY LIU is a freelance writer in Beijing. He also works at ARTEXB and *The Shanghai Literary Review*. Instagram: jadywhitesand

GEORGE LOONEY's books include the award-winning *What Light Becomes: The Turner Variations*, the award-winning novel *Report from a Place of Burning, Meditations Before the Windows Fail, Monks Beginning to Waltz,* and the Elixir Press Fiction Prize-winning *The Worst May Be Over.* He founded the BFA Program at Penn State Erie, where he is Distinguished Professor, editor of *Lake Effect*, and translation editor of *Mid-American Review.*

MARTA LÓPEZ-LUACES is a poet, writer, and translator with a PhD in Spanish and Latin American Literatures from NYU. Two of her five poetry books were translated into Italian and Romanian. Her poetry has appeared in English translation in different poetry journals. She has translated into Spanish the works of Robert Duncan, Dorothea Tanning, and Ann Lauterbach. She has also published two novels and one book of short stories.

JACK MARTIN lives and writes in Fort Collins, Colorado. His poems have appeared in *Georgia Review, Ploughshares, Agni,* and many other journals.

E.J. MCADAMS is a poet and artist, exploring language and mark-making in the urban environment using procedures and improvisation with found and natural materials. He has published four chapbooks, most recently *Middle Voice* (Dusie Kollectiv). He had a solo exhibition, *Trees Are Alphabets*, at The Bronx Museum. He curated the Social-Environmental-Aesthetics reading at EXIT ART and was founding board member of the interdisciplinary Laboratory of Art Nature and Dance (iLAND). He lives in Harlem, Ward's Island Sewershed, Manhattan, Lower Hudson Watershed, New York, USA, Earth.

ALICK MCCALLUM is a poet born and raised in Burnley, one among many de-industrialised towns in the county of Lancashire and across the north of England. He currently studies and teaches at Colorado State University where he is engaged in ethnographic excavations of his hometown through poetry. His chapbook *Waiting (Haunt)* was published in 2017 by Shirt Pocket Press.

Michael McClure was one of the major figures of the Beat Generation. A native of Kansas who grew up by the "blue-black waters" of Puget Sound, Michael McClure was a poet, playwright, novelist, and essayist. He collaborated with The Doors' keyboardist Ray Manzarek and contemporary composer Terry Riley. He overcame censorship laws with his Obie-winning play *The Beard*. Awards included a Guggenheim Fellowship, a Rockefeller grant for playwriting, and the Alfred Jarry award.

James McCorkle's collections of poetry include *Evidences* (2003), *The Subtle Bodies* (2014), and *In Time* (2020). "Locations / Echolocations" is part of a book-length collaboration with the artist and architect Gabriella D'Angelo. James McCorkle teaches in the Africana Studies Program at Hobart & William Smith Colleges.

Thomas McGuire's work has appeared in *North American Review*, *Southeast Review*, and *Open-Eyed, Full-Throated: An Anthology of American/Irish Poets* (Arlen House, 2019). He teaches at the US Air Force Academy and serves as Poetry Editor for *War, Literature & the Arts*. He lives in the rain shadow of Pike's Peak where he frequently writes about magpies and Native American culturally modified trees. His poem "Four Ways of Looking at Magpie—A Most Becoming Bird" was selected to appear in *Best New Poets 2020*.

Andrew Melrose is Emeritus Professor of Writing at the University of Winchester, UK. He has written animation films, books, including fiction and academic works on creativity, most recently *Writing Song Lyrics* (2019) and *Professional Writing* (2020), and contributed poetry to a number of collections and anthologies. He has also co-edited the *Writing in Practice* and *Meniscus* journals.

Nancy Mercado was named one of 200 living individuals who best embody Frederick Douglass's work and spirit by the Frederick Douglass Family Initiatives and the Antiracist Research and Policy Center at American University. She is the recipient of the 2017 American Book Award for Lifetime Achievement. Editor of the first *Nuyorican Women's Anthology* published in *Voices e/Magazine*, Hunter College-CUNY, her work is widely anthologized.

Sara Method lives with her husband and children in a tiny house in the mountains of western North Carolina. Her artwork engages environment through printmaking, drawing, and fibers, and she has exhibited in galleries regionally, nationally, and internationally. Method received her MFA in Studio Art at Western Carolina University. www.saramethod.com

Julian née Sara Mithra's *If the Color Is Fugitive* (Nomadic Press, 2018) was a finalist for a Lambda Literary Award in Transgender Poetry. English-to-English translations appear in *bæst* and *The Lifted Brow*, plant poetics in *Birds Fall Silent in the Mechanical Sea* and at *Entropy*, singsong at *meow meow pow pow*, and nonbinary embodiment in *Name and None*. They exhibit black-and-white collage zines and handmade chapbooks at festivals in the Bay Area.

Marcos Neroy (Vicente Lopez Abad) is a bilingual writer, translator, and PhD ABD of Spanish Literature with a minor in Creative Writing at the University of Wisconsin-Madison.

Among other distinctions, he is the recipient of a Fulbright grant and Kohler Fellowship at the Wisconsin Institute for Discovery. Under the pen-name Marcos Neroy, he writes poetry, theatre, short stories and dabbles in folk music composition.

BERNARD NOËL is a poet, novelist, essayist, historian, and art critic. He has received France's highest literary honors, including the poet laureateship and the Prix National de Poésie. His numerous books of poetry, novels, and essays include, most recently: *Comédie intime* (P.O.L, 2015), *Monologue du nous* (P.O.L, 2015), *La Place de l'autre* (P.O.L, 2013), *Le Roman d'un être* (P.O.L, 2012), and *Le Livre de l'oubli* (P.O.L, 2012).

VALERY OISTEANU was born in the USSR, educated in Romania, and immigrated to New York in 1973. He is the author of fifteen books of poetry. A new collection: *In the Blink of a Third Eye* is forthcoming from Spuyten Duyvil, 2020. He is a receiver of three awards, among them the Acker Award NYC 2013 for Poetry Performance.

PETER O'LEARY is the author of several books of poetry, including *Earth Is Best* (Cultural Society), and criticism, including *Thick and Dazzling Darkness: Religious Poetry in a Secular Age* (Columbia). He lives in Oak Park, Illinois and teaches at the School of the Art Institute of Chicago and the University of Chicago. With John Tipton, he edits Verge Books.

JOHN OLSON is the author of numerous books of poetry, essays, fiction, and prose poetry, including *Dada Budapest, Larynx Galaxy* and *Backscatter: New and Selected Poems*. He has also published four novels: including *In Advance of the Broken Justy, The Seeing Machine, The Nothing That Is,* and *Souls of Wind*, which was shortlisted for a *Believer Magazine* Book Award in 2008.

ANTÓNIO OSÓRIO is a Portuguese poet with Galician and Italian roots. From the very first books, *A Raiz Afectuosa* (The Tender Root) and *A Ignorância da Morte* (Ignorance of Death), published in the 1970s, Osório's work has explored childhood, the ephemerality of life, everyday objects, nearly extinct professions, animals, rural settings, joy, loss—all in familiar, refined detail. He divides his time between Lisbon and Azeitão. Translated by Patricio Ferrari and Susan Margaret Brown.

CATHERINE OWEN was born in Vancouver and now lives in Edmonton. The author of fifteen collections of poetry and prose, she also works in film, tutors, and engages in multimedia collaborations and event hosting. Her latest book of poems is *Riven* (ECW, 2020), on grief and the ecology of place. These pieces are from a work in progress titled *The Flowers Terminal.*

CHRIS PEDLER teaches writing near the beach in California. He seeks to rearrange conventional views of landscape and animals by writing "songlines" that integrate history and ecology while tracing routes through specific locations that come to be seen anew. His poems have appeared, among other places, in *Hobart* and *you are here: a journal of creative geography.*

Craig Santos Perez is an indigenous Chamoru from the Pacific Island of Guåhan (Guam). He is the author of five books of poetry and the co-editor of five anthologies. He is an an associate professor in the English Department at the University of Hawai'i, Mānoa, where he teaches creative writing, Pacific literature, and environmental poetry.

Frances Presley's publications include *Paravane* (2004), *Myne* (2006), *Lines of Sight* (2009), *An Alphabet for Alina* (2012), *Halse for Hazel* (2014), and *Sallow* (2016). *Ada Unseen* (Shearsman, 2019), concerns Ada Lovelace and her life on Exmoor. Presley's work is in the anthologies *Infinite Difference* (2010), *The Ground Aslant: An Anthology of Radical Landscape Poetry* (2011), and *Out of Everywhere 2* (2015). These poems are from a new sequence called "channels."

Kristin Prevallet is the author of five collections of poetry including *I, Afterlife: Essay In Mourning Time* (Essay Press), published in French as *D'Un Devenir Fantôme*, and most recently *Everywhere Here and in Brooklyn* (The Belladonna Collaborative). She is the recipient of residencies and awards from the New York Foundation for the Arts, Poet's House, Spalding University and Bard College's Institute for Writing and Thinking.

Evan Pritchard (Mi'kmaq) is the author of *Greetings from Mawenawasic* (Foothills), *Red Head Band* (Resonance Books) and many more. A contributor to *Tending the Fire* (University of New Mexico Press), he was editor of *Resonance Magazine*. His poetry was included as part of a production of "Cedars" at LaMaMa in 2015 and a Chris Felver documentary called *Tending the Fire*.

George Quasha: poet & artist. Thirty+ books include *Poetry in Principle* (poetics); ongoing series of invented poetic genre "preverbs": *Verbal Paradise, Glossodelia Attract, The Daimon of the Moment, Things Done for Themselves, Not Even Rabbits Go Down This Hole*; art: *Axial Stones: An Art of Precarious Balance; An Art of Limina: Gary Hill's Works and Writings* (with Charles Stein). Guggenheim, NEA Fellow. Co-publisher Station Hill Press.

Kester Reid is a writer and nature-based teacher living in British Columbia, Canada. As a settler, his cultural work with Indigenous communities proposes the question of "decolonization": of society and individuals. Dislodging our imperial bias requires deep internal reflection alongside a revival of our pre-rational ways of knowing and relating. Poetry, myth, and place emerge as essential commentaries in this landscape of postcolonial healing.

Evelyn Reilly's books include *Styrofoam, Apocalypso,* and *Echolocation*, all published by Roof Books. Her work has been widely anthologized, and she has taught at the Poetry Project at St. Mark's Church and Naropa's Summer Writing Program, and has been a curator of the Segue Reading Series. Portuguese translations of *Styrofoam* and *Echolocation* will be published by Douda Correria (Lisbon) in 2021.

Eléna Rivera was born in Mexico City and raised in Paris, France. Her third full-length collection of poetry *Scaffolding* (2017) was published by Princeton University Press in the Princeton Series of Contemporary Poets. Her book *Epic Series* is forthcoming from Shearsman

Books. She received a National Endowment for the Arts Literature Fellowship in Translation and was a recent recipient of fellowships from the MacDowell Colony (2020) and the Trelex Paris Poetry Residency (2019).

Born in Subic Bay, Philippines, MG ROBERTS is the author of the poetry collections *Anemal Uter Meck* and *not so, sea*. She is a teacher, poet, and multimedia artist. Her work has appeared or is forthcoming in the *Academy of American Poets*, the *Stanford Journal of Asian American Studies*, *Web Conjunctions*, *Elderly*, and elsewhere. She lives in the Pacific Northwest with her three daughters.

LINDA RUSSO co-edited, with Marthe Reed, *Counter-Desecration: A Glossary for Writing Within the Anthropocene* (Wesleyan, 2018). At Washington State University, on the traditional homelands of the Nimiipuu (Nez Perce) Tribe and the Pelëuc Band of Indigenous People, she teaches and also directs EcoArtsonthePalouse.com.

MARK RUTTER grew up in the UK and lived in Maine between 1990 and 2002, during which time two collections of his poetry were published. Mark has published several collaborative artist's books, most recently *Homage to Andrei Tarkovsky*, in collaboration with Walter Tisdale, and *Oorts Cloud*, in collaboration with Kate Dicker. A new collection of visual and minimal poems, *Simple Cells*, is forthcoming from inkConcrete.

JOHN CHARLES RYAN is a poet, botanist, and environmental humanities scholar. His creative work has been published by Fremantle Press and Margaret River Press in Australia, and in the journals *Arc Poetry Magazine*, *Australian Geographic*, *Axon*, *Cordite Poetry Review*, *Griffith Review*, and *Philosophy Activism Nature*. His co-edited book, *The Language of Plants*, explores scientific, philosophical, and literary perspectives on vegetal communication.

JIMMY SAEKKI is an American citizen or rootless cosmopolitan, born and partially raised in Seoul, South Korea, and in various parts of the United States. He now resides and works in Shanghai, PRC. He was educated in the United States, England, and Scotland, from where he earned a BA, MA, and PhD, respectively.

SAM SAMPSON was born in Auckland, Aotearoa–New Zealand, and raised in South Titirangi, next to Little Muddy Creek (Paruiti) where he still lives. *Everything Talks* (Auckland University Press and Shearsman, 2008), his first collection, won the NZSA Jessie Mackay Award for the Best First Book of Poetry. He has collaborated with visual artists and photographers, which has seen the production of chapbooks, photobooks, and artworks. Sampson's most recent collection of poems, *Halcyon Ghosts*, was published in 2014. For more information on the author and associated collaborations: http://www.samsampson.co.nz.

ANDREW SCHELLING lives along Colorado's Front Range, studying languages, ecology, and animal tracks. He teaches at Naropa University, writes poetry and essays, and translates Sanskrit and other poetry of ancient India. His twenty-odd titles include *Tracks Along the Left Coast: Jaime de Angulo and Pacific Coast Culture*, a folkloric account of linguistics, native lore, cattle rustling, and bohemian poets.

MARK SCROGGINS is the author of four books of poetry, a critical biography of the poet Louis Zukofsky, two scholarly monographs, and two collections of essays and reviews. He has recently edited a selection of the erotic poetry of Algernon Charles Swinburne. He writes a monthly poetry column for *Hyperallergic Weekend* and "La Dernière mode," a fashion column for *Dispatches from the Poetry Wars*.

ANTHONY SEIDMAN is a poet translator from the San Fernando Valley, with additional homes in the deserts of Mexicali and Ciudad Juárez, Mexico. His most recent poetry collections are *A Sleepless Man Sits Up In Bed* (Eyewear Publishing, 2016) and *Cosmic Weather*, forthcoming from Spuyten Duyvil, late 2020. His full-length translations include *Confetti-Ash: Selected Poems of Salvador Novo*, and *A Stab in the Dark* by Facundo Bernal.

KELLY SHEPHERD's second full-length poetry collection, *Insomnia Bird: Edmonton Poems* (Thistledown Press, 2018) won the 2019 Robert Kroetsch City of Edmonton Book Prize, and was shortlisted for the 2019 Stephan G. Stephansson Award for Poetry. Kelly has written seven poetry chapbooks and is the poetry editor for the environmental philosophy journal *The Trumpeter.* Originally from Smithers, BC, Kelly lives and teaches in Edmonton, Alberta.

JOHN SHOPTAW was raised in the Mississippi floodplain of "swampeast Missouri." His book *Times Beach* (2015) won the Northern California Book Award in Poetry. He teaches (eco)poetry reading and writing at the University of California at Berkeley. He is finishing *Near-Earth Object*, a book of poems.

MURALI SIVARAMAKRISHNAN, poet, painter, and literary critic, was former Professor and Chair of the Department of English, Pondicherry University. He has authored several books, a number of critical essays, and six volumes of poetry. As artist and poet he is also a committed environmentalist. He has held fifteen solo exhibitions of his paintings. He is the founding President of ASLE India.

JONATHAN SKINNER is a poet, field recordist, editor, and critic, best known for founding the journal *ecopoetics*. His poetry collections include *Birds of Tifft* (BlazeVOX, 2011) and *Political Cactus Poems* (Palm Press, 2005). *Earth Shadow* is forthcoming from Ahsahta Press. He has published numerous ecocritical essays. Skinner teaches in the Department of English and Comparative Literary Studies at the University of Warwick.

ISABEL SOBRAL CAMPOS is the author of the poetry collection *Your Person Doesn't Belong to You* (V. A. Press, 2018). Her latest chapbook, *Autobiographical Ecology*, is out with above/ground press, and work is forthcoming with Sutra Press and The Magnificent Field. She is the co-founder of the Sputnik & Fizzle publishing series.

ANDRÉ SPEARS is the director of the Maud/Olson Library in Gloucester (MA) and a senior editor at *Dispatches From the Poetry Wars*. His most recent book, *XIII: Ship of State* , excerptedfrom a Tarot-based work-in-progress, was published by Dispatches Editions (2019) in conjunction with the "virtual-chapbook" republication of his short epic *XO: A Tale for the New Atlantis* (1983).

STEPHANIE STRICKLAND's ten books of poetry include *How the Universe Is Made: Poems New & Selected* (2019) and *Ringing the Changes* (2020), a code-generated project for print based on the ancient art of tower bell-ringing. She has published twelve collaborative digital poems, most recently *Liberty Ring!* (2020), a companion to *Ringing the Changes*, and *House of Trust,* a poem in praise of free public libraries.

COLE SWENSEN has seventeen volumes of poetry, most recently *On Walking On*, and the forthcoming *Art in Time*, a collection of hybrid lyric writings on visual art. The author of a collection of critical essays, *Noise That Stays Noise,* and the co-editor of the Norton anthology *American Hybrid*, she has been awarded the Iowa Poetry Prize, the SF State Poetry Center Book Award, and the National Poetry Series. She divides her time between Paris and Providence, RI, where she teaches at Brown University.

ARTHUR SZE's ten books of poetry include *Sight Lines* (2019), which won the National Book Award; *Compass Rose*, a Pulitzer Prize finalist; and *The Ginkgo Light*, selected for the PEN Southwest Book Award. Sze's honors include the Jackson Poetry Prize, a Lannan Literary Award, a Lila Wallace–Reader's Digest Writers' Award, a Guggenheim Fellowship, and two National Endowment for the Arts fellowships. His translation *The Silk Dragon* won the Western States Book Award.

In 2019, CavanKerry Press published MARGO TAFT STEVER's second full-length book, *Cracked Piano*, and Kattywompus Press published her chapbook, *Ghost Moose*. Her other poetry collections are *The Lunatic Ball* (2015), *The Hudson Line* (2012), *Frozen Spring* (2002), and *Reading the Night Sky* (1996). She is the founder of the Hudson Valley Writers Center and the founding editor of Slapering Hol Press. www.margotaftstever.com.

HARRIET TARLO is a poet and academic interested in place, landscape, environment and gender. Her poetry appears with Shearsman Books and her artists' books with Judith Tucker with Wild Pansy Press. Critical work is published in books and journals such as *Jacket, Critical Survey; Classical Review,* and the *Journal of Ecocriticism*. She is Reader in Creative Writing at Sheffield Hallam University, UK.

BRIAN TEARE is the author of six books, most recently *Companion Grasses*, *The Empty Form Goes All the Way to Heaven,* and *Doomstead Days*, longlisted for the National Book Award and a finalist for the National Book Critics Circle and Kingsley Tufts Awards. He's an associate professor at the University of Virginia, and lives in Charlottesville, where he makes books by hand for Albion Books.

ORCHID TIERNEY is an Aotearoa–New Zealand poet, scholar, and consulting editor for the *Kenyon Review*. Publications include *a year of misreading the wildcats* (Operating System, 2019), *ocean plastic* (BlazeVOX, 2019), and *blue doors* (Belladonna* Press), among others. She is Assistant Professor of English at Kenyon College.

EDWIN TORRES is the author of ten books of poetry including *XoeteoX: the infinite word object* (Wave Books) and *Ameriscopia* (University of Arizona Press), and editor of *The Body In Language: An Anthology* (Counterpath Press). His work appears in the anthologies *American Poets in the 21st Century: The Poetics of Social Engagement, Post-Modern American Poetry*, and *Aloud: Voices From The Nuyorican Poets Café.*

JEAN-THOMAS TREMBLAY is Assistant Professor of English at New Mexico State University. An excerpt from their monograph in progress, *Breathing Aesthetics*, appeared in the thirtieth-anniversary issue of *differences*. Jean-Thomas is coediting, with Drew Strombeck, the collection *Avant-Gardes in Crisis: Art and Politics in the Long 1970s* (forthcoming from SUNY Press). A full list of refereed and para-academic publications is available at http://jttremblay.wordpress.com.

JOHN TRITICA has published five books of poetry: *How Rain Records Its Alphabet* (1998), *Sound Remains* (2008), *Standing in Astonishment* (2012), and *Spruce Bark Text* (2018). He translated Swedish poet Niklas Törnlund's *All Things Measure Time* (1992). He worked closely with Gene Frumkin and Mary Rising Higgins for over twenty years. He lives with his family in Albuquerque, NM.

KEITH TUMA's books include *Climbing into the Orchestra* (The Mute Canary, 2017), *On Leave: A Book of Anecdotes* (Salt, 2011), and *Holiday in Tikrit* (Critical Documents, 2005, with Justin Katko). He teaches at Miami University, where he edits The Miami University Press.

PAUW VOS holds a BA in Photography from the AKV Sint Joost Breda and a BA in English Language and Culture from the Utrecht University. He is currently a master's student in Comparative Literary Studies at Utrecht University in the Netherlands. He is a founding member and an editor of the student-driven magazine *Paratext*. His academic focus and literary interests are in the interrelated fields of ecocriticism and animal studies.

JEN WEBB is Distinguished Professor of Creative Practice and Dean of Graduate Research at the University of Canberra, Australia. Her research and practice address creativity, representation, and material poetics. Recent publications include *Art and Human Rights: Contemporary Asian Contexts* (Manchester University Press, 2016), the edited volume *Publishing and Culture* (with D. Baker and D. L. Brien, CSP, 2019), and the poetry collection *Moving Targets* (Recent Work Press, 2018). Her forthcoming collection of poetry is *Flight Mode* (Recent Work Press, Oct. 2020).

KATHRYN WELD is a mathematician and poet. Her chapbook is *Waking Light* (Kattywompus Press). Her writing appears in *Connotations Press, The Critical Flame, Bellevue Literary Review, The Cortland Review, Valparaiso Poetry Review, Midwest Quarterly*, and elsewhere. She has a PhD in Mathematics (CUNY) and an MFA from Sewanee School of Letters.

Laurie Wilcox-Meyer's third poetry collection is forthcoming in 2020, *Conversation In The Key Of Blue* (Main Street Rag Publishing, 2020). She lives in the mountains of Western North Carolina where she often spots bears while hiking and meditating about her next poem. She is Co-Founder of Poetry Pathways, a project intended to celebrate poetry and make poetry accessible along Asheville City Greenways.

Tyrone Williams teaches literature and theory at Xavier University in Cincinnati, Ohio. He is the author of several chapbooks and six books of poetry: *c.c., On Spec, The Hero Project of the Century, Adventures of Pi, Howell,* and *As Iz*. A limited-edition art project, *Trump l'oeil*, was published by Hostile Books in 2017. He and Jeanne Heuving edited the anthology *Inciting Poetics* (2019).

Morgan Grayce Willow has published three poetry collections, including *Dodge & Scramble,* which addresses the demise of the small family farm in rural American culture. Her poem "Driving Home to Garfield Street, Northeast Minneapolis" appeared in *Resist Much/Obey Little* in 2017. Morgan's essay "(Un)Document(ing)," examining the fallacy of land "ownership," which appeared in *Water~Stone Review* #22 in 2019, was nominated for a Pushcart Prize.

Daniel Wolff's poetry has appeared in *The Paris Review, APR,* and *Raritan*, among others. The illustrated ecopoem *CURRENTCY* was published in 2019 as was the chapbook *AYITI* (Finishing Line Press). As well as three collections of poetry, he has authored a half-dozen acclaimed nonfiction books, most recently *Grown-Up Anger: Bob Dylan, Woody Guthrie, and the Calumet Massacre of 1913* (Harper Collins).

Jeffrey Yang is the author of *Hey, Marfa* (winner of the Southwest Book Award), *Vanishing-Line*, and *An Aquarium* (winner of the PEN/Osterweil Award). He is the translator, most recently, of Bei Dao's autobiography *City Gate, Open Up* (honorable mention for the Aldo and Jeanne Scaglione Prize for Translation), and the editor of several volumes from New Directions Press.

Soohyun Yang is a freelance translator based in Seoul, South Korea.